W9-BVM-398

Managerial Economics
Tenth Edition

Mark Hirschey

University of Kansas

THOMSON

SOUTH-WESTERN

Australia · Canada · Mexico · Singapore · Spain · United Kingdom · United States

THOMSON

™

SOUTH-WESTERN

Study Guide

to accompany

Managerial Economics, 10e

Mark Hirschey

Editor-in-Chief:
Jack Calhoun

VP, Team Director:
Michael P. Roche

Sr. Acquisitions Editor:
Peter Adams

Sr. Developmental Editor:
Jan Lamar

Sr. Production Editor:
Elizabeth A. Shipp

Executive Marketing Manager:
Lisa L. Lysne

Media Developmental Editor:
Peggy Buskey

Media Production Editor:
Pam Wallace

Manufacturing Coordinator:
Sandee Milewski

Cover Designer:
Rik Moore

Cover Photograph:
© PhotoDisc, Inc.

Printer:
Phoenix Color/Book Technology Park

PREFACE

This *Study Guide* has been prepared to accompany *Managerial Economics*, Tenth Edition. Use of this *Study Guide* can significantly enhance comprehension of the material presented in *Managerial Economics*, Tenth Edition and make easier the process of learning the tools and techniques of economic analysis. It is designed as a supplement to the text, and will not substitute for it.

Although there are numerous ways in which to incorporate the use of the *Study Guide* in a program of academic study, many have found the following four-step approach to be especially beneficial.

1.   Read the chapter theme and outline in the *Study Guide* to obtain a quick preview of the material to be presented. This introduction to the chapter alerts students to key concepts being developed.

2.   Read the chapter in *Managerial Economics*, Tenth Edition. Many find that a rapid pass through the chapter, followed by a more careful and deliberate reading, leads to greater comprehension and understanding.

3.   Work through the problems in the *Study Guide* and check solutions obtained with those provided. While arriving at correct solutions is certainly important at this stage, real facility in the use of the tools and techniques of economic analysis comes only with an understanding of why the problems were set up and solved as indicated in the *Study Guide* solution. It is crucial to grasp the underlying logic of sample problems and solutions. Only after one has developed such economic intuition does it become possible to transfer the skills demonstrated in the solution of a given problem to other, perhaps more complex, managerial decision problems.

4.   Work through the end-of-chapter problems in the textbook. Again, an analysis of why the problem is set up and solved in a particular fashion, as well as an interpretation of the results, enhances both comprehension and the ability to use the concepts developed in real-world applications.

Use of this *Study Guide* in a comprehensive study of managerial economics is aimed at easing the burden in learning what is for some a difficult subject. This *Study Guide* has proven helpful to students in my own classes and the extensive feedback they have provided has led to significant improvements. Of course, comments from many other users--both professors and students alike--have been very helpful over the years, and continue to be welcome. Please let me hear your suggestions for improvement.

Finally, I would like to thank Christine Hauschel and Nicholas H. Hirschey for help with proofreading and problem checking.

Mark Hirschey
e-mail: mhirschey@ku.edu
July, 2002

TABLE OF CONTENTS

Chapter 1

NATURE AND SCOPE OF MANAGERIAL ECONOMICS

How do managers make good decisions? What pitfalls must be avoided? When are the characteristics of a market, a line of business, or an industry so attractive that entry becomes appealing? When are these attributes so unattractive that growth is not warranted and exit is preferable to continued operation? Why do some professions continue to pay well, while others offer only minimal financial rewards? How do you effectively motivate employees? All of these questions involve important economic issues that pose a continuing challenge to the managerial decision making process. Providing a logical and consistent framework that can be used to derive an appropriate answer to each of these questions is a task for which managerial economics is ideally suited. Managerial economics tells managers how things should be done to achieve objectives efficiently, and helps them recognize how economic forces affect organizations.

The nature and scope of managerial economics is laid out in this chapter. A primary emphasis of managerial economics is the application of economic theory and methodology to the practice of business decision making. Because managers of not-for-profit and government agencies must also efficiently employ scarce resources, managerial economics is an important tool for them as well. An important secondary emphasis in managerial economics is the study of how managerial decisions are affected by the economic environment. Managerial economics is applied economics; it is the use of economics theory and methodology to solve practical decision problems.

CHAPTER OUTLINE

I.   HOW IS MANAGERIAL ECONOMICS USEFUL?

    A.   Evaluating Choice Alternatives: Managerial economics links economic concepts with quantitative methods to develop vital tools for managerial decision making.

        1.   Managerial economics identifies ways to efficiently achieve goals.

        2.   Managerial economics can be used to specify pricing and production strategies.

        3.   Managerial economics provides production and marketing rules to help maximize net profits.

    B.   Making the Best Decision: To establish appropriate decision rules, managers must understand the economic environment in which they operate.

1.   Once management has set relevant goals, managerial economics can be used to efficiently attain those objectives.

2.   Managerial economics can be used to deduce the underlying logic of company, consumer, and government decisions.

II.   THEORY OF THE FIRM

A.   **Expected Value Maximization:** Firms exist because they are useful for producing and distributing goods and services. The basic model of business is called the theory of the firm.

1.   In its simplest version, the firm's owner-manager is assumed to be working to maximize short-run profits.

2.   In a more complete model, the primary goal of the firm is long-term expected value maximization.

3.   The value of the firm is the present value of the firm's expected future net cash flows.

a.   If cash flows are equated to profits for simplicity, the value of the firm today, or its present value, is the value of expected profits or cash flows, discounted back to the present at an appropriate interest rate.

B.   **Constraints and the Theory of the Firm:** Managerial decisions are often made in light of constraints imposed by technology, resource scarcity, contractual obligations, and government laws and regulations.

1.   To make decisions that will maximize value, managers must consider both short-run and long-run implications and how external constraints affect their ability to achieve organizational objectives.

2.   The value of the firm is given by the equation:

$$\text{Value} = \sum_{t=1}^{n} \frac{TR_t - TC_t}{(1 + i)^t}$$

Total revenue   *Total cost*

t = period of time
i = risk adjusted discount

where TR is total revenue, TC is total cost, and i is a risk-adjusted discount rate, all during period t.

C. **Limitations of the Theory of the Firm:** In practice, it is difficult to determine whether managers actually maximize firm value or merely attempt to satisfy stockholders while pursuing other goals.

    1. Alternative theories, or models, of managerial behavior have added to our understanding of the firm.

        a. Still, the basic value maximization model is a foundation for analyzing managerial decisions.

    2. Vigorous competition in markets for goods and services typically forces managers to seek value maximization in their operating decisions.

    3. Competition in the capital markets forces managers to seek value maximization in their financing decisions.

    4. Managers who pursue their own interests instead of stockholders' interests run the risk of being replaced.

        a. Hostile takeovers are especially unfriendly to inefficient management, which is usually replaced.

    5. What sometimes appears to be satisficing on the part of management can be interpreted as value-maximizing behavior once the costs of information gathering and analysis are considered.

    6. Short-run growth maximization strategies are often consistent with long-run value maximization when the production, distribution, or promotional advantages of large firm size are better understood.

III. PROFIT MEASUREMENT

A. **Business Versus Economic Profit:** The free enterprise system would fail to operate without profits and the profit motive. Even in planned economies, where state ownership rather than private enterprise is typical, the profit motive is increasingly used to spur efficient resource use.

    1. The general public and the business community typically define profit using an accounting concept.

        a. The amount available to fund equity capital after payment for all other resources the firm uses is called accounting profit, or business profit.

      b.   The risk-adjusted normal rate of return on capital is the minimum return necessary to attract and retain investment.

      2.   Economic profit is business profit minus the implicit costs of capital and other owner-provided inputs used by the firm.

B.   **Variability of Business Profits:** The observed variation in business profits makes it clear that many firms earn significant economic profits or experience meaningful economic losses at any point in time.

      1.   The business profit concept is typically measured in percentage terms by net income divided by the book value of stockholders' equity, or the return on equity (ROE).

$$\frac{NI}{ROE} = \text{business profit}$$

IV.   WHY DO PROFITS VARY AMONG FIRMS?

A.   **Frictional Theory of Economic Profits:** Markets are sometimes in disequilibrium because of unanticipated changes in demand or cost conditions.

      1.   Profits are sometimes above or below normal because of factors that prevent instantaneous adjustment to new market conditions.

B.   **Monopoly Theory of Economic Profits:** Monopoly profits exist when firms are sheltered from competition by high barriers to entry.

      1.   Economies of scale, high capital requirements, patents, or import protection, among other factors, enable some firms to build monopoly positions that allow above-normal profits for extended periods.

C.   **Innovation Theory of Economic Profits:** Innovation profit theory, describes the above-normal profits that arise following successful invention or modernization.

      1.   As in the case of frictional or disequilibrium profits, innovation profits are susceptible to the onslaught of competition from new and established competitors.

D.   **Compensatory Theory of Economic Profits:** Compensatory profit theory describes above-normal rates of return that reward firms.

      1.   Superior firms provide goods and services that are better, faster or cheaper than the competition.

E. **Role of Profits in the Economy:** Each of the preceding theories describe economic profits obtained for different reasons. In some cases, several might apply.

    1. Above-normal profits signal that firm or industry output should be increased.

    2. Below-normal profits provide a signal for contraction and exit.

V. ROLE OF BUSINESS IN SOCIETY

A. **Why Firms Exist:** Business contributes significantly to social welfare.

    1. These contributions stem directly from the efficiency of business in serving the economic needs of customers.

B. **Role of Social Constraints:** Regulation is sometimes imposed to promote economic fairness.

    1. Regulation is sometimes seen as a necessary means for stemming unwarranted monopoly profits, worker exploitation, environmental degradation, and so on.

C. **Social Responsibility of Business:** Firms exist by public consent to serve the needs of society.

    1. The firm can be viewed as a collaborative effort on the part of management, workers, suppliers, and investors on behalf of consumers.

    2. Taxes and restrictions on firms are taxes and restrictions on those people associated with the firm.

    3. The economic model of the firm emphasizes the close relation between the firm and society, and suggests the importance of business participation in the development and achievement of social objectives.

VI. STRUCTURE OF THIS TEXT

A. **Objectives:** This text will help you accomplish the following objectives:

    1. Develop a clear understanding of economic theory and methods as they relate to managerial decision making;

2.   Acquire a framework for understanding the nature of the firm as an integrated whole as opposed to a loosely connected set of functional departments;

3.   Recognize the relation between the firm and society and the key role of business as a tool for social betterment.

B.   **Development of Topics:**   The value maximization framework is useful for characterizing actual managerial decisions and for developing rules that can be used to improve those decisions.

1.   The basic test of the value maximization model, or any model, is its ability to explain real-world behavior.

2.   This text highlights the complementary relation between theory and practice.

a.   Theory is used to improve managerial decision making, and practical experience leads to the development of better theory.

VII.   SUMMARY

Chapter 2

ECONOMIC OPTIMIZATION

The purpose of managerial economics is to furnish a systematic framework for problem analysis and solution. This means that the pluses and minuses of various decision alternatives must be carefully measured and weighed. Costs and benefits must be reliably measured; time differences must be accurately reflected. The collection and characterization of relevant information is the most important step of this process. After all relevant information has been gathered, managers must accurately state the goal or goals that they seek to achieve. Without a clear understanding of managerial objectives, effective decision making is impossible. Once all relevant information has been gathered, and managerial objectives have been clearly stated, the managerial decision making process can proceed to the consideration of decision alternatives. Effective managerial decision making is the process of efficiently arriving at the best possible solution to a given problem. If only one solution is possible, then no decision problem exists. When alternative courses of action are available, the decision that produces a result most consistent with managerial objectives is the optimal decision. The process of arriving at the best managerial decision, or best problem resolution, is the focus of managerial economics.

This chapter introduces fundamental principles of economic analysis, which are essential to all aspects of managerial economics and form the basis for describing demand, cost, and profit relations. Once basic economic relations are understood, the tools and techniques of optimization can be applied to find the best course of action.

CHAPTER OUTLINE

I. **ECONOMIC OPTIMIZATION PROCESS**

    A. **Optimal Decisions:** The best decision produces the result most consistent with managerial objectives.

        1. Economic concepts and methodology are used to select the optimal course of action in light of available options and objectives.

    B. **Maximizing the Value of the Firm:** In managerial economics, the primary objective of management is maximization of the value of the firm. Influences that must be considered include:

        1. prices and the quantity sold,

        2. cost relations

3.   the appropriate discount rate.

II.   BASIC ECONOMIC RELATIONS

A.   Functional Relations: Equations: Functional relations show the causal relation between the variable to the left of the equal sign, called the dependent variable, and independent X variables.

1.   The values of independent variables are determined outside or independently of the functional relation expressed by the equation.

B.   Total, Average, and Marginal Relations: Total, average, and marginal relations are very useful in optimization analysis. A marginal relation is the change in the dependent variable caused by a one-unit change in an independent variable.

1.   When the marginal is positive, the total is increasing; when the marginal is negative, the total is decreasing.

2.   Maximization of any function occurs at the point where the marginal switches from positive to negative.

3.   When the marginal is greater (less) than the average, the average must be increasing (decreasing).

C.   Graphing Total, Marginal, and Average Relations: Geometric relations among totals, marginals, and averages provide insight in managerial decision making.

1.   At any point along a total curve, the corresponding average figure is given by the slope of a straight line from the origin to that point.

2.   The marginal rise (or fall) in total profit associated with a one-unit increase in output is the slope of the total profit curve at that point.

D.   Deriving Totals from Marginal and Average Curves: There are simple direct relations among totals, marginals, and averages.

1.   Total profit at any given output level is the sum of marginal profits up to that point.

2.   Total profit is average profit multiplied by the corresponding number of units of output.

III.   MARGINALS AS THE DERIVATIVES OF FUNCTIONS

    A.   Concept of a Derivative: A marginal is the change in the dependent variable associated with a one-unit change in an independent variable.

        1.   A derivative is a marginal relation.

IV.   MARGINAL ANALYSIS IN DECISION MAKING

    A.   Finding Maximums and Minimums: Managerial decision making frequently requires one to find the maximum or minimum value of a function.

        1.   Maximization or minimization of a function occurs where its marginal value (slope) is equal to zero. For example, revenue is maximized when MR = 0.

    B.   Distinguishing Maximums from Minimums: Second derivatives distinguish maximums from minimums.

        1.   Maximums occur if the first derivative equals zero, and the second derivative is negative.

        2.   Minimums occur if the first derivative equals zero, and the second derivative is positive.

    C.   The Use of Marginals to Maximize the Difference Between Two Functions: Total profit is equal to total revenue minus total cost and is equivalent to the vertical distance between these two curves at any output level.

        1.   Profit is maximized at the output level where the slopes of the revenue and cost curves are equal.

        2.   The slopes of the total revenue and total cost curves measure marginal revenues (*MR*) and marginal costs (*MC*). Where these slopes are equal, *MR* = *MC* and profit is maximized.

    D.   Marginal Analysis of Operating Curves: Operating decisions are made on the basis of marginal analysis.

        1.   Revenue is maximized where MR = 0.

        2.   Average cost is minimized where MC = AC.

V.   THE INCREMENTAL CONCEPT IN ECONOMIC ANALYSIS

    A.   Definition: Incremental analysis involves examining the impact of alternative managerial decisions on revenues, costs, and profit. It focuses on changes or differences between available alternatives.

        1.   The incremental change is the difference resulting from a decision.

        2.   Marginal relations measure only the effect associated with *unitary changes* in output.

    B.   Incremental Profits: Incremental profit is the profit gain or loss associated with a given managerial decision.

        1.   When incremental profit is negative, total profit declines.
        2.   Incremental profit is positive (and total profit increases) if the incremental revenue associated with a decision exceeds incremental cost.

    C.   Incremental Concept Example: The incremental concept is important for managerial decision making because it focuses attention on the differences among available alternatives.

        1.   Revenues and costs that are unaffected by a decision are irrelevant and should be excluded from analysis.

VI.   SUMMARY

PROBLEMS & SOLUTIONS

P2.1   ***Marginal Analysis.*** *Characterize each of the following statements as true or false, and explain your answer.*

   A.   *If marginal revenue is greater than average revenue, the demand curve is downward sloping.*

   B.   *Profit is minimized when total revenue equals total cost.*

   C.   *Given a downward-sloping demand curve and positive marginal costs, profit-maximizing firms always sell more output at lower prices than revenue-maximizing firms.*

   D.   *Marginal cost must be less than average cost for average cost to decline as output expands.*

   E.   *Marginal profit is the difference between marginal revenue and marginal cost, and always exceeds zero at the profit-maximizing activity level.*

P2.1   **SOLUTION**

   A.   False. Because average revenue is falling along a downward sloping demand curve, marginal revenue must be less than average revenue for the demand curve to slope downward.

   B.   False. Profits are maximized when marginal revenue equals marginal cost. Profits equal zero at the breakeven point where total revenue equals total cost. Profits are minimized when the difference between total revenue and total cost is at a maximum.

   C.   False. Profit maximization involves setting marginal revenue equal to marginal cost. Revenue maximization involves setting marginal revenue equal to zero. Given a downward sloping demand curve and positive marginal costs, revenue maximizing firms charge lower prices and offer greater quantities of output than firms that maximize profits.

   D.   True. Average cost falls as output expands so long as marginal cost is less than average cost. If this condition is met, average costs decline whether marginal costs are falling, rising or constant.

E.   False. Marginal profit equals marginal revenue minus marginal cost, and equals zero at the profit maximizing activity level.

P2.2   ***Revenue Maximization: Tables.*** *Doug Heffernan, marketing director for Arthur's Bedroom, Inc., has just received the following price/demand information from a market experiment for a new closet-space organizer product called Max Headroom:*

Price	Product Demand
$500	0
475	1
450	2
425	3
400	4
375	5
350	6
325	7
300	8
275	9
250	10
225	11
200	12
175	13
150	14
125	15

A.   *Use a spreadsheet to calculate total and marginal revenue at each level of product demand.*

B.   *At what price level is total revenue maximized? Why?*

P2.2   SOLUTION

A.   Total and marginal revenue at each level of product demand are as follows:

Price P	Product Demand Q	Total Revenue TR=P×Q	Marginal Revenue MR=∂TR/∂Q
$500	0	---	---
475	1	$475	$475
450	2	900	425
425	3	1,275	375
400	4	1,600	325
375	5	1,875	275
350	6	2,100	225
325	7	2,275	175
300	8	2,400	125
275	9	2,475	75
250	10	2,500	25
225	11	2,475	(25)
200	12	2,400	(75)
175	13	2,275	(125)
150	14	2,100	(175)
125	15	1,875	(225)

B. At a price level of $250 and product demand of 10 units, total revenue is maximized at a level of $2,500. Prior to that point, the added sales from a decrease in price more than compensate for the loss in revenue from charging current customers a lower price. At prices lower than $250, the loss in revenue from charging current customers a lesser price is greater than the gain in revenues from new customers, and total revenue declines. As seen from the marginal revenue column, total revenue increases so long as marginal revenue is positive, but declines when marginal revenue is negative.

P2.3 *Average Cost Minimization: Tables. Seinfeld Construction, Ltd., has been asked to submit a bid on the projected cost of sophisticated production machinery. To help in the bid development process, Gerry Seinfeld, head of product quality control, has prepared the following schedule of projected volume and production costs:*

Output	Total Cost
0	$50,000
1	51,750
2	54,000
3	56,750
4	60,000
5	63,750
6	68,000
7	73,250
8	79,500
9	86,250
10	93,500
11	102,250
12	111,500
13	122,250
14	134,500
15	150,000

A. *Use a spreadsheet to calculate the marginal and average cost at each level of production.*

B. *At what level of production is average cost minimized? Why?*

P2.3 *SOLUTION*

A. Marginal and average cost at each level of production appear as follows:

Output	Total Cost	Marginal Cost	Average Cost
0	$50,000	---	---
1	51,750	$1,750	$51,750.00
2	54,000	2,250	27,000.00
3	56,750	2,750	18,916.67
4	60,000	3,250	15,000.00
5	63,750	3,750	12,750.00
6	68,000	4,250	11,333.33
7	73,250	5,250	10,464.29
8	79,500	6,250	9,937.50
9	86,250	6,750	9,583.33
10	93,500	7,250	9,350.00
11	102,250	8,750	9,295.45
12	111,500	9,250	9,291.67
13	122,250	10,750	9,403.85
14	134,500	12,250	9,607.14
15	150,000	15,500	10,000.00

B. Minimum average costs of $9,291.67 are realized at an activity level of 12 units of output. Notice from the marginal cost column that average cost falls so long as marginal cost is less than average cost. Average cost rises so long as marginal cost is greater than average cost. Average cost reaches a minimum when marginal cost switches from being lower than average cost to being greater than average cost.

P2.4 **Profit Maximization: Spreadsheet Analysis.** *Roz Doyle, chief financial officer (CFO) of Seattle-based Frasier & Niles, Inc., has been asked to project the profit-maximizing activity level for a given product during the coming period. Relevant demand and cost information are as follows:*

Q	*P*	*TC*
0	*$1,000*	*$500*
1	*960*	*740*
2	*920*	*980*
3	*880*	*1,220*
4	*840*	*1,460*
5	*800*	*1,700*
6	*760*	*1,940*
7	*720*	*2,180*
8	*680*	*2,420*
9	*640*	*2,660*
10	*600*	*2,900*
11	*560*	*3,140*
12	*520*	*3,380*
13	*480*	*3,620*
14	*440*	*3,860*
15	*400*	*4,100*

A. *Construct a table (or spreadsheet) showing total revenue, marginal revenue, marginal cost, average cost, total profit, marginal profit, and average profit for this product at the various activity levels indicated previously.*

B. *Identify the profit-maximizing activity level.*

C. *Is the profit-maximizing activity level the same activity level as that at which minimum average costs are experienced? Why? or Why not?*

P2.4 SOLUTION

A. A table (or spreadsheet) showing total revenue, marginal revenue, marginal cost, average cost, total profit, marginal profit, and average profit for this product at the various activity levels is as follows:

Q	P	TR = P×Q	MR = ∂TR/∂Q	TC	MC = ∂TC/∂Q	AC = TC/Q	π = TR-TC	Mπ = ∂π/∂Q	Aπ = π/Q
0	$1,000	$0	---	$500	---	---	($500)	---	---
1	960	960	$960	740	$240	$740.00	220	$720	$220.00
2	920	1,840	880	980	240	490.00	860	640	430.00
3	880	2,640	800	1,220	240	406.67	1,420	560	473.33
4	840	3,360	720	1,460	240	365.00	1,900	480	475.00
5	800	4,000	640	1,700	240	340.00	2,300	400	460.00
6	760	4,560	560	1,940	240	323.33	2,620	320	436.67
7	720	5,040	480	2,180	240	311.43	2,860	240	408.57
8	680	5,440	400	2,420	240	302.50	3,020	160	377.50
9	640	5,760	320	2,660	240	295.56	3,100	80	344.44
10	600	6,000	240	2,900	240	290.00	3,100	0	310.00
11	560	6,160	160	3,140	240	285.45	3,020	(80)	274.55
12	520	6,240	80	3,380	240	281.67	2,860	(160)	238.33
13	480	6,240	0	3,620	240	278.46	2,620	(240)	201.54
14	440	6,160	(80)	3,860	240	275.71	2,300	(320)	164.29
15	400	6,000	(160)	4,100	240	273.33	1,900	(400)	126.67

B. Production and sale of 10 units at a price of $600 (or 9 units and a price of $640) is the profit-maximizing activity level. Profits are maximized at a level of $3,100. Prior to this point, the marginal revenue associated with additional sales exceeds their associated marginal cost, marginal profit is positive, and total profit rises with an expansion in output. Subsequent to this point, the marginal revenue associated with additional sales is less than their associated marginal cost, marginal profit is negative, and total profit falls with an expansion in output.

C. No, the profit-maximizing activity level is not the same activity level as that at which minimum average costs are experienced. In this problem, marginal costs are a constant $240 per unit. With fixed costs of $500, average costs continue to fall as output expands; they approach $240 as a lower limit. Although average costs continue to diminish as output expands, ever lower prices must be offered to generate these added sales. Total profits fall as output expands beyond 10 units because marginal revenues are less than marginal costs beyond that point. It is important to recognize that profit maximization requires a comparison of marginal revenues *and* marginal costs; average cost minimization involves a comparison of marginal cost and average cost relations only (revenue effects are not considered).

P2.5 **Marginal Analysis: Tables.** *Rachel Green, a student at Minnesota State University, is preparing for final exams and has decided to devote five hours to the study of* *managerial economics and finance. Green's goal is to maximize the average grade earned in the two courses, and must decide how much time to spend on each exam. Green realizes that maximizing the average grade in the two courses is equivalent to maximizing the sum of the grades. According to Green's best estimates, the grades achieved will vary according to the schedule shown below.*

Managerial Economics		Finance	
Hours of Study	*Grade*	*Hours of Study*	*Grade*
0	25	0	50
1	45	1	62
2	65	2	72
3	75	3	81
4	83	4	88
5	90	5	93

A. *Describe the manner in which Green could make use of the marginal concept in managerial economics to assist in determining the optimal allocation of five hours between the two courses.*

B. *How much time should Green spend studying each subject?*

C. *In addition to managerial economics and finance, Green is also taking a marketing course. Green estimates that each hour spent studying marketing will result in an eight point increase on the marketing examination score. Green has tentatively decided to spend three hours preparing for the marketing exam. Is Green's attempt to maximize the average grade in all three courses with three hours devoted to marketing and five hours devoted to managerial economics and finance (allocated as in part B) an optimal decision? Why? or Why not?*

P2.5 **SOLUTION**

A. An optimal allocation of study time is one that will permit Green to maximize the average grade earned in the managerial economics and finance courses. This maximization will occur when Green allocates each hour of study time to that course where the marginal grade value of study time is greatest.

B. To determine how much time Green should spend studying each subject a table illustrating the marginal grade value of each hour of study time must be constructed. This table reads as follows:

Managerial Economics			Finance		
Hours of Study	Grade	Marginal Grade Value	Hours of Study	Grade	Marginal Grade Value
0	25	--	0	50	--
1	45	20	1	62	12
2	65	20	2	72	10
3	75	10	3	81	9
4	83	8	4	88	7
5	90	7	5	93	5

With only five hours to study, Green should spend three hours on managerial economics and two hours on finance.

C. No, Green's decision to spend three hours studying for the marketing exam is incorrect if the objective is to maximize the average grade received in managerial economics, finance and marketing. Only two hours should be allocated to studying marketing because an additional hour spent on finance would increase the total grade achieved by nine points; one point more than the eight point gain associated with the third hour spent preparing for the marketing exam, and will lead to a maximum average grade.

P2.6 ***Marginal Analysis: Tables.*** *Monica Geller is a regional media consultant for Friendly Images, Inc., a New York-based media consultant. Geller has gathered the following data on weekly advertising media expenditures and gross sales for a major client, Greenwich Village's Central Perk Coffeehouse.*

| | Gross Sales Following Promotion in the Following Media: | | |
Advertising Expenditure	Newspaper	Radio	Television
$0	$10,000	$10,000	$10,000
100	12,000	14,000	13,000
200	13,800	17,600	15,600
300	15,400	20,200	18,000
400	16,600	22,000	18,600
500	17,200	22,400	18,800

A. Construct a table (or spreadsheet) showing marginal sales following promotion in each media. (Assume here and throughout the problem that there are no synergistic effects across different media.)

B. If the Central Perk Coffeehouse has an advertising budget of $500 per week, how should it be spent? Why?

C. Calculate the profit maximizing advertising budget and media allocation assuming the Central Perk Coffeehouse enjoys an average profit contribution before media expenditures of 6% on store-wide sales. How much are maximum weekly profits (before taxes)?

P2.6   SOLUTION

A.   A table showing marginal sales generated by promotion in each media appears as follows:

| | Marginal Sales Following Promotion in the Following Media: | | |
Advertising Expenditure	Newspaper	Radio	Television
$0	---	---	---
100	$2,000	$4,000	$3,000
200	1,800	3,600	2,600
300	1,600	2,600	2,400
400	1,200	1,800	600
500	600	400	200

B. Using the data in part A, and given a $500 advertising budget, gross sales and profit contribution are maximized by allocating $300 to radio and $200 to television advertising. Irrespective of whether the Central Perk Coffeehouse seeks to maximize revenues or profit, this expenditure allocation is optimal.

C. Given an average profit contribution before media expenditures of 6% on store-wide sales, an additional dollar of advertising will be profitable so long as it returns more than $16.67 in additional revenues. That is, the profit contribution on additional revenues of $16.67 is just sufficient to cover media costs of $1 (= $16.67 × 0.06). The profit maximizing advertising budget is $900 per week allocated as: $200 on newspaper, $400 on radio, and $300 on television.

Maximum weekly profits are:

Base sales	$10,000
+ Newspaper sales	3,800
+ Radio sales	12,000
+ Television sales	8,000
	$33,800
× Gross margin	0.06
Gross profit	2,028
- Media costs	900
Net profit	$ 1,128

(before tax)

P2.7   ***Marginal Analysis: Equations.*** *Buffay Products, Inc., has developed a new pocket-sized wireless communications device. This product's reliability level, measured by its failure rate, is a function of the amount of on-site preventive maintenance and warranty work:*

$$\text{Failure Rate} = 0.1 - 0.01t + 0.001t^2,$$

$$\text{Marginal Failure Rate} = \partial F/\partial t = -0.01 + 0.002t,$$

where t represents the amount of time devoted to on-site preventive maintenance and warranty work:

A.   *Set the marginal failure rate equal to zero to determine the failure rate-minimizing level of on-site preventive maintenance and warranty work.*

B.   *What is the optimal failure rate?*

P2.7   **SOLUTION**

A.   Set MF = 0 to find the failure rate-minimizing level of on-site preventive maintenance and warranty work:

$$MF = -0.01 + 0.002t$$

$$0 = -0.01 + 0.002t$$

$$0.002t = 0.01$$

$$t = 5 \text{ hours}$$

For this to be a failure-rate minimizing, rather than maximizing, level of on-site preventive maintenance and warranty work, the failure rate must be increasing beyond this point. This is indeed the case, as can be illustrated with a simple numerical example (see part B).

B.   At t = 5, note that:

$$F = 0.1 - 0.01t + 0.001t^2$$

$$= 0.1 - 0.01(5) + 0.001(5^2)$$

$$= 0.075 \text{ (or } 7.5\%)$$

To confirm that this is failure-rate minimizing level of t, notice that F is increasing for t > 5, e.g., F = 0.076 or 7.6% when t = 6.

P2.8   ***Profit Maximization: Equations.*** *Reggie's Diner Products, Inc., operates with the following revenue and cost functions:*

$$TR = \$100Q - \$0.5Q^2, \qquad (Total\ Revenue)$$

$$MR = \partial TR/\partial Q = \$100 - \$1Q, \qquad (Marginal\ Revenue)$$

$$TC = \$1,500 - \$10Q + \$0.5Q^2, \qquad (Total\ Cost)$$

$$MC = \partial TC/\partial Q = -\$10 + \$1Q, \qquad (Marginal\ Cost)$$

where Q represents the quantity of output produced and sold.

A.   *Set Mπ = MR - MC = 0 to determine the profit-maximizing price-output combination for Reggie's Diner Products, Inc.*

B.   *Show that marginal revenue equals marginal cost at this profit-maximizing output level.*

P2.8   **SOLUTION**

A.   Set Mπ = MR - MC = 0 to maximize profits, where:

$$M\pi = MR - MC$$

$$0 = \$100 - \$1Q + \$10 - \$1Q$$

$$2Q = 110$$

$$Q = 55$$

And,

$$P = TR/Q$$

$$= (\$100Q - \$0.5Q^2)/Q$$

$$= \$100 - \$0.05Q$$

$$= \$100 - \$0.05(55)$$

$$= \$72.50$$

B.   At Q = 55, note that:

$$MR = \$100 - \$1Q = \$100 - \$55 = \$45$$

$$MC = -\$10 + \$1Q = -\$10 + \$55 = \$45$$

This numerical finding illustrates the general result that if $M\pi = MR - MC = 0$, then MR = MC will always be true.

P2.9   ***Profit Versus Revenue Maximization.*** *West Wing Products, Inc., based in Durham, New Hampshire, produces and sells a wide variety of replacement parts and equipment for light aircraft. Leo McGarry, a product line specialist for the company, is reviewing the company's Internet marketing strategy for a popular flight manual. Demand and cost relations for the guidebook are given by the equations:*

$$P = \$155 - \$0.05Q, \qquad \text{(Demand)}$$

$$MR = \partial TR/\partial Q = \$155 - \$0.1Q, \qquad \text{(Marginal Revenue)}$$

$$TC = \$75,000 + \$5Q + \$0.0125Q^2, \qquad \text{(Total Cost)}$$

$$MC = \partial TC/\partial Q = \$5 + \$0.025Q, \qquad \text{(Marginal Cost)}$$

where Q is the quantity produced and sold per week.

A.   *Calculate the revenue-maximizing price/output combination.*

B.   *Calculate the profit-maximizing price/output combination.*

C.   *Are the differences in your answers to parts A and B typical or atypical? Explain.*

P2.9   ***SOLUTION***

A.   Set MR = 0 to find the revenue-maximizing output level:

$$MR = \$155 - \$0.1Q$$

$$0 = \$155 - \$0.1Q$$

$$0.1Q = 155$$

$$Q = 1,550$$

Because total revenue is declining beyond this point, Q = 1,550 is a point of maximum revenues. And,

$$P = \$155 - \$0.05(1,550)$$

$$= \$77.50$$

B.   Set Mπ = MR - MC = 0 to find the profit-maximizing output level:

$$M\pi = MR - MC$$

$$0 = \$155 - \$0.1Q - \$5 - \$0.025Q$$

$$0.125Q = 150$$

$$Q = 1,200$$

Because total profit is declining for Q > 1,200, Q = 1,200 is a point of maximum profits. And,

$$P = \$155 - \$0.05(1,200)$$

$$= \$95$$

C.   This is a typical result; so long as the product demand curve slopes downward and marginal cost exceeds zero, revenue maximization results in greater output (here, 1,550 versus 1,200) and lower prices (here, $77.50 versus $95) than is true with profit maximization.

P2.10   ***Profit Maximization Versus Average Cost Minimization.*** *Immensely popular mystery writer Jessica Fletcher has just published a new book titled "Diagnosis: Murder." Relevant monthly demand and cost relations for this hard cover title are:*

$$P = \$35 - \$0.00075Q, \qquad (Demand)$$

$$MR = \partial TR/\partial Q = \$35 - \$0.0015Q, \qquad (Marginal\ Revenue)$$

$$TC = \$50,000 + \$5Q + \$0.0005Q^2, \qquad (Total\ Cost)$$

$$MC = \partial TC/\partial Q = \$5 + \$0.001Q, \qquad (Marginal\ Cost)$$

where Q is the number of books produced and sold per month.

A. *Calculate the profit-maximizing price/output combination and profit level.*

B. *Calculate the average cost-minimizing price/output combination and profit level.*

C. *Contrast your answers to parts A and B.*

P2.10 **SOLUTION**

A. To find the profit-maximizing activity level, set $M\pi = MR - MC = 0$:

$$M\pi = MR - MC$$

$$0 = \$35 - \$0.0015Q - \$5 - \$0.001Q$$

$$0.0025Q = 30$$

$$Q = 12,000.$$

$$P = \$35 - \$0.00075(12,000)$$

$$= \$26.$$

$$\pi = TR-TC$$

$$= \$35Q - \$0.00075Q^2 - \$50,000 - \$5Q - \$0.0005Q^2$$

$$= -\$50,000 + \$30Q - \$0.00125Q^2$$

$$= -\$50,000 + \$30(12,000) - \$0.00125(12,000^2)$$

$$= \$130,000$$

Because total profit is declining for $Q > 12,000$, $Q = 12,000$ is a point of maximum profits per month. (*Note*: A publisher's price of $26 is consistent with a bookstore price of roughly $35.)

B. To find the average cost-minimizing activity level, set $MC = AC$:

$$MC = AC = TC/Q$$

$$\$5 + \$0.001Q = (\$50,000 + \$5Q + \$0.0005Q^2)/Q$$

$$\$5 + \$0.001Q = \$50,000/Q + \$5 + \$0.0005Q$$

$$0.0005Q = 50,000/Q$$

$$Q^2 = 100,000,000$$

$$Q = 10,000$$

$$P = \$35 - \$0.00075(10,000)$$

$$= \$27.50$$

$$\pi = -\$50,000 + \$30(10,000) - \$0.00125(10,000^2)$$

$$= \$125,000$$

Because average cost is rising for Q > 10,000, Q = 10,000 is a point of minimum average costs per month.

C.   Profit maximization involves a comparison of the marginal revenues and marginal costs of production. Average-cost minimization involves a consideration of cost relations only. Therefore, it is not surprising that these two approaches often yield different price/output combinations. In this instance, the added revenues associated with an additional 2,000 units beyond the average cost-minimizing level of 10,000 is so great as to overcome the disadvantage of somewhat higher average costs at the 12,000 units versus 10,000 units activity level.

Chapter 3

DEMAND AND SUPPLY

Nothing is more important to the economic survival of any organization than the need to effectively identify and respond to product demand and supply conditions. In economic terms, demand refers to the amount of a product that people are willing and able to buy under a given set of conditions. Need or desire is a necessary component but must be accompanied by financial capability before economic demand is created. Thus, economic demand requires potential buyers with a desire to use or possess something and the financial ability to acquire it. With vibrant demand for its products, the firm is able to attract the necessary resources to expand and grow. Without demand for a firm's products, no revenues are generated to pay suppliers, workers, and stockholders. Without demand, no amount of efficiency in production can ensure the firm's long-term survival. Without demand, the firm simply ceases to exist.

Once demand for the firm's products has been identified or created, the firm must thoroughly understand supply conditions to efficiently meet customer needs. Supply is the amount of a good or service that firms make available for sale under a given set of economic conditions. Just as demand requires a desire to purchase combined with the economic resources to do so, supply requires a desire to sell along with the economic capability to bring a product to market. Supply increases when additional profits are generated; supply decreases when production results in losses. The concepts of demand, supply, and equilibrium described in this chapter provide the fundamentals for analyzing interactions among buyers and sellers in the markets for all goods and services.

CHAPTER OUTLINE

I.   **THE BASIS FOR DEMAND**

         A.   **Definition:** Demand is the quantity of a good or service that customers are willing and able to purchase during a given period and under a given set of economic conditions.

                1.   Demand is created when customers perceive value (have desire) and the financial capability to make purchase decisions.

                2.   The success of any organization depends on a clear understanding of the demand and supply conditions for goods and services provided to customers.

         B.   **Direct Demand:** Demand for personal goods and services is based on the utility gained through consumption.

                1.   Consumers demand products that yield satisfaction.

C. **Derived Demand:** Demand for inputs that can be used in production is derived from the demand for consumer goods and services.

    1. Firms demand inputs that can be profitably employed.

II. THE MARKET DEMAND FUNCTION

A. **Determinants of Demand:** A demand function shows the relation between the quantity demanded and all factors that affect it.

    1. Important demand determinants include: price, price of other goods, income, advertising, and so on.

B. **Industry Demand Versus Firm Demand:** Demand functions can be specified for an entire industry or an individual firm.

    1. Industry Demand: Overall industry demand is subject to general economic influences (population, GDP, interest rates, and so on).

    2. Firm Demand: Firm demand is affected by general economic influences and competitor decisions (prices, advertising, and so on).

III. THE DEMAND CURVE

A. **Definition:** A demand curve shows the price-quantity relation, holding constant the effects of all other demand-determining influences.

B. **Demand Curve Determination:** To derive a demand curve, simply insert values for all nonprice variables into the demand function and determine the price/quantity relation.

C. **Relation Between The Demand Curve and Demand Function:** A demand curve can be plotted when all variables other than price and quantity in a given demand function are fixed at specific levels.

    1. A change in the quantity demanded reflects movement along a given demand curve following a price change.

    2. A shift in demand occurs when change in a nonprice variable leads to a shift from one demand curve to another.

IV.   **THE BASIS FOR SUPPLY**

    A.   **Definition:** Supply is the quantity of a good or service that producers are willing and able to sell during a given period.

        1.   Supply is offered when producers are able to at least cover the marginal cost of production.

    B.   **Factors That Influence Supply:** Anything that influences the profitability of production has the potential to influence supply.

        1.   Supply determinants include the price of the product itself, prices of competing products, technology, input prices, and weather, among other such factors.

V.   **THE MARKET SUPPLY FUNCTION**

    A.   **Determinants of Supply:** A supply function describes the relation between the quantity supplied and all factors that affect it.

        1.   Relevant factors include: price, price of related products, technology, input prices, and so on.

    B.   **Industry Versus Firm Supply:** Industry supply is affected by prices, prices of other products, advertising, and macroeconomic conditions.

        1.   Firm supply is affected by these factors *and* competitive influences.

        2.   Industry supply is the sum total of firm supply.

VI.   **SUPPLY CURVE**

    A.   **Definition:** A supply curve shows the price-quantity relation, holding constant the effects of all other supply-determining influences.

    B.   **Supply Curve Determination:** To derive a supply curve, simply insert values for all nonprice variables into the supply function and calculate the price/quantity relation.

    C.   **Relation Between Supply Curve and Supply Function:** A supply curve can be plotted when all variables other than price and quantity in a given supply function are fixed at specific levels.

1. A change in the quantity supplied reflects a movement along a given supply curve following a price change.

2. A shift in supply occurs when change in a nonprice variable leads to a switch from one supply curve to another.

VII. MARKET EQUILIBRIUM

A. **Definition:** Market Equilibrium is perfect balance in demand and supply under a given set of market conditions.

B. **Surplus and Shortage:** Both of these conditions reflect disequilibrium.

1. Surplus is excess supply.

2. Shortage is excess demand.

C. **Comparative Statics:** Comparative statics analysis is the study of the effect of changing demand and supply conditions.

D. **Comparative Statics: Changing Demand:** Equilibrium will change following a shift in the demand curve (change in demand).

E. **Comparative Statics: Changing Supply:** Equilibrium will also change following a shift in the supply curve (change in supply).

F. **Comparative Statics: Changing Demand *and* Supply:** Typically, changes in equilibrium reflect variation in demand and supply.

VIII. SUMMARY

PROBLEMS & SOLUTIONS

P3.1   ***Demand and Supply Concepts.*** *The market for oil is highly price sensitive. Indicate the effects of each of the following influences on demand and/or supply conditions:*

   A.   *A major oil discovery.*

   B.   *A $5 per barrel tax on oil.*

   C.   *An improvement in oil recovery technology.*

   D.   *An unusually hot summer causing an increase in the demand for air conditioning.*

   E.   *An increase in energy conservation.*

P3.1   ***SOLUTION***

   A.   Increase supply/rightward shift in supply curve. A major oil discovery will increase the quantity supplied at every price level.

   B.   Decrease supply/leftward shift in supply curve. A $5 per barrel tax on oil will reduce the share of total oil-related expenditures going to producers, and thus reduce the quantity supplied at every price level.

   C.   Increase supply/rightward shift in supply curve. An improvement in technology will make it possible to supply more oil at every price level.

   D.   Increase demand/rightward shift in demand curve. With an increase in air conditioning demand, electricity usage will rise, as will the demand for oil at every price level.

   E.   Decrease demand/leftward shift in demand curve. Increased energy conservation will cut oil usage at every price level.

P3.2   ***Demand and Supply Concepts.*** *Demand and Supply Concepts. Describe the effects of each of the following influences on demand and/or supply conditions in the new-hire market for MBAs.*

   A.   *An economic recession (fall in national income).*

   B.   *An increase in MBA graduate salaries.*

C. *An increase in the availability of low-cost student loans.*

D. *A rise in tuition costs.*

E. *A rise in relative productivity of MBA versus BA/BS job candidates.*

P3.2 **SOLUTION**

A. Decrease demand/leftward shift in demand curve and increase supply/rightward shift in supply curve. With a fall in national income, the profitability of added employment will fall, thereby causing a decline in the demand for labor. A recession can also reduce job opportunities for BAs and BSs, thereby reducing the income loss incurred while in graduate school, and thus can actually increase the supply of MBAs. Despite this often observed counter-cyclical relation between enrollment and economic activity, recessions can also limit the return to an MBA and thereby limit MBA supply. Thus, the net effect on supply can be uncertain.

B. Decrease in the quantity demanded/upward movement along demand curve and increase the quantity supplied/upward movement along supply curve. Rising prices cut the quantity demanded while increasing the quantity supplied.

C. Increase supply/rightward shift in supply curve. An increase in student loan availability will cut the cost of an MBA education, and increase the expected net return, and increase supply at every expected wage level.

D. Decrease supply/leftward shift in supply curve. A rise in tuition costs increases the cost of an MBA education, cuts the expected net return, and will decrease supply at each expected wage level.

E. Increase demand/rightward shift in demand. An increase in the relative productivity of MBAs will increase demand for MBAs at every price level.

P3.3 ***Surplus and Shortage.*** *The following relations describe monthly demand and supply conditions in the market for No. 1 grade cotton blue denim:*

$$Q_D = 100,000 - 40,000P \qquad \text{(Demand)}$$

$$Q_S = -5,000 + 30,000P \qquad \text{(Supply)}$$

where Q is quantity measured in thousands of square yards and P is price per square yard in dollars.

A. *Complete the following table:*

Price (1)	Quantity Supplied (2)	Quantity Demanded (3)	Surplus (+) or Shortage (-) (4) = (2) - (3)
$2.00			
1.75			
1.50			
1.25			
1.00			

P3.3 **SOLUTION**

A.

Price (1)	Quantity Supplied (2)	Quantity Demanded (3)	Surplus (+) or Shortage (-) (4) = (2) - (3)
$2.00	55,000	20,000	35,000
1.75	47,500	30,000	17,500
1.50	40,000	40,000	0
1.25	32,500	50,000	-17,500
1.00	25,000	60,000	-35,000

P3.4 **Quantity Demanded.** *Tim Taylor is a manager at Time Tools, Inc., a nation-wide supplier of tools and accessories to independent electricians and plumbers. A study of annual demand in several regional markets suggests the following demand function for a popular socket wrench set:*

$$Q = -500 - 10P + 0.001Pop + 0.05I + 20A$$

where Q is quantity, P is price ($), Pop is population, I is disposable income per person ($), and A is advertising measured in terms of personal selling days per year by Time Tools' sales staff.

A. *Determine the demand curve faced by Time Tools in a typical market where Pop = 1,000,000, I = $10,000, and A = 200 days.*

B. *Calculate the quantity demanded at prices of $250, $275, and $300.*

> C. *Calculate the prices necessary to sell 2,000, 3,000, and 4,000 units.*

P3.4 **SOLUTION**

> A. The demand curve can be calculated by substituting each respective variable into the firm's demand function:
>
> $$Q = -500 - 10P + 0.001Pop + 0.05I + 20A$$
>
> $$= -500 - 10P + 0.001(1,000,000)$$
>
> $$+ 0.05(10,000) + 20(200)$$
>
> $$Q = 5,000 - 10P$$
>
> Then, price as a function of quantity can be written:
>
> $$Q = 5,000 - 10P$$
>
> $$5,000 - Q = 10P$$
>
> $$P = \$500 - \$0.1Q$$
>
> B. At,
>
> $$P = \$250: Q = 5,000 - 10(250) = 2,500$$
>
> $$P = \$275: Q = 5,000 - 10(275) = 2,250$$
>
> $$P = \$300: Q = 5,000 - 10(300) = 2,000$$

C.   At,

$$Q = 2{,}000: P = \$500 - \$0.1(2{,}000) = \$300$$

$$Q = 3{,}000: P = \$500 - \$0.1(3{,}000) = \$200$$

$$Q = 4{,}000: P = \$500 - \$0.1(4{,}000) = \$100$$

P3.5   ***Quantity Demanded.*** *Joey Tribbian's Steakhouse, Inc., is a rapidly growing chain offering steak sandwiches at popular prices. An analysis of monthly customer traffic at its restaurants reveals the following:*

$$Q = 350 - 500P + 900P_F + 0.02Pop + 2{,}000S$$

where Q is quantity measured by the number of customers served per month, P is the average meal price per customer ($), P_F is the average meal price at fast-food restaurants, Pop is the population of the restaurant market area, and S, a binary or dummy variable, equals 1 in summer months and zero otherwise.

A.   *Determine the demand curve facing the company during the month of December if $P_F = \$6$, Pop = 300,000, and S = 0.*

B.   *Calculate the quantity demanded and total revenues during the summer month of August if P = $16, and all demand-related variables are as specified above.*

P3.5   SOLUTION

A.   With quantity expressed as a function of price, the firm demand curve can be calculated by substituting the value for each respective variable into the demand function:

$$Q = 350 - 500P + 900P_F + 0.02Pop + 2{,}000S$$

$$Q = 350 - 500P + 900(6) + 0.02(300{,}000) + 2{,}000(0)$$

$$Q = 11{,}750 - 500P$$

Then, with price as a function of quantity, the firm's demand curve is:

$$Q = 11{,}750 - 500P$$

$$500P = 11{,}750 - Q$$

$$P = \$23.5 - \$0.002Q$$

B. The total quantity demanded is found from the demand function:

$$Q = 350 - 500P + 900P_F + 0.02\text{Pop} + 2{,}000S$$

$$= 350 - 500(16) + 900(6) + 0.02(300{,}000) + 2{,}000(1)$$

$$= 5{,}750$$

Thus, total revenue is:

$$TR = P \times Q$$

$$= \$16(5{,}750)$$

$$= \$92{,}000$$

P3.6 **Quantity Supplied.** *A review of industry-wide data for the residential construction industry suggests the following industry supply function:*

$$Q = 1{,}000{,}000 + 5{,}000P - 3{,}500P_L - 30{,}000P_K$$

where Q is housing starts per year, P is the average price of new homes (in $ thousands), P_L is the average price paid for skilled labor ($), and P_K is the average price of capital (in percent).

A. *Determine the industry supply curve for a recent year when $P_L = \$40$, and $P_K = 12\%$, show the industry supply curve with quantity expressed as a function of price, and price expressed as a function of quantity.*

B. *Calculate the quantity supplied by the industry at new home prices of $100(000), $150(000), and $200(000).*

C. *Calculate the prices necessary to generate a supply of 1 million, 1.5 million, and 2 million new homes.*

P3.6   **SOLUTION**

    A.   With quantity expressed as a function of price, the industry supply curve can be written:

$$Q = 1,000,000 + 5,000P - 3,500P_L - 30,000P_K$$

$$= 1,000,000 + 5,000P - 3,500(40) - 30,000(12)$$

$$Q = 500,000 + 5,000P$$

With price expressed as a function of quantity, the industry supply curve can be written:

$$Q = 500,000 + 5,000P$$

$$5,000P = -500,000 + Q$$

$$P = -\$100 + \$0.0002Q$$

    B.   Industry supply at each respective price (in thousands) is:

$$P = \$100(000): Q = 500,000 + 5,000(100) = 1,000,000$$

$$P = \$150(000): Q = 500,000 + 5,000(150) = 1,250,000$$

$$P = \$200(000): Q = 500,000 + 5,000(200) = 1,500,000$$

    C.   The price necessary to generate each level of supply is:

$$Q = 1,000,000: P = -\$100 + \$0.0002(1,000,000) = \$100(000)$$

$$Q = 1,500,000: P = -\$100 + \$0.0002(1,500,000) = \$200(000)$$

$$Q = 2,000,000: P = -\$100 + \$0.0002(2,000,000) = \$300(000)$$

P3.7   ***Firm Supply.*** *Bing Uniform Supply, Inc., is a local supplier of uniform rental services. Chandler Bing, company controller, has estimated the following relation between its marginal cost per unit and weekly output:*

$$MC = \partial TC/\partial Q = \$3 + \$0.001Q$$

A. Calculate marginal costs per unit for 1,000, 2,000, and 3,000 uniform rentals per week.

B. Express output as a function of marginal cost. Calculate the level of output when MC = $5, $7.50, and $10.

C. Calculate the profit maximizing level of output if prices are stable in the industry at $7.50 per unit and, therefore, P = MR = $7.50.

D. Again assuming prices are stable in the industry, derive the company's supply curve. Express price as a function of quantity and quantity as a function of price.

P3.7 SOLUTION

A. Marginal production costs at each level of output are:

$$Q = 1,000: MC = \$3 + \$0.001(1,000) = \$4$$

$$Q = 2,000: MC = \$3 + \$0.001(2,000) = \$5$$

$$Q = 3,000: MC = \$3 + \$0.001(3,000) = \$6$$

B. When output is expressed as a function of marginal cost, one finds that:

$$MC = \$3 + \$0.001Q$$

$$0.001Q = -3 + MC$$

$$Q = -3,000 + 1,000MC$$

The level of output at each respective level of marginal cost is:

$$MC = \$5: Q = -3,000 + 1,000(5) = 2,000$$

$$MC = \$7.50: Q = -3,000 + 1,000(7.5) = 4,500$$

$$MC = \$10: Q = -3,000 + 1,000(10) = 7,000$$

C. Note from part B that MC = $7.50 when Q = 4,500. Therefore, when MR = $7.50, Q = 4,500 will be the profit-maximizing level of output. More formally:

$$MR = MC$$

$$\$7.50 \;=\; \$3 + \$0.001Q$$

$$0.001Q \;=\; 4.50$$

$$Q \;=\; 4{,}500$$

D. Because prices are stable in the industry, $P = MR$. This means that the company will supply output at the point where:

$$MR \;=\; MC$$

and, therefore, that:

$$P \;=\; \$3 + \$0.001Q$$

This is the supply curve for the company's service, where price is expressed as a function of quantity. When quantity is expressed as a function of price:

$$P \;=\; \$3 + \$0.001Q$$

$$0.001Q \;=\; \text{-}3 + P$$

$$Q \;=\; \text{-}3{,}000 + 1{,}000P$$

P3.8 *Industry Supply. Chips Ahoy, Inc., and Nehkdi Trading, Ltd., supply 256MB 16×8 DRAM chips to the computer industry. Confidential cost and output information for each company reveal the following relations between marginal cost and output:*

$$MC_S \;=\; \$10 + \$0.0004Q_S \qquad \textit{(Chips Ahoy)}$$

$$MC_N \;=\; \$2.50 + \$0.0001Q_N \qquad \textit{(Nehkdi)}$$

The wholesale market for these chips is vigorously price-competitive, and neither firm is able to charge a premium for its products. Thus, $P = MR$ in this market.

A. *Determine the supply curve for each firm. Express price as a function of quantity and quantity as a function of price.*

B. *Calculate the quantity supplied by each firm at prices of $5, $10, and $15. What is the minimum price necessary for each individual firm to supply output?*

C. *Determine the industry supply curve when $P < \$10$.*

D. *Determine the industry supply curve when P > $10. To check your answer, calculate quantity at an industry price of $15 and compare your answer with part B.*

P3.8 **SOLUTION**

A. Each company will supply output to the point where MR = MC. Because P = MR in this market, the supply curve for each firm can be written with price as a function of quantity as:

Chips Ahoy

$MR_S = MC_S$

$P = \$10 + \$0.0004Q_S$

Nehkdi

$MR_N = MC_N$

$P = \$2.50 + \$0.0001Q_N$

When quantity is expressed as a function of price:

Chips Ahoy

$P = \$10 + \$0.0004Q_S$

$0.0004Q_S = -10 + P$

$Q_S = -25,000 + 2,500P$

Nehkdi

$P = \$2.50 + \$0.0001Q_N$

$0.0001Q_N = -2.50 + P$

$Q_N = -25,000 + 10,000P$

B. The quantity supplied at each respective price is:

<u>Chips Ahoy</u>

$$P = \$5: Q_S = -25,000 + 2,500(5) = -12,500 \Rightarrow 0$$
(because $Q < 0$ is impossible)

$$P = \$10: Q_S = -25,000 + 2,500(10) = 0$$

$$P = \$15: Q_S = -25,000 + 2,500(15) = 12,500$$

<u>Nehkdi</u>

$$P = \$5: Q_N = -25,000 + 10,000(5) = 25,000$$

$$P = \$10: Q_N = -25,000 + 10,000(10) = 75,000$$

$$P = \$15: Q_N = -25,000 + 10,000(15) = 125,000$$

For Chips Ahoy, MC = $10 when $Q_S = 0$. Because marginal cost rises with output, Chips Ahoy will never supply a positive level of output unless a price in excess of $10 per unit can be obtained. Negative output is not feasible. Thus, Chips Ahoy will simply fail to supply output when P < $10. Similarly, $MC_N = \$2.50$ when $Q_N = 0$. Thus, Nehkdi will never supply output unless a price in excess of $2.50 per unit can be obtained.

C. When P < $10, only Nehkdi can profitably supply output. The Nehkdi supply curve will be the industry curve when P < $10:

$$P = \$2.50 + \$0.0001Q$$

or

$$Q = -25,000 + 10,000P$$

D. When P > $10, both companies can profitably supply output. To derive the industry supply curve in this circumstance, we simply sum the quantities supplied by each firm:

$$Q = Q_S + Q_N$$

$$= -25,000 + 2,500P + (-25,000 + 10,000P)$$

$$= -50,000 + 12,500P$$

To check, at P = $15:

$$Q = -50,000 + 12,500(15)$$

$$= 137,500$$

which is supported by the answer to part B, because $Q_S + Q_N = 12,500 + 125,000 = 137,500$.

(*Note*: Some students mistakenly add prices rather than quantities in attempting to derive the industry supply curve. To avoid this problem, it is important to remember that industry supply curves are found through adding up output (horizontal summation), not by adding up prices (vertical summation).)

P3.9 **Market Equilibrium.** *The HariKari is a subcompact sport utility vehicle exported to the U.S. by a leading Japanese automobile manufacturer. Demand and supply conditions for the vehicle are as follows:*

$$Q_D = 75,000 - 2P \qquad (Demand)$$

$$Q_S = 3P \qquad (Supply)$$

where P is average price per unit ($).

A. *Calculate the HariKari surplus or shortage when P = $14,000, $16,000, and $18,000.*

B. *Calculate the market equilibrium price/output combination.*

P3.9   **SOLUTION**

A.   The surplus or shortage can be calculated at each price level:

Price (1)	Quantity Supplied (2)	Quantity Demanded (3)	Surplus (+) or Shortage (-) (4) = (2) - (3)
$14,000	$Q_S = 3(14,000)$ $= 42,000$	$Q_D = 75,000-2(14,000)$ $= 47,000$	-5,000
16,000	$Q_S = 3(16,000)$ $= 48,000$	$Q_D = 75,000-2(15,000)$ $= 45,000$	3,000
18,000	$Q_S = 3(18,000)$ $= 54,000$	$Q_D = 75,000-2(17,500)$ $= 40,000$	14,000

B.   The equilibrium price is found by setting the quantity demanded equal to the quantity supplied and solving for P:

$$Q_D = Q_S$$

$$75,000 - 2P = 3P$$

$$75,000 = 5P$$

$$P = \$15,000$$

To solve for Q, set:

Demand: $Q_D = 75,000 - 2(15,000) = 45,000$

Supply: $Q_S = 3(15,000) = 45,000$

In equilibrium, $Q_D = Q_S = 45,000$.

P3.10   ***Market Equilibrium***. *Industry demand and supply functions for generic (unbranded) 12 ounce cans of cola are as follows:*

$$Q_D = 46,000,000 - 10,000,000P + 2,250,000P_C$$
$$+ 2,100Y + 200,000T, \qquad (Demand)$$

$$Q_S = 4,000,000 + 8,000,000P - 6000,000P_L$$
$$- 500,000P_K, \hspace{3cm} \textit{(Supply)}$$

where P is the average price of generic cola ($ per case), P_C is the average wholesale price of name-brand cola beverages ($ per case), Y is income (GNP in $ billions), T is the average daily high temperature (degrees), P_L is the average price of unskilled labor ($ per hour), and P_K is the average cost of capital (in percent).

A.   *When quantity is expressed as a function of price, what are the generic cola demand and supply curves if $P_C = 8, $Y = $10,000$ billion, $T = 75$ degrees, $P_L = 10, and $P_K = 12\%$.*

B.   *Calculate the surplus or shortage of generic cola when P = $5, $7, and $9.*

C.   *Calculate the market equilibrium price/output combination.*

P3.10   **SOLUTION**

A.   When quantity is expressed as a function of price, the demand curve for cola soft drinks is:

$$Q_D = 46,000,000 - 10,000,000P + 2,250,000P_C$$

$$+ 2,100Y + 200,000T$$

$$= 46,000,000 - 10,000,000P + 2,250,000(8)$$

$$+ 2,100(10,000) + 200,000(75)$$

$$Q_D = 100,000,000 - 10,000,000P$$

When quantity is expressed as a function of price, the supply curve for cola soft drinks is:

$$Q_S = 4,000,000 + 8,000,000P - 600,000P_L$$

$$- 500,000P_K$$

$$= 4,000,000 + 8,000,000P - 600,000(10)$$

$$- 500,000(12)$$

$$Q_S = -8,000,000 + 8,000,000P$$

B. The surplus or shortage can be calculated at each price level:

Price (1)	Quantity Supplied (2)	Quantity Demanded (3)	Surplus (+) or Shortage (-) (4) = (2) - (3)
$5	$Q_S = -8,000,000$ $+ 8,000,000(\$5)$ $= 32,000,000$	$Q_D = 100,000,000$ $- 10,000,000(\$5)$ $= 50,000,000$	-18,000,000
$7	$Q_S = -8,000,000$ $+ 8,000,000(\$7)$ $= 48,00,000$	$Q_D = 100,000,000$ $- 100,000,000(\$7)$ $= 30,000,000$	18,000,000
$9	$Q_S = -8,000,000$ $+ 8,000,000(\$9)$ $= 64,000,000$	$Q_D = 100,000,000$ $- 10,000,000(\$9)$ $= 10,000,000$	54,000,000

C. The equilibrium price is found by setting the quantity demanded equal to the quantity supplied and solving for P:

$$Q_D = Q_S$$

$$100,000,000 - 10,000,000P = -8,000,000 + 8,000,000P$$

$$18,000,000P = 108,000,000$$

$$P = \$6$$

To solve for Q, set:

Demand: $Q_D = 100,000,000 - 10,000,000(\$6) = 40,000,000$

Supply: $Q_S = -8,000,000 + 8,000,000(\$6) = 40,000,000$

In equilibrium $Q_D = Q_S = 40,000,000$.

Chapter 4

DEMAND ANALYSIS

Demand analysis and estimation is the most vital first responsibility of management. No matter how efficient the firm's production process, and regardless of overall managerial skill, it is impossible to operate profitably unless product demand exists or can be created. If any firm enjoys robust sales revenue growth, they possess the opportunity to capture a strong and growing level of profitability. If sales revenue growth is anemic, or worse yet if sales are falling, even dramatic restructuring and corporate downsizing seldom leads to higher profits. Successful stock-market investors have learned that over the long-run there is a 100% correlation between earnings growth and stock prices. Similarly, successful managers have learned that, again in the long-run, there is a 100% correlation between the growth in product demand and the firm's ability to enjoy high and expanding profitability.

Because demand is a fundamental determinant of profitability, management must have accurate information about demand conditions to make effective short-run operating decisions and strategic long-run planning decisions. To price the firm's products effectively, managers must know how changing prices affect the quantity demanded. Similarly, they must understand how advertising and credit terms affect demand to appraise the attractiveness of current or proposed credit and promotional strategies. Dependable estimates of the sensitivity of demand to changes in both population and income are helpful in the analysis of the firm's growth potential and, therefore, in the long-range planning process.

CHAPTER OUTLINE

I.   **BASIS FOR CONSUMER DEMAND**

      A.   **Utility Functions:** The ability of goods and services to satisfy consumer wants is the basis for consumer demand.

            1.   A utility function is a descriptive statement that relates satisfaction or well-being to the consumption of goods and services.

      B.   **Marginal Utility:** Marginal utility is the added satisfaction derived from a one-unit increase in consumption of a particular good or service.

            1.   In measuring marginal utility, it is necessary to hold consumption of other goods and services constant.

      C.   **Law of Diminishing Marginal Utility:** Marginal utility tends to diminish as consumption increases within a given time interval.

1.   This law gives rise to a downward-sloping demand curve for all goods and services.

II.   CONSUMER CHOICE

A.   **Indifference Curves:** Products are typically consumed as parts of a "market basket" of goods and services.

1.   An **indifference curve** represents all market baskets that provide a given consumer the same utility.

B.   **Marginal Rate of Substitution:** The marginal rate of substitution is the change in consumption of *Y* (goods) necessary to offset a given change in the consumption of *X* (services) if the consumer's overall level of utility is to remain constant.

1.   The marginal rate of substitution is given by the slope of an indifference curve.

2.   The marginal rate of substitution is usually not constant but diminishes as the amount of substitution increases.

C.   **Budget Lines:** A budget line represents all combinations of products that can be purchased for a fixed dollar amount.

1.   To derive a budget line, add up the amount of spending on goods and services that is feasible with a given budget.

D.   **Income and Substitution Effects:** The total effect of a price change on consumption is the sum of income and substitution effects.

1.   The income effect of a price change is the increase in overall consumption made possible by a price cut, or decrease in overall consumption that follows a price increase.

a.   The income effect shifts buyers to a higher indifference curve following a price cut or shifts them to a lower indifference curve following a price increase.

2.   The substitution effect of a price change describes the change in relative consumption that occurs as consumers substitute cheaper products for more expensive products.

a. The substitution effect results in an upward or downward movement along a given indifference curve.

III. OPTIMAL CONSUMPTION

A. **Utility Maximization:** The optimal market basket maximizes a consumer's utility for a given budget expenditure.

1. Utility maximization involves combining the consumer preference information provided by indifference curves with the cost considerations incorporated in budget lines.

2. At each point where goods and services are combined optimally, there is a tangency between the budget line and the indifference curve.

a. When consumption is optimal, the price ratios for goods and services must equal the ratios of their marginal utilities

IV. DEMAND SENSITIVITY ANALYSIS: ELASTICITY

A. **Elasticity Concept:** Elasticity measures the percentage change in a dependent *Y*-variable caused by a one percent change in an independent *X*-variable.

1. Demand analysis focuses on the percentage change in quantity sold due to a one percent change in some demand related factor *X*.

$$\text{Elasticity} = \frac{\%\Delta Q}{\%\Delta X} = \frac{\Delta Q/Q}{\Delta X/X} = \frac{\Delta Q}{\Delta X} \times \frac{X}{Q}.$$

where Δ designates change.

2. Endogenous factors are demand-related influences controlled by the firm.

3. Exogenous factors are demand-related influences outside the control of the firm.

B. **Point Elasticity and Arc Elasticity:** Elasticity can be measured in two different ways.

1. Point elasticity is a measure of elasticity at a given spot along a demand function:

$$\varepsilon = \frac{\partial Q}{Q} \div \frac{\partial X}{X} = \frac{\partial Q}{\partial X} \times \frac{X}{Q}$$

Point elasticities are useful in predicting the sales effect of "small" changes in X (i.e., $\partial X/X < 5\%$).

2. Arc elasticity is a measure of average elasticity over a range of the demand function:

$$E = \frac{Q_2 - Q_1}{(Q_2 + Q_1)/2} \div \frac{X_2 - X_1}{(X_2 + X_1)/2} = \frac{Q_2 - Q_1}{X_2 - X_1} \times \frac{X_2 + X_1}{Q_2 + Q_1}$$

Arc elasticities are useful in predicting the sales effect of "big" changes in X (i.e., $\Delta X/X \geq 5\%$).

C. **Advertising Elasticity Example:** Managers are sometimes concerned with the impact of substantial changes in a demand-determining factor, such as advertising. In these instances, the point elasticity concept suffers a conceptual shortcoming.

1. A problem sometimes occurs because elasticities are not typically constant but vary at different points along a given demand function.

2. To overcome the problem of changing elasticities along a demand function, the arc elasticity formula was developed to calculate an average elasticity for incremental as opposed to marginal changes.

V. **PRICE ELASTICITY OF DEMAND**

A. **Price Elasticity Formula:** The price elasticity of demand, or "own" price elasticity, measures the responsiveness of the quantity demanded to changes in price, holding constant all other variables in the demand function.

1. Because demand curves slope downward, price increases cause the quantity demanded to fall, and price decreases cause the quantity demanded to rise.

2. It follows that own price elasticities always have a negative sign.

3. Because the negative sign on own price elasticities is obvious, it is often ignored for convenience.

B. **Price Elasticity and Total Revenue:** Depending upon the degree of price elasticity, a given change in price will result in an increase, decrease, or no change in total revenue.

1. Total revenue is unaffected by changes in price if elasticity is unitary:

$$|\varepsilon_p| = 1.$$

2. Total revenue declines with price increases and rises with price decreases if demand is elastic:

$$|\varepsilon_p| > 1.$$

3. Total revenue rises with price increases and declines with price decreases if demand is inelastic:

$$|\varepsilon_p| < 1.$$

C. **Uses of Price Elasticity Information:** Price elasticity information is useful.

1. A profit-maximizing firm would never choose to lower its prices in the inelastic range of the demand curve. Such a price decrease would decrease total revenue and at the same time increase costs, because the quantity demanded would rise. A dramatic decrease in profits could result.

2. The profitability of a price cut in the elastic range of the demand curve depends on whether the marginal revenues generated exceed the marginal cost of added production.

3. Price elasticity of demand information has a multitude of useful application, including: inventory control, production planning, optimal pricing policy.

VI. **PRICE ELASTICITY AND MARGINAL REVENUE**

A. **Varying Elasticity at Different Points on a Demand Curve:** The price elasticity of demand varies along a given demand curve.

1. As price increases, the price elasticity of demand also increases.

2. As price decreases, the price elasticity of demand also decreases.

B. **Price Elasticity and Price Changes:** The revenue impact of a price change depends upon the price elasticity of demand.

    1.   In the elastic portion of the demand curve, $|\varepsilon_p| > 1$ and marginal revenue is greater than zero. Total revenue increases with reductions in price because this leads to a greater than proportional increase in quantity sold.

    2.   When $|\varepsilon_p| = 1$, marginal revenue equals 0 and total revenue is maximized.

    3.   In the inelastic range of the demand curve, $|\varepsilon_p| < 1$ and marginal revenue is negative. When price is reduced, output increases but revenue declines.

VII.   **PRICE ELASTICITY AND OPTIMAL PRICING POLICY**

A. **Optimal Price Formula:** Profits are maximized when MR = MC. Price elasticity estimates represent vital information because these data reveal the marginal revenue tied to price changes.

    1.   There is a simple direct relation between marginal revenue, price and the price elasticity of demand:

$$MR = P\left(1 + \frac{1}{\varepsilon_p}\right).$$

    2.   Because profits are maximized when MC = MR, the optimal or profit-maximizing price is:

$$P^* = \frac{MC}{\left(1 + \dfrac{1}{\varepsilon_p}\right)}.$$

B. **Optimal Pricing Policy Example:** Optimal prices can be easily calculated on the basis of marginal cost and point price elasticity of demand information.

C. **Determinants of Price Elasticity:** Demand tend to be less (more) elastic when:

    1.   A good is considered to be a necessity (nonessential).

    2.   Few (many) substitutes exist.

3. A small (large) proportion of income is spent on the product.

D. Price Elasticity of Demand For Airline Passenger Service: Airline passenger service has highly elastic demand.

VIII. CROSS-PRICE ELASTICITY OF DEMAND

A. Substitutes and Complements: The responsiveness of demand for one product to changes in the price of some other product, holding all other variables constant, is the cross-price elasticity of demand:

$$\varepsilon_{PX} = \frac{\partial Q_Y}{Q_Y} \div \frac{\partial P_X}{P_X} = \frac{\partial Q_Y}{\partial P_X} \times \frac{P_X}{Q_Y}$$

1. If $\varepsilon_{PX} > 0$, goods are substitutes and the price of one good and demand for another move in the same direction.

2. If $\varepsilon_{PX} < 0$, goods are complements and the price of one good and demand for another move in opposite directions.

   $P_y \uparrow \ D_x \downarrow$

3. If $\varepsilon_{PX} = 0$, goods are unrelated.

B. Cross-Price Elasticity Example: Cross-price elasticity information is useful for a number of purposes.

   a. Pricing strategy is dependent on how demand is affected by changes in the prices of other goods.

   b. Cross-price elasticity data is used in industry studies to define markets.

IX. INCOME ELASTICITY OF DEMAND

A. Normal Versus Inferior Goods: Income elasticity measures the responsiveness of demand to changes in income, holding all other variables constant:

$$\varepsilon_I = \frac{\partial Q}{Q} \div \frac{\partial I}{I} = \frac{\partial Q}{\partial I} \times \frac{I}{Q}.$$

1. If $\varepsilon_I > 0$, products are normal or superior goods, and demand rises with rising personal income and economic growth.

2.   If $\varepsilon_I < 0$, products are inferior goods, and demand falls with rising personal income and economic growth.

B.   Types of Normal Goods:

1.   Noncyclical normal goods display $0 < \varepsilon_I < 1$; producers of such products do not share proportionally in economic growth.

2.   Cyclical normal goods are characterized by $\varepsilon_I > 1$; producers of such products gain (lose) more than a proportionate share of increases (decreases) in income.

X.   SUMMARY

PROBLEMS & SOLUTIONS

P4.1   ***Basic Demand Concepts.*** *A recent study of the Fargo, North Dakota market by Chemyard, Inc., found that the local demand for weed control and fertilizer services is described by the following elasticities: price elasticity = -1.5, cross-price elasticity with department store fertilizer = 2, income elasticity = 5, TV advertising elasticity = 3. Indicate whether each of the following statements is true or false, and explain your answer.*

A.   *A price reduction for Chemyard services will increase both the number of units demanded and Chemyard revenues.*

B.   *A 15% reduction in Chemyard prices would lead to a 10% increase in unit sales.*

C.   *The cross-price elasticity indicates that a 10% increase in Chemyard prices would lead to a 20% increase in department store fertilizer demand.*

D.   *The demand for Chemyard services is price elastic and typical of noncyclical normal goods.*

E.   *A 4% increase in TV advertising would be necessary to overcome the negative effect on Chemyard sales caused by a 6% decrease in department store fertilizer prices.*

P4.1   **SOLUTION**

A.   True. Quantity demanded always rises following a price reduction. In the case of elastic demand (here $|\varepsilon_p| = 1.5 > 1$), the percentage increase in quantity will be greater than the percentage decrease in price, and total revenue will rise.

B.   False. Given $\varepsilon_p = -1.5$, a 15% reduction in Chemyard prices would lead to a 22.5% increase in unit sales.

C.   False. The $\varepsilon_{PX} = 2$ indicates that a 10% reduction in department store fertilizer prices would lead to a 20% reduction in the demand for Chemyard services.

D.   False. The demand for Chemyard services is price elastic, but $\varepsilon_I = 5 > 1$ indicates that service demand is cyclical.

E.   True. A 4% increase in TV advertising would increase service demand by 12%. Conversely, a 6% decrease in department store prices would decrease service demand by 12%. Therefore, these changes would be mutually offsetting.

P4.2   **Demand Analysis.** *Woody Boyd, owner-manager of The Lilly Pad, Inc., has estimated the following demand and marginal revenue relations for its deluxe model waterbed in the Hanover, Indiana area:*

$$P = \$500 - \$0.25Q \qquad (Demand)$$

$$MR = \$500 - \$0.5Q \qquad (Marginal\ Revenue)$$

where Q is quantity (in units).

A.   *Plot the demand, marginal, and total revenue curves.*

B.   *At what price would the Lilly Pad fail to sell any waterbeds?*

C.   *What is the maximum quantity that the Lilly Pad could give away?*

D.   *What is the maximum revenue that the firm could receive?*

E.   *For a given percentage change in price, what would be the percentage change in quantity demanded at the output level Q = 600?*

F.   *What is the arc price elasticity of demand for the quantity range of 600-700 units?*

P4.2   **SOLUTION**

A.   Note that:

Demand Curve = P = $500 - $0.25Q

Total Revenue Curve = TR = P × Q = $500Q - $0.25Q^2

Marginal Revenue Curve = MR = $\partial TR/\partial Q$ = $500 - $0.5Q

Q	P	Total Revenue = P × Q
0	$500	$0
400	400	160,000
800	300	240,000
1,000	250	250,000
1,200	200	240,000
1,600	100	160,000
2,000	0	0

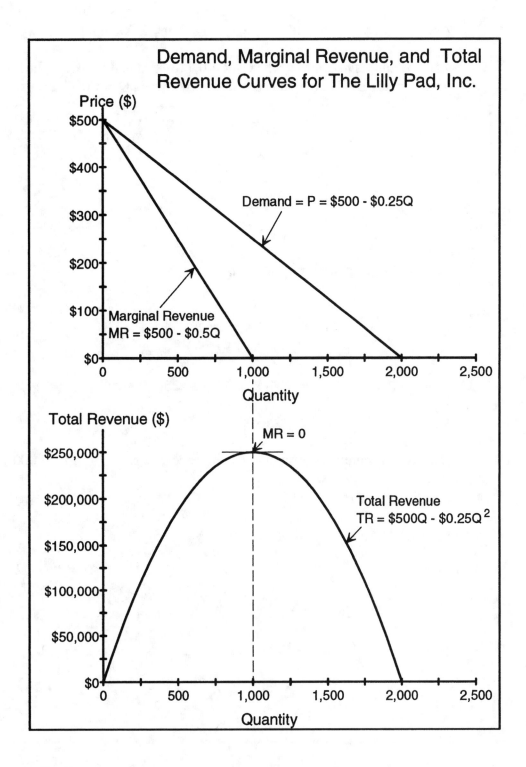

Demand, Marginal Revenue, and Total Revenue Curves for The Lilly Pad, Inc.

B. At P = $500, Q = 0 because P = $500 - $0.25(0) = $500.

C.   At a price of $0, Q = 2,000 - 4P = 2,000 - 4(0) = 2,000 units.

D.   Total revenue is maximized when MR = 0, provided that total revenue is falling as output increases. Here, revenue is maximized when Q = 1,000 because:

$$MR = \partial TR/\partial Q = \$500 - \$0.5Q$$

$$0 = \$500 - \$0.5Q$$

$$0.5Q = 500$$

$$Q = 1,000$$

At Q = 1,000, TR = $250,000, because:

$$TR = P \times Q$$

$$= \$500Q - \$0.25Q^2$$

$$= \$500(1,000) - \$0.25(1,000)^2$$

$$= \$250,000$$

(This is a maximum because marginal revenue is negative for Q > 2,000.)

E.   First, determine $\partial Q/\partial P$ as:

$$P = \$500 - \$0.25Q$$

$$Q = 2,000 - 4P$$

$$\partial Q/\partial P = -4$$

Then, at Q = 600 and P = 350:

$$\varepsilon_P = \partial Q/\partial P \times P/Q$$

$$= -4 \times (\$350/600)$$

$$= -2.33$$

The percentage change in quantity demanded is -2.33 times the percentage change in price. The point price elasticity is -2.33.

F.   Because P = $500 - $0.25Q,

At Q = 600: P = $500 - $0.25(600) = $350

At Q = 700: P = $500 - $0.25(700) = $325

Therefore:

$$\text{Arc Price Elasticity} \quad = \quad \frac{Q_2 - Q_1}{P_2 - P_1} \times \frac{P_2 + P_1}{Q_2 + Q_1}$$

$$= \quad \frac{700 - 600}{\$325 - \$350} \times \frac{\$325 + \$350}{700 + 600}$$

$$= \quad -2.1$$

As is typical, the price elasticity of demand is decreasing in absolute terms, here from $\varepsilon_P = -2.33$ to $\varepsilon_P = -2.1$, as price decreases.

P4.3   ***Demand Curve Determination.*** *Security Systems, Inc., markets electronic surveillance equipment used to control inventory "shrinkage" (shoplifting, employee theft) at retail clothing stores. The demand function for a new portable tag sensor is:*

$$Q = 100 - 20P + 0.4A + 0.025I$$

where Q = quantity demanded, P = price, A = advertising expenditures, and I = disposable income per family.

A.   *Assuming A = $6,000, and I = $60,000, what is the demand curve for the tag sensor?*

B.   *What are the total and marginal revenue functions for the tag sensor?*

C.   *What is the point price elasticity of demand, and the point income elasticity of demand under the assumptions in part A and if P = $150?*

P4.3   ***SOLUTION***

A.   The demand curve for the tag sensor is simply:

$$Q = 100 - 20P + 0.4A + 0.025I$$

$$= 100 - 20P + 0.4(6,000) + 0.025(60,000)$$

$$= 4,000 - 20P$$

or

$$P = \$200 - \$0.05Q$$

B. $TR = P \times Q$

$$= (\$200 - \$0.05Q)Q$$

$$= \$200Q - \$0.05Q^2$$

$$MR = \partial TR/\partial Q = \$200 - \$0.1Q$$

C.   Note that:

$$Q = 100 - 20P + 0.4A + 0.025I$$

$$= 100 - 20(150) + 0.4(6,000) + 0.025(60,000)$$

$$= 1,000$$

Thus, the own price elasticity is:

$$\varepsilon_P = \partial Q/\partial P \times P/Q$$

$$= -20 \times (\$150/1,000)$$

$$= -3$$

The income elasticity of demand is:

$$\varepsilon_I = \partial Q/\partial I \times I/Q$$

$$= 0.025 \times (\$60,000/1,000)$$

$$= 1.5$$

Because $\varepsilon_I = 1.5 > 0$, the tag sensor is a cyclical normal good.

P4.4 ***Arc Price Elasticity.*** *During September, in an effort to reduce end-of-the-model-year inventory, Newark Mercedes-Benz offered a $12,000 discount from the $120,000 sticker price on the Mercedes CL600 2-door coupe. Due to the success of the promotion, monthly sales rose from 15 to 23 units.*

A. *Calculate the arc price elasticity for the CL600 2-door coupe.*

B. *Calculate the sticker price reduction necessary to eliminate Newark's remaining inventory of 27 units during the month of October.*

P4.4 **SOLUTION**

A. $$E_P = \frac{\Delta Q}{\Delta P} \times \frac{P_2 + P_1}{Q_2 + Q_1}$$

$$= \frac{23 - 15}{\$108,000 - \$120,000} \times \frac{\$108,000 + \$120,000}{23 + 15}$$

$$= -4$$

B. The new price P_2 required to sell 27 units during October can be calculated from the arc price elasticity formula:

$$E_P = \frac{\Delta Q}{\Delta P} \times \frac{P_2 + P_1}{Q_2 + Q_1}$$

$$-4 = \frac{27 - 15}{P_2 - \$120,000} \times \frac{P_2 + \$120,000}{27 + 15}$$

$$-4 = \frac{12(P_2 + 120,000)}{42(P_2 - 120,000)}$$

$$-168P_2 + 20,160,000 = 12P_2 + 1,440,000$$

$$180P_2 = 18,720,000$$

$$P_2 = \$104,000$$

A new $P_2 = \$104,000$ implies a sticker price reduction of $16,000 because:

$$\Delta P = P_2 - P_1$$

$$= \$104,000 - \$120,000$$

$$= -\$16,000$$

P4.5   ***Cross-Price Elasticity.*** *The L&O Paper Company conducted a research study to determine how the demand for high strength paper boxes, product X, is affected by price changes of paper towels, product Y. Research staff member Nora Lewin estimates the relation between sales of X and the price of Y, holding other things constant, as: $Q_Y = 1,000 - 0.6P_X$.*

   A.   *How would you classify the relation between X and Y: substitute, complement, or independent?*

   B.   *Determine the quantities demanded of Y for the following prices of X: $P_X = \$100, \$80, \$60, \$40.*

   C.   *Determine the point cross-price elasticity of demand at $P_X = \$80$ and at $P_X = \$40$.*

   D.   *Determine the arc cross-price elasticity for these price ranges: $P_X = \$100$ to $80; $60 to $40*

P4.5   **SOLUTION**

   A.   X and Y are complement products. A rise in P_X causes a decrease in the demand for Y. Apparently, Adirondack's customers are more likely to buy its paper boxes if they are already a paper towel customer.

   B.   Given the functional relation $Q_Y = 1,000 - 0.6P_X$:

P_X	Y(units)
$100	940
80	952
60	964
40	976

C. At $P_X = 80$,

$$\varepsilon_{PX} = \partial Q_Y/\partial P_X \times P_X/Q_Y$$

$$= -0.6 \times (\$80/952)$$

$$= -0.05$$

At $P_X = 40$,

$$\varepsilon_{PX} = -0.6 \times (\$40/976)$$

$$= -0.02$$

D. For the range $100 to $80:

$$E_{PX} = \frac{Y_2 - Y_1}{P_{X2} - P_{X1}} \times \frac{P_{X2} + P_{X1}}{Y_2 + Y_1}$$

$$= \frac{952 - 940}{\$80 - \$100} \times \frac{\$80 + \$100}{952 + 940}$$

$$= -0.06$$

For the range $60 to $40:

$$E_{PX} = \frac{964 - 976}{\$60 - \$40} \times \frac{\$60 + \$40}{964 + 976}$$

$$= -0.03$$

P4.6 ***Cross-Price Elasticity.*** *Laguna Sporting Goods sells Roller-Ball roller skates at a wholesale price of $120 per pair. Last year, its sales volume was 10,000 pairs. This* *year, a competitor, Oceanside Sports, cut the wholesale price of Roller-Ball skates from $130 to $110 per pair. As a result, Laguna sales fell to only 8,000 pairs of skates.*

A.   *Determine the arc cross-price elasticity of demand between Laguna's and Oceanside's roller skates. (Assume that Laguna's price is held constant.)*

B.   *Assume that the arc price elasticity for Laguna's skates is $E_P = -2$. Assume also that Oceanside keeps the price of its skates at $110. What price cut must be made by Laguna in order to increase its annual sales volume back to 10,000 pairs?*

P4.6   **SOLUTION**

A.   Using the arc cross-price elasticity formula:

$$E_{PX} = \frac{Q_2 - Q_1}{P_{X2} - P_{X1}} \times \frac{P_{X2} + P_{X1}}{Q_2 + Q_1}$$

$$= \frac{8{,}000 - 10{,}000}{\$110 - \$130} \times \frac{\$110 + \$130}{8{,}000 + 10{,}000}$$

$$= 1.33$$

Because $E_{PX} > 0$, a substitute good relation exists between Laguna and Oceanside roller skates (as expected).

B.   Using the formula for arc price elasticity of demand:

$$E_P = \frac{Q_2 - Q_1}{P_2 - P_1} \times \frac{P_2 + P_1}{Q_2 + Q_1}$$

$$-2 = \frac{10{,}000 - 8{,}000}{P_2 - \$120} \times \frac{P_2 + \$120}{10{,}000 + 8{,}000}$$

$$-2 = \frac{2{,}000}{18{,}000} \times \frac{P_2 + 120}{P_2 - 120}$$

$$-18 = \frac{P_2 + 120}{P_2 - 120}$$

$$2{,}160 - 18P_2 = P_2 + 120$$

$$19P_2 = 2{,}040$$

$$P_2 = \$107.37$$

Thus, \$107.37 is the price required to again sell 10,000 pairs. This involves a \$12.63 price reduction because,

$$\Delta P = P_2 - P_1$$

$$= \$107.37 - \$120$$

$$= -\$12.63$$

P4.7   ***Optimal Pricing Policy.*** *Captain Video, Inc., sells video recording of recent movies and blank video cassettes for home recording use. During recent years, Captain Video has run a Christmas special on its products, reducing average prices of first-run movie videos from \$19.99 to \$14.99, and five-packs of blank cassettes from \$12.69 to \$9.99. Captain Kirk, manager of a new Captain Video outlet, questions the wisdom of this pricing policy in light of a recent trade association study that reports point price elasticity estimates of $\varepsilon_P = -2.5$ for first-run movie videos, and $\varepsilon_P = -4$ for blank cassettes.*

A.   *Is a price reduction likely to increase unit sales of movie videos and blank cassettes?*

B.   *What is the likely impact on total revenues of the Christmas price reductions?*

C.   *Determine optimal average prices if movie videos cost Captain Video \$9 and five-packs of blank video cassettes cost \$7.50?*

D.   *Is the Christmas special pricing policy desirable?*

P4.7   **SOLUTION**

A.   Yes, price reductions will always increase unit sales.

B.   Given $|\varepsilon_P| > 1$ for both movie videos and blank cassettes, demand is elastic and price reductions will increase both units sold and total revenues.

C. Because MC = MR at the profit-maximizing level of output, the optimal pricing formula is:

$$P = \frac{MC}{\left(1 + \dfrac{1}{\varepsilon_P}\right)}.$$

<u>Movie videos</u>

$$P = \frac{MC}{\left(1 + \dfrac{1}{\varepsilon_P}\right)}$$

$$\$14.99 \overset{?}{=} \frac{\$9}{\left(1 + \dfrac{1}{-2.5}\right)}$$

$$\$14.99 \overset{\checkmark}{=} \$15 \text{ (or } \$14.99)$$

<u>Blank Cassettes</u>

$$P = \frac{MC}{\left(1 + \dfrac{1}{\varepsilon_P}\right)}$$

$$\$9.99 \overset{?}{=} \frac{\$7.50}{\left(1 + \dfrac{1}{-4}\right)}$$

$$\$9.99 \overset{\checkmark}{=} \$10 \text{ (or } \$9.99)$$

D. Given these data, Kirk is wrong to question the Christmas special pricing policy. At P = $14.99, MR = MC for movie videos. Similarly, prices for blank video cassettes will maximize profits when P = $9.99 for blank cassettes. Captain Video's pricing policy is optimal.

P4.8   ***Arc Income Elasticity.*** *Kitchen Art, Ltd., sells its basic food processor for $300. The company's experience indicates that sales volume is affected by changes in consumers' income as well as by the price of the product. Specifically, the market research department estimates that the arc price elasticity of demand is -9, whereas the arc income elasticity is 4. These relations are expected to remain stable in the near future over the contemplated range of price and incomes.*

Last year, sales volume for the food processor was 100,000 units, and disposable income per capita was $37,500.

    A.   *Using the arc elasticity of demand formula, and holding all else equal, calculate the effect on sales of a rise in disposable income per capita from $37,500 to $42,500.*

    B.   *Using the arc price elasticity of demand formula, and holding all else equal, estimate the quantity effect of a $50 price reduction.*

    C.   *Based on your answers to parts A and B, calculate the total effect on unit sales of a $37,500 to $42,500 increase in disposable income per capita and a $50 price reduction.*

P4.8   **SOLUTION**

    A.   Using the arc income elasticity of demand formula to find Q:

$$E_I = \frac{Q_2 - Q_1}{I_2 - I_1} \times \frac{I_2 + I_1}{Q_2 + Q_1}$$

$$4 = \frac{Q_2 - 100{,}000}{\$42{,}500 - \$37{,}500} \times \frac{\$42{,}500 + \$37{,}500}{Q_2 + 100{,}000}$$

$$4 = \frac{Q_2 - 100{,}000}{Q_2 + 100{,}000} \times \frac{80{,}000}{5{,}000}$$

$$4Q_2 + 400{,}000 = 16Q_2 - 1{,}600{,}000$$

$$12Q_2 = 2{,}000{,}000$$

$$Q_2 = 166{,}667 \text{ units}$$

B. Using the arc price elasticity of demand formula to find Q:

$$E_P = \frac{Q_2 - Q_1}{P_2 - P_1} \times \frac{P_2 + P_1}{Q_2 + Q_1}$$

$$-9 = \frac{Q_2 - 100,000}{\$250 - \$300} \times \frac{\$250 + \$300}{Q_2 + 100,000}$$

$$-9 = \frac{Q_2 - 100,000}{Q_2 + 100,000} \times \frac{550}{(-50)}$$

$$-9Q_2 - 900,000 = -11Q_2 + 1,100,000$$

$$2Q_2 = 2,000,000$$

$$Q_2 = 1,000,000 \text{ units}$$

C. To estimate sales when disposable income per capita rises from $37,500 to $42,500 and price falls from $300 to $250, simply calculate the price effect from the Q = 166,667 base, or the income effect from the Q = 1,000,000 base.

Using the first approach:

$$E_P = \frac{Q_2 - Q_1}{P_2 - P_1} \times \frac{P_2 + P_1}{Q_2 + Q_1}$$

$$-9 = \frac{Q_2 - 166,667}{\$250 - \$300} \times \frac{\$250 + \$300}{Q_2 + 166,667}$$

$$-9 = \frac{Q_2 - 166,667}{Q_2 + 166,667} \times \frac{550}{(-50)}$$

$$-9Q_2 - 1,500,000 = -11Q_2 + 1,833,337$$

$$2Q_2 = 3,333,337$$

$$Q_2 = 1,666,667 \text{ units}$$

Using the second approach:

$$E_I = \frac{Q_2 - Q_1}{I_2 - I_1} \times \frac{I_2 + I_1}{Q_2 + Q_1}$$

$$4 = \frac{Q_2 - 1{,}000{,}000}{\$42{,}500 - \$37{,}500} \times \frac{\$42{,}500 + \$37{,}500}{Q_2 + 1{,}000{,}000}$$

$$4Q_2 + 4{,}000{,}000 = 16Q_2 - 16{,}000{,}000$$

$$12Q_2 = 20{,}000{,}000$$

$$Q_2 = 1{,}666{,}667 \text{ units}$$

P4.9   ***Arc Cross-Price Elasticity.*** *Spiel, Inc., is a catalog retailer of distinctive women's clothing. In an audit of Christmas season sales data, the company noted that sales of its popular $276 Harris Tweed sports jacket fell to 2,000 units from the 5,000 units sold last season. Apparently, this sales downturn was caused by department store competitors who reduced their average price on similar items from $300 to $225 per unit.*

A.   *Calculate the arc cross-price elasticity of demand for this product.*

B.   *Calculate Spiel's arc price elasticity of demand for this product if sales rebounded from 2,000 to 4,000 units following a price reduction to $241.50 per unit.*

C.   *Calculate the additional price reduction Spiel must offer on this item to fully recover lost sales (i.e., regain a volume of 5,000 units).*

P4.9   **SOLUTION**

A. $$E_{PX} = \frac{Q_{Y2} - Q_{Y1}}{P_{X2} - P_{X1}} \times \frac{P_{X2} + P_{X1}}{Q_{Y2} + Q_{Y1}}$$

$$= \frac{2{,}000 - 5{,}000}{\$225 - \$300} \times \frac{\$225 + \$300}{2{,}000 + 5{,}000}$$

$$= 3 \text{ (substitutes)}$$

B. $E_P = \dfrac{Q_2 - Q_1}{P_2 - P_1} \times \dfrac{P_2 + P_1}{Q_2 + Q_1}$

$\qquad\qquad = \dfrac{4{,}000 - 2{,}000}{\$241.50 - \$276} \times \dfrac{\$241.50 + \$276}{4{,}000 + 2{,}000}$

$\qquad\qquad = -5 \text{ (Elastic)}$

C. $E_P = \dfrac{Q_2 - Q_1}{P_2 - P_1} \times \dfrac{P_2 + P_1}{Q_2 + Q_1}$

$\qquad -5 = \dfrac{5{,}000 - 4{,}000}{P_2 - \$241.50} \times \dfrac{P_2 + \$241.50}{5{,}000 + 4{,}000}$

$\qquad -5 = \dfrac{P_2 + \$241.50}{9(P_2 - \$241.50)}$

$-45P_2 + \$10{,}867.50 = P_2 + \$241.50$

$\qquad 46P_2 = \$10{,}626$

$\qquad\quad P_2 = \$231$

Thus, \$231 is the price required to again sell 5,000 units. This involves a further price reduction of \$10.50 because,

$$\Delta P = P_3 - P_2$$

$$= \$231 - \$241.50$$

$$= -\$10.50$$

P4.10   ***Other Demand Elasticities.*** *Last year, a 1% increase in overall economic activity (GDP) caused a 5% increase in equipment sales at Empire State Manufacturing. George Costanza, executive vice-president, believes that during the coming year the anticipated 1% downturn in GDP will require a 2.5% increase in advertising to maintain current sales.*

A.   *Calculate the point income elasticity of demand for Empire State's products.*

B.   *Calculate the point advertising elasticity assumption underlying Costanza's projection.*

P4.10   **SOLUTION**

A. $\varepsilon_I = \dfrac{\text{Percentage Change in Q}}{\text{Percentage Change in I}}$

$= \dfrac{0.05}{0.01}$

$= 5$ (A cyclical normal good)

B.   All else equal, a 1% decrease in income would cause a 5% decrease in equipment demand because:

$$\varepsilon_I = \dfrac{\text{Percentage Change in Q}}{\text{Percentage Change in I}}$$

Percentage Change in Q $= \varepsilon_I \times$ (Percentage Change in I)

$= 5(-0.01)$

$= -0.05$ or -5%

If this income effect is to be offset by a 2.5% increase in advertising, the relevant advertising elasticity is:

$\varepsilon_A = \dfrac{\text{Percentage Change in Q}}{\text{Percentage Change in Advertising}}$

$= \dfrac{0.05}{0.025}$

$= 2$

Chapter 5

DEMAND ESTIMATION

Accurate estimation of demand relations is among the most challenging responsibilities that managers must meet in a dynamic economic environment. Demand is difficult to measure because consumers often react in unexpected ways to price changes, innovative advertising campaigns, changes in the pace of economic activity, and so on. Derived demand for intermediate products is similarly difficult to characterize because corporate customers frequently shift from one supplier to another on the basis of modest changes in product price and quality characteristics. Most firms simply don't have the resources to continuously monitor all current and potential customers. Others that closely monitor customer purchase decisions and perceptions are stymied by customers that have neither the time nor inclination to respond to detailed surveys. For both of these reasons, demand estimation is a difficult task.

In this chapter, three approaches to demand estimation are explored, including: consumer interviews, market experiments, and regression analysis. Consumer interviews and market experiments yield best results when skilled interviewers deal with carefully selected samples. An advantage of both techniques is that they can glean meaningful information from only limited data; a drawback to each is that they simulate actual customer decisions only imperfectly. With the present revolution in personal computing and user-friendly software, regression analysis and the statistical analysis of demand relations is now within the domain of even the smallest organization. Managers are often directly responsible for the design and execution of statistical studies, and the material contained in this chapter helps one become skillful at these tasks.

CHAPTER OUTLINE

I.   **IDENTIFICATION PROBLEM**

        A.   **Changing Nature of Demand Relations:** Demand estimation is sometimes relatively simple, especially in the case of stable short-run demand relations. In most situations, however, the changing nature of demand relations makes it difficult to compile accurate short-run estimates.

            1.   More difficult still is the problem of determining the effect on demand of changes in specific variables such as price, advertising expenditures, credit terms, prices of competing products, and so on.

            2.   The unpredictable nature of general economic conditions makes demand estimation difficult for many products. When the income elasticity of demand is high, demand tends to vary more than the parallel change in economic activity.

B. **Interplay of Demand and Supply:** It is sometimes difficult to obtain accurate estimates of demand relations because linkages exist among most economic variables.

    1. To plot a demand curve, it is necessary to vary price to obtain data on the price/quantity relation, while keeping fixed the effects of all factors in the demand function.

C. **Shifts in Demand and Supply:** If the demand curve has not shifted but the supply curve *has* shifted, price/quantity data can be utilized to estimate demand relations.

    1. If sufficient information exists to determine how demand and supply curves shift between data observations, both curves can be estimated.

D. **Simultaneous Relations:** At any point in time, a simultaneous relation, or coincident association, exists between demand and supply.

    1. The problem of estimating any given economic relation in the presence of important simultaneous relations is the identification problem.

    2. To separate shifts in demand or supply from changes or movements along a single curve, it is necessary to have more than just price/quantity data.

    3. Advanced statistical techniques, such as two-stage least squares (2SLS) or seemingly unrelated regression (SUR) analysis, are sometimes required to solve the identification problem.

II. **INTERVIEW AND EXPERIMENTAL METHODS**

A. **Consumer Interviews:** The consumer interview, or survey, method requires questioning customers or potential customers to estimate demand relations.

    1. Unfortunately, the quantity and quality of survey information are typically limited because consumers are often unable or unwilling to provide accurate answers to hypothetical questions.

B. **Market Experiments:** Market experiments examine consumer behavior in actual "test" markets or in laboratory settings.

    1. Market experiments are expensive and usually undertaken on a scale too small to allow high levels of confidence in the results.

2.   Market experiments are seldom run for sufficiently long periods to indicate the long-run effects of various price, advertising, or packaging strategies.

3.   Controlled laboratory experiments have the advantages of lower cost and greater control of extraneous factors. However, the value of consumer clinics or laboratory experiments suffers because such tests often distort shopper buying habits.

C.   **Demand for Oranges: An Illustrative Market Experiment:** The purpose of this classic market experiment was to examine the nature of competition between California and Florida oranges.

1.   The experiment provides estimates of the price elasticities of demand for various varieties of oranges and measures the cross-price elasticities of demand among types.

III.   **REGRESSION ANALYSIS**

A.   **Value of Regression Analysis:**

1.   This technique is often used to provide successful managers with valuable insight concerning demand, cost and profit relations.

B.   **What Is a Statistical Relation?:** A statistical relation exists between two economic variables if the average of one is related to another, but it is impossible to exactly predict the value of one based on the value of another.

1.   A deterministic relation is an association between variables that is known with certainty.

2.   Regression analysis is a powerful technique used to describe the statistical relation among important economic variables.

a.   A time series of data is a daily, weekly, monthly, or annual sequence of data on an economic variable such as price, income, cost, or revenue.

b.   A cross section of data is a group of observations on an important economic variable at any given point in time.

3.   The simplest and most common means for analyzing a sample of historical data is to plot and visually study the data.

a. A scatter diagram is a plot of data where the *dependent* variable is plotted on the vertical axis (*Y* axis), and the *independent* variable is plotted on the horizontal axis (*X* axis).

C. **Specifying the Regression Model:** The first step in regression analysis is to specify the variables to be included in the regression equation or model. The second step in regression analysis is to obtain reliable estimates of the variables. Once variables have been specified and the data have been gathered, the functional form of the regression equation must be determined.

1. The most common specification is a linear model where unit demand is assumed to change in a straight-line fashion with changes in each independent variable.

    a. Linear models imply a constant marginal effect on the *Y* variable due to one-unit changes in the various independent *X* variables.

    b. Elasticity varies along linear demand functions.

2. Another common regression model form is the multiplicative model where the marginal effect of each independent variable depends on the value of all independent variables.

    a. Multiplicative models can be transformed into a linear relation using logarithms and then estimated by the least squares technique.

    b. Multiplicative models imply a changing absolute effect on the *Y* variable due to one-unit changes in the various independent *X* variables.

    c. Multiplicative demand functions implicitly assume constant elasticities.

    d. The specific form of any regression model--linear, multiplicative, or otherwise--must be consistent with economic theory.

D. **Least Squares Method:** Regression equations are typically estimated, or "fitted," by the method of least squares. This method fits the regression line that minimizes the sum of the squared deviations between the best-fitting line and the set of original data points.

1. The minimization of squared deviations avoids the problem of having positive and negative deviations cancel one another out.

IV.   **MEASURES OF REGRESSION MODEL SIGNIFICANCE**

A.   **Standard Error of the Estimate:**   A very useful measure for examining the accuracy of any regression model is the standard error of the estimate (SEE), or the standard deviation of the dependent Y variable after controlling for the influence of all X variables.

1.   The standard error of the estimate increases with the amount of scatter about the sample regression line.

2.   If each data point were to lie exactly on the regression line, then the standard error of the estimate would equal zero because each $\hat{Y}_t$ would exactly equal Y_t.

3.   The standard error of the estimate is used to determine a range within which the dependent Y variable can be predicted with varying degrees of statistical confidence based on the regression coefficients and values for the X variables.

a.   The best estimate of the tth value for the dependent variable is $\hat{Y}_t$, as predicted by the regression equation.

b.   There is a 95% probability that observations of the dependent variable will lie within the range $\hat{Y}_t \pm (1.96 \times \text{SEE})$, or within roughly 2 standard errors of the estimate.

c.   The probability is 99% that any given $\hat{Y}_t$ will lie within the range $\hat{Y}_t \pm (2.576 \times \text{SEE})$, or within roughly 3 standard errors of its predicted value.

B.   **Goodness of Fit, *r*, and *R^2*:**   In a simple regression model with only one independent variable, the correlation coefficient, r, measures goodness of fit. In multiple regression models where more than one independent X variable is considered, the coefficient of determination, or R^2, shows how well a multiple regression model explains changes in the value of the dependent Y variable.

1. R^2 is the proportion of total variation in the dependent variable that is explained by the full set of independent variables.

a.   If $R^2 = 0$, the regression model is unable to explain *any* variation in the dependent Y variable.

b.   If $R^2 = 1$, the regression model is able to explain *all* variation in the dependent Y variable.

c.   In judging R^2, the type of analysis conducted and the anticipated use of statistical results must be considered.

C.   **Corrected Coefficient of Determination, $\bar{R}^2$:** R^2 always equals 100% when the number of estimated coefficients equals or exceeds the number of observations because each data point can then be placed exactly on the regression line. The corrected coefficient of determination, denoted by the symbol $\bar{R}^2$, is an adjustment to R^2 based upon the number of observations (data points) and the number of estimated coefficients.

1.   The downward adjustment to R^2 is large when n, the sample size, is small relative to k, the number of coefficients being estimated.

2.   The downward adjustment to R^2 is small when n is large relative to k.

D.   **F Statistic:** The F statistic provides evidence on whether a statistically significant proportion of total variation in the dependent variable has been explained by the regression model.

1.   Like $\bar{R}^2$, the F statistic is adjusted for sample size and coefficient number.

2.   The F test is used to determine whether a given F statistic is statistically significant.

a.   Performing F tests involves comparing F statistics with critical values from a table of the F distribution.

b.   If a given F statistic *exceeds* the critical value from the F distribution table, the hypothesis of no relation between the dependent Y variable and the set of independent X variables can be rejected.

V.   **MEASURES OF INDIVIDUAL VARIABLE SIGNIFICANCE**

A.   *t* **statistic:** The *t* statistic (or test statistic) has an *approximately* normal distribution with a mean of zero and a standard deviation of 1. It describes the difference between an estimated coefficient and some hypothesized value in terms of "standardized units," or by the number of standard deviations of the coefficient estimate.

1.   It is rare to find a calculated t statistic that falls outside the bounds ± 1.96, or roughly ± 2, when the true value of $t = 0$. This occurs less than 5% of the time.

2.   It is very rare to find a calculated t statistic that falls outside the bounds ± 2.576, or roughly ± 3, when the true value of $t = 0$; this happens less than 1% of the time.

B.   **Two-Tail t Tests:** In regression analysis, the most common t-test is performed to learn if an individual slope coefficient estimate $b = 0$. If X and Y are unrelated, then the b slope coefficient for a given X variable equals zero.

1.   If the $b = 0$ hypothesis can be rejected, then it is possible to infer that $b \neq 0$ and that a relation exists between Y and a given X variable.

   a.   Calculated t statistics greater than 2 usually permits rejection of the hypothesis that there is no relation between the dependent Y variable and a given X variable with 95% confidence.

   b.   A calculated t statistic greater than 3 typically permits rejection of the hypothesis that there is no relation between the dependent Y variable and a given X variable with 99% confidence.

2.   Critical t values are adjusted upward when sample size is small in relation to the number of estimated coefficients.

   a.   Precise critical t values can be obtained from a t table, such as that found in Appendix C.

   b.   If the calculated t statistic is greater than the relevant critical t value, the $b = 0$ hypothesis can be rejected.

   c.   If the calculated t statistic is not greater than the critical t value, it is not possible to reject the $b = 0$ hypothesis. In that case, there is no evidence of a relation between Y and a given X variable.

3.   Tests of the hypothesis $b = 0$ are referred to as two-tail t tests because either very small negative t values or very large positive t values can lead to rejection.

C.   **One-Tail t tests:** Some managerial questions go beyond the simple matter of whether X influences Y. Tests of direction (positive or negative) or comparative magnitude are called one-tail t tests.

1.   In a two-tail t test, rejection of the null hypothesis occurs with a finding that the t statistic is not in the *region around zero*.

2.   In one-tail t tests, rejection of the null hypothesis occurs when the t statistic is in one specific tail of the distribution.

VI.   PRACTICAL SOLUTIONS TO REGRESSION PROBLEMS

A.   **Choosing the Best Model:** The specific form of a regression equation is typically based on a demand or cost model derived from economic theory. Nevertheless, some experimentation might sometimes prove appropriate.

1.   The specific functional form of the regression model is often subject to experimentation.

2.   Some careful experimentation with the range of independent X variables incorporated in the regression model might also be proper.

3.   When using an experimental method, it is appropriate to retain a hold out, or test sample, of data where the experimental model can be verified.

B.   **Dealing with Multicollinearity:** A multicollinearity problem exists when the regression model indicates a significant relation between the dependent Y variable and the group of independent X variables, but the least squares technique is unable to identify the various X variables as uniquely important.

1.   Multicollinearity is a situation in which two or more independent variables are very highly correlated.

2.   One practical approach for dealing with multicollinearity is to deflate or otherwise transform the independent variables.

C.   **Residual Analysis:**   The least squares regression technique makes four assumptions about the distribution of the error term, or residual, u_t. Residuals are assumed to have a random distribution that is normal, an expected value of zero, and constant variance. A violation of any one of these assumptions impairs the validity of the technique.

1.   The problem of serial correlation (or autocorrelation) exists when residuals are related sequentially and, therefore, not independent.

2.   If the variance of the residuals is not constant over the entire sample, a heteroskedasticity problem exists.

    a.   To correct a heteroskedasticity problem, the regression variables are often transformed into logarithmic or ratio form prior to estimation, or more sophisticated weighted least squares regression methods are used.

VII.   SUMMARY

PROBLEMS & SOLUTIONS

P5.1   ***Demand Concepts.*** *Identify each of the following as true or false and explain why.*

    A.   *The effect of a one-unit change in advertising is constant along a linear demand curve.*

    B.   *An increase in income increases the quantity demanded for normal goods and services.*

    C.   *A demand curve is revealed if prices fall while demand conditions are held constant.*

    D.   *The price elasticity of demand is constant along a linear demand curve.*

    E.   *A rise in price tends to reduce the quantity demanded.*

P5.1   **SOLUTION**

    A.   True.   The effect of a one-unit change in advertising is constant, but the advertising elasticity of demand varies along a linear demand curve.

    B.   False.   An increase in income causes an upward shift in the demand curve for normal goods and services.

    C.   True.   A demand curve is revealed if prices fall while demand conditions are held constant.

    D.   False.   The effect of a one-unit change in price is constant, but the elasticity of demand varies along a linear demand curve.

    E.   True.   A rise in price causes an upward movement along the demand curve and a decrease in the quantity demanded.

P5.2   ***Regression Analysis.*** *Identify each of the following as true or false and explain why.*

    A.   *A parameter is a sample characteristic.*

    B.   *A one-tail F test is used to indicate whether or not the independent variables as a group explain a significant share of demand variation.*

C. *The estimated demand relation can be used to derive a predicted value for demand.*

D. *A two-tail t test is an appropriate means for testing whether or not individual independent variables have an influence on the dependent variable.*

E. *The coefficient of determination shows the share of total variation in demand that can be explained by the regression model.*

P5.2   **SOLUTION**

A. False. A parameter is a population characteristic that is estimated by a coefficient derived from a sample of data.

B. True. An *F* test is used to indicate whether or not the independent variables as a group explain a significant share of demand variation.

C. True. Given values for independent variables, the estimated demand relation can be used to derive a predicted (or fitted) value for demand.

D. True. A two-tail t test is an appropriate means for tests concerning the influences of independent variables on *Y*.

E. True. The coefficient of determination (R^2) shows the share of total variation in demand that can be explained by the regression model.

P5.3   ***Demand Curve Analysis.*** *Game-Gear, Inc., is a leading supplier of video games for hand-held video game players. Average wholesale price and unit sales data for the "Game-Gear Football" over the past five-month period are shown in the table.*

	June	July	August	Sept.	Oct.
Price ($)	$36	$34	$33	$35	$34
Units sold	350,000	400,000	425,000	375,000	400,000

A. *Complete the following table, and use these data to derive intercept and slope coefficients for a linear demand curve.*

Month	Price	Quantity	∂Price	∂Quantity	Slope = ∂P/∂Q
June	$36	350,000	---	---	---
July	34	400,000			
August	33	425,000			
Sept.	35	375,000			
Oct.	34	400,000			

B.   *Assuming that demand conditions are held constant, use the preceding data to plot a linear demand curve.*

P5.3   **SOLUTION**

A.   A linear demand curve is based on the assumption that a one-unit change in price leads to a constant change in the quantity demanded. From the monthly price/output data note that:

Month	Price	Quantity	∂Price	∂Quantity	Slope = ∂P/∂Q
June	$36	350,000	---	---	---
July	34	400,000	-$2	50,000	-0.00004
August	33	425,000	-1	25,000	-0.00004
Sept.	35	375,000	2	-50,000	-0.00004
Oct.	34	400,000	-1	25,000	-0.00004

When a linear demand curve is written as:

$$P = a + bQ$$

a is the intercept and b is the slope coefficient. By definition, slope equals ∂P/∂Q. From the above data note:

$$b = \partial P/\partial Q = -0.00004$$

Therefore,

$$P = a - \$0.00004Q$$

Under the assumption of a liner demand relation, each of the data points given in the table fall exactly along the linear demand curve. The value of the intercept term can therefore be easily calculated using data for any of the data points given in the table. For example, using the June data point where P = $36 and Q = 350,000,

$$P = a - \$0.00004Q$$

$$\$36 = a - \$0.00004(350,000)$$

$$\$36 = a - \$14$$

$$a = \$50$$

Therefore, in general:

$$P = \$50 - \$0.00004Q$$

or

$$Q = 1,250,000 - 25,000P$$

B. The linear demand curve can be plotted as:

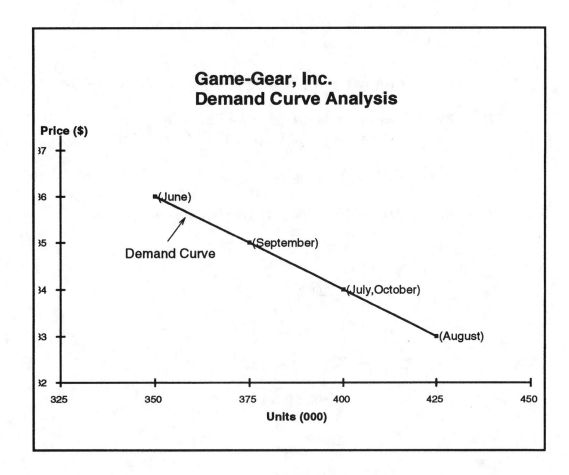

P5.4 ***The Identification Problem.*** *Complex Circuits, Inc., is a small but rapidly growing supplier of analog/digital circuits and systems used for measurement and control. The average price received by CCI for the XKE device, and the number sold (output) per quarter over the past five years given in the table.*

	Year				
	1	*2*	*3*	*4*	*5*
Price	*$100*	*$110*	*$120*	*$130*	*$140*
Quantity	*500*	*600*	*700*	*800*	*900*

Annual demand and supply curves for CCI services are:

$$Q_D = 625 - 2.5P + 125T \qquad (Demand)$$

$$Q_S = -500 + 10P \qquad (Supply)$$

where Q is output (000), P is price, T is a trend factor, and T = 1 during Q-1 and increases by one unit per quarter.

A.   *Express each demand and supply curve in terms of price as a function of output.*

B.   *Plot the quarterly demand curves for the last six quarterly periods. (Hint: Let T=1 to find the Y-intercept for Q-1, T = 2 for Q-2, and so on.)*

C.   *Plot the CCI supply curve on the same graph.*

D.   *What is this problem's relation to the identification problem?*

P5.4   **SOLUTION**

A.   Demand

$$Q_D = 625 - 2.5P + 125T$$

$$2.5P = 625 - Q_D + 125T$$

$$P = \$250 - \$0.4Q_D + \$50T$$

Supply

$$Q_S = -500 + 10P$$

$$10P = 500 + Q_S$$

$$P = \$50 + \$0.1Q_S$$

B.,C.

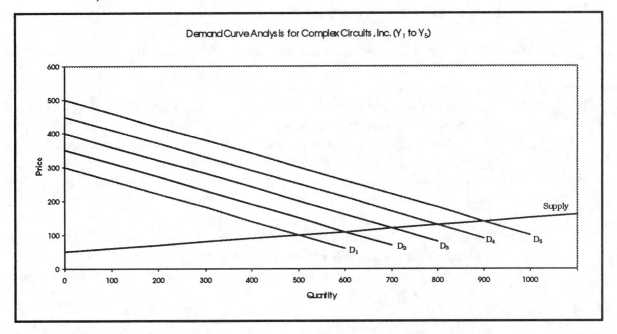

Demand Curve Analysis for Complex Circuits, Inc. (Y₁ to Y₅)

D. This example illustrates the identification problem. If we know that either the demand or supply function is shifting while the other is stable, then the price/output data can be used to trace out the stable curve. Here the supply curve is stable while demand is growing rapidly (shifting to the right). Therefore, the price/output data given in the problem can be used to trace out the relevant supply curve.

P5.5   *Regression Statistics. The Travel Company, Inc., has hired a management consulting firm to analyze demand in 26 regional markets for one of its major products. A preliminary report from the consultant contained the following regression results (standard errors in parentheses):*

$$Q = 260 + 2A + 6.4I + 3P_X - 4P$$
$$(400)\ (0.4)\ (2.4)\ (0.9)\ (1.2)$$

$$R^2 = 90\%$$

Standard Error of the Estimate = 10

Here, Q is the annual demand for the tour in question, P is the price charged by TTC in dollars, A is thousands of dollars of advertising expenditures, P_X is the average price *of another product (unidentified), also measured in dollars, and I is thousands of dollars of disposable income per family in the market area.*

A.   *Interpret the demand equation and explain the use of the regression statistics provided.*

B.   *Assume that the consultant is not available and the management of TTC is unsure whether the P_X variable in the equation is the price of a complementary or competing product. (Both were used in different regression runs and, because of a mixup in labeling, the P_X variable is unidentified.) Can you determine at the 99% confidence level whether X is a complement or a substitute? Why or why not? If so, which is it?*

C.   *Assuming that the current price is $400, advertising expenditures are $20,000, P_X is $500, and disposable income per family is $62,500, what is the point price elasticity of demand? Would a reduction in price result in an increase in total revenues? Why?*

D.   *Given the data in part C, what is the point cross-price elasticity between the tour and product X?*

E.   *If TTC wished to use this equation for forecasting purposes, what is the size of the 99% confidence interval for predicting Q?*

P5.5   **SOLUTION**

A.   The regression equation relates the number of tours sold annually to the value of four variables: advertising expenditures, A, per family income, I, the average price of the unidentified product, P_X, and the price charged by TTC, P. More specifically, the expected sales quantity for any year is equal to 260 plus 2 times the advertising expenditures (measured in thousands of dollars), plus 6.4 times the per family income in the market area (in thousands of dollars), plus 3 times the average price of another unidentified product (in dollars), minus 4 times the price charged by TTC (also measured in dollars).

The individual coefficients of the equation provide estimates of the marginal relationships between the annual number of tours sold and each of the independent variables in the model. All of the other information provided relates to the accuracy of the empirical estimation of the demand equation. $R^2 = 90\%$ is the coefficient of determination. It measures the proportion of the total variation in the annual number of tours sold that has been explained by the regression model as a whole. That is, it measures the percentage of total variation in Q that has been accounted for by variation in A, I, P_X and P taken together.

The standard error of the estimate provides information about the level of accuracy one can expect when using the equation for forecasting purposes. The standard error of the estimate corresponds to the standard deviation of a probability distribution and thus can be used to develop a confidence interval for sales predictions.

Letting $\hat{Q}_t$ represent the sales forecast for a given set of values for A, I, P_X and P, there is approximately a 95% probability that actual sales, Q_t, will fall in the range $Q_t = \hat{Q}_t \pm 2.08$ standard errors (where $t^*_{26 - 5 = 21, \alpha = 0.05} = 2.08$), and a 99% probability that $Q_t = \hat{Q}_t \pm 2.831$ standard errors of the estimate (where $t^*_{26 - 5 = 21, \alpha = 0.01} = 2.831$).

For simplicity, these critical t values are often rounded off to t = 2 (for 95% confidence), and t = 3 (for 99% confidence).

The standard errors of the coefficient estimate provide information about the level of accuracy with which the individual relationships between the independent variables and sales of the tour have been estimated. The standard errors of the coefficients can be used to estimate confidence intervals within which the true parameter relating each independent variable to sales will lie with varying degrees of probability. For example, there is a 95% probability that the true parameter relating price to quantity sold lies in the interval -1.5 (= - 4 + 2.08(1.22)) to -6.5 (= - 4 - 2.08(1.22)) which is the estimated parameter -4 ± 2.08 times the coefficient standard error of 1.22. Thus, the smaller the relative size of a coefficient's standard error, the greater the level of accuracy that can be ascribed to the parameter estimate.

B.   The fact that the coefficient of P_X is positive indicates that there is a substitute relation between tours and product X. As the price of X increases so too does the demand for the tour in question. In order to conclude that product X is in fact a substitute, one must be able to reject $H_0 : b_{P_X} < 0$ (one-tail test).

At the 99% confidence level, this hypothesis can be rejected because:

$$t = \frac{b - 0}{\sigma_b} = \frac{3}{0.9} = 3.33 > 2.518 = t^*_{21, \alpha = 0.01}$$

Thus, a substitute relation exists between X and tours.

(*Remember*: the *t* table at the back of the text shows rejection regions for *two*-tail tests. Thus, the $\alpha = 0.1$ column shows critical *t* values for $\alpha = 0.1$ (one-tail) *and* for $\alpha = 0.05$ (two-tail). Here t* = 2.518 because the relevant hypothesis involves a one-tail test and $\alpha = 0.01$ or 99% confidence).

C. To calculate the point price elasticity one must first substitute the values of the independent variables into the demand model to obtain $\hat{Q}$.

$$\hat{Q} = 260 + 2A + 6.4I + 3P_X - 4P$$

$$= 260 + 2(20) + 6.4(62.5) + 3(500) - 4(400)$$

$$= 600$$

Therefore,

$$\varepsilon_P = \partial Q/\partial P \times P/Q$$

$$= -4 \times (\$400/600)$$

$$= -2.67$$

A price reduction would increase total revenue because demand is elastic ($|\varepsilon_P| > 1$).

D. Using the point cross-price elasticity formula:

$$\varepsilon_{PX} = \partial Q_Y/\partial P_X \times P_X/Q_Y$$

$$= 3 \times (\$500/600)$$

$$= 2.5$$

Because $\varepsilon_{PX} = 2.5 > 0$, a substitute good relation exists between X and tours. This is consistent with the individual coefficient analysis of Part B.

E. The 99% confidence interval for Q is $\hat{Q} \pm 2.831$ times the standard error of the estimate (where $t^*_{26-5=21,\alpha=0.01} = 2.831$). Given the current values for A, I, P_X and P, the 99% confidence interval would be Q = 600 ± 2.831(10) = 600 ± 28.

P5.6 *Elasticity Estimation. The Washington Life Insurance Company offers a wide variety of insurance products, including whole-life and term policies. The company has compiled the following data concerning policy sales during recent years:*

Year	Whole-life		Term	
	Price*	*Quantity*	*Price**	*Quantity*
1998	$2.00	240,000	$1.50	100,000
1999	2.00	200,000	1.45	130,000
2000	1.90	230,000	1.45	150,000
2001	1.80	280,000	1.40	200,000
2002	1.80	238,000	1.33	270,000

*Price is quoted in terms of cost per $1,000 of coverage.

A. Calculate the point price elasticity of demand for whole-life insurance?

B. Calculate the point price elasticity of demand for term insurance?

C. Evaluate the percentage change in whole-life demand given a 1% change in the price of term insurance. Is term insurance a substitute for whole-life?

P5.6 **SOLUTION**

A. To evaluate the point price elasticity of demand for whole-life insurance, one must only consider years when the price of whole-life changed but the price of term remained constant. Therefore, only the 1999-2000 period is relevant.

$$\varepsilon_P = \partial Q/\partial P \times P/Q$$

$$= \frac{230,000 - 200,000}{\$1.90 - \$2} \times \frac{\$2}{200,000}$$

$$= -3 \text{ (Elastic)}$$

B. To evaluate the point price elasticity of demand for term insurance, one must only consider years when the price of term changed, but the price of whole-life remained constant. Therefore, only the 1998-1999 and 2001-2002 periods are relevant.

<u>1998-1999</u>

$$\varepsilon_P = \partial Q/\partial P \times P/Q$$

$$= \frac{130,000 - 100,000}{\$1.45 - \$1.50} \times \frac{\$1.50}{100,000}$$

$$= -9$$

2001-2002

$$\varepsilon_P = \partial Q/\partial P \times P/Q$$

$$= \frac{270,000 - 200,000}{\$1.33 - \$1.40} \times \frac{\$1.40}{200,000}$$

$$= -7$$

<u>Average</u>: $\varepsilon_P = (-9 + -7)/2 = -8$ (Highly elastic)

C. To evaluate the relevant cross-price elasticity of demand, it is necessary to consider periods when only the price of term insurance changed.
   Thus, only the 1998-1999 and 2001-2002 periods are relevant.

1998-1999

$$\varepsilon_{PX} = \partial Q_Y/\partial P_X \times P/Q$$

$$= \frac{200,000 - 240,000}{\$1.45 - \$1.50} \times \frac{\$1.50}{240,000}$$

$$= 5$$

2001-2002

$$\varepsilon_{PX} = \partial Q_Y/\partial P_X \times P/Q$$

$$= \frac{238,000 - 280,000}{\$1.33 - \$1.40} \times \frac{\$1.40}{280,000}$$

$$= 3$$

<u>Average</u>: $\varepsilon_{PX} = (5 + 3)/2 = 4$ (Substitutes)

Yes, term insurance appears to be a substitute for whole-life insurance.

P5.7   ***Standard Error of the Estimate.*** *Body Fit, Inc., runs a California-based chain of health clubs featuring aerobic exercise, racket sports, swimming and weight training* *facilities. An in-house study of monthly sales by three outlets during the past year (a total of 36 observations) revealed the following (standard errors in parentheses):*

$$Q_Y = 410 - 20P_Y + 12P_X + 8A + 50T - 5W$$
$$\quad\quad (250)\ (7.5)\ \ (7)\ \ (3.5)\ \ (10)\ \ (2.8)$$

$$R^2 = 96\%$$

Standard Error of the Estimate = 10

Here Q_Y = membership sales (in units), P_Y = average membership price (in dollars), P_X = average membership price charged by competitors (in dollars), A = advertising expenditures (in hundreds of dollars), T = time (in months of continuous operation), W = weather (in average monthly temperature).

A. *What share of overall variation in membership sales is explained by the regression equation? What share is left unexplained?*

B. *Using a 95% confidence level criterion, which independent factors have an influence on membership sales?*

C. *During this period, the San Diego outlet's average monthly price was $150, the average competitor's monthly price was $100, advertising was $6,750, the outlet had been in operation for 3 years, and the average temperature was 70°. Assuming this was a typical observation included in the study, derive the relevant demand curve for Body Fit memberships.*

D. *Assume the model and data given above are relevant for the coming period. Calculate the range within which you would expect to find actual monthly sales revenue with 95% confidence.*

P5.7   **SOLUTION**

A. $R^2 = 96\%$ means that 96% of the total variation in demand is explained by the regression model. This implies that 4% of demand variation remains unexplained.

B. With a sample size $n = 36$ and a model featuring $k = 6$ coefficients, the relevant number of degrees of freedom is $d.f. = n - k = 30$. Roughly speaking, this means that a coefficient estimate more than twice as large as the coefficient's standard deviation, or a t-statistic of more than two, is necessary before we can conclude that a given independent variable influences Q at the 95% confidence level (assuming a two-tail test).

More precisely, $t^*_{30,\alpha=0.05} = 2.042$. Therefore, from the regression equation:

	Variable		Influence
Price:	$t = \dfrac{b_{P_Y}}{\sigma_{P_Y}} = \dfrac{20}{7.5} = 2.67 > t^*_{30,\alpha=0.05}$		Yes.
Competitor Price:	$t = \dfrac{b_{P_X}}{\sigma_{P_X}} = \dfrac{12}{7} = 1.71 \ngtr t^*_{30,\alpha=0.05}$		No.
Advertising:	$t = \dfrac{b_A}{\sigma_A} = \dfrac{8}{3.5} = 2.29 > t^*_{30,\alpha=0.05}$		Yes.
Time:	$t = \dfrac{b_T}{\sigma_T} = \dfrac{50}{10} = 5.00 > t^*_{30,\alpha=0.05}$		Yes.
Weather:	$t = \dfrac{b_W}{\sigma_W} = \dfrac{5}{2.8} = 1.79 \ngtr t^*_{30,\alpha=0.05}$		No.

C.   The demand curve for Body Fit memberships is given by the expression:

$$Q_Y = 410 - 20P_Y + 12P_X + 8A + 50T - 5W$$

$$= 410 - 20P_Y + 12(100) + 8(67.5) + 50(36) - 5(70)$$

$$= 3{,}600 - 20P_Y$$

D.   Given a monthly membership price $P_Y = \$150$, the estimated value for membership demand (in units) is:

$$\hat{Q} = 3{,}600 - 20(150)$$

$$= 600$$

Therefore, using the standard error of the estimate SEE = 10, the 95% confidence region for membership sales (in units) is:

$$Q_Y = \hat{Q} \pm t_{30,\alpha=0.05} \times SEE \quad \text{(with 95\% confidence)}$$

$$= 600 \pm 2.042(10)$$

$$= 600 \pm 20.42, \text{ or } 579.58 \text{ to } 620.42$$

Finally, given a membership price P_Y = $150, the 95% confidence region for annual sales revenue is:

$$579.58 \times \$150 \text{ to } 620.42 \times \$150$$

or

$$\$86,937 \text{ to } \$93,063$$

P5.8 *Demand Curve Estimation. Z-Box Toys Company manufactures and sells educational toys. An empirical demand function for one of the firm's products has just been estimated over the last 21 quarters using regression analysis. The demand function is:*

$$Q_Y = -800 - 500P_Y + 24A + 15I + 200P_X$$
$$(600) \ (100) \quad (12) \quad (30) \ (80)$$

$$R^2 = 91\%$$

Standard Error of the Estimate = 50

Here Q_Y is quantity (measured in units) of Product Y demanded in the current period, A is hundreds of dollars of advertising ($00), I is thousands of dollars of disposable income per capita ($000), and P_X is the price ($) of another toy manufactured by ABC. The terms in parentheses are the standard errors of the coefficients.

A. *How would you characterize the ability of this empirical demand function to explain demand for Product Y?*

B. *Currently, P_Y = $8, advertising is $20,000, disposable income per capita is $40,000 and P_X = $7. What are expected sales of Y in this period, and what range of sales would you specify for the current period if you wanted to establish a 99% confidence interval?*

C. *What is the demand curve currently facing Z-Box for Product Y? (Note: Be careful to properly account for the units in which advertising and income appear in the estimated demand function.)*

D. *What is the point price elasticity of demand for Y at the current price?*

E. *Given the current price elasticity of demand, would a price reduction increase Z-Box profits? Explain.*

F. *What demand curve would Z-Box face for Product Y if it raised advertising expenditures to $30,000?*

P5.8 **SOLUTION**

A. The regression equation appears to explain the relation between demand for the product and the independent variables quite well. The coefficient of determination $R^2 = 91\%$ indicating that 91% of the variation in sales has been explained by the variation in the independent variables.

B. Note that:

$$\hat{Q}_Y = -800 - 500P_Y + 24A + 15I + 200P_X$$

$$= -800 - 500(8) + 24(200) + 15(40) + 200(7)$$

$$= 2,000 \text{ units}$$

The 99% confidence interval for Q is $\hat{Q} \pm 2.921$ times the standard error of the estimate (where $t^*_{21 - 5 = 16, \alpha = 0.01} = 2.921$). Given the current values for P_Y, A, I, and P_X, the 99% confidence interval is:

$$Q = \hat{Q} \pm 2.921 \times SEE$$

$$= 2,000 \pm 2.921(50)$$

$$= 2,000 \pm 146 \text{ units}$$

C. The relevant demand curve is found by noting:

$$Q_Y = -800 - 500P_Y + 24A + 15I + 200P_X$$

$$= -800 - 500P_Y + 24(200) + 15(40) + 200(7)$$

$$= 6,000 - 500P_Y$$

$$P_Y = 12 - 0.002Q_Y$$

D. Using the point price elasticity formula, it is obvious that:

$$\varepsilon_{P_Y} = \partial Q_Y/\partial P_Y \times P_Y/Q_Y$$

$$= -500 \times (8/2{,}000)$$

$$= -2$$

E. With $|\varepsilon_p| > 1$, the relative change in quantity is greater than that of price so a price reduction will lead to an increase in total revenue. However, to determine whether such a price reduction is appropriate, one would need information concerning the marginal cost of increased output. In other words, the marginal revenue of added sales is positive, but one can't know whether MR > MC. Thus, although revenue would be increased with a price reduction, profits might be reduced. Without further information, no recommendation concerning the profit implications of a price reduction can be made.

F. With an increase in advertising of $15,000, the demand curve for product Y becomes:

$$Q_Y = -800 - 500P_Y + 24A + 15I + 200P_X$$

$$= -800 - 500P_Y + 24(300) + 15(40) + 200(7)$$

$$= 8{,}400 - 500P_Y$$

or

$$P_Y = \$16.8 - \$0.002Q_Y$$

P5.9 *z-Statistics. Martin's Footware, Inc., of Boston, Massachusetts has retained you to aid the firm in an evaluation of its marketing strategy. Martin's "Happy Feet" running shoes are marketed through local retail outlets in the eastern United States. A move to extend Martin's market to midwestern and western states is currently being contemplated.*

A marketing research group conducted an empirical analysis of demand for Martin's "Happy Feet" during 2002 in thirty-six regional markets and found the following (standard errors in parentheses):

$$Q = 982 - 10P + 12.5I + 5W - 0.5CA + 5A$$
$$\quad\ (240)\ (1.3)\quad (8.6)\quad (2.8)\quad (0.4)\quad (2.5)$$

$$R^2 = 85\%$$

Standard error of the estimate = 200

$$cov(I,W) = 3.5, \; cov(I,CA) = 8.6, \; cov(I,A) = 2.8$$

where Q = quantity sold (in pairs of shoes), P = price (in dollars), I = disposable income per capita (in thousands of dollars), W = weather measured by average temperature (in degrees), CA = competitor advertising (in thousands of dollars), A = Martin's "own" advertising (in thousands of dollars).

A. Fully evaluate and interpret the empirical results reported above on an overall basis. Include in your analysis a discussion of:

(i) R^2

(ii) $\bar{R}^2$

(iii) F statistic

(iv) Standard error of the estimate

B. Will a recession hurt sales?

C. Is demand more dependent on local income than on weather conditions?

D. Champaign-Urbana, Illinois is a potential Midwestern market with economic characteristics typical of those eastern markets included in the empirical analysis. In Champaign-Urbana, expected levels are: disposable income per capita of $60,000, average temperature of 54°, competitor advertising of $64,000, and Martin's advertising of $6,000. Given these data,

(i) Derive the demand curve for the Champaign-Urbana market.

(ii) Calculate the probability of Martin's generating at least $35,525 in revenues in the Champaign-Urbana market given a wholesale price of $25 per pair.

P5.9 **SOLUTION**

A. (i) Coefficient of determination = R^2 = 85% implying that 85% of demand variation is explained by the regression model.

(ii) Corrected coefficient of determination = $\bar{R}^2$ = $R^2 - (k - 1/n - k)(1 - R^2)$ = 0.85 - (5/30)(1 - 0.85) = 0.825 implying that 82.5% of demand variation is explained by the regression model when both coefficient number, k, and sample size, N, are controlled for.

(iii)   *F* statistic $= F = (n - k/k - 1)(R^2/1 - R^2) = (30/5)\,(0.85/0.15) = 34 > F^*_{5,30,\alpha}$
$_{= 0.01} = 3.70$ implying that we can reject null hypothesis $H_0\!:\!b_1 = b_2 = ... = b_5 = 0$ and conclude with 99% confidence that the independent variables as a group explain a significant share of demand variation.

(iv)   Standard error of the estimate = SEE = 200 implying that:

$$Q = \hat{Q} \pm 2.042 \times 200 \text{ with 95\% confidence.}$$

$$Q = \hat{Q} \pm 2.750 \times 200 \text{ with 99\% confidence.}$$

(Note: Here d.f. $= n - k = 36 - 6 = 30$).

B.   To learn whether a recession will hurt sales, one must ask is $b_I > 0$? At first this may seem counter intuitive, but we must remember that a recession is associated with a fall in income, just as "hurting" sales is associated with a fall in sales. The only way falling income could cause sales to fall is if $b_I > 0$. If $b_I < 0$, then evidence exists that a fall in income would increase sales. For testing purposes, the null hypothesis which one seeks to reject is the converse of the initial question:

$$H_0\!:\!b_I < 0 \qquad \text{(One-tail test)}$$

where

$$t = \frac{b_I}{\sigma_{b_I}} = \frac{12.5}{8.6} = 1.453 > 1.31 = t^*_{30,\alpha=0.1}$$

which means that we can reject $H_0\!:\!b_I < 0$ with 90% confidence and conclude that yes, a recession will hurt sales.

C.   For demand to be more dependent upon income than upon weather conditions the coefficient for I would have to be larger than the coefficient for W. Therefore, the relevant question is $|b_I| > |b_W|$ or is $|b_I| - |b_W| > 0$? If $|b_I| > |b_W|$, then a change in local income will have a bigger affect on demand than will a change in weather conditions. Absolute values are considered in the questions above because either positive or negative impacts on demand are possible. For testing purposes, the null hypothesis which one seeks to reject is the converse of the above question:

$$H_0\!:\!|b_I| < |b_W| \text{ or } H_0\!:\!|b_I| - |b_W| < 0 \text{ (One-tail test)}$$

where,

$$t = \frac{|b_I| - |b_W|}{\sigma|b_i| - |b_W|} = \frac{12.5 - 5}{\sqrt{8.6^2 + 2.8^2 - 2(3.5)}}$$

$$= \frac{7.5}{\sqrt{74.8}} = 0.867 \ngtr 1.13 = t^{*}_{30,a=0.10}$$

which means that we cannot reject $H_0:|b_I| < |b_W|$ nor $H_0:|b_I| - |b_W| < 0$ with even 90% confidence and conclude that no, there is no evidence that demand is more sensitive to changes in income than to changes in weather conditions.

D.   (i)   The demand curve for the Champaign-Urbana market is found simply by substituting relevant independent variable values into the demand function.

$$Q = 982 - 10P + 12.5I + 5W - 0.5CA + 5A$$

$$= 982 - 10P + 12.5(60) + 5(54) - 0.5(64) + 5(6)$$

$$= 2,000 - 10P$$

(ii)   At a price of $25, the estimated value of Q is:

$$\hat{Q} = 2,000 - 10P$$

$$= 2,000 - 10(25)$$

$$= 1,750$$

and the estimated value of total revenues is:

$$T\hat{R} = P\hat{Q}$$

$$= \$25(1,750)$$

$$= \$43,750$$

To generate revenues of $35,525, Martin's would have to sell Q = TR/P = 35,525/25 = 1,421 pairs of shoes in the Champaign-Urbana market.

Because expected sales are $\hat{Q} = 1,750$, there is a greater than 50/50 chance of reaching the target sales level of $Q = 1,421$. To learn the exact probability, note that $Q = 1,421$ is $\hat{Q} = 1,750$ minus 1.645 standard deviations because:

$$z = \frac{x - \hat{Q}}{\text{S.E.E.}}$$

$$= \frac{1,421 - 1,750}{200}$$

$$= -1.645$$

where z is the relative distance from $\hat{Q}$ (or standard normal), x is the point of interest, $\hat{Q}$ is the expected value or mean, SEE is the standard error of the estimate or standard deviation.

With $z = -1.645$, only 0.05 or 5% of the total area under the normal curve will lie to the left of or below $Q = 1,421$. Thus, there is a 95% chance that actual Q in Champaign-Urbana will meet or exceed $Q = 1,421$, and generate at least $35,525 in revenues.

P5.10 **Multiplicative Model Estimation.** *A study of the demand for imported motorcycles recently appeared in an industry newsletter. According to the study, demand for motorcycle imports is described by the function:*

$$Q_Y = 1.5 P_Y^{-4} P_X^{3} A_Y^{2} A_X^{2} I^{3}$$

$$R^2 = 95\%$$

Standard error of the estimate = 30

Here Q_Y is the quantity of motorcycles imported (000), P_Y is average motorcycle price ($), P_X is the average price of imported compact cars, A_Y is motorcycle industry advertising ($000,000), A_X is industry advertising of compact cars ($000,000), and I is average disposable family income ($000). The standard errors of the exponents in the multiplicative demand function above are:

$$b_{P_Y} = 1, \; b_{P_X} = 1.5, \; b_{A_Y} = 0.8, \; b_{A_X} = 1.5, \; b_I = 1.2$$

And finally, this demand function was estimated using two years of monthly data (24 observations).

A. *Is the demand for imported motorcycles elastic with respect to price?*

B. *Are imported motorcycles a normal good?*

C. *Are motorcycles and compact cars substitutes?*

D. *Given your answer to part A, can you explain why the coefficients for both A_Y and A_X are positive?*

P5.10 **SOLUTION**

A. The exponents of multiplicative demand functions are elasticity estimates. Therefore, motorcycle demand is elastic with respect to price provided:

$|b_{P_Y}| > 1$ or $|b_{P_Y}| - 1 > 0$. For testing purposes, the null hypothesis to reject is: $H_0:|b_{P_Y}| < 1$ or $|b_{P_Y}| - 1 < 0$ (One-tail test)

where:

$$t = \frac{|b_{P_Y}| - 1}{\sigma|b_{P_Y}|} = \frac{4 - 1}{1} = 3 > 2.552 = t^*_{18,\alpha=0.01}$$

meaning one can reject H_0 with 99% confidence and conclude that motorcycle demand is elastic with respect to price.

B. Because exponents in multiplicative models are elasticity estimates, motorcycles will be a normal good provided $b_I > 0$. For testing purposes, the null hypothesis to reject is:

$$H_0: b_I < 0 \quad \text{(One-tail test)}$$

where

$$t = \frac{|b_I|}{\sigma|b_{P_I}|} = \frac{3}{1.2} = 2.5 > 1.734 = t^*_{18,\alpha=0.05}$$

meaning one can reject H_0 with 95% confidence and conclude motorcycles are a normal good.

C. Because exponents here are elasticity estimates, motorcycles and compact cars will be substitutes provided $b_{P_X} > 0$, and complements if $b_{P_X} < 0$. To test the substitute good hypothesis, the hypothesis to reject is:

$$H_0: b_{P_X} < 0 \quad \text{(One-tail test)}$$

where

$$t = \frac{b_{P_X}}{\sigma b_{P_X}} = \frac{3}{1.5} = 2 > 1.33 = t^*_{18, \alpha = 0.1}$$

meaning one can reject H_0 with 90% confidence, and conclude motorcycles and compact cars are substitutes.

D. Recall that an increase in price by a competitor leads to an increase in units sold, and that a decrease in price by a competitor leads to a decrease in units sold. From the perspective of the firm's demand curve, units sold and the price moves of competitors are inversely related. Similarly, in most instances an increase in "own advertising" leads to an increase in sales revenue and profits, whereas an increase in competitor advertising leads to a decrease in sales revenue and profits. In fact, it is common to consider such negative influences as *prima facie* evidence that another firm is in fact a competitor.

Both "own" and compact car advertising appear to increase sales. Although relatively uncommon, this is not a rare occurrence. Advertising of substitutes can sometimes raise sales for competitor products due to beneficial spillover effects following increased customer awareness regarding, for example, the quality of foreign-produced goods.

Chapter 6

FORECASTING

Success in business depends on management's ability to develop and execute long-range strategic plans that take advantage of the organization's comparative strengths. This planning process involves a number of important related activities. Management must decide the range of products that the firm will offer customers, and then forecast the level of demand under assorted conditions. Typically, the effects of pricing policy, promotional activity, competition, and general economic conditions must all be considered. In addition to compiling a range of demand forecasts, management must also forecast costs of producing different levels of output in light of changing technology, wage rates, and raw materials prices. After all relevant data have been collected and analyzed, managers must pick and choose from among a range of reasonable decision scenarios to select the value-maximizing operating plan.

If forecasts about demand, the cost of inputs, technology, and other planning considerations are seriously in error, operating plans will be of little practical value. When forecast errors have the potential to adversely affect the realization of planning objectives, the control phase of the planning process must allow for necessary changes and modifications. At the same time, the planning and control process must be sufficiently structured to facilitate the realization of firm objectives. Managerial economics has developed a number of forecasting techniques that have proven successful in a variety of real-world applications. The purpose of this chapter is to help students understand how managers can make better forecasts.

CHAPTER OUTLINE

I.   **WHAT IS ECONOMIC FORECASTING?**

      A.   **Why is Forecasting Useful?** Everybody forecasts, whether they realize it or not. Businesses must forecast future events before preparing even the simplest business plan or making the most mundane decision.

          1.   A primary advantage of the wide variety of statistical techniques commonly employed in economic forecasting is that they separate the forecasting process from the firm's goal-setting activity.

          2.   Forecasting that is objective provides firms with the backdrop necessary for optimal decisions.

II.   COMMON TYPES OF FORECASTING PROBLEMS

A.   **Macroeconomic Forecast Problems:**   Macroeconomic forecasting involves predicting aggregate measures of economic activity at the international, national, regional, or state level.

1.   In the case of macroeconomic forecasting, uncontrollable factors loom large in influence.

B.   **Microeconomic Forecast Problems:**   Microeconomic forecasting involves the prediction of desegregate or partial economic data at the industry, firm, plant, or product level.

1.   Trained and experienced analysts often find it easier to accurately forecast microeconomic trends, like the demand for new cars, than macroeconomic trends in the overall economy, such as GDP growth.

2.   Microeconomic forecasts abstract from the profusion of variables and variable interrelationships that determine the macroeconomy.

3.   When the influence of uncontrollable factors is significant, as in macroeconomic forecasting, it is prudent to allow for large forecast error.

C.   **Problem of Changing Expectations**:   The expectations of purchasing agents and other managers can become a self-fulfilling prophesy because the macroeconomic environment represents the sum of the investment and spending decisions of business, government and the public.

1.   The link between expectations and realizations has the potential to create an optimistic bias in government-reported statistics.

2.   It is important for managers to appreciate the link between economic expectations and realizations, and to be wary of the potential for forecast bias.

D.   **Data Quality Problems**:   It is impossible to derive accurate forecasts from data that are carelessly collected.

1.   Accurate forecasts require pertinent data that are current, complete, and free from error.

2.   The quantity and quality of data analyzed must be sufficient to shed meaningful light on the forecast problem being addressed.

       a.   The acid test is: Can useful forecasts be generated?

    E.   **Common Forecast Techniques:** Multiple forecasting tools are available; their strengths and weaknesses must be understood if accurate forecasts are to be obtained. Common methods of forecasting include:

       1.   Qualitative analyses,

       2.   Trend analysis and projection,

       3.   Exponential smoothing,

       4.   Econometric methods.

III.   QUALITATIVE ANALYSES

    A.   **Expert Opinion:** When quantitative information is not available, qualitative analysis must be relied upon to prepare required forecasts. Prevalent qualitative forecast methods include:

       1.   Personal insight from a knowledgeable individual.

       2.   Panel consensus from a group of informed individuals.

       3.   The Delphi method in which an independent expert tries to elicit the unspoken consensus from a panel of informed individuals.

    B.   **Survey Techniques:** Accurate forecasting using survey techniques requires the careful selection of a sample that is fully representative of the entire population, as well as a skillful interpretation of sample results.

       1.   Samples may be drawn in a random fashion, or stratified in an explicit attempt to match overall population characteristics.

       2.   Advantages: Surveys based on mailed questionnaires or individual interviews can be a low cost way of adding valuable background and depth to the sometimes superficial data available for statistical analyses.

       3.   Limitations: Unlike "hard" market transactions data, survey data can be "soft" if consumers are unwilling or unable to reveal true preferences prior to actual purchase decisions.

IV.   TREND ANALYSIS AND PROJECTION

   A.   **Trends in Economic Data:** Trend projection assumes that economic relations will be maintained subject to historical patterns of variability. There are a number of causes of historical variability.

   1.   Secular trends reflect long-run growth or decline.

   2.   Cyclical fluctuations show rhythmic variations from boom to recession.

   3.   Seasonal variations are caused by weather or custom.

   4.   Irregular or random influences often result in unpredictable variation.

   B.   **Linear Trend Analysis:** Linear trend analysis assumes a constant *unit* change in an important economic variable over time.

   1.   Accurate forecasts can sometimes be obtained from linear trend analysis because some economic variables display roughly constant change per period.

   2.   Exogenous shocks to the economic system (such as oil embargoes) have unanticipated consequences and reduce the accuracy of trend forecasts.

   C.   **Growth Trend Analysis:** Growth trend analysis assumes constant *percentage* change in an important economic variable over time.

   1.   Growth trend analysis often gives a realistic view of economic growth patterns.

   D.   **Linear and Growth Trend Comparison:** Both methods offer useful insight concerning the economic growth.

   1.   Both methods suffer from a failure to incorporate the effects of exogenous shocks.

V.   BUSINESS CYCLE

   A.   **What is the Business Cycle?** The business cycle is a rhythmic pattern of contraction and expansion in the overall economy.

   1.   Many important economic time series are also subject to additional variation caused by weather and custom.

B.   Economic Indicators: Series of data that successfully describe the pattern of projected, current, or past economic activity are called economic indicators.

1.   A composite index is a weighted average of leading, coincident, or lagging economic indicators.

C.   Economic Recessions: An economic recession is a significant decline in activity spread across the economy that lasts more than a few months.

1.   In the United States, economic recessions are defined by the National Bureau of Economic Research (NBER), a private nonprofit research organization.

a.   Recessions are rare and brief, usually less than a year in duration.

2.   Economic expansion is a period of rising economic activity.

a.   Expansion is the typical state of the U.S. economy.   Expansions typically last roughly four years.

D.   Common Sources of Forecast Information: Forecasts of economic trends are regularly reported by the U.S. government, industry trade groups, and the business press.

1.   The world-wide web features a plethora of relevant sites. For example, check out the *USA Today* money section at http://www.usatoday.com

VI.   EXPONENTIAL SMOOTHING TECHNIQUES

A.   Exponential Smoothing Concept: Exponential smoothing is a method for forecasting time series of data.

1.   This technique identifies historical trends in the data series one wishes to forecast, and then extrapolates these patterns forward into the forecast period.

2.   Its accuracy depends on the degree to which established patterns of change are operative and consistent over time.

B.   One-Parameter (Simple) Exponential Smoothing: In one-parameter (simple) exponential smoothing, the sole regular component is the level of the forecast data series.

1. It is implicitly assumed that the data consist of irregular fluctuations around a constant or very slowly changing level.

2. Simple exponential smoothing is appropriate for forecasting sales in mature markets with stable activity.

3. Simple exponential smoothing is not appropriate for forecasting data that exhibit trends.

C. **Two-Parameter (Holt) Exponential Smoothing:** In two-parameter (Holt) exponential smoothing, the data are assumed to fluctuate around a level that is changing with some constant or slowly drifting linear trend.

1. Two-parameter exponential smoothing is appropriate for forecasting sales in established markets with stable growth.

2. It is inappropriate in either stable or rapidly growing markets.

D. **Three-Parameter (Winters) Exponential Smoothing:** The three-parameter (Winters) exponential smoothing method extends the two- parameter technique by including a smoothed multiplicative index to account for seasonal behavior.

1. Because much economic data involves both growth trend and seasonal considerations, three-parameter exponential smoothing is one of the most commonly used forecasting methods employed in business today.

2. Three-parameter exponential smoothing is best suited for forecasting problems that involve rapid and/or changing rates of growth combined with seasonal influences.

3. Three-parameter exponential smoothing is suitable for forecasting sales in both rapidly growing markets and in rapidly decaying markets with seasonal influences.

E. **Practical Use of Exponential Smoothing:** In practical application various exponential smoothing methods are typically used in tandem with other forecast techniques.

VII. ECONOMETRIC METHODS

A. **Advantages of Econometric Methods:** Econometric forecasting relies on theoretically derived economic relations as the basis for statistical forecasts.

1.   Econometric methods benefit from insights provided by economic theory.

2.   Forecast error information can also be used to improve subsequent forecasts.

B.   **Single Equation Models:** Single equation econometric models offer a simple but powerful technique for regression-based forecasts.

   1.   Forecasting with a single-equation model consists of evaluating the equation with specific values for the independent variables.

C.   **Multiple Equation Systems:** Multiple equation systems offer a means for considering interrelated influences among a variety of dependent Y-variables and independent X-variables.

   1.   Although forecasting problems can often be analyzed with a single-equation model, complex relations among economic variables sometimes require use of multiple-equation systems.

      a.   Variables whose values are determined within such a model are *endogenous*, meaning originating from within.

      b.   Variables determined outside, or external to, the system are referred to as *exogenous*.

   2.   Identities express relations that are true by definition (e.g., π = TR - TC).

   3.   Behavioral equations may indicate how individuals and institutions are expected to react to various stimuli (e.g., Q = a - bP).

VIII.   **JUDGING FORECAST RELIABILITY**

A.   **Tests of Predictive Capability:** To test predictive capability, a model generated from one set of data is used to predict a second set of data.

1.   Data used to generate a forecast model are called the test group.

2.   Data used to examine a forecast model are called the forecast group.

B.   **Correlation Analysis:** The simple correlation between actual and forecast values provides an attractive index of forecast accuracy:

$$r = \frac{\sigma_{fx}}{\sigma_f \sigma_x},$$

where r is the correlation coefficient, σ_{fx} is the covariance between the forecast and actual series, and σ_f and σ_x are the standard deviations of the forecast and actual series, respectively.

1. Generally speaking, when $r \geq 0.95$ or 0.99 (95 or 99%), a high level of forecast accuracy has been achieved in terms of predicting variation in an important series.

C. **Sample Mean Forecast Error Analysis:** This index of forecast reliability, denoted by U, provides valuable insight regarding the absolute level of forecast accuracy:

$$U = \sqrt{\frac{1}{n}\sum_{i=1}^{n} (f_i - x_i)^2},$$

where n is the number of sample observations, f_i is a forecast value, and x_i is the corresponding actual value.

1. Generally speaking, when the mean or average forecast error is a small fraction, 0.05 or 0.01 (5 or 1%), of actual values, a high level of absolute forecast accuracy has been achieved.

IX. CHOOSING THE BEST FORECAST TECHNIQUE

A. **Data Requirements:** Complex forecasting methods require extensive data.

1. Limited data mandates use of simple techniques.

B. **Time Horizon Considerations:** Very long-term forecasts often require qualitative insight.

1. Quantitative methods work best for monthly or annual forecast problems.

C. **Computer and Related Costs:** Computing costs have plummeted with the invention of powerful desktop computers.

       1.   Computing costs do not represent an impediment to the use of sophisticated forecasting methods.

D.   **Role of Judgment:** Don't dismiss the importance of informed judgment.

       1.   Experienced professionals often achieve enviable results with simple forecast techniques.

       2.   The objective of economic forecasting is to improve on the subjective judgments made by managers.

       3.   All managers forecast; the goal is to make better forecasts.

X.   **SUMMARY**

PROBLEMS & SOLUTIONS

P6.1   Sales Trend Analysis.   *The following figures show the trend in annual sales for Josh Bartlet's Steak House over the 1992-2002 period.*

Year	Sales
1992	$284,000
1993	266,000
1994	287,000
1995	315,000
1996	353,000
1997	384,000
1998	427,000
1999	462,000
2000	520,000
2001	575,000
2002	568,000

A.   *Calculate the rate of growth in sales for 1992-2002 using the constant rate of change model with annual compounding. (Note: $t = 0$ in 1992).*

B.   *Forecast Sales for 2007 and 2012.*

P6.1   SOLUTION

A.
$$S_t = S_0(1 + g)^t$$

$$\$568,000 = \$284,000(1 + g)^{10}$$

$$568,000/284,000 = (1 + g)^{10}$$

$$2 = (1 + g)^{10}$$

$$\ln 2 = 10 \times \ln(1 + g)$$

$$0.693/10 = \ln(1 + g)$$

$$e^{0.0693} = 1 + g$$

$$g = 0.0718 \text{ or } 7.18\%$$

B. 5-year Forecast

$$S_t = S_0(1 + g)^t$$

$$= \$284,000(1 + 0.0718)^{15}$$

$$= \$284,000(2.829)$$

$$= \$803,436$$

10-year Forecast

$$S_t = S_0(1 + g)^t$$

$$= \$284,000(1 + 0.0718)^{20}$$

$$= \$284,000(4.002)$$

$$= \$1,136,568$$

P6.2 **Growth Rate Estimation.** *Durable Products, Inc., is a leading manufacturer and distributor of polyethylene liners for pickup truck beds. Annual sales revenue has grown rapidly from $30 million to $60 million during the past five-year period.*

A. *Calculate the five-year growth rate in sales using the constant rate of change model with annual compounding.*

B. *Calculate the five-year growth rate in sales using the constant rate of change model with continuous compounding.*

C. *Compare your answers to parts A and B, and discuss any differences.*

P6.2 **SOLUTION**

A.
$$S_t = S_0(1 + g)^t$$

$$\$60 = \$30(1 + g)^5$$

$$2 = (1 + g)^5$$

$$\ln(2) = 5 \times \ln(1 + g)$$

$$0.693/5 = \ln(1 + g)$$

$$e^{0.139} = 1 + g$$

$$1.149 - 1 = g$$

$$g = 0.149 \text{ or } 14.9\%$$

B.
$$S_t = S_0 e^{gt}$$

$$\$60 = \$30 e^{5g}$$

$$2 = e^{5g}$$

$$\ln(2) = 5g$$

$$g = 0.693/5$$

$$= 0.139 \text{ or } 13.9\%$$

C. If annual sales revenue doubles from \$30 million to \$60 million over a five-year period, a 14.9% rate of sales growth is indicated when annual compounding is assumed. With continuous compounding, a 13.9% rate of growth leads to a doubling in sales over a five-year period. The difference, of course, is the amount of "interest-on-interest." Either method can be employed to measure the rate of growth, the analyst must simply be sure to make growth comparisons using a consistent basis.

P6.3   ***Growth Rate Analysis.*** *The Coat Factory Warehouse, Inc., is a leading retailer of off-price women's clothing, predominately outer wear. Ross Geller, general sales manager for the company, is concerned about the company's erratic revenue pattern during recent years.*

       A. *Complete the following table showing annual sales data for the Coat Factory during the 1997-2002 period.*

Year (1)	Sales ($ millions) (2)	Current Sales/Previous Period Sales (3)	Growth Rate (4)=[(3)-1]×100
1997	$50	--	--
1998	40		
1999	80		
2000	100		
2001	100		
2002	50		

B. Calculate the geometric average annual rate of growth for the five-year 1997-2002 period. (Hint: Calculate this growth rate using sales from 1997 and 2002.)

C. Calculate the arithmetic average annual rate of growth for the five-year 1997-2002 period. (Hint: This is the average of column (4) figures.)

D. Discuss any differences in your answers to parts B and C.

P6.3 **SOLUTION**

A.

Year (1)	Sales ($ millions) (2)	Current Sales/Previous Period Sales (3)	Growth Rate (4)=[(3)-1]×100
1997	$50	--	--
1998	40	0.80	-20%
1999	80	2.00	100
2000	100	1.25	25
2001	100	1.00	0
2002	50	0.50	-50

B. From column (3) of part A, the geometric average rate of return is calculated as:

$$\bar{g} = \left[\prod_{t=1}^{n}(1 + g_t) \right]^{\frac{1}{n}} - 1$$

$$= [(0.80)(2.00)(1.25)(1.00)(0.50)]^{1/5} - 1$$

$$= 1^{1/5} - 1$$

$$= 0 \text{ or } 0\% \text{ (No growth)}$$

Alternatively, the geometric average rate of return is:

$$S_t = S_0(1 + g)^t$$

$$\$50,000,000 = \$50,000,000(1 + g)^5$$

$$1 = (1 + g)^5$$

$$g = 0 \text{ or } 0\% \text{ (No growth)}$$

C. From column (4) of part A, the arithmetic average rate of return is calculated as:

$$\bar{g} = \frac{1}{n}\sum_{t=1}^{n} g_t$$

$$= \frac{1}{5}(-20 + 100 + 25 + 0 - 50)$$

$$= 11\%$$

D. The zero geometric average rate of growth is consistent with the zero growth in sales observed for the Coat Factory over the 1997-2002 period. The arithmetic average rate of return of 11% is greater than the geometric (true) mean. This is always the case, and results from the changing base used from one period to another. Note that when sales increase from $50,000,000 to $100,000,000 (a 100% gain), but then fall back to $50,000,000 (a 50% loss), the arithmetic average growth is 25% (= (100% - 50%)/2) despite the fact that no net growth has occurred. As a result, when compound growth rates are considered, managers rely on the geometric average rather than the arithmetic average rate of return.

P6.4 *Cost Forecasting.* *Robert Romano is a quality-control supervisor for Rocket Merchandise, Inc. Romano is concerned about unit cost increases for imported components. Costs for components imported from Germany have increased from $10* to $12.21 per unit over the last two years. Romano thinks that buying from domestic suppliers at a cost of $16.49 per unit may soon be desirable.

A.   Calculate the company's unit cost growth rate during the past two years using the constant rate of change model with continuous compounding.

B.   Forecast when costs for imported units are expected to equal $16.49, the domestic supplier cost.

P6.4   SOLUTION

A. $C_t = C_0e^{gt}$

$$\$12.21 = \$10e^{2g}$$

$$1.221 = e^{2g}$$

$$\ln(1.221) = 2g$$

$$g = 0.1997/2$$

$$= 0.1 \text{ or } 10\%$$

B.   Domestic Cost $= C_0e^{gt} =$ Forecast Cost

$$\$16.49 = \$12.21e^{(0.1)t}$$

$$1.35 = e^{(0.1)t}$$

$$\ln(1.35) = 0.1t$$

$$t = 0.3/0.1$$

$$= 3 \text{ years}$$

P6.5   *Unit Sales Forecast Modeling.* *The change in the quantity of product A demanded in any given year is inversely proportional to the change in sales of product B in the previous year. That is, if sales of B rose by X% last year, sales of A can be expected to fall by X% this year.*

A. *Write the equation for next year's sales of A, using the symbols A = sales of product A, B = sales of product B, and t = time. Assume that there will be no shortages of either product.*

B. *Last year, 500 units of A and 400 units of B were sold. Two years ago, 250 units of product B were sold. What would you predict the sales of A to be this year?*

P6.5 **SOLUTION**

A. $$A_t = A_{t-1} + \Delta A_{t-1}$$

$$A_t = A_{t-1} - \left(\frac{B_{t-1}}{B_{t-2}} - 1 \right) A_{t-1}$$

B. For A_t, forecast sales are:

$$A_t = A_{t-1} - \left(\frac{B_{t-1}}{B_{t-2}} - 1 \right) A_{t-1}$$

$$= 500 - \left(\frac{400}{250} - 1 \right) 500$$

$$= 500 - 300$$

$$= 200$$

P6.6 **Unit Sales Forecast Modeling.** *The quantity demanded of product A in any given week is inversely proportional to the sales of product B in the previous week. That is, if sales of B rose by X% last week, sales of A can be expected to fall by X% this week.*

A. *Write the equation for next week's sales of A, using the symbols A = sales of product A, B = sales of product B, and t = time. Assume there will be no shortages of either product.*

B. *Two weeks ago, 200 units of product A and 150 units of product B were sold. Last week, 160 units of A and 180 units of B were sold. What would you predict sales of A to be this week?*

C. *What is the significance of the error term? What property must the error term have to allow use of regression results in forecasting?*

P6.6   **SOLUTION**

   A.   An equation for next week's sales of A is:

$$A_t = A_{t-1} + \Delta A_{t-1}$$

$$= A_{t-1} - \left(\frac{B_{t-1}}{B_{t-2}} - 1 \right) A_{t-1}$$

   B. A_t is forecast as follows:

$$A_t = A_{t-1} - \left(\frac{B_{t-1}}{B_{t-2}} - 1 \right) A_{t-1}$$

$$= 160 - \left(\frac{180}{150} - 1 \right) 160$$

$$= 128 \text{ units}$$

   C.   The error term represents the "margin of error" in forecasting. For forecasting to be viable, the average value of the error term must be zero or $E(u) = 0$.

P6.7   *Sales Forecasting. Jing-Mei Chen, manager of the Beijing Garden Restaurant, knows that sales of Egg Rolls appetizers average 40 orders per day. Recently, however, sales declined to 20 orders per day. During this period, Beijing was running a special that reduced the price on Crab Rangoons appetizers, a competing product, from $5 to $4.*

   A.   *What is the arc cross-price elasticity between Egg Rolls and Crab Rangoons?*

   B.   *What level of Egg Rolls sales would you forecast if the regular price on Crab Rangoons were raised from $5 to $6?*

P6.7   **SOLUTION**

   A. $E_{PX} = \dfrac{\Delta Q}{\Delta P_X} \times \dfrac{P_{X2} + P_{X1}}{Q_2 + Q_1} = \dfrac{(20 - 40)}{(\$4 - \$5)} \times \dfrac{(\$4 + \$5)}{(20 + 40)} = 3$

   B. $E_{PX} = \dfrac{\Delta Q}{\Delta P_X} \times \dfrac{P_{X2} + P_{X1}}{Q_2 + Q_1}$

$$3 = \frac{Q_2 - 40}{(\$6 - \$5)} \times \frac{(\$6 + \$5)}{(Q_2 + 40)}$$

$$3(Q_2 + 40) = 11(Q_2 - 40)$$

$$3Q_2 + 120 = 11Q_2 - 440$$

$$8Q_2 = 560$$

$$Q_2 = 70 \text{ units}$$

(*Note:* The arc cross-price elasticity formula is used in this problem given the large percentage changes in price being considered).

P6.8 **Sales Forecast Modeling.** *Gil Grissom, president of CSI, Inc., in Las Vegas, Nevada, believes that sales in the coming year are closely related to disposable income.*

A. *Write an equation for next year's sales, using the symbols S = sales, Y = income, t = time, a_0 = constant term, a_1 = regression slope coefficient, and u = random disturbance term.*

B. *Now assume that sales in the coming year increase by the same percentage as income increased during the past year. Write an equation for predicting next year's sales.*

C. *This year, sales totaled $1.4 million, while income per capita in Las Vegas increased from $35,000 to $36,050. Forecast next year's sales using your forecast equation from part B.*

P6.8 **SOLUTION**

A. A forecast equation for next year's sales is:

$$S_{t+1} = a_0 + a_1 Y_t$$

B. A forecast equation relating percent changes in sales and income is:

$$S_{t+1} = S_t + \Delta S$$

$$= S_t + \left(\frac{Y_t}{Y_{t-1}} - 1 \right) S_t$$

$$= \left(\frac{Y_t}{Y_{t-1}} \right) S_t$$

C.   Next year's sales are:

$$S_{t+1} = (\$36,050/\$35,000)\$1,400,000$$

$$= \$1,442,000$$

P6.8   *Sales Forecast Modeling. Dr. Kerry Weaver, sole proprietor of the Westwood Physical Therapy Center, would like to generate a sales forecast. Based on the assumption that next-period sales are a function of current-period local disposable income, own advertising, and advertising by a competing hospital:*

A.   *Specify a general demand equation, assuming that sales rise with income and own advertising but fall with competitor advertising.*

B.   *Write an equation for predicting sales if you assume that the percentage growth (or decline) in sales is twice as large as the sum of the current period's percentage changes in local disposable income and own advertising, minus one-half of the current period's percentage change in competitor advertising.*

C.   *Forecast sales if current period sales total $900,000, average disposable income per household is $82,800, own advertising is $33,000, and competitor advertising is $63,000. Previous period levels were $80,000 for disposable income, $30,000 for own advertising, and $60,000 for competitor advertising.*

P6.8   **SOLUTION**

A.   A general demand equation can be written:

$$S_{t+1} = b_0 + b_1 Y_t + b_2 A_t + b_3 A_{Xt}$$

B. $S_{t+1} = S_t + \Delta S$

$$= S_t + 2 \left(\frac{Y_t}{Y_{t-1}} - 1 \right) S_t + 2 \left(\frac{A_t}{A_{t-1}} - 1 \right) S_t$$

$$- \frac{1}{2} \left(\frac{A_{Xt}}{A_{Xt-1}} - 1 \right) S_t$$

$$= S_t + 2S_t \left(\frac{Y_t}{Y_{t-1}} \right) - 2S_t + 2S_t \left(\frac{A_t}{A_{t-1}} \right) - 2S_t$$

$$- \frac{1}{2}S_t \left(\frac{A_{Xt}}{A_{Xt-1}} \right) + \frac{1}{2}S_t$$

$$= 2S_t \left(\frac{Y_t}{Y_{t-1}} \right) + 2S_t \left(\frac{A_t}{A_{t-1}} \right) - \frac{1}{2}S_t \left(\frac{A_{Xt}}{A_{Xt-1}} \right)$$

$$- 2.5S_t$$

C. Forecast sales are:

$$S_{t+1} = 2(\$900,000)(1.035) + 2(\$900,000)(1.1)$$

$$- \frac{1}{2}(\$900,000)(1.05) - 2.5(\$900,000)$$

$$= \$1,120,500$$

P6.10 **Simultaneous Equations.** *Macrosoft, Inc., is a leading provider of software and technical services to business and government. The company has found that demand for its products tends to be closely related to aggregate economic activity. The company has collected the following data in order to forecast economic activity during the coming year:*

$$\text{Last Year's Corporate Profits, } P_{t-1} = \$1,100$$

$$\text{This Year's Federal Government Spending, } G = \$2,400$$

$$\text{Annual Consumption Expenditures, } C = \$2,175 + 0.7Y$$

$$\text{Annual Investment Expenditures, } I = \$550 + 1.5P_{t-1}$$

$$\text{Annual Federal Tax Receipts, } T = 0.25 \, GDP$$

$$\text{Income, } Y = GDP - T$$

$$\text{Net Exports, } X = \$1,350 - 0.15\ GDP$$

$$\text{Gross Domestic Product, } GDP = C + I + G + X$$

Assuming that all random disturbances average out to zero, forecast each of the above variables through the simultaneous relations expressed in the multiple equation system. All dollar values are in billions of dollars.

P6.10   SOLUTION

Investment

$$I = \$550 + 1.5 P_{t-1}$$

$$= \$550 + 1.5(\$1,100)$$

$$= \$2,200 \text{ billion}$$

Gross Domestic Product (GDP)

$$GDP = C + I + G + X$$

$$GDP = \$2,175 + 0.7(GDP - T) + \$2,200 + \$2,400 + \$1,350 - 0.15 GDP$$

$$GDP = \$8,125 + 0.7(GDP - (0.25 GDP)) - 0.15 GDP$$

$$GDP = \$8,125 + 0.375 GDP$$

$$0.625 GDP = \$8,125$$

$$GDP = \$13,000 \text{ billion}$$

Consumption

$$C = \$2,175 + 0.7Y$$

$$= \$2,175 + 0.7(GDP - T)$$

$$= \$2,175 + 0.7(GDP - 0.25\ GDP)$$

$$= \$2,175 + 0.525 \ GDP$$

$$= \$2,175 + 0.525(\$13,000)$$

$$= \$9,000 \ billion$$

Taxes

$$T = 0.25 \ GDP$$

$$= 0.25(\$13,000)$$

$$= \$3,250 \ billion$$

Income

$$Y = GDP - T$$

$$= \$13,000 - \$3,250$$

$$= \$9,750 \ billion$$

Net Exports

$$X = \$1,350 - 0.15 \ GDP$$

$$= \$1,350 - 0.15(\$13,000)$$

$$= -\$600 \ billion \ (\text{which implies a trade deficit})$$

Chapter 7

PRODUCTION ANALYSIS AND COMPENSATION POLICY

Given product demand conditions, how does a firm determine the optimal level of output during any given production period? When several alternative production methods are available, how does a firm choose the best one? How will investment in new manufacturing equipment affect worker productivity and the unit costs of production? If the firm undertakes an expansion program to increase productive capacity, will cost per unit be higher or lower after the expansion? Each of these questions can be critically important to firm success. Valuable insights and further questions that make ultimate answers obvious are provided by the study of production.

Production concepts have broad application and are equally relevant to the manufacture of physical goods and to the provision of services. In each instance, production analysis focuses on the efficient use of inputs to create outputs that meet the demonstrated demand of customers. Technical and economic characteristics of production methods used in the manufacture of both goods and services are studied to determine the low-cost means of meeting specific customer needs. It is worth emphasizing that the study of production involves much more than the simple physical transformation of resources. Production involves all the activities associated with providing goods and services. The hiring of workers (from unskilled labor to top management), personnel training, and the organizational structure adopted to maximize efficiency are all part of the production process. The efficient employment of capital resources is also part of production, as are the design and use of appropriate accounting and management information systems.

CHAPTER OUTLINE

I.   **PRODUCTION FUNCTIONS**

      A.   **Properties of Production Functions:** A production function specifies the maximum output that can be produced from a given combination of inputs; or alternatively, the minimum quantity of inputs necessary to produce a given level of output.

            1.   Production functions are determined by technology, equipment, and input prices.

            2.   Discrete production functions have distinct or "lumpy" input patterns.

            3.   Continuous production functions have the potential to employ inputs in small increments.

B. Returns to Scale and Returns to a Factor: Returns to scale and returns to a factor measure the effects of changes in inputs on output.

1. The relation between changes in output and a percentage change in *all* inputs is the returns to scale attribute of a production function.

2. The relation between changes in output and change in a *single* input identifies the factor returns attribute of a production function.

II. TOTAL, MARGINAL AND AVERAGE PRODUCT

A. Total Product: Total product is the quantity of output that results from employing a specific level of resources in a production system.

B. Marginal Product: Marginal product is the change in output caused by a unit change in a given input, holding all else constant:

$$MP_X = \frac{\partial Q}{\partial X}.$$

1. MP_X is the slope of the total product curve.

a. Total product rises when $MP_X > 0$, and falls when $MP_X < 0$.

b. When $MP_X = 0$, total product is maximized.

C. Average Product: Average product is simply total product divided by the amount of input employed:

$$AP_X = \frac{Q}{X}.$$

1. Average product rises when $MP_X > AP_X$, and falls when $MP_X < AP_X$.

2. When $MP_X = AP_X$, average product is maximized.

III.   **THE LAW OF DIMINISHING RETURNS TO A FACTOR**

   A.   Diminishing Returns to a Factor Concept: If use of a given variable factor input rises while all other inputs are held constant, the marginal product of that factor (MP_X) eventually diminishes.

   1.   Diminishing returns imply positive but falling marginal products.

   a.   *Negative* marginal products are never observed because it would be irrational to expand input use if doing so causes total output to fall.

   2.   Diminishing returns exist for each factor in every known production system.

   B.   Illustration of Diminishing Returns to a Factor: Input combinations in the range of diminishing returns are commonly observed.

   1.   Theoretically, when input usage is very low, increased specialization and better utilization of other factors in the production process allow factor productivity to grow.

   2.   In practice it is very rare to see input combinations that exhibit increasing returns for any factor. With increasing returns to a factor, an industry would come to be dominated by one very large producer--and this is seldom the case.

IV.   **INPUT COMBINATION CHOICE**

   A.   Production Isoquants: An isoquant curve shows all possible input combinations which, when used efficiently, produce a given quantity of output.

   1.   Technical efficiency is achieved when output is produced in a least-cost fashion.

   B.   Input Factor Substitution: The shape of an isoquant indicates the degree of substitutability among input factors.

   1.   A straight line isoquant implies perfect substitutability.

   2.   Isoquants that are made up of two straight lines perpendicular to each other (L-shaped) imply complete non-substitutability.

   3.   C-shaped or curved isoquants imply limited substitutability.

C. **Marginal Rate of Technical Substitution:** The marginal rate of technical substitution ($MRTS_{XY}$) measures the amount of one input factor (X) that must be substituted for some other input factor (Y) to hold output constant.

1. $MRTS_{XY}$ can be thought of as the marginal productivity of X relative to the marginal productivity of Y:

$$MRTS_{XY} = -\frac{MP_X}{MP_Y}$$

2. $MRTS_{XY}$ is -1 times the slope of an isoquant drawn on a graph where X is on the horizontal axis and Y is on the vertical axis:

$$MRTS_{XY} = -\frac{MP_X}{MP_Y}$$

$$= -\frac{\partial Q/\partial X}{\partial Q/\partial Y}$$

$$= -\frac{1/\partial X}{1/\partial Y}$$

$$= -\frac{\partial Y}{\partial X}$$

D. **Rational Limits of Input Substitution:** Ridge lines show the rational limits on resource use.

1. Activity will never be observed the range where $MP_X < 0$ or $MP_Y < 0$.

2. Outside the ridge lines, output can be increased by reducing use of the relatively more abundant factor employed.

V. **MARGINAL REVENUE PRODUCT AND OPTIMAL EMPLOYMENT**

A. **Marginal Revenue Product:** Optimal input use requires a careful consideration of productive capability and economic cost.

1.   Marginal Revenue Product (MRP) is the revenue gain to increasing input X usage by one unit.

   a.   Algebraically,

$$MRP_X = MP_X \times MR_Q$$

$$= \frac{\partial Q}{\partial X} \times \frac{\partial TR}{\partial Q}$$

$$= \frac{\partial TR}{\partial X}$$

where X is any single input and Q is output.

B.   Optimal Level of a Single Input: The profit-maximizing level of usage is at the point where the marginal revenue product of the last input unit employed is equal to input price.

   1.   Algebraically,

$$\begin{array}{ccc} \text{Marginal} & & \text{Marginal} \\ \text{Input Revenue} & = & \text{Input Cost} \end{array}$$

$$\frac{\partial TR}{\partial X} = \frac{\partial TC}{\partial X}$$

$$MRP_X = P_X$$

VI.   **Illustration of Optimal Employment:** Firm employment is optimal when it equates the marginal revenue product and marginal cost of each input.

   1.   Economic efficiency is achieved in the overall economy when all firms employ resources so as to equate each input's marginal revenue product and marginal cost.

VII.   **INPUT DEMAND FUNCTION**

   A.   **Input Demand Illustration:** The input demand schedule is derived by calculating the profit-maximizing level of output, and then determining the level of input required to produce that output level.

1.   Input demand grows when profits rise with expanded output.

B.   **Input Demand and Optimal Output:** The optimal level of employment can be derived by calculating the profit-maximizing level of output and then determining the amount of labor required to produce that output level.

    1.   This is similar to setting $MR = MC$ for each input.

VIII.   **OPTIMAL COMBINATION OF MULTIPLE INPUTS**

A.   **Budget Lines:** The optimal input combination occurs at the point of tangency between a budget (isocost) line and a production isoquant.

    1.   The least-cost combination of inputs requires that the marginal-product-to-price ratio be equal for all inputs (or relative marginal products equal relative price):

$$\frac{MP_X}{P_X} = \frac{MP_Y}{P_Y} \text{ or } \frac{MP_X}{MP_Y} = \frac{P_X}{P_Y}$$

B.   **Expansion Path:** The expansion path depicts optimal input combinations as the scale of production expands.

    1.   For optimal input combinations, the ratio of input prices must equal the ratio of input marginal products.

C.   **Illustration of Optimal Input Proportions:** Optimal input proportions are employed when an additional dollar spent on any input yields the same increase in output.

    1.   No other input combination that can be purchased for the same cost produces as much output.

    2.   When input proportions are optimal, a given level of output is produced efficiently. However, this does not ensure than an optimal *total amount* of output is produced.

IX.   **OPTIMAL LEVELS OF MULTIPLE INPUTS**

A.   **Optimal Employment and Profit Maximization:** Profits are maximized when inputs are employed so that price equals marginal revenue product for each input.

1.   Algebraically, for all inputs X and Y:

$$MRP_X = P_X$$

$$MRP_Y = P_Y$$

2.   When optimal levels of multiple inputs are employed, output is produced efficiently and the optimal *total amount* of output is produced.

B.   **Illustration of Optimal Levels of Multiple Inputs:** At the optimal employment level, marginal revenue product equals marginal for each input.

1.   At the optimal employment level, an optimal combination of inputs is employed.

2.   At the optimal employment level, optimal levels of each input are employed.

3.   At the optimal employment level, a profit-maximizing level of output is produced.

X.   **RETURNS TO SCALE**

A.   **Evaluating Returns to Scale:** Returns to scale are measured in terms of the output response to a given percentage increase in *all* inputs.

1.   If the percentage increase in output is greater than the percentage increase in inputs, increasing returns prevail.

2.   If the percentage increase in output is precisely equal to the percentage increase in inputs, constant returns prevail.

3.   If the percentage increase in output is less than the percentage increase in inputs, decreasing returns prevail.

4.   Returns to scale can be evaluated graphically by considering the distance between consecutive isoquants.

a.   If the distance between successive isoquants diminishes, then doubling output requires less than a doubling of inputs, and increasing returns are indicated.

    b.   If the distance between isoquants for successive output quantities is constant, then output doubles when input usage doubles, and constant returns prevail.

    c.   If the distance between successive isoquants increases, then doubling output requires more than a doubling of inputs, and diminishing returns are indicated.

B.   **Output Elasticity and Returns to Scale:** Output elasticity, ε_Q, is the percentage change in output associated with a 1% increase in all inputs.

    1.   By definition:

$$\varepsilon_Q = \frac{\partial Q}{Q} \div \frac{\partial X}{X} = \frac{\partial Q}{\partial X} \times \frac{X}{Q}$$

where $\underline{X}$ represents all inputs (capital, labor, etc.). Possibilities include:

    a. $\varepsilon_Q > 1$ implies increasing returns to scale.

    b. $\varepsilon_Q = 1$ implies constant returns to scale.

    c. $\varepsilon_Q < 1$ implies diminishing returns to scale.

C.   **Returns to Scale Estimation:** In most instances, returns to scale can be easily estimated.

    1.   If a 1% increase in all inputs causes more than a 1% increase in output, returns to scale are increasing.

    2.   If a 1% increase in all inputs causes a 1% increase in output, returns to scale are constant.

    3.   If a 1% increase in all inputs causes less than a 1% increase in output, returns to scale are diminishing.

XI.   **PRODUCTION FUNCTION ESTIMATION**

A.   **Cubic Production Functions:** Cubic production functions exhibit stages of first increasing and then diminishing returns to scale.

B. Power Production Functions: The power (or multiplicative) function is probably the most popular structural form employed.

    1.   Power functions allow the marginal productivity of individual inputs to vary depending upon employment levels for all inputs.

C. Functional Form Selection for Empirical Studies: As in demand estimation, an appropriate model for production function estimation is derived from economic theory and practical experience.

XII.   PRODUCTIVITY MEASUREMENT

A. How is Productivity Measured?: Studies of output per hour in individual industries and the overall economy have been a responsibility of the Bureau of Labor Statistics (BLS) since the 1800s.

    1.   Productivity growth is the rate of increase in output per unit of input

    2.   Labor productivity refers to the relationship between output and the worker time used to generate that output.

        a.   It is the ratio of output per worker hour.

    3.   In multifactor productivity measures, output is related to combined inputs of labor, capital and intermediate purchases.

B. Trends in Industry Productivity: Industry productivity measures describe the relationship between output and the labor time involved in its production.

    1.   Although these measures relate output to hours of employees or all persons engaged in an industry, they do not measure the specific contribution of labor, capital, or any other factor of production.

    2.   They reflect the joint effects of many influences, including changes in technology; capital investment; level of output; utilization of capacity, energy, and materials; the organization of production; managerial skill; and the characteristics and effort of the workforce.

C. Uses and Limitations of Productivity Data: Measures of output per hour are useful for analyzing trends in labor costs across industries, comparing productivity progress among countries, examining the effects of technological improvements, and analyzing related economic and industrial activities.

1. Productivity measures of output per hour may not fully take into account changes in the quality of goods and services produced.

2. Year-to-year changes in output per hour are sometimes irregular and not indicative of basic changes in long-term trends.

XIII. SUMMARY

PROBLEMS & SOLUTIONS

P7.1   ***Production Function Concepts.*** *Indicate whether each of the following statements is true or false. Explain why.*

    A.   *The law of diminishing returns states that returns to scale are diminishing in all known production systems.*

    B.   *Decreasing returns to scale and increasing average costs are indicated when $\varepsilon_Q > 1$.*

    C.   *Straight line-shaped isoquants describe production systems in which inputs are perfect substitutes.*

    D.   *The marginal rate of technical substitution is not affected by a given percentage decrease in the marginal productivity of all inputs.*

    E.   *Returns to a factor describe the percentage change in output relative to a percentage change in all inputs.*

P7.1   **SOLUTION**

    A.   False. The law of diminishing returns states that as the quantity of any *single* variable input increases, holding other inputs constant, the marginal product of that single input eventually decreases. Returns to scale are often constant or increasing over limited ranges of output.

    B.   False. When $\varepsilon_Q > 1$, the percentage change in output is greater than a given percentage change in all inputs. Thus, increasing returns to scale and decreasing average costs are indicated.

    C.   True. Straight line-shaped production isoquants reflect a perfect substitute relation among inputs.

    D.   True. The marginal rate of technical substitution is measured by the relative marginal productivity of input factors. This relation is unaffected by a commensurate decrease in the marginal productivity of all inputs.

    E.   False. Returns to scale describe the percentage change in output relative to a percentage change in *all* inputs.

P7.2   ***Returns to Scale Estimation.*** *Determine whether the following production functions exhibit constant, increasing or decreasing returns to scale.*

    A. $Q = 0.6X + 20Y + 10Z$

    B. $Q = 200 + 4L$

    C. $Q = 20L + 16K + 10LK$

    D. $Q = 2A^2 + 3AB + 5B^2$

    E. $Q = 20L^{0.25}K^{0.70}$

    F. $Q = \sqrt{3X^2 + 2Y^2 + 15Z^2}$

P7.2   **SOLUTION**

    A.   Returns to scale can be determined by evaluating the percentage increase in output which follows any given percentage increase in inputs. Answers to parts A, B and C reflect this approach. Alternatively, returns to scale can be evaluated using the more general algebraic approach of parts D, E and F. Both approaches work; use the one that is easiest for you.

        If $X = Y = Z = 100$, then:

$$
\begin{aligned}
Q_1 &= 0.6X + 20Y + 10Z \\
&= 0.6(100) + 20(100) + 10(100) \\
&= 3{,}060
\end{aligned}
$$

        Increasing each input by 1% yields:

$$
\begin{aligned}
Q_2 &= 0.6(101) + 20(101) + 10(101) \\
&= 3{,}090.6
\end{aligned}
$$

        which implies a 1% increase in output ($Q_2/Q_1 = 3{,}090.6/3{,}060 = 1.01$), and therefore the function exhibits constant returns to scale.

    B.   If $L = 100$, then:

$$Q_1 = 200 + 4L$$

$$= 200 + 4(100)$$

$$= 600$$

Increasing labor by 2% yields:

$$Q_2 = 200 + 4(102)$$

$$= 608$$

which implies a 1.3% increase in output ($Q_2/Q_1 = 608/600 = 1.013$, and therefore the function exhibits diminishing returns to scale. (Note: $Q = 200$ even though $L = 0$ could be descriptive of an agricultural production function).

C.   If $L = K = 100$, then:

$$Q_1 = 20L + 16K + 10LK$$

$$= 20(100) + 16(100) + 10(100)(100)$$

$$= 103,600$$

Increasing each input by 3% yields:

$$Q_2 = 20(103) + 16(103) + 10(103)(103)$$

$$= 109,798$$

which implies a 5.98% increase in output ($Q_2/Q_1 = 109,798/103,600 = 1.0598$), and therefore the function exhibits increasing returns to scale.

Alternatively, for a k proportionate increase in all inputs (where $k > 1$):

$$Q = 20L + 16K + 10LK$$

$$hQ = 20(kL) + 16(kK) + 10(kL)(kK)$$

$$= k^1(20L + 16K + 10kLK)$$

$$= k^1(Q^*)$$

Here, returns to scale would be constant if $Q^* = Q$. However, because $k > 1$, it is clear that $Q^* > Q$. This implies that returns to scale for this production function are increasing (as before).

D. For a k proportionate increase in all inputs:

$$Q = 2A^2 + 3AB + 5B^2$$

$$hQ = 2(kA)^2 + 3(kA)(kB) + 5(kB)^2$$

$$= k^2(2A^2 + 3AB + 5B^2)$$

$$= k^2Q$$

$$h = k^2$$

Therefore, $h > k$ and the production function demonstrates increasing returns to scale.

E. For a k proportionate increase in all inputs:

$$Q = 20L^{0.25}K^{0.70}$$

$$hQ = 20(kL)^{0.25}(kK)^{0.70}$$

$$= k^{0.25 + 0.70}(20L^{0.25}K^{0.70})$$

$$= k^{0.95}Q$$

$$h = k^{0.95}$$

Because $h < k$, the production function exhibits diminishing returns to scale.

F. For a k proportionate increase in all inputs:

$$Q = \sqrt{3X^2 + 2Y^2 + 15Z^2}$$

$$hQ = \sqrt{3(kX)^2 + 2(kY)^2 + 15(kZ)^2}$$

$$= \sqrt{k^2(3X^2 + 2Y^2 + 15Z^2)}$$

$$= k\sqrt{3X^2 + 2Y^2 + 15Z^2}$$

$$= kQ$$

$$h = k$$

Therefore, h = k and the production function demonstrates constant returns to scale.

P7.3   ***Marginal and Total Product.*** *The patient insurance record processing department for St. Eligius Hospital has a production function described by the relation:*

$$Q = 0.4K^2 + 0.2KL + 0.3L^2$$

where Q is output in records processed, K is capital in terms of the number of computer hours, and L is the number of labor hours employed.

Assume a weekly rate of use where K = 40 computer hours and L = 150 labor hours.

A.   *What is total product per week?*

B.   *What are the marginal products for computer hours and for labor hours?*

P7.3   **SOLUTION**

A. $Q = 0.4K^2 + 0.2KL + 0.3L^2$

$$= 0.4(40^2) + 0.2(40)(150) + 0.3(150^2)$$

$$= 8{,}590 \text{ records processed}$$

B.   Marginal product of computer time $= MP_K = \partial Q/\partial K$

$$= 0.8K + 0.2L$$

$$= 0.8(40) + 0.2(150)$$

$$= 62 \text{ records processed}$$

Marginal product of labor $= MP_L = \partial Q/\partial L$

$$= 0.2K + 0.6L$$

$$= 0.2(40) + 0.6(150)$$

$$= 98 \text{ records processed}$$

P7.4 ***Optimal Wages.*** *Shortcuts, Inc., is a regional chain offering walk-in haircut services at popular prices. The company currently has two employee job classifications. Inexperienced haircutters (I) have six months or less job experience, and, on average, are able to cut a customer's hair in 20 minutes. Experienced haircutters (E), employees with more than six months experience, can provide one haircut in 15 minutes.*

A. *If inexperienced haircutters are readily available at a wage of $10 per hour, what is the maximum hourly wage that could be justified for experienced haircutters?*

B. *What would be your employment recommendation to the company if experienced haircutters can be readily employed at a wage of $12 per hour?*

P7.4 **SOLUTION**

A. The rule for optimal relative employment of inexperienced (I) and experienced (E) haircutters is:

$$\frac{MP_I}{P_I} = \frac{MP_E}{P_E} \text{ or } \frac{MP_I}{MP_E} = \frac{P_I}{P_E}$$

Because inexperienced haircutters can provide one haircut in 20 minutes, or 1/3 hour, their marginal product per hour is $MP_I = 3$. Because experienced haircutters can provide one haircut in 15 minutes, or 1/4 hour, their marginal product per hour is $MP_E = 4$. Therefore, given $P_I = \$10$ per hour, the maximum hourly wage that could be justified for experienced haircutters is:

$$\frac{MP_I}{MP_E} = \frac{P_I}{P_E}$$

$$\frac{3}{4} = \frac{\$10}{P_E}$$

$$P_E = \$13.33 \text{ per hour}$$

B.   If experienced haircutters can be readily employed at a wage of $12 per hour, then relative to inexperienced haircutters, the experienced haircutters represent an employment bargain. Whereas the labor cost per haircut with inexperienced haircutters is $3.33 (= P_I/MP_I), the labor cost per haircut with experienced haircutters is only $3 (= P_E/MP_E). The superior productivity of experienced haircutters more than compensates for their higher wages. Shortcuts should employ relatively more experienced haircutters. Indeed, if the marginal productivity of each employment class is independent, experienced haircutters would be employed exclusively.

P7.5   ***Marginal Rate of Technical Substitution.*** *Bush's Broccoli Farm is a moderate-sized Connecticut broccoli grower. Bush's estimates that broccoli output would increase by 600 bushels with an additional 1,000 gallons of water provided to its irrigation system. Alternatively, broccoli output could be increased by 500 bushels with an additional 2 tons of lime fertilizer.*

A.   *Estimate the marginal products of water and fertilizer.*

B.   *What is the marginal rate of technical substitution between these inputs?*

C.   *Assuming the cost of water is 6¢ per gallon and the cost of fertilizer is $25 per ton, is Bush's currently using an optimal combination of fertilizer and water?*

P7.5   SOLUTION

A.
$$\text{Marginal product of water} = MP_W = \frac{\partial Q}{\partial W}$$

$$= \frac{600}{1,000}$$

$$= 0.6 \text{ bushels per gallon}$$

$$\text{Marginal product of fertilizer} = MP_F = \frac{\partial Q}{\partial F}$$

$$= \frac{500}{2}$$

$$= 250 \text{ bushels per ton}$$

B. Marginal rate of technical substitution

$$MRTS = -\frac{MP_W}{MP_F}$$

$$\frac{\partial Q/\partial W}{\partial Q/\partial F} = -\frac{0.6}{250}$$

$$\frac{\partial F}{\partial W} = -0.0024$$

which implies:

$$\partial F = -0.0024\partial W \text{ or } \partial W = -416.6\partial F$$

C. Yes, Bush's current combination of water and fertilizer is optimal because:

$$\frac{MP_W}{MP_F} = \frac{P_W}{P_F}$$

$$\frac{0.6}{250} \stackrel{?}{=} \frac{\$0.06}{\$25}$$

$$0.0024 \stackrel{\checkmark}{=} 0.0024$$

P7.6 ***Optimal Input Mix.*** *Lockheart Laboratories, Inc., offers medical tests to private employers and government agencies. To better serve the rapidly growing demand for its services, LLI is considering hiring a new lab technician, leasing new testing equipment, or both. The cost of hiring a new lab technician is $8,000 per month (including fringes); the cost of leasing additional testing equipment is $10,000 per month. A new lab technician would allow LLI to increase output from 60,000 to 62,000 tests per month; a new piece of testing equipment is capable of increasing current staff output by 2,500 tests per month.*

A. *Does MLI's current employment of lab technicians and testing equipment reflect an optimal mix of labor and equipment?*

B. *If each test provides a $6 net marginal revenue before labor and capital costs, is expansion advisable?*

P7.6   SOLUTION

A.   The rule for an optimal mix of labor and capital is:

$$\frac{MP_L}{P_L} = \frac{MP_K}{P_K} \quad \text{or} \quad \frac{MP_L}{MP_K} = \frac{P_L}{P_K}$$

On a monthly basis, the relevant question is:

$$\frac{MP_L}{P_L} \stackrel{?}{=} \frac{MP_K}{P_K}$$

$$\frac{2,000}{\$8,000} \stackrel{?}{=} \frac{2,500}{\$10,000}$$

$$0.25 \stackrel{\checkmark}{=} 0.25$$

Therefore, the marginal effect on output of one dollar spent on either labor technicians or capital equipment is 0.25 tests. This indicates an *optimal mix* of labor and capital because output could not be increased by changing the relative usage of labor and capital.

B.   Yes, expansion would be profitable. The rule for an optimal level of input employment is:

$$MRP = MP \times MR_Q = \text{Input Price}$$

In this instance, for each input:

$$MRP_L = MP_L \times MR_Q \stackrel{?}{=} P_L$$

$$2,000 \times \$6 \stackrel{?}{=} \$8,000$$

$$\$12,000 > \$8,000$$

$$MRP_K = MP_K \times MR_Q \stackrel{?}{=} P_K$$

$$2,500 \times \$6 \stackrel{?}{=} \$10,000$$

$$\$15,000 \ > \ \$10,000$$

Both inputs generate net marginal revenues in excess of marginal costs. As a result, expansion would be profitable.

P7.7   ***Optimal Input Level.*** *Enron Natural Resources, Ltd., is a leading energy provider with vast coal holding in western states. The company is in the process of negotiating a new labor agreement, and is relying upon an engineering analysis that suggests the following production and marginal product relations:*

$$Q \ = \ 1,000L^{0.5}K^{0.5}$$

$$MP_L \ = \ \partial Q/\partial L = 500L^{-0.5}K^{0.5}$$

$$MP_K \ = \ \partial Q/\partial K = 500L^{0.5}K^{-0.5}$$

where

> Q = *Coal output (in thousands of tons).*
>
> L = *Labor (in hundreds of employees).*
>
> K = *Capital (in billions of dollars).*
>
> MP_L = *Marginal product of labor (in hundreds of employees).*
>
> MP_K = *Marginal product of capital (in billions of dollars).*

Enron employs 10,000 workers and maintains a $16 billion capital investment. Coal output is sold in competitive markets at an expected price of $33.75 per ton.

A.   *Determine and interpret returns to scale.*

B.   *Determine and interpret returns to each factor input.*

C.   *What is the maximum annual salary Enron is willing to pay a labor force of 10,000 employees?*

D.   *How many workers would Enron willingly employ at a $75,000 annual salary?*

    (Note: Interpret your units of measurement carefully!)

P7.7   SOLUTION

A. $Q = 1{,}000L^{0.5}K^{0.5}$

               $hQ = 1{,}000(kL)^{0.5}(kK)^{0.5}$

                    $= k^{0.5+0.5}(1{,}000L^{0.5}K^{0.5})$

                    $= k^{1}Q$

               $h = k^{1}$

Therefore, $h = k$ and the above production exhibits constant returns to scale.

B.   Returns to each factor can be determined by looking at how each marginal product changes with increased input usage.

Returns to Labor:

$$\text{Marginal product of labor} = MP_{L} = \partial Q / \partial L = 500L^{-0.5}K^{0.5}$$

$$= \frac{500(16^{0.5})}{100^{0.5}}$$

$$= 200$$

Because $\partial^{2}Q / \partial L^{2} = -250L^{-1.5}K^{0.5} < 0$, MP_{L} is decreasing beyond this point, and returns to the labor factor are diminishing.

Returns to Capital:

$$\text{Marginal product of capital} = MP_{K} = \partial Q / \partial K = 500L^{0.5}K^{-0.5}$$

$$= \frac{500(100^{0.5})}{16^{0.5}}$$

$$= 1{,}250$$

Because $\partial^2 Q/\partial K^2 = -250L^{0.5}K^{-1.5} < 0$, MP_K is decreasing beyond this point, and returns to the capital factor are diminishing.

C.   The optimal employment rule, $P_i = MRP_i$, is used to determine the maximum annual salary that Enron would willingly pay 10,000 employees.

$$\frac{\text{Price}}{\text{of labor}} = \frac{\text{Marginal revenue}}{\text{product of labor}}$$

$$P_L = MP_L \times MR_Q$$

$$= (500L^{-0.5}K^{0.5})(\$33.75 \times 1,000)$$

$$= \frac{500K^{0.5}}{L^{0.5}} \times 33,750$$

$$= \frac{500(16^{0.5})}{100^{0.5}} \times 33,750$$

$$= \$6,750,000 \text{ per hundred workers or } \$67,500 \text{ per worker}$$

These numerical calculations must reflect the fact that Q is in thousands of tons, L is in hundreds of employees, and K is in billions of dollars of capital. Given that coal sells for \$33.75 per ton, the $MR_Q = \$33,750$ because Q is one thousand tons of coal. Similarly, the P_L derived above is for one hundred employees because the MP_L is also for one hundred employees. At first, making such unit adjustments may seem confusing. With practice, however, you will become able to deal with "units problems" and be able to interpret and use productivity studies compiled by subordinates, consultants, government agencies, and others.

D.   Again, using the optimal employment rule:

$$\frac{\text{Price}}{\text{of labor}} = \frac{\text{Marginal revenue}}{\text{product of labor}}$$

$$P_L = MP_L \times MR_Q$$

$$\$75,000 \times 100 = (500L^{-0.5}K^{0.5})(\$33.75 \times 1,000)$$

$$7,500,000 = \frac{500K^{0.5}}{L^{0.5}} \times 33,750$$

$$7,500,000 \; = \; \frac{500(16^{0.5})}{L^{0.5}} \times 33,750$$

$$7,500,000 \; = \; \frac{67,500,000}{L^{0.5}}$$

$$L^{0.5} \; = \; \frac{67,500,000}{7,500,000}$$

$$L^{0.5} \; = \; 9$$

$$L \; = \; 81(00) \text{ or } 8,100 \text{ workers}$$

At a salary of $75,000, Enron would be willing to employ only 8,100 workers.

P7.8   ***Optimal Employment.*** *Both Senior Claims Analysts and Junior Claims Analysts process claims at the Wakarusa Insurance Company. Senior Claims Analysts earn $30 while processing an average of 5 claims per hour. Junior Analysts earn $16 while processing an average of 2 claims per hour.*

   A.   *Calculate the marginal labor cost per claim processed by Senior and Junior Analysts.*

   B.   *Is the firm operating efficiently? Explain.*

   C.   *Should Wakarusa increase or decrease the relative number of Senior Analysts? Explain.*

   D.   *Holding all else unchanged, what Senior Analyst wage would make the current ratio of Senior Analysts to Junior Analysts optimal?*

P7.8   **SOLUTION**

   A.   The marginal labor cost per claim processed is given by the ratio:

$$\begin{matrix} \text{Marginal labor} \\ \text{cost per unit} \end{matrix} = \frac{P_L}{MP_L} = \frac{\text{Labor cost per hour}}{\partial Q \text{ per hour}}$$

Therefore, for senior (SA) and junior (JA) claims analysts:

$$MC_{SA} = \frac{P_{SA}}{MP_{SA}} = \frac{\$30}{5} = \$6 \text{ per claim}$$

$$MC_{JA} = \frac{P_{JA}}{MP_{JA}} = \frac{\$16}{2} = \$8 \text{ per claim}$$

B. No, the firm is employing an inefficient combination of senior and junior analysts. The marginal labor cost per claim processed is only $6 for senior analysts, but $8 per claim processed by junior analysts. To be optimal, the employment of senior and junior analysts should be such that the marginal labor processing costs are equal for each type of employee.

C. Increase. If relatively more senior analysts are hired the firm will reduce its average labor processing cost per claim. Holding the number of junior analysts constant, additional senior analysts will be employed until the marginal product of senior analysts falls to 3.75 claims per hour. At that point, the marginal labor cost of claims processed by senior analysts would equal $8 per claim (= $30/3.75). If the number of senior analysts is held constant, the number of junior analysts should be reduced until the marginal product of junior analysts rises to 2.67 claims per hour. At that point, the marginal labor cost of claims processed by junior analysts would equal $6 (= $16/2.67).

In either case, the marginal labor processing costs would become equal across employee classifications, as is required for input proportions to be optimal.

D. Senior analysts are 2.5 (= MP_{SA}/MP_{JA} = 5/2) times as productive as junior analysts, while earning only 1.875 (= P_{SA}/P_{JA} = $30/$16) times as much pay. Given their relative productivity, a senior analyst pay level of $40 per hour or 2.5 times that of junior analysts can be justified. At that wage,

$$MC_{SA} = \frac{P_{SA}}{MP_{SA}} = \frac{\$40}{5} = \$8 \text{ per claim}$$

Optimality would be reached because, at that higher wage for senior analysts,

$$\frac{P_{SA}}{MP_{SA}} = \frac{P_{JA}}{MP_{JA}}$$

Therefore, a $10 per hour raise (= $40 - $30) for senior analysts could be justified.

P7.9   ***Power Production Functions.*** *Data Analysis, Inc., has engaged Ray Barone, a recent MBA graduate, to recommend a hiring policy for its soon to be opened office in Long Island, New York. Barone has conducted a statistical study of operations at twelve similar-sized DAI offices and found the following (standard errors in parentheses):*

$$\ln Q \;=\; 0.50 \ln L + 0.25 \ln C + 0.25 \ln B$$
$$\qquad\quad (0.13) \qquad (0.06) \qquad (0.11)$$

$$R^2 \;=\; 87\%$$

Q = data processing output.

L = labor hours for data processing staff.

C = computer time-sharing hours for data processing.

B = office building space in hundreds of square feet.

A.   *Describe the economic logic underlying Barone's choice of the above log-linear production relation as opposed to, say, a linear relation.*

B.   *Based on the above analysis, Barone projects the following marginal products for each input:*

$$MP_L = \partial Q/\partial L \;=\; 0.5 L^{-0.5} C^{0.25} B^{0.25}$$

$$MP_C = \partial Q/\partial C \;=\; 0.25 L^{0.5} C^{-0.75} B^{0.25}$$

$$MP_B = \partial Q/\partial B \;=\; 0.25 L^{0.5} C^{0.25} B^{-0.75}$$

Determine the optimal relation between total expenditures for L and C.

C.   *Barone projects computer time-sharing costs of $225 per hour, and anticipates needing to pay $90,000 per year to attract and retain data processing personnel. If a total labor and computer time budget of $1,350,000 has been established for the Long Island office, and staff members work 2,000 hours per year, how many staff members should be hired and how much computer time should be purchased?*

P7.9   **SOLUTION**

A.   Log-linear (or power) production relations are appropriate when the marginal products of individual inputs depend upon the levels of all inputs employed.

Although many other functional forms (quadratic and cubic, for example) also enjoy this feature, log-linear forms are easy to estimate and results are easily interpreted.

B. The optimal combination rate for L and C is determined by the relation:

$$\frac{MP_L}{MP_C} = \frac{P_L}{P_C}$$

$$\frac{0.5L^{-0.5}C^{0.25}B^{0.25}}{0.25L^{0.5}C^{-0.75}B^{0.25}} = \frac{P_L}{P_C}$$

$$\frac{2C}{L} = \frac{P_L}{P_C}$$

which implies an optimal relation between total expenditures for L and C of:

$$2C \times P_C = P_L \times L$$

$$2 \times \begin{array}{c} \text{Expenditures} \\ \text{on computer time} \end{array} = \begin{array}{c} \text{Expenditures} \\ \text{on labor} \end{array}$$

Thus, expenditures on labor will be twice the total level of expenditures on computer time. Alternatively, expenditures on computer time will be one-half total expenditures on labor.

C. From part B it is clear that:

$$\begin{array}{c} \text{Total} \\ \text{budget} \end{array} = \begin{array}{c} \text{Labor} \\ \text{expenditures} \\ \text{(two thirds)} \end{array} + \begin{array}{c} \text{Computer} \\ \text{expenditures} \\ \text{(one third)} \end{array}$$

Given a salary of \$90,000 per employee and assuming 2,000 worker hours per year, a wage of \$90,000/2,000 = \$45 per hour is implied. The number of staff members to be hired is determined as follows:

$$\text{Labor expenditures} = \$900,000$$

$$P_L \times L = 900,000$$

$$45 \times L = 900,000$$

$$L = 20,000$$

If each programmer works 2,000 hours per year, then:

$$\text{New programmers} = \frac{20,000}{2,000}$$

$$= 10 \text{ employees}$$

Similarly, the amount of computer time to be purchased is determined as:

$$\text{Computer time expenditures} = \$450,000$$

$$P_C \times C = 450,000$$

$$225 \times C = 450,000$$

$$C = 2,000 \text{ hours}$$

P7.10   ***Marginal Product Analysis.*** *Kenny Kramer, head of the engineering department of the Automatic Switch Company, estimates the following production and marginal product functions for assembly of the K-2 switch:*

$$Q = 30X + 2XY - 0.5X^2 - 0.5Y^2$$

$$MP_X = 30 + 2Y - X$$

$$MP_Y = 2X - Y$$

where Q = total output of K-2 switches, X = worker hours, and Y = machine tool hours.

A.   *Assume a weekly rate of use where X = 70 worker hours and Y = 30 machine tool hours. What is total product per week?*

B.   *Calculate the marginal product for each input at this rate of usage.*

C.   *Calculate the marginal revenue product for each input at these usage levels, assuming K-2 switches are sold at a competitive market price of 50¢ each.*

D. *Are these input usage levels optimal in light of wage costs of $25 per hour and machine tool costs of $40 per hour? If so, why? If not, calculate optimal input levels and explain your answer.*

P7.10 SOLUTION

A. At $X = 70$ and $Y = 30$,

$$Q = 30X + 2XY - 0.5X^2 - 0.5Y^2$$

$$= 30(70) + 2(70)(30) - 0.5(70^2) - 0.5(30^2)$$

$$= 3,400$$

B. In general,

$$MP_X = \partial Q/\partial X = 30 + 2Y - X$$

$$= 30 + 2(30) - 70$$

$$= 20$$

$$MP_Y = \partial Q/\partial Y = 2X - Y$$

$$= 2(70) - 30$$

$$= 110$$

C. In general,

$$MRP_X = MP_X \times MR_Q$$

$$= (30 + 2Y - X)(\$0.5)$$

$$= \$15 + Y - \$0.5X$$

$$= \$15 + \$30 - \$0.5(70)$$

$$= \$10$$

$$MRP_Y = MP_Y \times MR_Q$$

$$= (2X - Y)(\$0.5)$$

$$= X - \$0.5Y$$

$$= \$70 - \$0.5(30)$$

$$= \$55$$

D.   Input usage levels of $X = 70$ and $Y = 30$ will be optimal provided $MRP_i = P_i$. Here, usage of neither X nor Y is optimal because:

$MRP_X = \$10 < \$25$ and X usage should be reduced.

$MRP_Y = \$55 > \$40$ and Y usage should be expanded.

Optimal input usage will be achieved only when $MRP_X = P_X$ and $MRP_Y = P_Y$:

$$(1) \; MRP_X = \$15 + Y - \$0.5X = \$25 = P_X$$

$$(2) \; MRP_Y = X - \$0.5Y = \$40 = P_Y$$

This constitutes a system of two equations with two unknowns to be solved simultaneously. Taking equation (1) plus two times (2) yields:

$$(1) \qquad\qquad 15 + Y - 0.5X = 25$$

$$+ 2 \times (2) \qquad\qquad \underline{2X - Y = 80}$$

$$15 + 1.5X = 105$$

$$1.5X = 90$$

$$X = 60$$

And substituting $X = 60$ into (1) yields:

$$(1) \qquad\qquad 15 + Y - 0.5X = 25$$

$$15 + Y - 0.5(60) = 25$$

$$Y = 40$$

Chapter 8

COST ANALYSIS AND ESTIMATION

Corporate restructuring typically involves eliminating nonstrategic operations to redeploy assets and strengthen core lines of business. When nonessential assets are disposed of in a depressed market, there is often no relation between low "fire sale" proceeds and book value, historical cost, or replacement cost. Conversely, when assets are sold to others who can more effectively use such resources, sale proceeds can approximate replacement valuations and greatly exceed historical costs and book values. Even under normal circumstances, the link between economic and accounting values can be tenuous. Economic worth as determined by profit-generating capability, rather than accounting value, is always the most relevant consideration when determining the cost and use of specific assets. In cost analysis and estimation, historical accounting information provides a valuable starting point for evaluation. Nevertheless, these data must be constantly monitored and adjusted, when necessary, to reflect economic reality.

This chapter focuses on how costs and output are related on a conceptual level, and how practical knowledge about such relations can be used to accurately estimate cost relationships. Cost analysis and estimation plays an essential role in managerial economics because virtually every managerial decision requires a careful comparison between costs and benefits. Central to all economic analysis is the notion that relevant cost determination depends on a careful consideration of applicable decision alternatives.

CHAPTER OUTLINE

I.   **WHAT MAKES COST ANALYSIS DIFFICULT?**

      A.   **Link Between Accounting and Economic Valuations:** Cost analysis is made difficult by the effects of unforeseen inflation, unpredictable changes in technology, and the dynamic nature of input and output markets.

            1.   Divergences between economic costs and accounting valuations are common.

            2.   Accurate cost analysis involves careful consideration of all relevant decision alternatives.

      B.   **Historical Versus Current Costs:** The term *cost* can be defined in a number of ways; the correct definition varies from situation to situation.

            1.   For tax purposes, historical cost, or actual cash outlay, is the relevant cost.

            2.   Current costs are typically more relevant than historical costs.

a.   Current cost is the amount that must be paid under prevailing market conditions.

C.   Replacement Cost: Replacement cost is the cost of duplicating productive capability using current technology.

1.   In assessing the cost of using productive assets, the appropriate measure is the replacement cost.

II.   OPPORTUNITY COSTS

A.   Opportunity Cost Concept: Opportunity cost is value foregone with current rather than next-best use of a given asset.

1.   Opportunity cost is determined by the highest-valued *opportunity* that must be foregone to allow current use.

B.   Explicit and Implicit Costs: Resource costs often involve out-of-pocket expenses, or explicit costs, and other noncash expenses, called implicit costs.

1.   Wages, utility expenses, raw materials costs, interest expenses, and rent are all examples of explicit expenses.

2.   Implicit costs do not involve cash expenditures and can be wrongly overlooked in decision analysis.

III.   INCREMENTAL AND SUNK COSTS IN DECISION ANALYSIS

A.   Incremental Cost: The change in cost associated with a given managerial decision is called the incremental cost.

1.   Marginal cost involves a one-unit change in output; incremental cost can involve a multiple-unit change in output.

B.   Sunk Costs: Any cost that does not vary across decision alternatives is a sunk cost.

1.   Sunk costs arise from past decisions that are irreversible.

2.   Sunk costs are irrelevant for current and future decisions.

IV.   SHORT-RUN AND LONG-RUN COSTS

    A.   Cost Functions: A cost function is the functional relation between cost and output.

        1.   Technology, or the manner in which inputs are converted to output, plays a role in determining costs.

        2.   The level and rate of change in input prices also affect costs.

    B.   How is the Operating Period Defined?: The short run is the time-frame within which operating decisions are made. The long run is the time-frame within which planning decisions are made.

        1.   At least one input is fixed in supply during the short run.

        2.   Firms have complete input flexibility in the long run.

    C.   Fixed and Variable Costs: Fixed costs do not vary with output. Variable costs differ according to output.

        1.   Fixed costs exist in the short-run only; all costs are variable in the long-run.

V.   SHORT-RUN COST CURVES

    A.   Short-Run Cost Categories: Total, average, and marginal costs in short-run cost functions are described as:

        1.   Total Cost (TC) = Fixed Costs (TFC) + Total Variable Costs (TVC)

        2.   Average Fixed Cost (AFC) = TFC/Q.

        3.   Average Variable Cost (AVC) = TVC/Q.

        4.   Average Cost (or Average Total Cost) (AC) = TC/Q.

        5.   Marginal Cost (MC) = $\partial TC/\partial Q = \partial TVC/\partial Q$.

    B.   Short-Run Cost Relations: A short-run cost curve shows the minimum cost impact of output changes for a specific plant in a given operating environment.

        1.   The slope of the total cost curve is identical to the slope of the total variable cost curve.

        a.   A change in fixed costs merely shifts the total cost curve to a different level.

        b.   Marginal costs are independent of fixed costs.

    2.   Assuming constant input prices, the shape of the total variable cost curve is determined by the productivity of variable input factors employed.

VI.   LONG-RUN COST CURVES

A.   Long-Run Total Costs: All long-run cost curves are based on the assumption that an optimal scale of plant is used to produce any given output level.

    1.   If input prices are held constant, there is a direct relation between cost and production.

    2.   Long-run total cost functions and production functions both provide returns to scale information.

B.   Economies of Scale: The impact on total cost of a percentage change in output is the returns to scale attribute of a cost function.

    1.   Returns to scale are increasing, constant, or diminishing depending upon the relation between long-run total costs and output.

    2.   Economists often use the term economies of scale as synonymous with increasing returns to scale.

C.   Cost Elasticities and Returns to Scale: Cost elasticity, ε_C, measures the percentage change in total cost associated with a 1% change in output. By definition:

$$\varepsilon_C = \partial C/C \div \partial Q/Q = \partial C/\partial Q \times Q/C.$$

The relation between cost elasticity and returns to scale is straightforward.

    1.   If $\varepsilon_C < 1$, returns to scale are increasing.

    2.   If $\varepsilon_C = 1$, returns to scale are constant.

    3.   If $\varepsilon_C > 1$, returns to scale are decreasing.

D. Long-Run Average Costs: The long-run average cost curve is the envelope (or border) of the short-run average cost curves for various plant sizes. Given constant input prices and unchanging technology, there is a direct relation between long-run average costs and returns to scale.

1. If LRAC are falling, returns to scale are increasing.

2. If LRAC are constant, returns to scale are constant.

3. If LRAC are rising, returns to scale are decreasing.

VII. MINIMUM EFFICIENT SCALE

A. Competitive Implications of Minimum Efficient Scale: The minimum efficient scale concept has important implications for competition.

1. Minimum efficient scale is the plant size at which long-run average cost is first minimized.

   a. MES is the minimum point of a "U-shaped" LRAC curve.

   b. MES is the "corner" point of an "L-shaped" LRAC curve.

2. Competition tends to be most vigorous when:

   a. MES is small in absolute terms.

   b. MES is a small share of industry output.

   c. The cost disadvantage to less than MES operation is minor.

B. Transportation Costs and MES: High transportation costs can offset the cost advantages of MES-size operation.

1. Transportation costs include terminal, line-haul, and inventory charges associated with moving output from production facilities to customers.

   a. Terminal charges or loading and unloading expenses do not vary with the distance of shipment.

b. Line-haul expenses, including equipment, labor, and fuel costs, vary directly with the distance shipped.

c. The inventory cost component of transportation costs relates to the time element involved in shipping goods.

2. When transportation costs are high, even small, relatively inefficient local competitors can survive, if not prosper.

3. When transportation costs are low, markets are national or international in scope and significant economies of scale can cause output to be produced at only a few large plants.

VIII. FIRM SIZE AND PLANT SIZE

A. **Multiplant Economies and Diseconomies of Scale:** Multiplant economies are cost savings that arise from operating multiple facilities in the same line of business or industry.

1. Multiplant diseconomies are cost disadvantages that arise from the difficulty of coordinating multiple locations.

2. If long-run average costs decline, multiplant economies exist, and multiplant firms are more efficient than single-plant operations.

3. Constant average costs for multiplant operations indicate that there are no economies or diseconomies in combining plants.

4. If average costs first decline and then rise, economies of scale for the multiplant firm dominate initially, but eventually diseconomies result.

B. **Economics of Multiplant Operation: An Example:** This example illustrates the effects of multiplant economies on firm size.

1. Multiplant production is preferable to centralized production when it allows the firm to concentrate production at the minimum point on the single-plant U-shaped average cost curve.

C. **Plant Size and Flexibility:** In choosing a plant to produce a certain output, the firm should select the plant with the lowest expected average total cost over the range of possible output levels.

IX.   LEARNING CURVES

    A.   Learning-Curve Concept: Learning curves illustrate the predictable decrease in average production costs that often accompanies greater production experience.

        1.   Like any technical innovation, learning results in an inward (leftward) shift in the firm's LRAC curve.

    B.   Learning-Curve Example: The rate of learning is typically expressed in terms of the average cost reduction percentage following a doubling in total production.

    C.   Strategic Implications of the Learning-Curve Concept: Early in the development of important industries featuring new products and/or new production techniques, learning curve advantages have allowed industry leaders to enhance their relative cost advantage over nonleading firms.

        1.   To play an important role in competitive strategy, learning must be significant. Cost savings of 20% to 30% as cumulative output doubles must be possible.

        2.   If only modest effects of learning are present, product quality or customer service often plays a greater role in determining firm success.

X.   ECONOMIES OF SCOPE

    A.   Economies of Scope Concept: Economies of scope exist when it is cheaper on a per unit basis to produce and/or deliver goods or services in tandem rather than individually.

        1.   With scope economies, firms sell multiple outputs (e.g., copier machines and copier service).

        2.   Without scope economies, firms specialize (e.g., gourmet ice cream shops).

    B.   Exploiting Scope Economies: Scope economies are often an important element of competitive strategy for new products with standard characteristics where price is a key consideration.

XI.   COST-VOLUME-PROFIT ANALYSIS

    A.   Cost-Volume-Profit Charts: Cost-volume-profit (or breakeven) analysis is an analytical technique used to study relations among costs, revenues, and profits.

1.   The object of the analysis is to discover the output quantities where profit targets are realized.

2.   Cost-volume-profit charts and electronic spreadsheets depict cost and revenue categories as a function of the quantity produced and sold.

    a.   The point where total revenue equals total costs is the breakeven output level.

B.   Algebraic Cost-Volume-Profit Analysis: The breakeven quantity is defined as:

$$Q = \frac{TFC}{P - AVC},$$

where TFC is total fixed costs, P is price per unit sold, and AVC is average variable cost.

C.   Textbook Publishing: A Cost-Volume-Profit Example: Cost-volume-profit analysis is often used to make profit projections for projects that entail linear revenue and cost relations.

D.   Degree of Operating Leverage: The degree of operating leverage is the percentage change in profit that results from a 1% change in units sold.

1.   When price and variable costs per unit are constant, DOL is:

$$DOL = \frac{Q(P - AVC)}{Q(P - AVC) - TFC},$$

where P is price, AVC is average variable cost, and TFC is total fixed costs.

2.   Because profit contribution equals total revenue minus total variable cost, DOL is the profit contribution to net profit ratio.

3.   DOL is also the elasticity of profit with respect to output.

E.   Limitations of Linear Cost-Volume-Profit Analysis: Linear cost-volume-profit analysis is limited in its applications because:

1.   Linear cost and revenue relations often do not hold at all output levels.

2.   Because any given linear cost-volume-profit chart is based on constant prices and unit costs, a series of charts or spreadsheets is necessary to study profit possibilities under different scenarios.

XII.   SUMMARY

PROBLEMS & SOLUTIONS

P8.1   ***Cost Concepts.*** *Holding all else equal, describe the decline in average costs caused by each of the following as due to economies of scale, economies of scope, or learning curve advantages. Explain.*

      A.   *Increased worker specialization as output expands.*

      B.   *Growing levels of output per period.*

      C.   *Product line extension.*

      D.   *Better labor-management coordination over time.*

      E.   *Growing practical experience in production.*

P8.1   **SOLUTION**

      A.   Economies of Scale. Increased worker specialization as output expands is a prime cause of increasing returns to scale in production.

      B.   Economies of Scale. As output per period expands, increased worker specialization and other advantages of large size become operative. As in Part A, this involves a downward movement along the average cost curve.

      C.   Economies of Scope. Product line extension allows a firm to extend to related products the special productive capabilities and marketing skills gained in the production and sale of a given product. The cost savings which result are due to economies of scope.

      D.   Learning curve advantages. Better labor-management coordination over time is an example of how production experience can lead to substantial cost savings. Because such advantages are a function of time (cumulative output), they can be described as learning curve advantages.

      E.   Learning curve advantages. Growing practical experience in production is a prime source of learning curve advantages.

P8.2   ***Cost Concepts.*** *Determine whether each of the following is true or false. Explain why.*

      A.   *Average cost exceeds marginal cost at the minimum efficient scale of plant.*

B. *An increase in fixed cost will typically cause a reduction in the break-even activity level.*

C. *If $\varepsilon_C > 1$, increasing returns to scale and increasing average costs are indicated.*

D. *When long-run average cost is increasing, it can pay to operate larger plants with some excess capacity rather than smaller plants at their peak efficiency.*

E. *An increase in minimum efficient scale will typically increase the degree of operating leverage.*

P8.2 SOLUTION

A. False. The point of minimum average cost identifies the minimum efficient scale of plant. By definition, average and marginal costs are equal at this point.

B. False. The breakeven activity level is where $Q = TFC/(P - AVC)$. As total fixed cost (TFC) increases, this ratio and the breakeven activity level will increase.

C. False. When $\varepsilon_C > 1$, the percentage change in cost exceeds a given percentage change in output. This describes a situation of increasing average costs and diminishing returns to scale.

D. False. When long-run average costs are increasing, it can pay to operate smaller plants at above-minimum costs rather than larger plants at their peak efficiency.

E. True. An increase in minimum efficient scale is typically associated with an increase in fixed costs and the degree of operating leverage.

P8.3 Cost Curve Analysis. *Indicate whether each of the following involves an upward or downward shift in the long-run average cost curve, or instead involves a leftward or rightward movement along a given curve. Also indicate whether each will have an increasing, decreasing, or uncertain effect on the level of average cost.*

A. *A fall in wage rates*

B. *A rise in output*

C. *An labor-saving technical change*

D. *A rise in interest rates*

E.   *An increase in scope economies*

P8.3   **SOLUTION**

A.   A fall in wage rates causes a downward shift in the LRAC curve, and decrease LRAC.

B.   A rise in output is reflected in a rightward movement along a given LRAC curve, and involve an uncertain effect on the level of LRAC.

C.   Labor saving technical change causes a downward shift in the LRAC curve, and decrease LRAC.

D.   A rise in interest rates gives rise to a upward shift in the LRAC curve, and an increase in LRAC.

E.   Like any beneficial technical change or innovation, an increase in scope economies causes a downward shift in the LRAC curve, and decrease LRAC.

P8.4   **Incremental Analysis.** *One year ago, Will Truman quit a promising career with a major Manhattan-based law firm to set up his own law practice. Truman was a valued member of the firm, and his former employer has been persistent in its efforts to get Truman to return. They have offered Truman a promotion to the rank of partner with a starting salary of $150,000 per year. Truman has asked your opinion as to whether or not it would be financially wise to do so, and has provided the following data on his own law practice:*

Income Statement

Revenues		$315,000
Expenses:		
Materials, exhibits, etc.	$25,000	
Labor	90,000	
Rent, misc.	40,000	155,000
		$ 160,000

Balance Sheet

Assets:		
Accounts Receivable	$85,000	
Office Equipment, etc.	65,000	
Automobile	40,000	$190,000

<u>Liabilities:</u>

Accounts Payable	$5,000	
Note Payable	<u>15,000</u>	<u>20,000</u>
Net Book Value		$170,000

After making a few phone calls, you find out that Truman's office equipment and company car can be sold for 75% of book value, while a local factor will purchase Truman's accounts receivable for 90% of face value. In addition, a local real estate firm has offered to sublet Truman's office space, effectively letting Truman out of his office lease of $2,500 per month. As an alternative to dissolving Truman's law practice, Truman's former employer has offered to absorb the practice and pay Truman $175,000 for his interest.

A. Determine the economic value before taxes of the dissolution sale versus sale as ongoing concern alternatives.

B. If Truman sells his practice for more than its net book value he must pay a state plus federal capital gains tax of 40% on his profit. In light of this fact, what rate of return on investment of the sale proceeds would make Truman financially indifferent to selling his practice and returning to his former employer, versus continuing his solo career? (Note: Labor expenses itemized in the income statement do <u>not</u> include a salary for Truman.)

P8.4 SOLUTION

A. The economic value of the dissolution sale versus sale as ongoing concern alternatives can be determined as follows:

<u>Dissolution Sale Proceeds</u>	
Accounts Receivable (0.9 × $85,000)	$76,500
Office Equipment, Car (0.75 × $105,000)	<u>78,750</u>
Gross Proceeds	155,250
Debts	<u>(20,000)</u>
Net Proceeds	$135,250
<u>Ongoing Concern Sale Proceeds</u>	
Offer	$175,000

Thus, the sale as an ongoing concern dominates the dissolution sale alternative, and constitutes a measure of the economic value of the firm.

B.   The before tax interest rate necessary for Truman to be indifferent between selling his own law practice and returning to his former employer is calculated by comparing current profits with the current economic value of his own practice.

Actual profits can be obtained by adjusting reported profits to reflect Truman's employment opportunity costs.

Reported profits	$160,000
Truman's employment opportunity cost	(150,000)
Adjusted business profits	$10,000

The after-tax economic value of Truman's own practice is:

Sale Proceeds	$175,000
Capital gains tax 0.4($175,000 - $170,000)	(2,000)
	$173,000

Therefore, Truman's effective current rate of return on the realizable economic value of his own law practice is:

$$\frac{\$10,000}{\$173,000} = 0.058 \text{ or } 5.8\%$$

This means that Truman would be indifferent between the two alternatives of maintaining his own law practice versus returning to his former employer if investments with taxable returns and similar risks currently yield 5.8%. If they yield more, he would realize an economic gain from selling out and returning to his former employer. This problem points out the importance of considering the cost of owner-supplied capital. Capital isn't free, even when it's your own.

P8.5   ***Incremental Analysis.*** *Flintstones, Inc., markets a small solid cylinder of a spark-producing alloy used to ignite the fuel in residential and commercial furnaces. Currently, the company's products are sold to other manufacturers who then incorporate it in their merchandise. The yearly volume of output is 5,000 units produced and sold. The selling price and cost per unit are:*

<u>*Selling Price*</u>	*$250*
<u>*Costs:*</u>	

Direct material	$40	
Direct labor	60	
Variable overhead	30	
Variable selling expenses	25	
Fixed selling expenses	*20*	*175*
Unit profit before tax		$ 75

Barney Rubble, marketing director for Flintstones, is considering whether or not the company should use the Internet to market its product directly to end-users for $300 per unit. Although no added investment in productive facilities is required, there are additional costs for further packaging and marketing. Rubble estimates these costs as:

Direct labor	*$20 per unit*
Variable overhead	*$5 per unit*
Variable selling expenses	*$2 per unit*
Fixed selling expenses	*$20,000 per year*

Should Flintstones market its product directly to end-users?

P8.5 **SOLUTION**

This problem deals with the preferable extent of product marketing and packaging, and must be answered through incremental profit analysis. The analysis deals only with the incremental revenues and costs associated with the decision to market directly to end-users.

Incremental revenue per unit ($300 - $250)	$50
Incremental variable cost per unit ($20 + $5 + $2)	27
Incremental profit contribution per unit	$23
Yearly output volume in units	× 5,000
Incremental variable profit per year	$115,000
Incremental fixed cost per year	20,000
Yearly incremental profit	$ 95,000

Because incremental profit is positive, the decision to market directly to end-users is preferable to continuing the present operating policy.

P8.6   ***Learning or Experience.*** *Grace Adler Designs, Inc., has successfully completed a $2 million interior decorating project for the headquarters of a Silicon valley-based high tech firm. Adler believes that experience gained on the project will allow the company to now complete a similar job for $1.9 million.*

    A.   *In percentage terms, what is the learning or experience rate projected by Adler? (Hint: Learning rates are expressed as a cost savings percentage).*

    B.   *Assuming Adler's learning rate estimate is accurate, how would you explain actual costs of $1.95 million on a second project?*

P8.6   **SOLUTION**

    A.   In this problem, the learning rate projection is made using total costs because the project is the relevant scale of output.

$$\text{Learning rate} = \left(1 - \frac{\text{Cost}_2}{\text{Cost}_1} \right) \times 100$$

$$= \left(1 - \frac{\$1.9}{\$2.0} \right) \times 100$$

$$= 5\%$$

    B.   If actual costs were $1.95 million, or $500,000 above the $1.9 million projection, then one of two possible explanations could be offered. A first possibility is that the second project may not have been as efficiently carried out. The same level of operating efficiency must be achieved in both periods if learning curve advantages are to be fully realized. Secondly, higher costs could be due to increases in wage or interest rates, higher material costs, poorer weather conditions, etc. Learning curve calculations are made based on the assumption that all else is held equal in terms of operating conditions.

P8.7   ***Profit Contribution Analysis.*** *Cleo Finch, sales manager of Medical Supply, Inc., has informed the company president that if the price of MSI's disposable syringe is reduced, sales and profits will both increase. Currently, sales are 100,000 units per month, variable costs are 40% of total revenue, allocated fixed costs are 50% of total revenue, with profits making up the remaining 10%. The current syringe price is $2. According to Finch, a price reduction of 10% will result in profits one and one-half times what they are now. The firm has large amounts of excess capacity and, therefore, no increase in* *overhead is expected to accompany an increase in output. Unit variable costs are also expected to remain constant.*

A.   *How many units must be sold at the new price for Finch to be correct?*

B.   *What point price elasticity is implicit in Finch's forecast?*

P8.7   SOLUTION

A.   Currently,

$$TR = P \times Q = \$2(100,000) = \$200,000$$

$$\pi = 0.1(\$200,000) = \$20,000$$

$$TFC = 0.5(\$200,000) = \$100,000$$

$$TVC = 0.4(\$200,000) = \$80,000$$

$$AVC = \frac{TVC}{Q} = \frac{\$80,000}{100,000} = \$0.80$$

The projected profit is 150% of current profit, or:

$$\pi_P = 1.5(\$20,000)$$

$$= \$30,000$$

The new price is 90% of the current price, therefore:

$$P_P = 0.9(\$2)$$

$$= \$1.80$$

The unit profit contribution of the product is price minus variable cost, thus:

$$\pi_C = \$1.80 - \$0.80$$

$$= \$1$$

Dividing fixed costs plus the projected profit by the unit profit contribution determines the projected sales quantity:

$$Q_P = \frac{TFC + \pi_P}{\pi_C}$$

$$= \frac{\$100,000 + \$30,000}{\$1}$$

$$= 130,000 \text{ units}$$

B. Following a price decline from $2 to $1.80, the quantity purchased is projected to increase from 100,000 to 130,000. Therefore, the sales manager is projecting:

$$\varepsilon_P = \partial Q/\partial P \times P/Q$$

$$= \frac{\$130,000 - 100,000}{\$1.80 - \$2} \times \frac{\$2}{100,000}$$

$$= -3 \text{ (Elastic)}$$

P8.8 **Multiplant Operation.** *Jack McFarland is CEO of the Cola King Bottling Company, a small regional producer operating in the Pacific Northwest. McFarland is considering two alternative expansion proposals:*

1. *Construct a single bottling plant in Phoenix, Arizona with a capacity of 40,000 cases per month, at a monthly fixed cost of $20,000 and a variable cost of $2.50 per case.*

2. *Construct 3 plants, 1 each in Phoenix, Arizona; Las Vegas, Nevada; and Albuquerque, New Mexico, with capacities of 15,000, 14,000 and 13,000 respectively; and monthly fixed costs of $11,000, $10,000 and $9,000 each. Variable costs would be only $2.30 per case due to lower distribution costs, but sales from each plant would be limited to demand within the home state. The total estimated monthly sales volume in the southwestern states, 37,000 cases, is distributed as: Arizona, 15,000 cases; Nevada, 14,000 cases; and New Mexico, 8,000 cases.*

   A. *Using a wholesale price of $4 per case in each state, calculate the breakeven output quantities for each alternative.*

   B. *Which alternative expansion scheme should Cola King follow?*

C.   *If sales increase to production capacities, which alternative would prove to be more profitable?*

P8.8   **SOLUTION**

A.   Single-plant alternative

$$Q = \frac{TFC}{P - AVC}$$

$$= \frac{\$20,000}{\$4 - \$2.50}$$

$$= \frac{20,000}{1.5}$$

$$= 13,333 \text{ cases}$$

Multiple-plant alternative

$$\text{Phoenix: } Q = \frac{\$11,000}{\$4 - \$2.30}$$

$$= \frac{11,000}{1.70}$$

$$= 6,471 \text{ cases}$$

$$\text{Las Vegas: } Q = \frac{\$10,000}{\$1.70}$$

$$= 5,882 \text{ cases}$$

$$\text{Albuquerque: } Q = \frac{\$9,000}{\$1.70}$$

$$= 5,294 \text{ cases}$$

Thus, the breakeven quantity for the multiple-plant option would be:

$$6,471 + 5,882 + 5,294 = 17,647 \text{ cases}$$

Of course, this assumes that the demand is distributed among the states in amounts equal to the breakeven quantities for the individual plants.

B.   Single-plant alternative

$$\pi = TR - TC$$

$$= P(Q) - TFC - AVC(Q)$$

$$= \$4(37{,}000) - \$20{,}000 - \$2.50(37{,}000)$$

$$= \$35{,}500$$

Multiple-plant alternative

$$\pi = TR - TC$$

$$= P(Q) - TFC - AVC(Q)$$

$$= \$4(37{,}000) - \$30{,}000 - \$2.30(37{,}000)$$

$$= \$32{,}900$$

Management should elect the single-plant alternative because of its larger profit.

C.   Single-Plant at Full Capacity

$$\pi = TR - TC$$

$$= P(Q) - TFC - AVC(Q)$$

$$= \$4(40{,}000) - \$20{,}000 - \$2.50(40{,}000)$$

$$= \$40{,}000$$

Multiple-Plant at Full Capacity

	P(Q)	-	TFC	-	AVC(Q)	=	Profit
Phoenix Plant	$4(15,000)	-	$11,000	-	$2.30(15,000)	=	$14,500
Las Vegas Plant	$4(14,000)	-	$10,000	-	$2.30(14,000)	=	13,800
Albuquerque Plant	$4(13,000)	-	$9,000	-	$2.30(13,000)	=	13,100
					π	=	$41,400

In this case, management should select the multiple-plant alternative because of its larger profit potential.

P8.9   ***Cost-Volume-Profit Analysis.*** *Karen Walker is CFO of Rosario Products, Inc., a New England-based manufacturer of electrical components. RPI is currently producing and selling 40,000 units of output. Unfortunately, plant capacity is also 40,000 units and potential orders are being turned down. As a result, Walker is considering expanding capacity to 50,000 units. RPI's product sells for $6 per unit, and Walker expects to maintain that price if capacity is expanded. Currently, output has a variable cost of $2 per unit and fixed costs are $80,000. Expansion of capacity to 50,000 units will increase fixed costs by 50% to $120,000, but variable costs per unit will decline by 40% to $1.20.*

A.   *What is RPI's current breakeven output level?*

B.   *What is RPI's current degree of operating leverage at 40,000 units?*

C.   *Considered by itself (that is, assuming that variable cost per unit remains at $2), would the increase in fixed costs associated with expansion increase, decrease, or leave unchanged the degree of operating leverage at 40,000 units?*

D.   *Considered by itself (that is, assuming that fixed costs remain at $80,000), would the decrease in variable costs associated with expansion increase or leave unchanged the degree of operating leverage at 40,000 units?*

E.   *What is the importance of analyzing operating leverage in a decision problem such as this one?*

P8.9   **SOLUTION**

A.   The breakeven quantity is:

$$Q = \frac{TFC}{P - AVC} = \frac{\$80,000}{\$6 - \$2} = 20,000 \text{ units}$$

B.   The degree of operating leverage formula is:

$$DOL = \frac{Q(P - AVC)}{Q(P - AVC) - TFC}$$

$$= \frac{40,000(\$6 - \$2)}{40,000(\$6 - \$2) - 80,000}$$

$$= 2$$

C.   Because,

$$DOL = \frac{Q(P - AVC)}{Q(P - AVC) - TFC}$$

If TFC increases while Q, P and AVC remain constant, then DOL will increase. Proof:

$$DOL = \frac{Q(P - AVC)}{Q(P - AVC) - TFC}$$

$$\frac{\partial DOL}{\partial TFC} = \frac{[Q(P - AVC) - TFC] \times (0) - Q(P - AVC)(-1)}{(Q(P - AVC) - TFC)^2}$$

$$= \frac{Q(P - AVC)}{(Q(P - AVC) - TFC)^2} > 0$$

D.   If AVC decreases while holding Q, P and TFC constant, then DOL will decrease. Proof:

$$DOL = \frac{Q(P - AVC)}{Q(P - AVC) - TFC}$$

$$= \frac{Q(P) - Q(AVC)}{Q(P) - Q(AVC) - TFC}$$

$$\frac{\partial DOL}{\partial AVC} = \frac{[Q(P) - Q(AVC) - TFC](-Q) - [Q(P) - Q(AVC)](-Q)}{[Q(P) - Q(AVC) - TFC]^2}$$

$$= \frac{Q(TFC)}{(Q(P - AVC) - TFC)^2} > 0$$

E.   The study of operating leverage is important for operating and planning purposes. For example, the level of operating leverage can have an important effect on changes in operating profits, especially when projected changes in output are substantial. Remember:

$$DOL = \frac{\partial \pi / \pi}{\partial Q / Q}$$

$$\partial \pi / \pi = DOL \times \partial Q / Q$$

If the expected $\partial Q/Q$ over the next couple of years is positive, then one would want the highest DOL possible, thus achieving the highest $\partial \pi / \pi$. Unfortunately, it is seldom possible to know for certain that changes in output will be positive. A severe recession, for example, can cause output to fall. If this were the case and DOL were high, then a large negative change in operating profits would result. Because the expected change in output has an element of uncertainty attached to it in the real world, the desired level for DOL depends on the risk attitude of the managers and owners of the firm. By changing fixed and variable costs, the level of DOL can be changed to the desired level.

P8.10   ***Breakeven Analysis.*** *Korean Motor Works , Inc., recently converted an unused assembly plant in Pennsylvania to produce budget-priced compact sport-utility vehicles, thus adding to the number of foreign-owned auto makers in the United States. KMW's analysis indicate that variable production costs can be described by the function:*

$$TVC = \$13,500Q + \$10Q^2$$

Where TVC = total variable costs in thousands of dollars, and Q = output in thousands of SUVs. KMW's SUVs have been enthusiastically accepted in the market given their surprisingly good quality and low average price of $18,000 per unit.

Calculate the breakeven level of yearly output for KMW, assuming that fixed costs are $500 million.

P8.10   ***SOLUTION***

From the breakeven formula:

$$Q = \frac{TFC}{P - AVC}$$

$$Q = \frac{\$500,000}{\$18,000 - \left(\dfrac{\$13,500Q + \$10Q^2}{Q}\right)}$$

$$500,000 = (18,000 - 13,500 - 10Q)(Q)$$

$$0 = -10Q^2 + 4,500Q - 500,000$$

This is a quadratic equation in the form:

$$aQ^2 + bQ + c = 0$$

where a = -10, b = 4,500 and c = -500,000. Its two roots can be obtained from the quadratic formula:

$$Q = \frac{-b \pm \sqrt{b^2 - 4ac}}{2a}$$

$$= \frac{-4,500 \pm \sqrt{4,500^2 - 4(-10)(-500,000)}}{2(-10)}$$

$$= \frac{-4,500 \pm 500}{-20}$$

$$= 200(000) \text{ or } 250(000)$$

Thus, there are dual breakeven points of 200,000 and 250,000 cars.

A "unit's problem" may be encountered if one isn't careful in the solution to this problem. All dollar and output values must reflect the fact that TVC is in thousands of dollars and Q is in thousands of cars. Here, a P = $18,000 per car becomes $18,000,000 per unit of Q when expressed in dollars, and $18,000 per unit of Q when expressed in thousands of dollars. Thus, P = $18,000 is used in the breakeven formula.

Chapter 9

LINEAR PROGRAMMING

Managers analyze spreadsheet information using powerful desktop computers and user-friendly "solver" software that uses a proven optimization tool called linear programming (LP) to isolate the best, or optimal, solution to decision problems. LP is ideally suited to solving problems that involve an objective function to be maximized or minimized, where the relevant objective function is subject to a variety of underlying constraints. Product design and product mix decisions are often constrained by the availability of essential raw materials, production equipment, or key personnel. Plant location and delivery routing decisions must be made in light of production schedules, customer service requirements, and delivery costs. Inventory and cash management in accounting, capital budget decisions in finance, work scheduling and organization design in management, and media choice decisions in marketing all involve constraints on the allocation of scarce resources to achieve specific managerial goals. All are typical of the types of decision problems addressed using LP methods.

Just as important as the amazing power of LP techniques is the ease with which the method can be applied. Even complex LP problems can be set up and solved easily using popular LP "solver" software for the personal computer, such as What's Best and What-if-Solver. Before these software programs came along, a mainframe computer and an extensive background in mathematics were required to solve highly complex optimization problems. Now all that is needed is a desktop computer, a spreadsheet model, and a constrained decision problem with plenty of variables!

CHAPTER OUTLINE

I.   **BASIC ASSUMPTIONS**

   A.   **Inequality Constraints:** Linear programming handles constraint inequalities easily, making it a useful technique for finding the optimal solution to many management decision problems.

      1.   Constraints often limit the resource employed to less than or equal to ($\leq$) some fixed amount available.

      2.   Constraints sometimes specify that the quantity or quality of output must be greater than or equal to ($\geq$) some minimum requirement.

   B.   **Linearity Assumption:** As its name implies, linear programming is a tool designed to deal with optimization problems involving linear output, cost, revenue, and cost relations. To be applicable, the decision problems addressed must involve:

1. Constant output prices.

2. Constant input prices.

3. Constant returns to scale in production.

II.   PRODUCTION PLANNING FOR A SINGLE PRODUCT

A. **Production Processes:** If a production system exhibits constant returns to scale, and inputs can be combined in only a limited number of ways, these production combinations (processes) can be represented as linear rays in a labor and capital (*LK*) plane.

1. Equal distances along *the same* process ray imply equal output quantities.

2. Equal distances along *different* process rays do not necessarily imply equal output quantities.

B. **Production Isoquants:** Joining points of equal output on various production rays produces a set of isoquant curves.

1. Isoquants are linear segments that represent all combinations of L and K that can be used to produce a given quantity of output.

C. **Least-Cost Input Combinations:** Adding an isocost curve to a set of isoquants permits one to determine the point of tangency between them. This tangency point indicates the least cost method of producing output.

1. The point of tangency indicates the least cost method of producing output.

2. An isocost line shows all input combinations that result in a given level of total cost.

3. Because isocost lines are linear, they can be easily drawn by connecting the two endpoints. These endpoints can be found by dividing a given level of total cost by each input price, i.e., TC/P_L and TC/P_K.

D. **Optimal Input Combinations with Limited Resources:** Managers frequently face resource limitations that constrain the options available.

1. Adding constraints to a production process ray diagram defines the feasible space for the problem solution.

2.   In maximization LP problems, the optimal solution is the feasible point that is furthest from the origin.

3.   In minimization LP problems, the optimal solution is the feasible point that is closest to the origin.

III.   PRODUCTION PLANNING FOR MULTIPLE PRODUCTS

A.   Objective Function Specification: Assuming a two- product production problem for a firm attempting to maximize profits, the objective function is expressed as:

$$\text{Maximize } \pi = \begin{matrix}\text{Per unit}\\\text{profit}\\\text{contribution}\\\text{of product X}\end{matrix} \times Q_X + \begin{matrix}\text{Per unit}\\\text{profit}\\\text{contribution}\\\text{of product Y}\end{matrix} \times Q_Y$$

B.   Constraint Equation Specification: For each resource, the constraint equation is expressed as:

$$\begin{matrix}\text{Quantity}\\\text{of resource}\\\text{used in}\\\text{producing}\\\text{one unit}\\\text{of X}\end{matrix} \times Q_X + \begin{matrix}\text{Quantity}\\\text{of resource}\\\text{used in}\\\text{producing}\\\text{one unit}\\\text{of Y}\end{matrix} \times Q_Y \le \begin{matrix}\text{Amount of}\\\text{resource}\\\text{available}\\\text{for use in}\\\text{production}\\\text{of X}\\\text{and Y}\end{matrix}$$

C.   Nonnegativity Requirement: To prevent economically irrelevant results, all LP variables are constrained to non-negative values.

IV.   GRAPHIC SPECIFICATION AND SOLUTION

A.   Analytic Expression: The first step in setting up and solving an LP problem is its logical presentation.

B.   Graphing the Feasible Space: Constraint equations are graphed in the first quadrant to identify the feasible space of the program.

C.   Graphing the Objective Function: In a profit maximization LP problem, the objective function is graphed as a set of isoprofit curves, each illustrating all possible combinations of output X and output Y that result in a constant amount of profit.

D. Graphic Solution: When a set of isoprofit curves is superimposed on the feasible space determined by the constraints, the profit-maximizing solution is the highest point of tangency between a corner of the feasible space and the isoprofit line.

    1. Solutions within the interior of the feasible space are never optimal.

    2. The optimal solution is always at a corner of the feasible space.

    3. If the highest obtainable isoprofit curve lies along a boundary of the feasible space, multiple optimal solutions exist.

V. ALGEBRAIC SPECIFICATION AND SOLUTION

A. Slack Variables: Algebraic methods are used to find exact solutions for linear programming problems that are too complex to be solved graphically.

    1. Slack variables represent excess (unused) input capacity at optimal solution points. The use of slack variables converts constraint equations into equalities rather than inequalities (i.e., $\leq$ or $\geq$).

        a. Zero values for slack variables at the optimal solution represent inputs that are limiting factors in production.

        b. Positive values for slack variables at the optimal solution indicate excess capacity in the related input factor.

B. Algebraic Solution: Solution of any linear program requires that the number of constraint equations ("known relations") be at least as large as the number of unknown variables.

    1. At the corners of the feasible space enough slack variables take on zero values so that the number of unknown variables is equal to the number of constraint equations.

    2. With sufficient zero-valued slack variables, exact solution of the system of constraint equations becomes possible.

        a. The optimal solution always occurs at a corner point of the feasible space.

        b. At each corner point, the number of non-zero constraint variables is equal to the number of constraint equations.

c.   The corner point that produces the highest (lowest) value is the objective function maximum (minimum).

C.   Slack Variables at the Solution Point: At each corner solution the values of slack variables have a ready interpretation.

1.   When a given constraint is binding, its slack variable equals zero.

2.   When a given constraint is not binding, its slack variable exceeds zero.

D.   Computer-Based Solution Methods: Complex LP problems can be solved using readily available PC "solver" software.

1.   Graphic and combined algebraic-graphic methods of linear program solutions are highly useful, but limited to quite simple examples.

VI.   DUAL IN LINEAR PROGRAMMING

A.   Duality Concept: For every minimization (maximization) problem in linear programming there exists a symmetrical maximization (minimization) problem.

1.   Pairs of symmetrical LP problems are known as the primal and dual.

2.   Once the dual solution is obtained, the primal solution can be readily determined, and vice versa.

B.   Shadow Prices: The economic value of constrained resources is determined by value in use rather than by historical costs.

1.   Shadow prices represent the price a manager would pay for an additional unit of a given resource.

2.   When a resource constraint is binding, no excess capacity exists, and the resource shadow price is positive.

3.   When a resource constraint is not binding, excess capacity exists, and the resource shadow price is zero.

C.   Dual Objective Function: The dual of the profit maximization problem described previously attempts to minimize the imputed value of the firm's fixed (constrained) resources used in production. The dual objective function is to minimize:

$$
\begin{array}{c}
\text{Total imputed} \\
\text{value of} \\
\text{fixed resources}
\end{array}
=
\begin{array}{c}
\text{Amount of} \\
\text{input A} \\
\text{available}
\end{array}
\times
\begin{array}{c}
\text{Shadow} \\
\text{price} \\
\text{of A}
\end{array}
+
\begin{array}{c}
\text{Amount of} \\
\text{input B} \\
\text{available}
\end{array}
\times
\begin{array}{c}
\text{Shadow} \\
\text{price} \\
\text{of B}
\end{array}
$$

D.   **Dual Constraints:** The marginal value of inputs used in the production of one unit of output must not be less than the per unit profit contribution:

$$
\begin{array}{c}
\text{Units of A} \\
\text{required to} \\
\text{produce one} \\
\text{unit of X}
\end{array}
\times
\begin{array}{c}
\text{Shadow} \\
\text{price} \\
\text{of A}
\end{array}
+
\begin{array}{c}
\text{Units of B} \\
\text{required to} \\
\text{produce one} \\
\text{unit of X}
\end{array}
\times
\begin{array}{c}
\text{Shadow} \\
\text{price} \\
\text{of B}
\end{array}
$$

$$
+
\begin{array}{c}
\text{Units of C} \\
\text{required to} \\
\text{produce one} \\
\text{unit of X}
\end{array}
\times
\begin{array}{c}
\text{Shadow} \\
\text{price} \\
\text{of C}
\end{array}
\geq
\begin{array}{c}
\text{Profit} \\
\text{contribution} \\
\text{per unit} \\
\text{of X}
\end{array}
$$

E.   **Dual Slack Variables:** Dual slack variables are subtracted from each constraint equation, thus enabling one to express the constraints as equalities.

   1.   In the present example, slack variables represent the excess of input value over output value for each output.

   2.   If a slack variable is positive, marginal input value exceeds output value and the related output should not be produced.

   3.   If a slack variable is zero, marginal input value equals output value and the related output should not be produced.

F.   **Solving the Dual Problem:** In the present example, there are two constraints and the maximum permissible number of non-zero variables at any corner solution is two. If any three constraint variables are set equal to zero, the remaining two values can be determined.

   1.   The optimal solution is the best feasible solution.

G.   **Using the Dual to Solve the Primal:** The primal (dual) solution can be used to solve the dual (primal).

$$\begin{array}{c} \text{Primal} \\ \text{objective variable}_i \end{array} \times \begin{array}{c} \text{Dual} \\ \text{slack variable}_i \end{array} = 0$$

$$\begin{array}{c} \text{Primal} \\ \text{slack variable}_j \end{array} \times \begin{array}{c} \text{Dual} \\ \text{objective variable}_j \end{array} = 0$$

1. If a variable takes on a non-zero value in the primal (dual), its related slack variable in the dual (primal) equals zero.

VII. CONSTRAINED COST MINIMIZATION: ANOTHER LP EXAMPLE

A. **Background Information:** Constrained cost minimization problems are frequently encountered in managerial decision making, and it is useful to work through such a problem to gain facility in using the technique.

B. **Primal Problem:** The primal cost-minimization problem is set up and solved in precisely the same fashion as the product mix problem.

C. **Dual Problem:** The dual to the cost-minimization problem is a maximization problem.

1. The dual constraints are of a ≤ nature because the primal constraints are ≥.

D. **Solving the Dual:** Primal problem solution values can be used to easily solve for the dual solution.

E. **Interpreting the Dual Solution:** Both the dual variables and slack values have a ready economic interpretation.

1. The dual variables are shadow prices, or the marginal costs associated with each constraint condition (audience exposure requirement).

2. The dual slack variables represent opportunity costs associated with use of each advertising media.

VIII. SUMMARY

PROBLEMS & SOLUTIONS

P9.1   **LP Basics.** *Indicate whether each of the following statements is true or false, and explain your answer.*

     A.   *An unlimited number of isoprofit lines can be written in a given bounded feasible space.*

     B.   *The number of decision variables plus the number of slack variables must be less than the number of constraint conditions for a unique LP solution to exist.*

     C.   *Maximizing profit contribution will always result in maximum total profits.*

     D.   *Equal distances along different output rays indicate equal levels of output.*

     E.   *An increase in input prices would be reflected by an outward shift in the related isocost line.*

P9.1   **Solution**

     A.   True. An infinite number of parallel isoprofit lines can be drawn in any bounded feasible space.

     B.   False. For any system of equations to yield a unique solution, the number of variables (unknowns) must be just equal to the number of equations (known relations).

     C.   True. Profit contribution is the difference between total revenues and total variable costs. Profit, on the other hand, is the difference between total revenues and total variable plus fixed costs. Because fixed costs do not vary with output, either maximizing profit contribution or profit with respect to output will always identify a unique activity level.

     D.   False. Output along a given process ray increases proportionately with increases in the input factors. Therefore, equal distances along a given process ray indicate equal output quantities.

     E.   False. An increase in input prices is reflected by an inward shift in the related isocost line.

P9.2   **Duality.** *Indicate whether each of the following statements is true or false, and explain your answer.*

A. *The solution values to primal LP problems are most useful for long-run planning decisions.*

B. *The solution values to dual LP problems are most useful for short-run operating decisions.*

C. *When the slack variable associated with a given resource constraint is positive, excess capacity is present.*

D. *The optimal objective function solution values for related primal and dual LP problems are identical.*

E. *When excess capacity is present, the opportunity cost associated with an increase in resource usage is zero.*

P9.2   *Solution*

A. False. Solution values to primal LP problems provide the basis for short-run operating decisions made subject to a wide variety of constraint conditions. They suggest, for example, an optimal product mix or activity level.

B. False. Solution values to dual LP problems provide the basis for long-run planning decisions. They suggest, for example, the importance of various constraint conditions, and the profits that might be obtained through expanded resource usage.

C. True. When the slack variable associated with a given resource constraint is positive, excess capacity is present. When a given resource is fully employed, no slack or excess capacity is present.

D. True. The optimal solutions for related primal and dual LP objective functions have identical numerical values. For example, if the primal solution indicates a maximum profit contribution of $1,000, then the dual's $1,000 solution value is the minimum marginal value of inputs employed at that activity level.

E. True. When excess capacity is present, the opportunity cost associated with an increase in resource usage is zero.

P9.3   *LP Concepts.* *LP techniques have often been employed to help companies make efficient use of skilled labor. Consider the case of a hospital that wants your advice concerning the usefulness of LP methods for helping determine the optimal staffing of skilled nurses. Indicate whether each of the following potential characteristics of the hospital's staffing problem would allow or not allow use of LP techniques. Explain your answer.*

A. *The wage costs associated with constrained nursing staff are fixed.*

B. *The wage costs associated with constrained nursing staff are variable.*

C. *Nursing and medical staff can be employed in variable proportions.*

D. *The hospital is run on a not-for-profit basis.*

E. *A minimal level of staffing must be maintained 24 hours per day.*

P9.3   Solution

A.   Allow. When the availability of skilled nursing staff is constrained, the wage costs associated with employment are fixed. In such instances, the hospital has a constrained optimization problem where the goal is to derive an optimal employment pattern for its staff. Such a situation is well-suited to the use of LP techniques.

B.   Not Allow. When the availability of skilled nursing staff is not constrained, the wage costs associated with employment are variable. In such instances, the hospital does not have a constrained optimization problem. It must simply derive an optimal employment pattern for its staff based on the marginal costs and marginal benefits derived from employment. Such a situation is not well-suited to the use of LP techniques.

C.   Allow. When nursing and medical staff can be employed in variable proportions, the hospital is able to vary the input mix associated with a given level of output. In such instances, the hospital is able to construct various output rays to identify various employment possibilities. Such input use flexibility is a necessary ingredient for the successful application of LP methods.

D.   Allow. Irrespective of whether the hospital is run on a for-profit or not-for-profit basis, the use of LP techniques can lead to the optimal employment of scarce nursing staff.

E.   Allow. If a minimal level of nursing staff coverage must be maintained 24 hours per day, the hospital faces a staffing constraint. Use of LP techniques could, for example, allow the hospital to meet such staffing requirements at minimum cost.

P9.4   LP Assumptions. *Why can't LP techniques be employed in each of the following situations?*

A.   *Input prices rise at high activity levels.*

B. *Output prices must be reduced to expand sales.*

C. *All production costs are variable.*

D. *Diseconomies of large-scale production are evident.*

E. *The number of decision plus slack variables exceeds the total number of constraint conditions.*

P9.4 **Solution**

A. A rise in input prices at high activity levels would give rise to a nonlinear total cost function, and a violation of the LP requirement of linear objective functions.

B. When output prices must be reduced to expand sales, nonlinear total revenue and total profit functions result. As a result, the LP requirement of linear objective functions would be violated.

C. When all production costs are variable, the firm faces no constraints in input employment. As such, it faces no constrained optimization problem, and is completely free to vary input usage according to the rule that marginal revenue product must equal input price at the optimal activity level.

D. When diseconomies of large-scale production are evident, nonlinear total cost and total profit functions result. As a result, the LP requirement of linear objective functions would be violated.

E. If the number of decision plus slack variables exceeds the total number of constraint conditions, the number of unknown variables would exceed the number of known relations. In such instances, it is impossible to solve the LP problem and find a unique solution for all decision and slack variables.

P9.5 **Fixed Input Combinations.** *Production of a product Q requires use of two inputs, X and Y. These inputs must be combined in a fixed ratio with each unit of Q requiring 5 units of X and 9 units of Y.*

A. *What combination of X and Y would be used to produce 4 units of Q?*

B. *Assume that a firm has 26 units of X and 27 units of Y available. How much Q can be produced?*

C. *Determine the marginal products of X and Y in part B.*

 D.   *Are input prices irrelevant to the calculation of optimal input proportions in this problem?*

P9.5   SOLUTION

 A.   Because inputs must be combined in the ratio 5X to 9Y for each unit produced, production of 4 units of Q requires:

$$Q \times \frac{X}{Q} = 4(5) = 20 \text{ units of } X$$

$$Q \times \frac{Y}{Q} = 4(9) = 36 \text{ units of } Y$$

 B.   With 26 units of X, 5.2 units of Q could be produced before X is exhausted because:

$$Q = \frac{X}{X/Q}$$

$$= \frac{26}{5}$$

$$= 5.2$$

With 27 units of Y, 3 units of Q could be produced before Y is exhausted because:

$$Q = \frac{Y}{Y/Q}$$

$$= \frac{27}{9}$$

$$= 3$$

Clearly, Y will be exhausted before X, and Y is the scarce resource because it limits production to only 3 units of Q. Thus, with 26 units of X and 27 units of Y available, 3 units of Q will be produced, and:

<u>X Utilized:</u>

$$X = Q(X/Q)$$

$$= 3(5)$$

$$= 15$$

X Surplus:

$$26 - 15 = 9$$

Y Utilized:

$$Y = Q(Y/Q)$$

$$= 3(9)$$

$$= 27$$

Y Surplus:

$$27 - 27 = 0$$

C.   Because Q requires inputs in the required ratio 5X to 9Y,

$$Q = (1/5)X \quad \text{When X is scarce}$$

$$Q = (1/9)Y \quad \text{When Y is scarce}$$

This implies

Input	Marginal Product	When
X	$MP_X = 1/5$	X is scarce ($X < (5/9)Y$)
X	$MP_X = 0$	X is redundant (Surplus) ($X \geq (5/9)Y$)
Y	$MP_Y = 1/9$	Y is scarce ($Y < (9/5)X$)
Y	$MP_Y = 0$	Y is redundant (Surplus) ($Y \geq (9/5)X$)

Because X is redundant in part B, the $MP_X = 0$. Additional X will just add to excess capacity. Because Y is scarce in part B, the $MP_Y = 1/9$. An additional unit of Y would increase Q by 1/9.

D.   Yes. When inputs must be combined in some fixed ratio, say 5X to 9Y, input prices are irrelevant to the calculation of optimal input proportions because there is no substitutability between inputs.

P9.6   ***Profit Maximization.*** *Biogenetics, Inc., can produce a new high yield crop culture, product X, using any of three possible production processes. In order to produce one unit of X the following combinations of laboratory and greenhouse hours are required.*

Process	Laboratory Hours	Greenhouse Hours
1	4	1
2	3	2
3	2	4

The selling price for X is well-established at $P_X = \$40$. Furthermore, Biogenetics pays a variable rental fee of \$6 per laboratory hour and \$5 per greenhouse hour. Using the following notation:

X = *the number of units of output*

X_1 = *the number of units of X produced by process 1*

X_2 = *the number of units of X produced by process 2*

X_3 = *the number of units of X produced by process 3*

P_X = *fixed selling price per unit of X*

VC_1 = *variable cost per unit of X_1*

VC_2 = *variable cost per unit of X_2*

VC_3 = *variable cost per unit of X_3*

A.   *Draw the Biogenetic's process rays on a laboratory hours-greenhouse hours graph.*

B.   *On the above graph, draw isoquants for production levels of 10, 15, and 20.*

C. *Draw an isocost curve and visually determine what the least cost production process would be for any given output level.*

D. *On a new graph, draw the process rays. Allow for a laboratory constraint of 120 hours and a greenhouse constraint of 80 hours.*

E. *On the graph constructed in part D, draw some isoprofit curves and determine the level of maximum profits, given the laboratory and greenhouse constraints. (This can be done graphically and/or algebraically.)*

P9.6   **SOLUTION**

A,B. See Biogenetics graph (1).

C.   To draw the relevant isocost line note that:

Total Cost   = $6(Laboratory hours) + $5(Greenhouse hours)

= $6L + 5G$

$6L$ = $TC - 5G$

L = $1/6 \, TC - 5/6 \, G$

Isocost lines are parallel to each other; extending the isocost curves out to any isoquant would indicate (visually) that process 2 would be the least cost process.

D,E.   See Biogenetics graph (2).

Profit for process 1,

$$\pi_1 \;=\; P_X X_1 - VC_1(X_1)$$

$$=\; P_X X_1 - (\$6(L) + \$5(G))(X_1)$$

Because P_X and the costs of laboratory and greenhouse hours are fixed, unit profit will also be fixed. With process 1, unit profit will be $11. That is, if $X_1 = 1$:

$$\pi_1 \;=\; \$40 - (\$6(4) + \$5(1))(1)$$

$$=\; 40 - 29$$

$$= \$11$$

For example, a profit level of $100 involves: $X_1 = 9.09$, $L_1 = 36.36$, and $G_1 = 9.09$.

Profit for process 2,

$$\pi_2 = \$40X_2 - (\$6(L) + \$5(G))X_2$$

per unit profit will be $12. That is, if $X_2 = 1$,

$$\pi_2 = \$40 - (\$6(3) + \$5(2))(1)$$

$$= 40 - 28$$

$$= \$12$$

For example, a profit level of $100 involves: $X_2 = 8.33$, $L_2 = 24.99$, and $G_2 = 16.66$.

Profit for process 3,

$$\pi_3 = \$40X_3 - (\$6(L) + \$5(G))X_3$$

per unit profit will be $8. That is, if $X_3 = 1$,

$$\pi_3 = \$40 - (\$6(2) + \$5(4))(1)$$

$$= 40 - 32$$

$$= \$8$$

For example, a profit level of $100 involves: $X_3 = 12.5$, $L_3 = 25$, and $G_3 = 50$.

According to the isoprofit curve $\pi = \$100$, process 2 is the most profitable. The laboratory and greenhouse constraints also intersect process 2, so it appears that we can maximize profits by using only that process. Furthermore, both constraints will be binding.

Process 2 uses 3L and 2G for each output, so:

$$3X_2 \leq 120$$

$$2X_2 \leq 80$$

Because both constraints are binding, we can use the equality form:

(1) $3X_2 = 120$

- (2) $\underline{2X_2 = 80}$

                                         $X_2 = 40$

At $X_2 = 40$, $L_2 = 120$, $G_2 = 80$, and:

$$\pi_2 = P_X X_2 - 6L_2 - 5G_2$$

$$= \$40(40) - \$6(120) - \$5(80)$$

$$= 1{,}600 - 720 - 400$$

$$= \$480$$

For comparison purposes, it is interesting to note that $\pi = \$480$ would involve:

Using Process 1:

   $X_1 = 43.63$, $L_1 = 174.52$, $G_1 = 43.63$.
   (*Note*: See point X).

Using process 3:

   $X_3 = 60$, $L_3 = 120$, $G_3 = 240$.
   (*Note*: See point Z).

   However, only point Y on the process 2 ray is feasible given the greenhouse and laboratory constraints. Points X and Z, which would also give the firm $480 in profits, are not feasible because they lie outside the feasible region.

(*Note*: Part of the isoprofit curve $\pi_0 = \$480$ (curve XYZ) is superimposed on the laboratory constraint line from points Y to Z.)

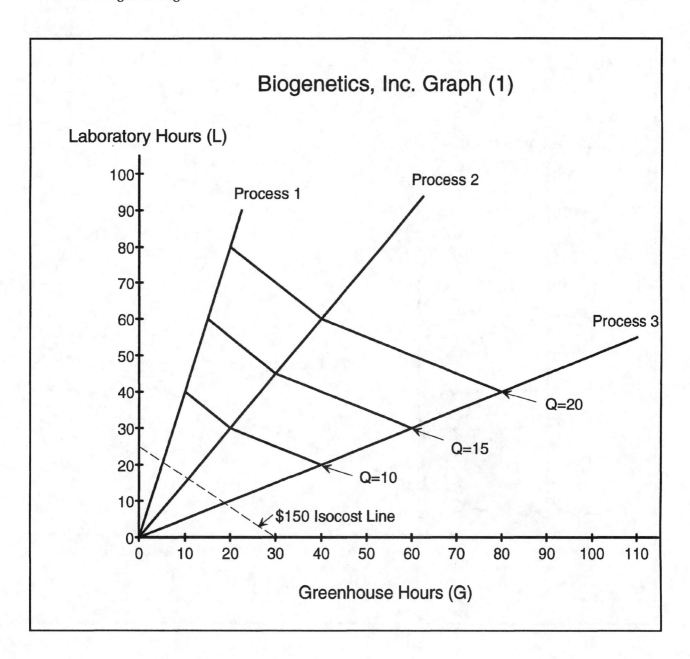

Biogenetics, Inc. Graph (1)

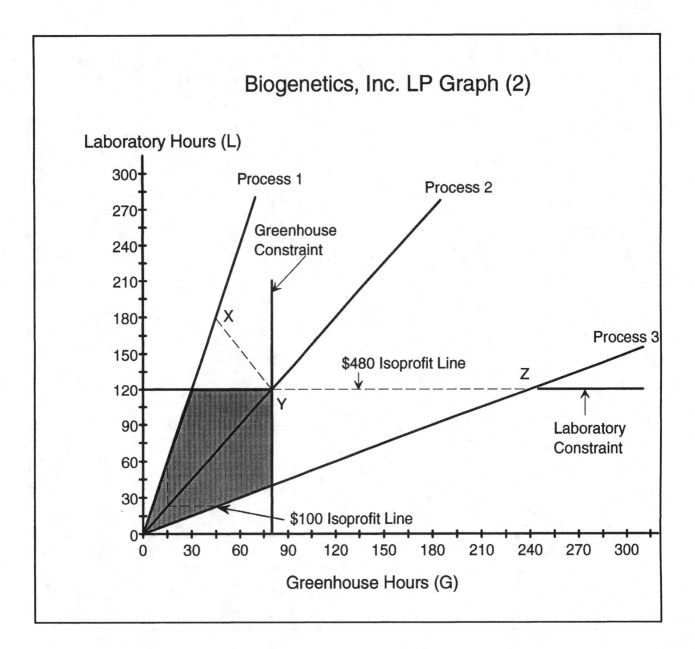

Biogenetics, Inc. LP Graph (2)

P9.7   ***Optimal Portfolio Decisions.*** *The Investors' Balanced Fund is an open-end investment company (mutual fund) designed to meet the needs of investors planning for future retirement. IBF seeks to provide current income plus capital growth by investing in a diversified portfolio of high-quality stocks and investment-grade bonds. The fund's bylaws state that at least 25% of the portfolio must be invested in bonds in order to reduce downside risk during bear markets. The fund's growth potential is maintained by a requirement that the share of the portfolio invested in common stocks must be at least as large as the share devoted to bonds. Like most mutual funds, IBF is prohibited from using leverage (borrowing) to enhance investor returns. Without leverage, stock and bond investments cannot exceed 100% of IBF's portfolio. And finally, the fund's investment management committee currently projects an expected return of 10% on stocks and 8% on bonds.*

    A.   *Set up and interpret the linear programming problem IBF would use to determine the optimal portfolio percentage holdings in stocks (S) and bonds (B). Use both the inequality and equality forms of the constraint conditions.*

    B.   *Use a graph to determine the optimal solution, and check your answer algebraically. Interpret the solution.*

    C.   *Holding all else equal, how much would the expected return on bonds have to rise before the optimal investment policy determined in part A would change?*

    D.   *What is the maximum share of the portfolio that could be converted into cash if management projects a downturn in both stock and bond prices?*

P9.7   **SOLUTION**

    A.   In this problem, the goal is to maximize expected return, R, subject to the various stock, bond and leverage constraints. The relevant linear programming problem is:

Maximize: $R = 0.1S + 0.08B$

Subject to: $B \geq 0.25$

                $S - B \geq 0 \text{ (or } S \geq B)$

                $S + B \leq 1$

or, in equality form:

$$(1) \qquad B - L_B \ = \ 0.25 \qquad\qquad \text{(Bond constraint)}$$

$$(2) \qquad S - B - L_S \ = \ 0 \qquad\qquad \text{(Stock constraint)}$$

$$(3) \qquad S + B + L_L \ = \ 1 \qquad\qquad \text{(Leverage constraint)}$$

$$S, B, L_S, L_B, L_L \ \geq \ 0$$

Here R is expected return, S is the portfolio share in common stocks, B is the portfolio share in bonds. L_S, L_B, and L_L are slack variables, representing excess stock investments, excess bond investments, and "slack leverage" or cash holdings, respectively.

B. From the graph, it is obvious that the bond investment (1) and leverage (3) constraints are binding and, therefore, that $L_B = L_L = 0$ at point X. Thus,

$$(1) \qquad\qquad B - 0 \ = \ 0.25$$

$$(2) \qquad\qquad S - 3B - L_S \ = \ 0$$

$$(3) \qquad\qquad S + B + 0 \ = \ 1$$

From (1),

$$(1) \qquad\qquad B + 0 \ = \ 0.25$$

$$B \ = \ 0.25$$

From (3),

$$(3) \qquad\qquad S + 0.25 + 0 \ = \ 1$$

$$S \ = \ 0.75$$

From (2),

$$(2) \qquad\qquad 0.75 - 0.25 - L_S \ = \ 0$$

$$L_S \ = \ 0.5$$

And the expected return is:

$$R = 0.1S + 0.08B$$

$$= 0.1(0.75) + 0.08(0.25)$$

$$= 0.095 \text{ or } 9.5\%$$

Solution values can be interpreted as follows:

$S = 0.75$ The optimal portfolio percentage in stocks is 75%.

$B = 0.25$ The optimal share of the portfolio in bonds is 25%.

$L_B = 0$ At optimum, IBF is holding the minimum percentage of bonds.

$L_S = 0.5$ At optimum, IBF is holding a 50% greater share of its portfolio in stocks than the minimum required in light of its bond holdings.

$L_L = 0$ At optimum, IBF is not employing leverage, and the fund is fully invested (holds no cash).

$R = 0.095$ Maximum expected return given constraints.

C. The isoreturn line $S = (R_0/R_S) - (R_B/R_S)B$, where R_0 is any return level, and R_S and R_B are returns on stocks and bonds, respectively. The isoreturn line in this problem has a slope equal to $-(R_B/R_S) = -(0.08/0.1) = -0.8$. Holding all else equal, this slope will become more negative as the return on bonds rises (or return on stocks falls). Similarly, this slope will move closer to zero as the return on bonds falls (or return on stocks rises).

Holding all else equal, if R_B rises to slightly more than 10%, the optimal feasible point will shift from point X(0.25B, 0.75S) to point Z(0.5B, 0.5S), because the isoreturn line slope will then be steeper than -1, the slope of the leverage constraint, $S = 1 - B$. Thus, a rise from 8% to more than 10%, or at least 2%, is necessary before the optimal solution derived above would change.

D. The bond investment constraint requires that a minimum of 25% of the overall portfolio be invested in bonds. From the stock constraint we know that stock investments must be at least as large as bond investments. Therefore, a minimum 50% of the overall portfolio must be invested in stocks (25%) plus bonds (25%), and the maximum share of the portfolio which could be converted into cash is 50% (point Y on the graph.)

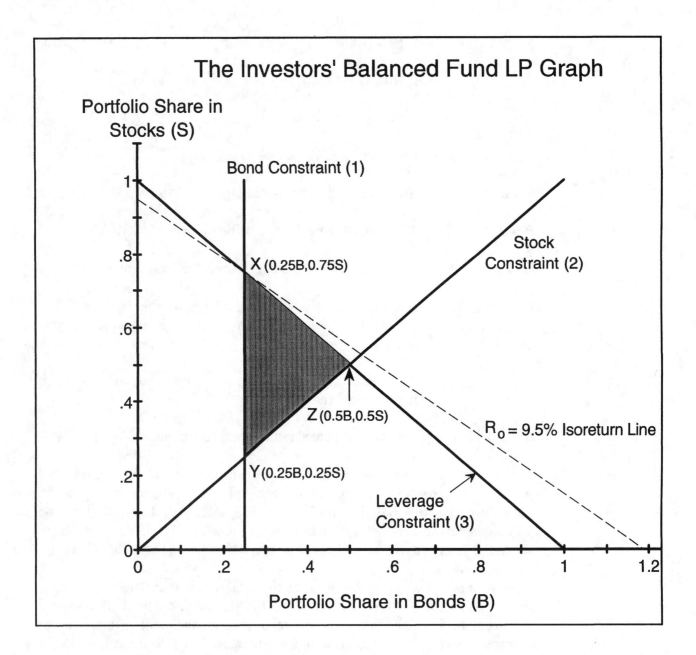

The Investors' Balanced Fund LP Graph

Portfolio Share in
Stocks (S)

Bond Constraint (1)

Stock
Constraint (2)

X (0.25B,0.75S)

R_o = 9.5% Isoreturn Line

Z (0.5B,0.5S)

Y (0.25B,0.25S)

Leverage
Constraint (3)

Portfolio Share in Bonds (B)

P9.8   **Profit Maximization.**   *The Michigan Boat Company manufactures two models of boats--an 8-foot jet ski, model X, and a 12-foot family sailboat, model Y.   The market for both models is competitive, so Michigan can sell all the boats it can produce at the going wholesale prices of $9,500 for the jet ski and $12,500 for the sailboat.   Because variable costs are $6,800 per unit for the jet ski and $8,900 for the sailboat, the profit contributions are $2,700 and $3,600, respectively.*

Fractional inputs and outputs are permissible and are carried over to the next monthly production period.   All inputs included as variable costs are available in unlimited quantities at constant prices, and the firm's production process provides constant returns to scale.   However, three resources, the power engine assembly shop, the dry dock, and the boat assembly shop are limited.   The number of boat-unit-hours of each of these resources, together with the requirements for each model, is given in the table below.

	Boat-unit-hours available per month	Hours Required per Boat Jet ski X	Sailboat Y
Boat assembly (A)	9,600	600	1,200
Dry Dock (D)	3,000	300	300
Engine Shop (E)	6,300	900	0

A.   *Set up and interpret the linear programming problem Michigan would use to determine the company's optimal output mix.   You can use a graph to help set up the model, but solve it algebraically for the values at the optimal corner as determined by the graph.   Use the equality form of the constraint conditions.*

B.   *Assuming Michigan can purchase additional fixed inputs, what is the maximum it would pay for an additional unit of each input?*

C.   *If dry-dock capacity is increased by 20%, would the output of sailboats increase or decrease? (Note: This can be seen easily from the graph.)*

P9.8   **SOLUTION**

A.   The problem requires finding the profit maximizing output combination.   The primal linear programming problem using the equality form of the constraint conditions is:

Maximize: $\pi = \$2,700X + \$3,600Y$

Subject to:

(1) $600X + 1,200Y + S_A = 9,600$ (Assembly constraint)

(2) $300X + 300Y + S_D = 3,000$ (Dry dock constraint)

(3) $900X + 0Y + S_E = 6,300$ (Engine shop constraint)

         $X, Y, S_A, S_D, S_E \geq 0$

Here X and Y represent jet ski and sailboat output, respectively. S_A, S_D and S_E represent excess capacity of assembly, dry dock, and engine shop resources, respectively. The total monthly profit contribution is represented by π.

To determine the optimal combination of X and Y we graph the constraints and objective function for the linear programming problem. As shown below, the shaded region represents the feasible space. To learn which constraints are binding at the optimal solution we graph the isoprofit line:

$$\pi = \$2,700X + \$3,600Y$$

$$3,600Y = \pi - 2,700X$$

$$Y = (\pi/3,600) - (2,700/3,600)Y$$

which has a slope $= -2,700/3,600 = -0.75$. Graphing successive isoprofit lines we find the optimal solution occurs at the point Z where constraints (1) and (2) are binding. Thus, $S_A = S_D = 0$.

Then, adding (1) plus negative 2 times (2):

(1) $600X + 1,200Y = 9,600$

$+ (-2) \times (2)$ $\underline{-600X - 600Y = -6,000}$

                   $600Y = 3,600$

                   $Y = 6$ sailboats

And substituting $Y = 6$ into (1) yields:

(1) $600X + 1,200(6) = 9,600$

$600X = 2,400$

$$X = 4 \text{ jet skis}$$

And finally, from the objective function we find:

$$\pi = \$2,700X + \$3,600Y$$

$$= 2,700(4) + 3,600(6)$$

$$= \$32,400$$

Therefore, Michigan's maximum monthly profit contribution is $32,400.

B. To determine the maximum Michigan would pay for an additional unit of each input, one must specify the dual linear programming problem. In the dual we seek to minimize the total value of inputs used in production. The dual can be written:

Minimize $\pi^* = 9,600V_A + 3,000V_D + 6,300V_E$

Subject to:

$$(4)\ 600V_A + 300V_D + 900V_E - L_X = 2,700$$

$$(5)\ 1,200V_A + 300V_D + 0V_E - L_Y = 3,600$$

$$V_A, V_D, V_E\ L_X, L_Y \geq 0$$

Here V_A, V_D and V_E represent the marginal values of additional assembly, dry dock and engine shop hours, respectively. L_X and L_Y represent the excess of input value over output value for X and Y, respectively. And finally, π^* represents the total value of resources used in production.

From the primal solution it is clear that input E is not used to capacity; therefore, $V_E = 0$. Also because both X and Y are produced, both have zero opportunity costs. In other words, the unit profit of X and Y is equal to the opportunity costs of producing them. This implies that $L_X = L_Y = 0$. This leaves just two unknowns, V_A and V_D, in the two equation dual constraint system.

Taking (4) minus (5):

$$(4) \qquad\qquad 600V_A + 300V_D = 2,700$$

$$-(5) \qquad\qquad \underline{1,200V_A + 300V_D = 3,600}$$

$$-600V_A = -900$$

$$V_A = 1.5$$

Substituting $V_A = 1.5$ into (4)

$$(4) \qquad 600(1.5) + 300V_D = 2,700$$

$$300V_D = 1,800$$

$$V_D = 6$$

Solving the dual objective function, we find:

$$\pi^* = 9,600V_A + 3,000V_D + 6,300V_E$$

$$= 9,600(1.5) + 3,000(6) + 6,300(0)$$

$$= \$32,400 \text{ (As it must)}$$

The minimum π^* value is, of course, equal to the maximum π. This step is necessary merely as a check.

So finally, it is obvious that Michigan would pay any amount up to the imputed values of each resource for additions to its fixed inputs.

Assembly value $= V_A = \$1.50$ per boat-unit-hour.

Dry dock shop value $= V_D = \$6.00$ per boat-unit-hour.

Engine shop value $= V_E = \$0$ per boat-unit-hour

(excess already exists).

C.   Referring back to the graph, one can see that if dry dock capacity were increased, this would amount to a parallel shift of constraint (2) upwards and to the right. The appropriate corner solution would shift down along the boat assembly constraint (1), which would become the binding constraint, until constraint (3) became binding. This would mean a reduction of sailboats and an increase in jet skis as Michigan took advantage of its unused engine shop capacity.

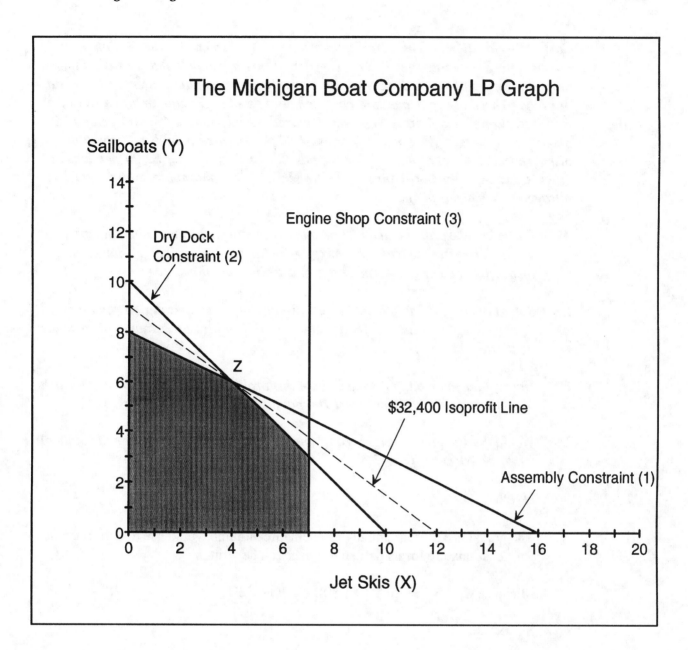

The Michigan Boat Company LP Graph

Sailboats (Y)

Engine Shop Constraint (3)

Dry Dock
Constraint (2)

Z

$32,400 Isoprofit Line

Assembly Constraint (1)

Jet Skis (X)

P9.9   ***Cost Minimization.*** *The Greenthumb Lawn & Garden Products Company is reformulating its garden fertilizer. The firm wants a product that has a minimum nitrogen content of 6 pounds per bag, and a minimum phosphate content of 12 pounds per bag. There are four possible base compounds that Greenthumb can use in its fertilizer. Compound A costs $1.20 per hundred pounds, and is 4% nitrogen and 6% phosphate by weight. Compound B costs $1.80 per hundred pounds and contains 2% nitrogen and 10% phosphate. Compounds C and D both cost $2.00 per hundred pounds. Compound C contains 4% nitrogen and 8% phosphate, while D is 10% nitrogen and 5% phosphate.*

   A.   *Formulate the primal and dual linear programming problems Greenthumb would use to determine the least cost mixture for its garden fertilizer. Show both the inequality and equality forms of the constraint conditions.*

   B.   *Solve both the primal and dual problems and interpret the solution you obtained as completely as possible. (Hint: Here it will be easiest to graph and solve the dual problem first).*

   C.   *How would you modify the analysis of this problem if Greenthumb wanted each bag of fertilizer to weigh at least 100 pounds?*

   D.   *Would the 100 pound weight requirement specified in Part C change the optimal mixture? Why or why not?*

P9.9   **SOLUTION**

   A.   The primal linear programming problem Greenthumb would use to determine the least cost mixture for its garden fertilizer can be written:

   Minimize Cost $=$ $1.20A + $1.80B + $2C + $2D

   Subject to:

   $$4A + 2B + 4C + 10D \geq 6$$

   $$6A + 10B + 8C + 5D \geq 12$$

   or, in equality form:

   (1) $4A + 2B + 4C + 10D - S_N = 6$ (Nitrogen constraint)

   (2) $6A + 10B + 8C + 5D - S_P = 12$ (Phosphate constraint)

$A, B, C, D, S_N, S_P \geq 0$

Here A, B, C and D are the amounts of the individual compounds used in the fertilizer mix. S_N and S_P represent the amounts of nitrogen and phosphates in the fertilizer mixture above and beyond minimum requirements.

Using the rules for forming the dual linear program (see appendix 9A), the dual can be written:

Maximize $C^* = 6V_N + 12V_P$

Subject to:

$$4V_N + 6V_P \leq 1.20$$

$$2V_N + 10V_P \leq 1.80$$

$$4V_N + 8V_P \leq 2$$

$$10V_N + 5V_P \leq 2$$

or, in equality form:

(3) $\quad 4V_N + 6V_P + L_A = 1.20 \quad$ (Value of inputs used in each unit of

(4) $\quad 2V_N + 10V_P + L_B = 1.80 \quad$ output should not exceed output value

(5) $\quad 4V_N + 8V_P + L_C = 2 \quad$ if output is to be produced.)

(6) $\quad 10V_N + 5V_P + L_D = 2$

$$V_N, V_P, L_A, L_B, L_C, L_D \geq 0$$

Here V_N and V_P are the marginal costs (in dollars) of increasing the nitrogen and phosphate content of the fertilizer mixture by one unit, respectively. L_A, L_B, L_C, L_D represent the shortfall between the total value in use of each compound and compound acquisition costs (in dollars). When this shortfall is positive, use of the compound in question will be inefficient. And finally, C^* can be interpreted as the total value of output.

B. In graphing the dual linear objective function, note:

$$C^* = 6V_N + 12V_P$$

$$6V_N = C^* - 12V_P$$

$$V_N = (C^*/6) - (12/6)V_P$$

This function has a slope of $-2 = (-12/6)$.

Graphing succeeding isovalue lines, one finds the optimal solution occurs at the point X where constraints (3) and (4) are binding and $L_A = L_B = 0$.

Taking 2 times (4) minus (3):

$$2 \times (4) \qquad 4V_N + 20V_P = 3.6$$

$$-(3) \qquad \underline{4V_N + 6V_P = 1.2}$$
$$14V_P = 2.4$$

$$V_P = 0.171$$

Substituting $V_P = 0.171$ into (4):

$$(4)\ 2V_N + 10(0.171) = 1.8$$

$$2V_N = 0.090$$

$$V_N = 0.045$$

Substituting $V_N = 0.045$ and $V_P = 0.171$ into (5):

$$(5)\ 4(0.045) + 8(0.171) + L_C = 2$$

$$L_C = 0.452$$

Substituting $V_N = 0.045$ and $V_P = 0.171$ into (6):

$$(6)\ 10(0.045) + 5(0.171) + L_D = 2$$

$$L_D = 0.695$$

And, the solution to the dual objective function is:

$$C^* = 6V_N + 12V_P$$

$$= 6(0.045) + 12(0.171)$$

$$= \$2.32$$

Because V_N, V_P, L_C, and L_D are nonzero valued variables in the dual problem solution, their related primal problem variables must also be zero-valued. Thus, $S_N = S_P = C = D = 0$. Only A and B in the primal can be nonzero valued.

Taking 5 times (1) minus (2):

$$5 \times (1) \qquad 20A + 10B \; = \; 30$$

$$- (2) \qquad \underline{6A + 10B \; = \; 12}$$

$$14A \; = \; 18$$

$$A \; = \; 1.286$$

Substituting A = 1.286 into (1):

$$(1) \; 4(1.286) + 2B \; = \; 6$$

$$2B \; = \; 0.856$$

$$B \; = \; 0.428$$

And finally, the solution to the primal objective function is:

$$Cost \; = \; \$1.2A + \$1.8B + \$2C + \$2D$$

$$= \; \$1.2(1.286) + \$1.8(0.428) + \$2(0) + \$2(0)$$

$$= \; \$2.32 \; (\text{As it must})$$

Summarizing from above, the solution to the primal and dual linear programming problems and an interpretation of their values reads:

Primal

Solution	Interpretation
A = 1.286	1.286 units of Compound A employed.
B = 0.428	0.428 units of Compound B employed.
C = 0	Compound C not employed.
D = 0	Compound D not employed.
S_N = 0	Nitrogen requirement exactly met.
S_P = 0	Phosphate requirement exactly met.
C = $2.32	Minimum cost of mixture.

Dual

Solution	Interpretation
L_A = $0	Marginal output value equals input value so A is employed.
L_B = $0	Marginal output value equals input value so B is employed.
L_C = $0.452	At margin, C input value (cost) exceeds output value by 45.2¢.
L_D = $0.695	At margin, D input value (cost) exceeds output value by 69.5¢.
V_N = $0.045	Marginal cost of increasing nitrogen content.
V_P = $0.171	Marginal cost of increasing phosphate content.
C* = $2.32	Maximum value of resources used.

C. A requirement of at least 100 pounds of weight in each bag of fertilizer would require the addition of another constraint to the problem. The constraint would be written as: $A + B + C + D \geq 1$.

D. Because the optimal solution to the problem requires that 128.6 pounds of Compound A be combined with 42.8 pounds of Compound B, we know that the

100 pound requirement is already exceeded. Therefore, adding such a constraint to the problem would not affect the optimal solution.

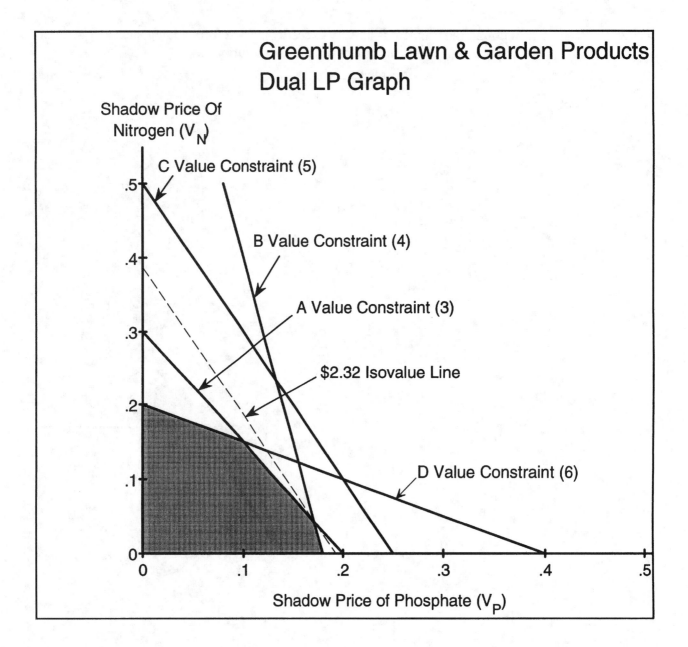

Greenthumb Lawn & Garden Products
Dual LP Graph

Shadow Price Of
Nitrogen (V$_N$)

C Value Constraint (5)

B Value Constraint (4)

A Value Constraint (3)

$2.32 Isovalue Line

D Value Constraint (6)

Shadow Price of Phosphate (V$_P$)

P9.10 **Optimal Output.** The Olympic Arms Company is a specialized producer of shotguns used by sportsmen for bird and small game hunting, and by competitors in target (skeet) competition. Currently, two shotgun models are produced. The hunting, H, model retails for $5,000, while the target, T, model retails for $6,000. Both are offered to consumers by retailers at a 100% markup on their cost from Olympic. Olympic's variable production costs are $2,350 for the H model, and $2,900 for the T model.

Each model uses scarce woodworking, W, and metalworking, M, capacity. The H model requires 2 hours each of woodworking and metalworking, while the T model requires only 1 hour of woodworking but 5 hours of metalworking. In addition, each T model requires 2 hours of hand finishing, F. Olympic currently has a monthly capacity of 1,000 hours for woodworking, 1,500 hours for metalworking, and 500 hours for hand finishing.

A. Set up the primal and dual linear programming problem which Olympic might use to determine optimal output levels for the H and T models in light of an operating philosophy of profit maximization. Be sure to completely interpret each program, and use the equality form of the constraint conditions.

B. Solve and completely interpret the solution values for the primal and dual linear programming problems.

C. How would the optimal output levels determined above differ if Olympic had an operating philosophy of sales rather than profit maximization? Explain.

P9.10 **SOLUTION**

A. Prior to specifying the primal and dual linear programming problems, we must calculate Olympic's profit contribution from the H and T models. These values are:

H Unit Profit Contribution $= \pi_H = 0.5(5,000) - 2,350 = \$150$

T Unit Profit Contribution $= \pi_T = 0.5(6,000) - 2,900 = \$100$

Using the equality form of the constraint conditions, the relevant primal linear programming problem can then be written:

Maximize $\pi^* = \$150H + \$100T$

Subject to:

(1) $2H + 1T + S_W = 1,000$ (Woodworking constraint)

(2) $2H + 5T + S_M = 1,500$ (Metalworking constraint)

(3) $0H + 2T + S_F = 500$ (Hand finishing constraint)

$H, T, S_W, S_M, S_F \geq 0$

Here H and T represent output of each model of shotgun. S_W, S_M and S_F represent excess capacity of woodworking, metalworking, and hand finishing inputs, respectively.

Using the rules for forming the dual linear program, the dual can be written:

Minimize $\pi^* = 1,000V_W + 1,500V_M + 500V_F$

Subject to:

(4) $2V_W + 2V_M + 0V_F - L_H = 150$ (Value of inputs used in each unit
(5) $1V_W + 5V_M + 2V_F - L_T = 100$ of output should not exceed output
                                                                          value if output is to be produced.)

$V_W, V_M, V_F, L_H, L_T \geq 0$

Here V_W, V_M and V_F are the marginal values of additional woodworking, metalworking and hand finishing inputs, respectively, in terms of dollars of profit generated. L_H and L_T, also in dollars of profits, represent the excess of input value over output value for each output. Obviously, should these values be positive, the output in question will not be produced. And finally, π^* represents the total value of inputs used in production.

B.   To learn which constraints are binding at the optimal solution, graph the isoprofit line:

$$\pi = \$150H + \$100T$$

$$150H = \pi - 100T$$

$$H = (\pi/150) - (100/150)T$$

which has a slope $= -100/150 = -0.67$. Graphing succeeding isoprofit lines we find the optimal solution occurs at the point X where constraints (1) and (2) are binding and $S_W = S_M = 0$.

Taking (1) minus (2):

$$
\begin{array}{lll}
(1) & 2H + 1T & = 1{,}000 \\
-(2) & \underline{2H + 5T} & \underline{= 1{,}500} \\
& -4T & = -500 \\
\\
& T & = 125
\end{array}
$$

Substituting T = 125 into (1):

$$
\begin{array}{rl}
(1)\ 2H + 1(125) &= 1{,}000 \\
2H &= 875 \\
H &= 437.5
\end{array}
$$

Substituting T = 125 into (3) yields:

$$
\begin{array}{rl}
(3)\ 2(125) + S_F &= 500 \\
S_F &= 250
\end{array}
$$

And finally, solving the primal objective function:

$$
\begin{array}{rl}
\pi &= \$150H + \$100T \\
&= 150(437.5) + 100(125) \\
&= \$78{,}125
\end{array}
$$

The dual can be solved directly, given the solution to the primal problem. Since H, T, and S_F are all nonzero values in the solution to the primal problem, $L_H = L_T = V_F = 0$ in the solution to the dual problem. This reduces the constraints in the dual from a system of 2 equations and 5 unknowns, to a system of 2 equations and 2 unknowns, V_W and V_M. These values can be determined algebraically.

Taking (4) minus 2 times (5):

$$\text{(4)} \qquad 2V_W + 2V_M \;=\; 150$$

$$-2 \times \text{(5)} \qquad \underline{2V_W + 10V_M \;=\; 200}$$

$$-8V_M \;=\; -50$$

$$V_M \;=\; 6.25$$

Substituting $V_M = 6.25$ into (4):

$$\text{(4)} \; 2V_W + 2(6.25) \;=\; 150$$

$$2V_W \;=\; 137.5$$

$$V_W \;=\; 68.75$$

And finally, solving the dual objective function:

$$\pi^* \;=\; 1{,}000V_W + 1{,}500V_M + 500V_F$$

$$=\; 1{,}000(68.75) + 1{,}500(6.25) + 500(0)$$

$$=\; \$78{,}125 \;\; \text{(As it must)}$$

Summarizing from above, the solution to the primal and dual linear programming problems and an interpretation of their values reads:

Primal

Solution	Interpretation
$H = 437.5$	437.5 hunting models will be produced.
$T = 125$	125 target models will be produced.
$S_W = 0$	No excess wood-working capacity.
$S_M = 0$	No excess metalworking capacity.
$S_F = 250$	250 hours of excess hand finishing capacity available.
$\pi = \$78{,}125$	Maximum profit given input constraints.

Dual

Solution	Interpretation
$L_H = 0$	At margin, input value equals output value so H produced.
$L_T = 0$	At margin, input value equals output value so T produced.
$V_W = \$68.75$	Marginal profit value of woodworking.
$V_M = \$6.25$	Marginal profit value of metalworking.
$V_F = 0$	Given excess capacity, an increase in hand finishing capacity wouldn't affect profits.
$\pi^* = \$78,125$	Minimum value of inputs required to produce H = 437.5 and T = 125.

C. No, in this problem output levels would remain the same with an operating strategy of revenue or profit maximization. This is easily seen if one considers the revenue function:

$$R = \$5,000H + \$6,000T$$

or

$$H = (R/5,000) - (6,000/5,000)T$$

This function has a slope = -6,000/5,000 = -1.2 which is somewhat "steeper" than the profit function shown above, but will still intersect the feasible region at the point *X* when maximized. Since this result will not always hold true, it always pays to graph alternative objective functions to determine their point of intersection with the feasible space.

Olympic Arms Company LP Graph

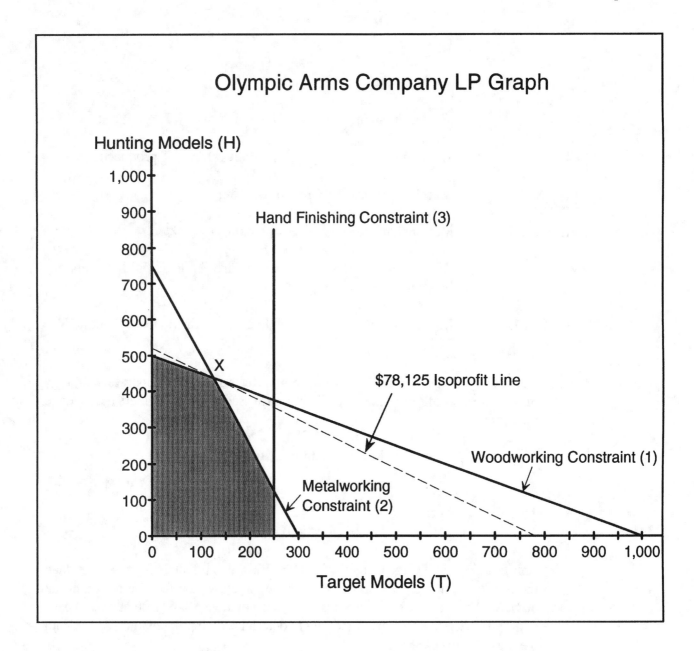

Hunting Models (H)

Hand Finishing Constraint (3)

$78,125 Isoprofit Line

Woodworking Constraint (1)

Metalworking
Constraint (2)

Target Models (T)

Chapter 10

PERFECT COMPETITION AND MONOPOLY

To this point, managerial decisions have been studied without attention to market structure considerations. In practice, the competitive environment or market structure faced by the firm is a factor of utmost importance. Market structure analysis is so important that this text devotes two full chapters to this topic. This chapter considers perfect (or pure) competition and monopoly. These market structure models can be viewed as endpoints along a continuum of decreasing competition, moving from the models of perfect competition to monopolistic competition to oligopoly to monopoly. The perfect competition model describes sectors of the economy in which widespread price competition drives profitability to a level just sufficient to maintain required investment. Agriculture, mining, and stock trading are good examples. In a monopoly environment, like that enjoyed by Intel and Microsoft, the firm can earn above-normal (economic) profits even in the long run. When economic profits are derived from market power rather than innovation, superior efficiency, or other socially valued activities, monopolies are sometimes subject to state and federal regulation. When direct government regulation is not desirable, market mechanisms such as countervailing power sometimes arise to combat monopoly abuse.

The study of perfect competition and monopoly is valuable as a necessary backdrop for understanding managerial decision making in each of these market settings, and as a framework for understanding monopolistic competition and oligopoly. Once market structure considerations are fully understood, it becomes possible to devise and execute a value-maximizing competitive strategy.

CHAPTER OUTLINE

I. **CONTRAST BETWEEN PERFECT COMPETITION AND MONOPOLY**

    A. **What is Market Structure?** The competitive environment in the market for any product is the market structure faced by the firm.

        1. Market structure is measured in terms of the number of actual buyers and sellers plus potential entrants, barriers to entry and exit, capital requirements, nonprice competition, and so on.

        2. Potential entrants pose a sufficiently credible threat of entry to affect price/output decisions of incumbents.

    B. **Perfect Competition:** A perfectly competitive market is characterized by a large number of buyers and sellers of an identical product.

1.   Price takers accept market prices as given.

C.   **Monopoly:** Monopoly exist in a market with a single seller of a highly differentiated product.

1.   Monopolists exert significant control over market prices.

II.   FACTORS THAT DETERMINE THE LEVEL OF COMPETITION

A.   **Effect of Product Characteristics on Market Structure:** Market competition increases with product standardization.

1.   When distribution costs are low, broad geographic markets and active competition are possible.

B.   **Effect of Production Characteristics on Competition:** Industries with production functions that exhibit increasing returns to scale are sometimes characterized by less competition than are industries with constant or decreasing returns.

C.   **Effect of Entry and Exit Conditions on Competition:** When entry and exit are easy, the threat of potential entry can effectively limit prices and profits for current competitors.

1.   A barrier to entry is any advantage for industry incumbents over new rivals.

2.   A barrier to exit is any limit on asset redeployment.

D.   **Effect of Buyers on Competition:** Competition is most vigorous when numerous highly informed buyers are present.

1.   Monopsony describes a market with one buyer.

E.   **Effect of Product Differentiation on Competition:** The extent of product differentiation is an important determinant of the competitive environment.

1.   Product differentiation includes all of the methods used by firms to distinguish their products from those produced by rivals.

a.   R&D, advertising, innovative product design, and imaginative customer service are all valuable means of product differentiation.

III.   PERFECT COMPETITION

A. **Characteristics of Perfectly Competitive Markets:** Perfect competition exists when individual producers in a market have no influence over prices. Basic requirements for perfect competition are:

1. Large number of buyers and sellers.

2. Product homogeneity.

3. Free entry into and exit from the market.

4. Perfect dissemination of information.

B. **Market Price Determination:** Industry supply and demand conditions determine market prices. Industry supply is the sum of the quantities that individual firms are willing to supply at different prices. Industry demand is the aggregate quantity that individual purchasers wish to buy at each price.

1. Under perfect competition, a single firm's output decisions do not affect price.

2. The firm demand curve is a horizontal line intersecting the vertical axis at the market price.

3. In competitive markets, price equals marginal revenue.

C. **Firm Price/Output Decision:** Management must determine the output that maximizes profit, given the prevailing market price.

1. A profit-maximizing firm in a competitive market operates at the point where market price (and MR) is equal to MC.

2. Above-normal profits can exist in the short-run, but in the long-run those profits attract competitors, who drive down prices and eliminate above-normal profits.

3. In long-run equilibrium, prices are stable, and each firm operates at the minimum point on its short-run and long-run average cost curve:

$$P = AR = MR = MC = AC$$

D. **Illustration of Price/Output Decisions in Perfectly Competitive Markets:** The optimal price/output combination can be determined by setting marginal revenue equal to marginal cost and solving for Q

E.   Firm Supply Curve: The short-run supply schedule corresponds with the portion of the marginal cost curve that lies above the average variable cost curve.

  1.   Profits are earned when price (average revenue) exceeds average cost.

  2.   In a perfectly competitive market where P < AC, losses can be reduced by expanding production so long as added revenues exceed added costs.

IV.   MONOPOLY

  A.   Characteristics of Monopoly Markets: Monopoly exists when a single firm is the sole producer of a product that has no close substitutes. Monopoly markets are described by:

  1.   A single seller.

  2.   Unique product.

  3.   Blockaded entry and exit.

  4.   Imperfect dissemination of information.

  B.   Price/Output Decision Under Monopoly: Management must determine the price and output combination that will maximize profits.

  1.   Under monopoly, the firm is the industry and, therefore, the downward sloping industry demand curve is identical to the firm demand curve.

  2.   The monopolist can set either price or quantity, the value of the other being determined by the relation expressed in the demand function.

  3.   Economic Profits: Monopolists operate at the point where MR = MC, so long as average variable costs are covered.

  4.   With P = AR > AC, economic profits result.

  C.   Illustration of Price/Output Decisions in Monopoly Markets: A monopoly uses the same profit-maximization rule as does any other firm: It operates at the output level at which marginal revenue equals marginal cost.

1.   Marginal revenue is always less than price for output quantities greater than one because of the negatively sloped demand curve.

2.   When a monopoly equates marginal revenue and marginal cost, it simultaneously determines the output level and the market price for its product.

D.   Long-Run Equilibrium Under Monopoly: Economic profits can persist even in the long-run for a monopolist protected by barriers to entry or exit.

1.   A natural monopolist emerges in an industry where long-run average costs are declining at the intersection of industry supply and demand curves.

E.   Is Monopoly Always Bad? Monopoly can be efficient, but monopoly can also lead to excess profits and under-production.

1.   The potential for superior efficiency but risk of monopoly abuse create a dilemma for regulators.

V.   COUNTERVAILING POWER: MONOPOLY/MONOPSONY CONFRONTATION

A.   Seller Versus Buyer Power: Countervailing power is any economic influence that creates a closer balance of power between sellers and buyers.

1.   Seller power creates high prices and low output.

2.   Buyer power limits prices and can restrict output.

B.   Compromise Solution: Seller/Buyer conflict often results in compromise and a more efficient market equilibrium.

1.   The balance of buyer and seller power is only exact in perfectly competitive markets.

VI.   MEASUREMENT OF BUSINESS PROFIT RATES

A.   Rate of Return on Stockholders' Equity: Business profit rates are best measured by the accounting rate of return on stockholders' equity measure.

1.   ROE is defined as net income divided by the book value of stockholders' equity, where stockholders' equity is the book value of total assets minus total liabilities.

2. ROE equals the firm's profit margin multiplied by the total asset turnover ratio, all times the firm's leverage ratio:

$$\text{ROE} = \frac{\text{Net Income}}{\text{Equity}}$$

$$= \frac{\text{Net Income}}{\text{Sales}} \times \frac{\text{Sales}}{\text{Total Assets}} \times \frac{\text{Total Assets}}{\text{Equity}}$$

$$= \text{Profit Margin} \times \frac{\text{Total Asset}}{\text{Turnover}} \times \text{Leverage}.$$

3. Profit margin is defined as accounting net income expressed as a percentage of sales revenue, and shows the amount of profit earned per dollar of sales.

    a. When profit margins are high, robust demand or stringent cost controls, or both, allow the firm to earn a significant profit contribution.

    b. Holding capital requirements constant, profit margin is a useful indicator of managerial efficiency in responding to rapidly growing demand and/or effective measures of cost containment.

4. Total asset turnover is sales revenue divided by the book value of total assets.

    a. When total asset turnover is high, the firm displays a wise use of assets because it is able to make its investments work hard in the sense of generating a large amount of sales volume.

5. Leverage reflects the extent to which debt and preferred stock is used in addition to common stock financing.

    a. Leverage is used to amplify firm profit rates over the business cycle.

B. **Typical Business Profit Rates:** For both large and small firms in the United States and Canada, ROE ranges between 10 per cent to 12 per cent during a typical year.

    1. Average ROE is comprised of a typical profit margin on sales revenue of roughly 4.0 per cent, a standard total asset turnover ratio of 1.0 times, and a common leverage ratio of roughly 3.0:1:

$$\frac{\text{Typical}}{\text{ROE}} = \text{Profit Margin} \times \frac{\text{Total Asset}}{\text{Turnover}} \times \text{Leverage}$$

$$= 4.0\% \times 1.0 \times 3.0$$

$$= 12\%.$$

2. The accounting return on assets, defined as net income divided by the book value of total assets, is another useful indicator of the business profit rate.

    a. Like ROE, ROA captures the effects of managerial operating decisions; unlike ROE, ROA is unaffected by the amount of leverage.

VII. LINK BETWEEN MARKET STRUCTURE AND BUSINESS PROFIT RATES

    A. **Business Profit Rates By Industry Group:** In a perfectly competitive market, profit margins are low because $P = MC$ and $MC = AC$. When profit margin is measured as $(P - AC)/P$, profit margins will tend to be high and reflect above-normal rates of return in monopoly markets.

        1. Without detailed firm-specific data, it is not possible to know if higher profit margins are due to higher prices (monopoly power), or due to lower costs (superior efficiency).

        2. Over time, entry into highly profitable industries and nonleading firm growth causes above-normal profits to regress toward the mean.

        3. Conversely, bankruptcy and exit allow the below-normal profits of depressed industries to rise toward the mean.

    B. **Business Profit Rates for Top Performing Large Firms:** ROE is high to the extent that the firm enjoys a high profit margin on sales, a high rate of total asset turnover, or benefits from financial leverage.

        1. Firm-specific factors, such as superior efficiency, and industry-related factors, such as market power, both contribute to the realization of above-normal rates of return.

VIII. COMPETITIVE STRATEGY IN PERFECTLY COMPETITIVE AND MONOPOLY MARKETS

A. **Competitive Strategy in Perfectly Competitive Markets:** Competitive strategy is the search for a favorable competitive position in an industry or line of business.

1. Survival of the fittest translates into success for the most able, and extinction of the least capable.

    a. In perfectly competitive markets, the ready imitation of rivals makes ongoing success a constant struggle.

    b. In monopoly markets, entry and growth by nonleading firms often eats away at proprietary advantages.

2. Above-normal returns in perfectly competitive industries typically reflect what is known as economic rents, or profits due to uniquely productive inputs.

    a. An exceptionally well-trained workforce, talented management, or superior land and raw materials can all lead to above-normal profits.

3. Disequilibrium profits are above-normal returns that can be earned in the time interval that often exists between when a favorable influence on industry demand or cost conditions first transpires, and the time when competitor entry or growth finally develops.

4. Disequilibrium losses are below-normal returns that can be suffered in the time interval that often exists between when an unfavorable influence on industry demand or cost conditions first transpires, and the time when exit or downsizing finally occurs.

5. Above-normal profits in perfectly competitive industries are transitory and reflect the influences of economic rents, luck or disequilibrium conditions.

6. If above-normal returns persist for extended periods in a given industry or line of business, elements of monopoly are probably at work.

B. **Competitive Strategy in Monopoly Markets:** Above-normal returns tend to be fleeting in perfectly competitive industries, but can be durable for efficient firms that benefit from meaningful monopoly advantages.

1. The protection of current monopoly advantages is only likely to succeed when firms can maintain the distinctive and valuable characteristics required by customers.

2.   The search for above-normal profits is only likely to be successful when firms can offer customers products that are faster, cheaper, or better than those offered by rivals.

C.   **Why Market Niches are Attractive:** Entry into a perfectly competitive industry is not apt to result in above-normal rates of return under the best of circumstances.

1.   A market niche is a segment of a market that can be successfully exploited through the special capabilities of a given firm.

2.   Lasting success requires exploitation of those segments of the market that can be best served using the special capabilities of a given firm or individual.

D.   **Information Barriers to Competitive Strategy:** Any use of market structure information as a guide to competitive strategy must address the challenge posed by measurement problems encountered in defining the magnitude and root cause of above-normal rates of return.

1.   Business practices create an information barrier that hides details about economic profit rates.

IX.   **SUMMARY**

PROBLEMS & SOLUTIONS

P10.1   **Market Structure Concepts.** *Identify each of the following statements as true or false, and explain why.*

      A.   *Profit maximization in perfectly competitive markets requires setting P = MC.*

      B.   *Profit maximization in monopoly markets requires setting MR = MC.*

      C.   *In long-run equilibrium, monopoly results in lower prices than would be typical of a perfectly competitive industry.*

      D.   *In monopoly markets, firm and industry demand curves always have an identical slope.*

      E.   *In long-run equilibrium, P > AC in perfectly competitive markets.*

P10.1   **Solution**

      A.   True. Profit maximization in perfectly competitive markets requires setting MR = MC. Because the horizontal demand curve that is faced by all firms results in P = MR, by setting MC = P, the firm is implicitly setting MR = MC.

      B.   True. Profit maximization in monopoly markets requires setting MR = MC. Because P > MR, this does not imply setting P = MC as is the case in perfectly competitive markets.

      C.   False. In long-run equilibrium, monopoly results in higher prices than would be typical of a perfectly competitive industry.

      D.   True. In monopoly markets, the firm is the industry. Therefore, firm and industry demand curves always have an identical slope.

      E.   False. In long-run equilibrium, P = AC in perfectly competitive markets and zero excess profits are earned.

P10.2   **Market Structure Concepts.** *Identify each of the following characteristics as typical of perfect competition and/or monopoly market structures, and explain why.*

      A.   *Downward sloping industry demand curves.*

      B.   *Horizontal firm demand curves.*

C.   *Differentiated output.*

D.   *High barriers to entry.*

E.   *Excess profits in short-run disequilibrium.*

P10.2   **Solution**

A.   Both perfect competition and monopoly. Both perfectly competitive and monopoly market structures are characterized by downward sloping industry demand curves. Downward sloping industry demand curves result from the law of diminishing marginal utility discussed earlier in the book.

B.   Perfect competition. Horizontal firm demand curves in perfectly competitive markets reflect the fact that such firms are price takers, and imply that $P = MR$ in these markets.

C.   Monopoly. Monopoly is characterized by a lack of competition from close substitutes. Thus, highly differentiated output is a key characteristic of monopoly markets.

D.   Monopoly. High barriers to entry limit competition from rivals able to offer close substitutes. Thus, high barriers to entry are a key characteristic of monopoly markets.

E.   Both perfect competition and monopoly. Excess profits in short-run disequilibrium reflect the effects of unexpected changes in industry demand and supply relations. They are observed in all types of market structures, including perfect competition and monopoly.

P10.3   **Market Structure Concepts.** *Indicate whether each of the following statements is true or false and why.*

A.   *A natural monopoly results when the intersection of industry demand and supply curves occurs at a point where long-run average costs are declining.*

B.   *In long-run equilibrium, every firm in a perfectly competitive industry earns zero profit.*

C.   *Perfect competition exists in a market when $MR = P$.*

D.   *Downward-sloping industry demand curves characterize perfectly competitive markets.*

E.   *The price elasticity of demand would rise following a decrease in monopoly power.*

P10.3   **SOLUTION**

A.   True. A natural monopoly occurs in a market when the market clearing price, or price where Demand (Price) = Supply (Marginal Cost), occurs at an output level where long-run average costs are declining.

B.   False. In long-run equilibrium, every firm in a perfectly competitive industry earns zero excess profit. However, firms can expect to earn a normal rate of return on investment.

C.   True. Perfect competition exists in a market when individual firms have no influence over price. Such firms take industry prices as a given, and MR = P.

D.   True. Downward sloping demand curves follow from the law of diminishing marginal utility and characterize both perfectly competitive and monopoly market structures.

E.   True. An increase in the price elasticity of demand would result following a decrease in monopoly power.

P10.4   **Equilibrium**. *Demand conditions for household chemical spray treatments to control insects and other pests in the St. Louis, Missouri market area are described as follows:*

Spray Treatments per year	Price
0	$25
1	24
2	23
3	22
4	21
5	20
6	19
7	18

The marginal cost of service is stable at $20 per spray treatment.

A.   Use the indicated price and output data to complete the following table.

Spray Treatments per year	Price	Total Revenue	Marginal Revenue
0	$25		
1	24		
2	23		
3	22		
4	21		
5	20		
6	19		
7	18		

B.   Determine price and the level of service per customer if a perfectly competitive market structure is present.

C.   Determine price and the level of service if the city grants a single firm a monopoly franchise.

P10.4   SOLUTION

A.

Spray Treatments per year	Price	Total Revenue	Marginal Revenue
0	$25	$0	--
1	24	24	$24
2	23	46	22
3	22	66	20
4	21	84	18
5	20	100	16
6	19	114	14
7	18	126	12

B.   In a perfectly competitive industry, P = MR, so the optimal activity level occurs where P = MC. Here, P = MC = $20 at Q = 5 treatments per year.

C.   A monopoly will maximize profits by setting MR = MC. Here, MR = MC = $20 at Q = 3 treatments and P = $22.

P10.5   ***Perfectly Competitive Equilibrium.*** *Demand and Supply conditions in the perfectly competitive domestic oil industry are:*

$$Q_S = 10P \qquad \textit{(Supply)}$$

$$Q_D = 1{,}000 - 40P \qquad \textit{(Demand)}$$

where Q is quantity in millions of barrels, and P is price per barrel.

A.   *Graph industry supply and demand curves.*

B.   *Determine both graphically and algebraically the equilibrium industry price/output combination.*

P10.5   SOLUTION

A.

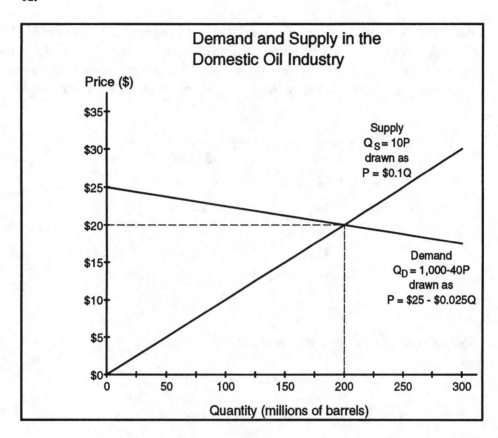

Demand and Supply in the Domestic Oil Industry

Price ($)

Supply
$Q_S = 10P$
drawn as
$P = \$0.1Q$

Demand
$Q_D = 1,000 - 40P$
drawn as
$P = \$25 - \$0.025Q$

Quantity (millions of barrels)

B.   From the graph, it is clear that $Q_D = Q_S = 200(000,000)$ at a price of $20 per barrel. Thus, P = $20 and Q = 200(000,000) is the equilibrium price-output combination.

Algebraically,

$$Q_D = Q_S$$

$$1,000 - 40P = 10P$$

$$50P = 1,000$$

$$P = \$20$$

Both demand and supply equal 200(000,000) because:

$$\text{Demand: } Q_S = 1,000 - 40(20) = 200(000,000)$$

$$\text{Supply: } Q_S = 10(20) = 200(000,000)$$

P10.6 **Perfectly Competitive Firm Supply.** *The market price for generic 256MB 144pin SDRAM chips used in computers and "intelligent" electronics fluctuates widely depending on changes in world-wide demand and supply conditions in this perfectly competitive industry. Market prices for a recent seven-month period were as follows:*

Month	Price
January	$29.00
February	30.00
March	33.50
April	35.50
May	42.50
June	37.50
July	35.00

Marginal cost conditions in the industry are:

$$MC = \$25 + \$0.0001Q$$

where MC is marginal cost and Q is output (in thousands).

A. *What is the minimum price necessary before domestic firms will supply chips?*

B. *Calculate the domestic supply of chips per month.*

P10.6 **SOLUTION**

A. $25. Given MC = $25 + $0.0001Q, a minimum price of $25 must be obtained before any domestic supply would be forthcoming.

B. In a perfectly competitive industry, P = MC. Therefore, when price is expressed as a function of output, the industry supply curve equals the marginal cost curve:

$$P = MC = \$25 + \$0.0001Q$$

To express quantity as a function of price, note that:

$$P = \$25 + \$0.0001Q$$

$$0.0001Q = -25 + P$$

$$Q = -250,000 + 10,000P$$

Therefore, domestic supply per month is:

Month	Supply (000)
January	$Q = -250,000 + 10,000(29) = 40,000$
February	$Q = -250,000 + 10,000(30) = 50,000$
March	$Q = -250,000 + 10,000(33.5) = 85,000$
April	$Q = -250,000 + 10,000(35.5) = 105,000$
May	$Q = -250,000 + 10,000(42.5) = 175,000$
June	$Q = -250,000 + 10,000(37.5) = 125,000$
July	$Q = -250,000 + 10,000(35) = 100,000$

P10.7   **Perfectly Competitive Firm and Industry Supply.** *Solar Systems, Inc., produces and sells solar heat panels for hot water heaters in a perfectly competitive industry and has the following total and marginal cost functions:*

$$TC = \$500Q - \$10Q^2 + Q^3$$

$$MC = \partial TC/\partial Q = \$500 - \$20Q + \$3Q^2$$

where TC is total cost (in thousands of dollars) and Q is output (in thousands of units). Included in this cost function is a normal return of 15% on invested capital.

A. *Assuming that the firm and the industry are in equilibrium, what is the price charged by Solar Systems for its product?*

B. *What is the value of economic profits, average cost, and marginal cost at this equilibrium price?*

C. *Graph the marginal revenue, marginal cost, and average cost curves.*

D. *What is the supply function for Solar Systems' output?*

P10.7   **SOLUTION**

A. If the firm and the industry are in equilibrium, then P = AC where average costs are minimized. To find the point of minimum average costs, set MC = AC where:

$$MC = AC$$

$$\$500 - \$20Q + \$3Q^2 = \frac{\$500Q - \$10Q^2 + Q^3}{Q}$$

$$500 - 20Q + 3Q^2 = 500 - 10Q + Q^2$$

$$2Q^2 = 10Q$$

$$2Q = 10$$

$$Q = 5(000)$$

At Q = 5(000),

$$AC = 500 - 10Q + Q^2$$

$$= 500 - 10(5) + 5^2$$

$$= \$475$$

Therefore, because P must equal AC:

$$P = AC$$

$$= \$475$$

(*Note*: $\partial AC/\partial Q = -10 + 2Q > 0$ for Q > 5, so AC is rising beyond that point and Q = 5 is a point of minimum average costs.)

B. In equilibrium, economic profits equal zero, and average cost equals marginal cost.

$$\pi = TR - TC$$

$$= P \times Q - 500Q + 10Q^2 - Q^3$$

$$= \$475(5) - \$500(5) + \$10(5^2) - \$1(5^3)$$

$$= \$0$$

$$AC = \$500 - \$10Q + Q^2$$

$$= 500 - 10(5) + 5^2$$

$$= 500 - 50 + 25$$

$$= \$475$$

$$MC = \$500 - \$20(5) + \$3(5^2)$$

$$= \$475$$

C.

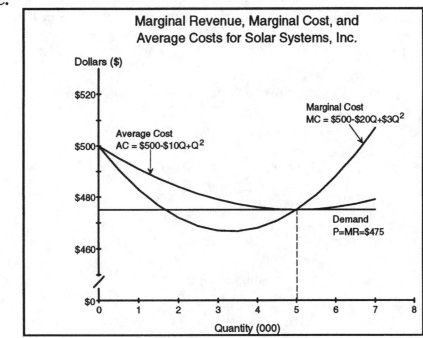

D.   A competitive firm's supply function is defined by that portion of the marginal cost curve lying above the average variable cost curve. Because Solar Systems' total cost function does not contain a fixed cost component, average costs and average variable costs are identical. Thus, Solar Systems' supply curve would be that portion of its marginal cost curve lying above the average cost curve.

P10.8   *Monopoly Equilibrium. MicroProducts, Inc., a Chicago-based supplier of micro-electronic products, has retained an independent management consulting firm to provide*

advice concerning supply and demand conditions in the industry. Using Department of Commerce data the consultant estimates:

$$Q_S = 4,000P \qquad\qquad (Supply)$$

$$Q_D = 1,500,000 - 2,000P \qquad\qquad (Demand)$$

A. *Assuming the industry is perfectly competitive, calculate the industry equilibrium price/output combination.*

B. *Now assume that import restrictions have eliminated MicroProduct's leading competitors, thereby giving the company a monopoly position in its home market. Based on the same supply and demand conditions stated above, calculate the new monopoly equilibrium price/output combination for the industry.*

P10.8 **SOLUTION**

A. The perfectly competitive industry equilibrium price is:

$$Q_S = Q_D$$

$$4,000P = 1,500,000 - 2,000P$$

$$6,000P = 1,500,000$$

$$P = \$250$$

At P = \$250, industry equilibrium output is:

$$Q_S = 4,000(\$250)$$

$$= 1,000,000$$

B. The new monopoly equilibrium price/output combination is found at the profit-maximizing activity level where MC = MR. It is important to recognize that the industry supply curve represents the horizontal sum of the marginal cost curves for individual producers. When the industry is transformed into a monopoly, the industry supply curve represents the relevant marginal cost curve:

$$Q_S = 4,000P \qquad\qquad (Supply)$$

$$MC = P = \$0.00025Q$$

And the profit maximizing activity level is where:

$$MC = MR$$

$$\partial TC/\partial Q = \partial TR/\partial Q$$

$$\$0.00025Q = \$750 - \$0.001Q$$

$$0.00125Q = 750$$

$$Q = 600,000$$

$$P = \$750 - \$0.0005(600,000)$$

$$= \$450$$

From parts A and B, it is clear that import restrictions reduce the level of industry output from 1,000,000 to 600,000 units, and increase prices from $250 to $450 per unit. Generally, speaking, monopolists offer consumers too little output at too high a price.

P10.9 *Dr. Elizabeth Corday is head of Corday Pharmaceuticals, Ltd., a company that enjoys an exclusive patent on a drug used to treat peptic ulcers. Total and marginal revenues for the product is:*

$$TR = \$100Q - \$0.0002Q^2$$

$$MR = \partial TR/\partial Q = \$100 - \$0.0004Q$$

Marginal costs for production and distribution are stable at $20 per unit. All other costs have been fully amortized.

A. *As a monopoly, calculate Corday's output, price, and profits at the profit maximizing activity level.*

B. *What price and profit levels would prevail following expiration of patent protection based on the assumption that perfectly competitive pricing would result?*

P10.9 SOLUTION

A. Set MR = MC to find the profit maximizing activity level:

$$MR = MC$$

$$\$100 - \$0.0004Q = \$20$$

$$0.0004Q = 80$$

$$Q = 200,000$$

$$P = TR/Q$$

$$= (\$100Q - \$0.0002Q^2)/Q$$

$$= 100 - 0.0002Q$$

$$= 100 - 0.0002(200,000)$$

$$= \$60$$

$$\pi = TR - TC$$

$$= \$60(200,000) - \$20(200,000)$$

$$= \$8,000,000$$

B. In a perfectly competitive industry, $P = MR = MC$ in equilibrium. Thus, after expiration of patent protection, $P = MC = \$20$ would result. Because $MC = AC$, $P = MC$ implies that $\pi = 0$.

P10.10 *Monopoly Versus Perfectly Competitive Equilibrium.* The Hotpoint Inspection & Insurance Company is the leading underwriter of boiler and machinery insurance. Market demand for the company's insurance given by the relation:

$$P = \$7,500 - \$1.1Q$$

$$MR = \partial TR/\partial Q = \$7,500 - \$2.2Q$$

All costs are variable, and average $2,000 per policy (Q).

A. Calculate the profit-maximizing price/output combination and economic profits if the company enjoys a monopoly due to state licensing requirements.

B. *Calculate the profit-maximizing price/output combination if a relaxation of entry restrictions transforms the industry into one that is perfectly competitive.*

P10.10 SOLUTION

A. The profit-maximizing price/output combination is found by setting MR = MC. Because AVC is constant, MC = AVC = $2,000. Therefore:

$$MR = \partial TR/\partial Q = MC$$

$$\$7,500 - \$2.2Q = \$2,000$$

$$2.2Q = 5,500$$

$$Q = 2,500$$

$$P = \$7,500 - \$1.1(2,500)$$

$$= \$4,750$$

$$\text{Economic Profits} = P \times Q - AVC \times Q$$

$$= \$4,750(2,500) - \$2,000(2,500)$$

$$= \$6,875,000$$

(*Note*: As a monopolist, Hotpoint is the industry. Also remember that the marginal revenue curve has the same intercept but twice the slope as the demand curve.)

B. In a perfectly competitive market, P = MC. In this instance where AVC is constant and, therefore, MC = AVC, perfectly competitive equilibrium will occur when:

$$P = MC = AVC$$

$$\$7,500 - \$1.1Q = \$2,000$$

$$1.1Q = 5,500$$

$$Q = 5,000$$

$$P = \$7,500 - \$1.1(5,000)$$

$$= \$2,000$$

$$\text{Economic Profits} = P \times Q - AVC \times Q$$

$$= \$2,000(5,000) - \$2,000(5,000)$$

$$= \$0$$

In words, the transformation of the industry from monopoly to perfect competition has brought a $2,750 reduction in price and a 2,500 unit expansion in output. At the same time, economic profits have been eliminated.

Chapter 11

MONOPOLISTIC COMPETITION AND OLIGOPOLY

Perfect competition and monopoly seldom exist in actual markets. Even Intel and Microsoft are subject to rivalry, though clearly not as robust as would exist under perfect competition. However, even though most firms compete with a large number of other firms producing highly substitutable products, many still have some control over the price of their product. They cannot sell all that they want at a fixed price, nor would they lose all their sales if they raised prices slightly. In other words, most firms face downward-sloping demand curves. This means that above-normal returns are possible, at least during the short-run time frame. For this reason, study of the partly-competitive, partly-monopolistic market structures of monopolistic competition and oligopoly is integral to managerial economics.

When vigorous price and product competition from firms offering close substitutes eliminates the potential for above-normal or economic profits in long-run equilibrium, a market is called monopolistically competitive. Oligopoly markets involve competition among only a handful of competitors. Products offered could be homogeneous, as in aluminum and steel, or differentiated, as in soft drinks and cigarettes. In both instances, limits on the number of competitors stem from meaningful impediments to new entry or nonleading firm growth. Competition among the few has the potential to result in excess profits if so-called "competitors" make implicit or explicit agreements not to compete. This chapter illustrates the nature of competition in imperfectly competitive markets, and shows how the principles of managerial economics can be used to develop an effective competitive strategy.

CHAPTER OUTLINE

I.   **CONTRAST BETWEEN MONOPOLISTIC COMPETITION AND OLIGOPOLY**

      A.   **Monopolistic Competition:** This market structure is characterized by a large number of sellers of a differentiated product.

            1.   Only a risk-adjusted normal rate of return is possible in monopolistically competitive long-run equilibrium.

      B.   **Oligopoly:** Oligopoly is a market structure characterized by few sellers.

            1.   Economic profits are possible in oligopoly markets, even in long-run equilibrium.

      C.   **Dynamic Nature of Competition:** In many formerly oligopolistic markets, the market discipline provided by a competitive fringe of smaller domestic and foreign rivals is sufficient to limit the potential abuse of a few large competitors.

1. Timely and accurate market structure information is required to form the basis for managerial investment decisions that relate to entry or exit from specific lines of business.

II.   MONOPOLISTIC COMPETITION

A. **Characteristics of Monopolistically Competitive Markets:** Monopolistic competition exists when a large number of firms offer close but not identical substitutes. Elements of perfect competition and monopoly are involved because monopolistically competitive markets feature:

1. Large numbers of buyers and sellers.

2. Product heterogeneity.

3. Free entry and exit.

4. Perfect dissemination of information.

B. **Price/Output Decisions Under Monopolistic Competition:** Profit maximization requires that firms operate at a point where marginal revenue equals marginal cost.

1. Monopolistic competition causes zero economic profits in the long-run because $P = AR = AC$.

2. Equilibrium prices are found within a range.

    a. The high-price/low-output solution is the point of tangency between the LRAC curve and a new firm demand curve created through a parallel leftward shift in the original (monopoly) demand curve.

    b. The low-price/high-output solution is the point of tangency between the minimum LRAC point and a new horizontal firm demand curve.

        (1) This is also the perfectly competitive solution.

3. Average cost is higher with monopolistic competition than in the case of pure competition.

    a. These higher costs can be viewed as the value of product diversity.

III. ILLUSTRATION OF MONOPOLISTICALLY COMPETITIVE EQUILIBRIUM

    A.   **Skyhawk Trailer Company:** The process of price/output adjustment and the concept of equilibrium in monopolistically competitive markets can be further illustrated by example.

        1.   As a first step in the analysis, one might determine the optimal price/output combination if Skyhawk were to take full advantage of its monopoly position and maximize short-run profits

        2.   In the long run, if competition from distinctive products produced by competitors eliminates any potential for economic profits, $P = AC$ at a point above minimum long-run average costs.

        3.   In the long run, if competition from homogenous products produced by competitors eliminates any potential for economic profits, $P = AC$ at minimum long-run average costs.

IV. OLIGOPOLY

    A.   **Characteristics of Oligopoly Markets:** Oligopoly is a market structure with few competitors; individual price/output decisions often produce reactions from rivals. Oligopoly markets feature:

        1.   Few sellers.

        2.   Homogenous or unique products.

        3.   Blockaded entry and exit.

        4.   Imperfect dissemination of information.

    B.   **Price/Output Decisions Under Oligopoly:** Under oligopoly, a price change by one firm often induces price changes by other firms.

        1.   By changing its price, a firm shifts from one demand curve to another, rather than moving along a single demand curve.

        2.   Despite oligopolist uncertainty regarding the reactions of competitors, economic profits are typical because $P = AR > AC$.

C.   **Cartel Arrangements:** A cartel is an explicit agreement among competitors not to compete in order to enhance collective profitability.

    1.   Collusion is a covert or informal agreement among competitors to fix price and output levels.

D.   **Price Leadership:** With price leadership, one firm tacitly establishes itself as the industry leader, and all other firms follow its pricing policy.

    1.   The leader faces a price/output problem similar to a monopolist, while the other firms face a competitive price/output problem under the "dominant firm" price leadership model.

E.   **Kinked Demand Curve:** According to this theory of oligopoly pricing, rival firms are assumed to follow any price decrease so as to maintain market share, but refrain from following price increases, thereby allowing their market share to increase at the expense of the firm making the initial price increase.

    1.   A discontinuity in the marginal revenue curve associated with a kink in the demand curve explains the price rigidity of some oligopolistic markets.

V.   NONPRICE COMPETITION

A.   **Advantages of Nonprice Competition:** Oligopolists often use nonprice competition to boost demand through product innovation, advertising, personal selling, and so on.

    1.   Although competitors often quickly match price cuts, innovative nonprice competition is difficult to counter.

B.   **Optimal Level of Advertising:** Profit maximization requires that the net marginal revenue derived from advertising, or any other nonprice method of competition, be set equal to its marginal cost.

    1.   An expansion in advertising is wise so long as the added profit margin gained is sufficient to at least cover promotional expenses.

C.   **Example of Optimal Advertising:** This optimal advertising example shows how marginal analysis can be used to determine an efficient level of nonprice competition.

    1.   The optimal level of advertising is found where the marginal benefits of advertising just equal the marginal costs of advertising.

VI.   GAME THEORY

A.   **Prisoner's Dilemma:** The Prisoner's Dilemma is a classic conflict-of-interest situation: To confess, or not to confess–that is the question. In game theory, there are a number of important broad categories of games.

1.   In a simultaneous-move game, each decision maker makes choices without specific knowledge of competitor counter moves.

2.   In a sequential-move game, decision makers make their move after observing competitor moves.

3.   In a one-shot game, the underlying interaction between competitors occurs only once; in a repeat game, there is an ongoing interaction between competitors.

4.   A dominant strategy results in the best outcome for either decision maker regardless of the action taken by the other.

5.   A secure strategy, sometimes called the maximin strategy, guarantees the best possible outcome given the worst possible scenario.

B.   **Nash Equilibrium:** A Nash equilibrium exists when neither firm can improve its own payoff by unilaterally changing its own strategy.

1.   This is often a business manifestation of the prisoner's dilemma because Nash equilibrium is often inferior from the firms' viewpoint to a collusive outcome where both competitors agree to charge higher prices.

C.   **Nash Bargaining:** A Nash bargaining game is another application of the simultaneous-move, one-shot game.

1.   In Nash bargaining, two competitors or players "bargain" over some item of value.

2.   In a simultaneous-move, one-shot game the players have only one chance to reach an agreement.

D.   **Repeat Games:** Competitors often interact on a continuous basis. In such circumstances, firms are said to be involved in repeat games.

1.   When a competitive game is repeated over and over, firms receive sequential payoffs that shape current and future strategies.

VII.   MARKET STRUCTURE MEASUREMENT

    A.   How are Economic Markets Measured?   An economic market consists of all individuals and firms willing and able to buy or sell competing products during a given time period.

        1.   Large positive cross-price elasticities indicate substitute products and competitors.

    B.   Economic Censuses: Economic censuses by the U.S. Department of Commerce provide a comprehensive view of economic activity across a number of important sectors.

        1.   Census data can be useful to firms, government regulators, and academic researchers.

    C.   How Economic Census Data are Collected and Published: Economic census statistics are collected and published primarily at the "establishment" level of aggregation.

        1.   An establishment is a business or industrial unit at a single physical location that produces or distributes goods or performs services.

        2.   Up to date census information can be obtained on the Internet (http://www.census.gov).

        3.   Census data are organized in ever increasing levels of detail from broad industry groups to narrow product classifications using the using the North American Industry Classification System (NAICS).

VIII. CENSUS MEASURES OF MARKET CONCENTRATION

    A.   Concentration Ratios: Concentration ratios are an empirical measure of the degree of concentration or centralization in productive resources within industries.

        1.   Concentration ratios are commonly measured at the four-firm level using four-digit industry sales data.

        2.   By definition:

$$CR_i = \sum_{i=1}^{n} X_i,$$

here CR is a concentration ratio for the ith number of firms and X_i is a relative percentage measure of firm input or output (employment, sales, etc.).

3. If the four largest firms account for 80 per cent of industry sales, then the four firm concentration ratio (CR_4) is 80.

B. **Herfindahl Hirschmann Index (HHI):** Is a measure of market concentration that measures market share inequality among all firms in the industry:

$$HHI = \sum_{i=1}^{n} \left(\frac{Firm\ Sales_i}{Industry\ Sales} \times 100 \right)^2$$

1. HHI = 10,000 for a monopoly.

2. HHI → 0 for a perfectly competitive industry.

C. **Limitations of Concentration Ratios and HHI Information:** Among the important limitations of concentration ratio data are:

1. The Census is notoriously slow in collecting data.

2. Only domestic production is considered, thereby ignoring possible foreign competition.

3. Only national concentration ratios are published. This ignores the regional character of many markets.

4. Competitive pressures are measured only imperfectly because even a few firms in an industry can compete vigorously.

5. Despite limitations, concentration ratios sometimes provide a useful measure of competitive pressure in industry.

IX. **COMPETITIVE STRATEGY IN MONOPOLISTIC COMPETITION AND OLIGOPOLY MARKETS**

A. **Competitive Strategy in Imperfectly Competitive Markets:** Not all industries offer the same potential for sustained profitability; not all firms are equally capable of exploiting the profit potential that is available.

1. An effective competitive strategy in imperfectly competitive markets must be founded on the firm's competitive advantage.

2. A competitive advantage is a unique or rare ability to create, distribute, or service products valued by customers.

    a. It is the business-world analog to what economists call comparative advantage, or when one nation or region of the country is better suited to the production of one product than to the production of some other product.

3. Above-normal rates of return require a comparative advantage in production, distribution, or marketing that cannot easily be copied.

    a. Such success is difficult to achieve and is often rather fleeting.

B. **Most Profitable Companies in America:** Business profit rates for a sample of top performing large firms demonstrate that market leaders earn truly extraordinary profits.

1. Superior performers clearly are doing something faster, better, or cheaper than the competition. Wonderful businesses tend to have:

    a. strong franchises

    b. enjoy pricing flexibility

    c. high ROE

    d. high cash flow

    e. owner-oriented management

    f. predictable earnings growth

    g. little regulation

2. Since 1900, the rate of return on common stocks has averaged roughly 10 per cent per year.

a.   Steady returns of 15 per cent to 20 per cent per year are very rare over extended periods.

b.   When business profits are measured using the ROE measure, 12 per cent per year is the approximate average business profit rate.

   (1)   A correspondence between the average ROE and average investor returns is to be expected.

   (2)   Firms must generate a 12 per cent profit rate if investors are to earn a 12 per cent rate of return.

C.   **When Large Size is a *Disadvantage:*** When diseconomies of scale are operative, larger firms suffer a cost disadvantage when compared to smaller rivals.

1.   Smaller firms are then able to translate the benefits of small size into a distinct competitive advantage.

2.   The trend towards a higher level of efficiency for smaller companies has become widespread. Many larger companies find that meeting the needs of the customer sometimes requires a dramatic downsizing of the large-scale organization.

D.   **Threat of Potential Competition:** Imitation may be the sincerest form of flattery, but it is also the most effective enemy of above-normal rates of return.

1.   Regression to the mean is the rule rather than the exception for above-normal corporate profit rates over time.

2.   Price and nonprice methods of competition are often vigorous, even in imperfectly competitive industries with few active or potential competitors.

X.   **SUMMARY**

PROBLEMS & SOLUTIONS

P11.1 Market Structure Concepts. *Identify each of the following characteristics as typical of monopolistic competition and/or oligopoly market structures, and explain why.*

    A.   *Downward sloping industry demand curves.*

    B.   *Kinked firm demand curves.*

    C.   *Differentiated output.*

    D.   *High barriers to entry.*

    E.   *Excess profits in long-run equilibrium.*

P11.1 Solution

    A.   Both monopolistic competition and oligopoly. Both monopolistically competitive and oligopoly market structures are characterized by downward sloping industry demand curves. Downward sloping industry demand curves result from the law of diminishing marginal utility discussed earlier in the book.

    B.   Oligopoly. Kinked firm demand curves in oligopoly markets reflect competitor matching of price cuts, but a failure by competitors to match price increases. This stems from the oligopoly firm's desire to maintain market share, and results in somewhat sticky market prices.

    C.   Both monopolistic competition and oligopoly. Monopolistic competition and oligopoly markets are characterized by a lack of competition from identical substitutes. Differentiated output is a key characteristic of both types of market structure.

    D.   Oligopoly. High barriers to entry limit rivals' ability to offer close substitutes. High barriers to entry are a key characteristic of oligopoly markets.

    E.   Oligopoly. Excess profits in long-run equilibrium reflect the effects of high barriers to entry. They are observed in oligopoly market structures, but not in those markets characterized as monopolistically competitive.

P11.2 Equilibrium. *Indicate whether each of the following statements is true or false and why.*

    A.   *Equilibrium in oligopoly markets requires that firms be operating at the point where marginal revenue equals marginal cost.*

B. *A high ratio of distribution cost to total cost tends to increase competition by widening the geographic area over which any individual producer can compete.*

C. *The price elasticity of demand tends to fall as new competitors introduce substitute products.*

D. *An efficiently functioning cartel achieves the monopoly price/output combination.*

E. *An increase in price advertising tends to increase the slope of firm demand curves.*

P11.2 SOLUTION

A. True. Stable equilibrium in all market structures requires that firms operate at the point where marginal revenue equals marginal cost.

B. False. A low ratio of distribution cost to total cost tends to increase competition by widening the geographic area over which any individual producer can compete.

C. False. The price elasticity of demand rises as new competitors introduce substitute products.

D. True. A perfectly functioning cartel achieves the monopoly price-output combination.

E. False. An increase in price advertising decreases the slope of individual firm demand curves.

P11.3 *Monopolistically Competitive Equilibrium.* Information Systems, Inc., is a small supplier of computer software information systems to hospitals.

A. *Use ISI's price, output, and weekly total cost data to complete the following table:*

Price	Output	Total Revenue	Marginal Revenue	Total Cost	Marginal Cost	Average Cost
$7,500	0	$0	--	$2,500	--	--
5,000	1			5,000		
3,500	2			7,000		
2,800	3			8,100		
2,400	4			9,600		
2,000	5			12,500		
1,700	6			16,500		

B.   *What is the monopolistically competitive high-price/low-output equilibrium?*

C.   *What is the monopolistically competitive low-price/high-output equilibrium?*

P11.3   SOLUTION

   A.

Price	Output	Total Revenue	Marginal Revenue	Total Cost	Marginal Cost	Average Cost
$7,500	0	$0	--	$2,500	--	--
5,000	1	5,000	$5,000	5,000	$2,500	$5000
3,500	2	7,000	2,000	7,000	2,000	3,500
2,800	3	8,400	1,400	8,100	1,100	2,700
2,400	4	9,600	1,200	9,600	1,500	2,400
2,000	5	10,000	400	12,500	2,900	2,500
1,700	6	10,200	200	16,500	4,000	2,750

   B.   The monopolistically competitive high-price/low-output equilibrium is at P = AC = $3,500, Q = 2 and π = TR - TC = 0. No excess profits are being earned, and there would be no incentive for either expansion or contraction because MR = MC = $2,000. Such an equilibrium is typical of monopolistically competitive industries where each individual firm retains some pricing discretion in the long-run.

   C.   The monopolistically competitive low-price/high-output equilibrium is at P = AC = $2,400, Q = 4 and π = TR - TC = 0. No excess profits are being earned, and there would be no incentive for either expansion or contraction. This is similar to the perfectly competitive equilibrium. (Note that MR < MC and average cost is rising for Q > 4.)

P11.4   Short-run Equilibrium. *CATV, Inc., has been granted a limited-term exclusive license to operate a cable television system in Jackson, Wyoming. Recent operating experience in similar locations suggests a close relation between the monthly price for basic service and the number of residential subscribers.*

   A.   *Complete the following table based on CATV's projected price, output, and monthly total cost data:*

Price	Output (000)	Total Revenue	Marginal Revenue ($000)	Total Cost ($000)	Marginal Cost ($000)
$50	0			$0	
40	1			20	
30	2			40	
25	3			60	
20	4			80	
15	5			100	

B. *Calculate the short-run equilibrium monopoly price/output combination and profit level.*

C. *Calculate the long-run equilibrium price/output combination and profit level if competitive bidding for the franchise resulted in a perfectly competitive market outcome.*

P11.4 SOLUTION

A.

Price	Output (000)	Total Revenue	Marginal Revenue ($000)	Total Cost ($000)	Marginal Cost ($000)
$50	0	$0	--	$0	--
40	1	40	$40	20	$20
30	2	60	20	40	20
25	3	75	15	60	20
20	4	80	5	80	20
15	5	75	-5	100	20

B. The profit maximizing activity level is found where MR = MC. As a monopoly, MR = MC = $20,000 at the Q = 2(000) activity level. This implies P = $30 and π = TR = TC = $60 - $40 = $20,000 per month.

C. The perfectly competitive equilibrium occurs where P = MC = AC and zero excess profits are earned, and TR = TC. Here, MR = MC = $20(000) and TR = TC = $80(000) at Q = 4(000) units per month, with P = $20 and π = TR - TC = $0 per month.

P11.5   ***Market Share Analysis.***   *No-reservation (shuttle) airline passenger service is currently provided in the Washington, D.C. to New York city-pair market by only three firms. Weekly output measured in passengers flown and the marginal cost per passenger are as follows:*

	Marginal Cost of Service:		
Weekly Output (000,000)	*Apple Airlines, Inc. (A)*	*Big Bird, Inc. (B)*	*Continuity Airlines, Ltd. (C)*
1	$40	$20	$50
2	30	25	40
3	25	30	45
4	35	35	55
5	50	40	65
6	60	50	75

The current fare (market price) of $45 cannot be raised given the threat of competitor entry. Nevertheless, each airline is able to greatly expand service without lowering prices. Thus, P = MR = $45.

A.   *Calculate current industry output and the market share of each airline.*

B.   *Calculate industry output if the introduction of a high-speed passenger train forces airline industry prices down to $35.*

P11.5   SOLUTION

A.   Each industry participant will produce to the point where MR = MC, but never where MR < MC. Given P = MR = $45, each firm will produce such that MC = MR = $45. A total Q = 12 units will be produced as follows:

Firm	Output	Market Share
Apple Airlines (A)	4	33%
Big Bird, Inc. (B)	5	42%
Continuity Airlines, Ltd. (C)	3	25%
Total	12	100%

B.   Following a decrease in industry prices to P = MR = $35, industry output will fall to Q = 8 distributed as follows:

Firm	Output	Market Share
Apple Airlines (A)	4	50%
Big Bird, Inc. (B)	4	50%
Continuity Airlines, Ltd. (C)	0	0%
Total	8	100%

Note that a fare reduction has the most severe effect on Continuity, the high-cost carrier.

P11.6 ***Monopolistically Competitive Equilibrium.*** Sifuentes Foundry, Inc., is a medium-sized foundry specializing in heavy duty pipe for industrial use. Sifuentes demand and cost information are as follows:

$$P = \$4,500 - Q \qquad \text{(Demand)}$$

$$MR = \partial TR/\partial Q = \$4,500 - \$2Q \qquad \text{(Marginal Revenue)}$$

$$TC = \$150,000 + \$400Q \qquad \text{(Total Cost)}$$

$$MC = \partial TC/\partial Q = \$400 \qquad \text{(Marginal Cost)}$$

where Q is output (thousand feet of heavy gauge pipe), P is price, MR is marginal revenue, TC is total costs and MC is marginal cost. Both cost functions include a normal return of 12% on capital investment.

A. Determine the profit-maximizing price/output combination and profit level.

B. Compute price, output and profits under the assumption that Sifuentes seeks to maximize revenue. Assuming that Sifuentes operates in a monopolistically competitive industry, is the industry in equilibrium?

C. If not, what output, price, and economic profits will occur in equilibrium? Assume equilibrium occurs through a parallel leftward shift in the demand curve. (Hint: The slope of the average cost curve $\partial AC/\partial Q = -\$150,000/Q^2$.)

D. Calculate Sifuentes' new equilibrium demand curve.

P11.6 SOLUTION

A. Set MR = MC to determine the profit-maximizing level of output:

$$MR = MC$$

$$\$4,500 - \$2Q = \$400$$

$$2Q = 4,100$$

$$Q = 2,050 \text{ units}$$

$$P = \$4,500 - Q$$

$$= 4,500 - 2,050$$

$$= \$2,450$$

$$\pi = TR - TC$$

$$= \$4,500Q - Q^2 - \$150,000 - \$400Q$$

$$= -\$150,000 + \$4,100Q - Q^2$$

$$= -150,000 + 4,100(2,050) - 2,050^2$$

$$= \$4,052,500$$

(*Note*: Profits are decreasing for Q > 2,050, thus Q = 2,050 is a profit maximum).

B.   Set MR = 0 to determine the revenue-maximizing level of output:

$$MR = \$0$$

$$4,500 - 2Q = 0$$

$$2Q = 4,500$$

$$Q = 2,250$$

$$P = \$4,500 - Q$$

$$= 4,500 - 2,250$$

$$= \$2,250$$

$$\pi = -\$150,000 + \$4,100Q - Q^2$$

$$= -150,000 + 4,100(2,250) - 2,250^2$$

$$= \$4,012,500$$

No, the industry is not in equilibrium. Under monopolistic competition, only normal profits can be earned in equilibrium. Sifuentes is earning substantial economic profits.

(*Note*: Total revenue is falling for $Q > 2,250$, thus $Q = 2,250$ is a revenue maximum.)

C. Sifuentes' economic profits will attract new firms to the foundry industry. These new firms will attract business away from Sifuentes, with the result being that Sifuentes' demand curve will shift in a leftward direction until P = AC and economic profits are eliminated. This process is described graphically below. (Note: Here there is no low-price/high-output equilibrium point because the AC curve declines continuously, i.e., there is no minimum AC point.)

Algebraically, we can determine equilibrium output, price and profit by following a few simple steps:

Step 1: The problem specifies that the demand curve shifts in a parallel fashion, so the demand curve intercept changes but the slope remains constant and equal to -1, so the new demand curve is Q = a - P. We do not need to determine the intercept a at this point because we are only interested in the slope of the new demand curve.

Step 2: Find the point of tangency between the AC curve and the demand or AR curve. This occurs where the slope of the AC curve (given as $\partial AC/\partial Q = -150,000/Q^2$) equals the slope of the new demand curve:

$$\frac{\text{Average cost}}{\text{curve slope}} = \frac{\text{New demand}}{\text{curve slope}}$$

$$\frac{-150,000}{Q^2} = -1$$

$$Q^2 = 150,000$$

$$Q = \sqrt{150,000}$$

$$Q = 387.3 \text{ units}$$

Step 3: In equilibrium,

$$P = AC$$

$$= \frac{\$150,000 + \$400Q}{Q}$$

$$= \frac{150,000 + 400(387.3)}{387.3}$$

$$= \$787.30$$

D.   Step 4: Because P = AR = AC, excess profits in equilibrium are zero.

Because Q = 387.3, P = \$787.30 and π = 0. Another point on the linear demand curve is P = \$787.30 and Q = 387.3, is where Q = a - P (and b = -1). Thus,

$$387.3 = a - 787.3$$

$$a = 1,174.6$$

Therefore, Q = 1,174.6 - P represents Sifuentes' new equilibrium demand curve.

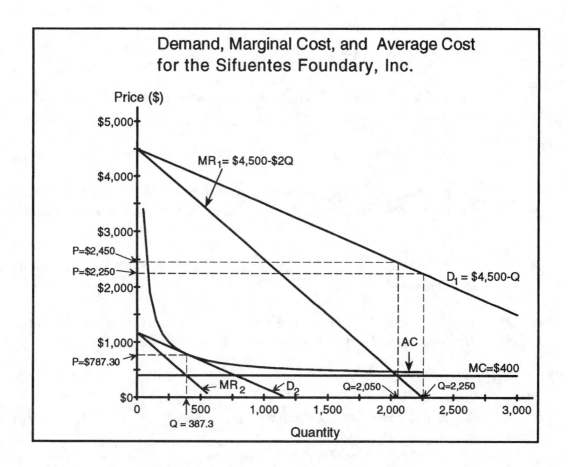

Demand, Marginal Cost, and Average Cost for the Sifuentes Foundary, Inc.

Price ($)

$5,000

$MR_1 = \$4,500 - \$2Q$

$4,000

$3,000

P=$2,450

P=$2,250

$2,000

$D_1 = \$4,500 - Q$

$1,000

P=$787.30

AC

MC=$400

$0

MR$_2$ D_2 Q=2,050   Q=2,250

0   500   1,000   1,500   2,000   2,500   3,000

Q = 387.3

Quantity

P11.7 **Kinked Demand Curve.** *Quality Electronics, Inc., faces the following segmented demand curve for a new printed circuit board:*

<u>Over the range 0 - 50(000) units:</u>

$$P_1 = \$300 - \$1Q$$

$$MR_1 = \partial TR_1/\partial Q = \$300 - \$2Q$$

<u>When output exceeds 50(000) units:</u>

$$P_2 = \$400 - \$3Q$$

$$MR_2 = \partial TR_2/\partial Q = \$400 - \$6Q$$

The company cost functions are:

$$TC = \$250 + \$50Q + \$1Q^2$$

$$MC = \partial TC/\partial Q = \$50 + \$2Q$$

where P is price (in dollars), Q is output (in thousands) and TC is total cost (in thousands of dollars).

A.   *Graph the company's demand, marginal revenue and marginal cost curves.*

B.   *How would you describe the market structure of QEI's industry? Explain your answer in some detail, including an explanation of why the demand curve takes the shape given above.*

C.   *What is the firm's optimal price and quantity, and what will its profits or losses be at this output?*

D.   *How much could marginal costs rise before the optimal price would increase? How much could they fall before the optimal price would decrease?*

P11.7   SOLUTION

A.   A graph of revenue and cost relations for Quality Electronics, Inc. is as follows:

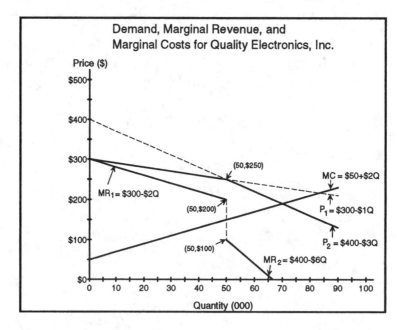

B.   The firm is in an oligopolistic industry. It faces a kinked demand curve meaning that competitors react to price reductions by cutting their own prices, thereby causing the segment of the demand curve below the kink to be relatively inelastic. Price increases are not followed, causing the portion of the demand curve above the kink to be relatively elastic.

C. An examination of the graph indicates that the marginal cost curve passes through the gap in the marginal revenue curve. Graphically, this indicates that optimal P = $250 and Q = 50(000).

    Analytically,

$$MR_1 = \$300 - \$2Q \qquad\qquad Q \leq 50(000)$$

$$MR_2 = \$400 - \$6Q \qquad\qquad Q > 50(000)$$

$$MC = \$50 + \$2Q$$

If one solves for the output levels where MR = MC, it becomes obvious that MR_1 > MC over the range $Q \leq 50(000)$, and MR_2 < MC for the range $Q \geq 50(000)$. Therefore, we QEI will produce 50(000) units of output and market them at P = $250.

    And finally,

$$\pi = P \times Q - TC$$

$$= \$250(50) - \$250 - \$50(50) - \$1(50^2)$$

$$= \$7,250(000) \text{ or } \$7,250,000$$

D. At Q = 50(000),

$MR_1 = \$300 - \$2Q$	$MR_2 = \$400 - \$6Q$
$= \$300 - \$2(50)$	$= \$400 - \$6(50)$
$= \$200$	$= \$100$

This implies that if marginal costs at Q = 50(000) exceed $200, the optimal price would increase.

    Conversely, if marginal costs at Q = 50(000) fall below $100, the optimal price would decrease. So long as marginal cost at Q = 50(000) is in the range of $100 to $200, QEI will have no incentive to change its price.

P11.8   ***Supply Reactions.*** *Computer Management Corporation specializes in the development of management information and decision assistance computer programs. CMC has just finished development of a new software package that will permit small retail firms to computerize their inventory management at a lower cost than has previously been possible. On the basis of sales data for similar software packages, management believes that demand for the product will be greatly influenced by the reactions of other computer software companies to the introduction of CMC's new product. No reaction will result in the monthly demand and marginal revenue functions:*

$$P = \$150 - \$0.1Q$$

$$MR = \partial TR/\partial Q = \$150 - \$0.2Q$$

A major reaction will lead to the more elastic curves:

$$P = \$130 - \$0.4Q$$

$$MR = \partial TR/\partial Q = \$130 - \$0.8Q$$

CMC's total monthly cost for marketing this product is composed of $3,000 additional administrative expenses and $50 per unit for production and distribution costs. That is, the relevant total cost and marginal cost functions are given by the expression:

$$TC = \$3,000 + \$50Q$$

$$MC = \partial TC/\partial Q = \$50$$

A.   *What is the profit-maximizing price for CMC's product, assuming no competitor reaction?*

B.   *Calculate this price based on the assumption competitors will react.*

C.   *In light of CMC's cost conditions, and absent any substantial barriers to entry, which scenario is more likely?*

P11.8   SOLUTION

A.   With no competitor reaction, set:

$$MR = MC$$

$$\$150 - \$0.2Q = \$50$$

$$0.2Q = 100$$

$$Q = 500$$

$$P = \$150 - \$0.1(500)$$

$$= \$100$$

B.   With a major competitor reaction, set:

$$MR = MC$$

$$\$130 - \$0.8Q = \$50$$

$$0.8Q = 80$$

$$Q = 100$$

$$P = \$130 - \$0.4(100)$$

$$= \$90$$

C.   In this situation, a reaction is probable. Note that:

$$MC = \$50$$

Therefore, CMC prices of P = $100 (in part A) or P = $90 (in part B) are both substantially above marginal costs, and likely to attract substantial entry. Still, the industry does not have the potential to achieve a stable perfectly competitive long-run equilibrium because average costs will decline continuously as output expands. Therefore, a monopolistically competitive long-run equilibrium where P = AC > MC and no excess profits seems likely.

Of course, in real world markets where software packages enjoy copyright protection, and assuming that copyright laws are effectively enforced, software publishing companies may have at least a short-run opportunity to earn above-normal profits.

P11.9 **Price Leadership.** *In the inland waterways shipping industry, bulk carriers (barges) are chartered on an annual basis to haul grain, oil, ore, and other bulk commodities. As far as the shippers are concerned, the service provided by barges of any given class are homogeneous products. Industry demand for carriers varies over time, depending on grain and oil movements. At present, industry demand is estimated as:*

$$Q = 40,000 - 0.2P$$

The industry consists of one large firm, Mississippi Barge Transport Company (MBT), and ten smaller firms of roughly equal size. MBT is the industry leader with regard to pricing decisions, and its marginal cost curve is given by:

$$MC_L = -\$20,000 + \$6Q$$

The following firms' marginal cost curve, derived by summing the MC curves of the ten follower firms, is given by:

$$MC_F = \$44,000 + \$4Q$$

It must be stressed that these curves are approximations, empirically derived over a limited range of outputs. If observations were available over the full range of outputs, the curves would not be linear. However, these are good approximations over probable output ranges.

MBT has several interesting characteristics. First, it controls most port facilities, and has a reputation for fairness and good business judgment. Following firms are permitted to use these facilities on a fee basis, but this permission could be terminated. And finally, MBT has great financial strength. Should the need arise, it could conduct an extended price war.

A.   *Construct a graph showing:*

  (i)   *The industry demand curve,*

  (ii)   *The leader's and the followers' marginal cost curves.*

  (iii) *The leader's demand and marginal revenue curves. To construct this graph, make the following calculations and use them to help draw the relevant curves:*

$$Q_F, \text{ when } P = \$113,333$$

$$Q_F, \text{ when } P = \$60,000$$

$$Q_L, \text{ when } P = \$113,333$$

$$Q_L, \text{ when } P = \$60,000$$

B.   *What price will MBT establish, and what will be its output at this price?*

C.   *How many units of output will the following firms supply?*

D.   *Is price leadership as described here consistent with the kinked demand curve theory of oligopoly behavior?*

E.   *Reconsider your graph. Could a price leadership situation exist, given the other facts of this problem, if MC_L were to lie above MC_F for all output quantities where the MC_F curve is below the industry demand curve?*

P11.9   **SOLUTION**

A.   (i)   The industry demand curve is simply:

$$Q = 40,000 - 0.2P$$

$$0.2P = 40,000 - Q$$

$$P = \$200,000 - \$5Q$$

(ii)   The following firms will take price as a given, then determine their outputs by setting MR = MC. Because followers take P as given, then P = MR = AR, and each following firm faces a horizontal demand curve once the leader establishes a price. Therefore, MC = MR = P, or P = MC.

When, P = \$113,333, the followers set P = 113,333 = MC_F:

$$P = MC_F$$

$$\$113,333 = \$44,000 + \$4Q_F$$

$$4Q_F = 69,333$$

$$Q_F = 17,333$$

When, P = $60,000,

$$P = \$60,000 = \$44,000 + \$4Q_F = MC_F$$

$$4Q_F = 16,000$$

$$Q_F = 4,000$$

From this, one has two points on the linear MC_F curve, and thus, can easily graph it.

(iii)   Whatever market demand is not supplied by followers, the leader can supply. Therefore, the leader's demand is comprised of residual demand. When P = $113,333, followers supply 17,333 units, which is the entire amount demanded at this price. Thus, the leader can supply only zero, because:

Leader demand = Market demand - Follower supply

$$Q_L = 17,333 - 17,333$$

$$= 0$$

This establishes one point on the leader's demand curve -- the vertical axis intercept, P = $113,333 and $Q_L = 0$. When P = $60,000, followers supply 4,000 units. The leader will then supply:

$$Q_L = 28,000 - 4,000$$

$$= 24,000$$

This establishes another point on the leader's demand curve: P = $60,000 and $Q_L = 24,000$. With these two points on can construct the leader's demand curve. Note that at any P < $44,000, followers drop out and the leader has the entire market demand to itself. Thus, D_L is kinked at P = $44,000. However, note that these calculations are only valid as linear approximations.

One can also find the leader's demand curve directly:

$$Q_L = \text{Total demand - Followers' supply}$$

where followers' supply S_F, is given by the relations:

$$MC = P = \$44,000 + \$4Q$$

or

$$Q = 0.25P - 11,000$$

and, therefore, leader demand is:

$$Q_L = 40,000 - 0.2P - (0.25P - 11,000)$$

$$= 51,000 - 0.45P$$

or

$$P = \$113,333 - \$2.22Q$$

Also note that:

$$MR_L = \partial TR / \partial Q = \$113,333 - \$4.44Q$$

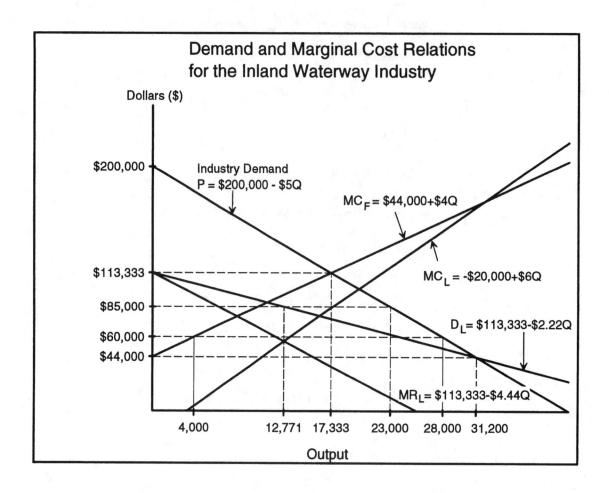

B. To determine a profit-maximizing output level, MBT will set $MR_L = MC_L$, where:

$$MR_L = \$113{,}333 - \$4.44Q_L = -\$20{,}000 + \$6Q_L = MC_L$$

$$10.44Q_L = 133{,}333$$

$$Q_L = 12{,}771 \text{ units}$$

$$P_L = \$113{,}333 - \$2.22Q$$

$$= 113{,}333 - 2.22(12{,}771)$$

$$= \$84{,}981$$

C. Following firms will take the $85,000 price as given, and will supply:

$$S_F = 0.25P - 11,000$$

$$= 0.25(84,981) - 11,000$$

$$= 10,245$$

To check,

$$\text{Industry demand} = \text{Industry supply}$$

$$Q_T = 40,000 - 0.2P = Q_L + Q_F$$

$$40,000 - 0.2(84,981) = 12,771 + 10,245$$

$$23,004 \overset{\checkmark}{\approx} 23,016 \text{ (Rounding error)}$$

D. This type of price leadership is not consistent with the kinked demand theory of oligopoly behavior. Under the kinked demand curve theory, no leader exists and prices are sticky. Under dominant firm price leadership, prices change as the leader's MC curve shifts, and followers behave as though they are strictly price-takers.

Price leadership theory is often quite consistent with reality when one firm is clearly dominant, and following firms are small factors in the market. Kinked demand curve theory is more realistic when no firm dominates, and all firms are relatively large.

E. If MC_L lies above MC_F at the point where $MR_L = MC_L$, the only change that would occur is that the leader would then supply less than half the total market. This situation could still be consistent with price leadership, as explained in Part D. However, the larger and more dominant the leader, the more likely price leadership is to exist.

P11.10 *Price Leadership. The industry supplying precision cast parts to mechanical robot manufacturers is comprised of one large firm and a number of small firms. The large firm acts as a price leader and sets the industry price. The small firms are price followers and can sell all they want at the industry price. The demand curve for the industry is:*

$$Q = 2,000 - 0.1P$$

The total and marginal cost curves for the large firm and the aggregate curves for the smaller firms are as follows:

$$TC_L = \$10,000 + \$2,000Q_L \qquad\qquad MC_L = \partial TC_L/\partial Q_L = \$2,000$$

$$TC_S = \$1,000Q_S + \$20Q_S^2 \qquad\qquad MC_S = \partial TC_S/\partial Q_S = \$1,000 + \$40Q_S$$

A. *What is the aggregate supply curve of the price followers?*

B. *Determine the relevant demand curve for the large firm.*

C. *Determine the price/output combination that maximizes the price leader's profit. (Note: If $TR_L = \$16,200Q_L - \$8Q_L^2$ then $MR_L = \partial TR_L/\partial Q = \$16,200 - \$16Q_L$.)*

D. *What output would be supplied by the smaller firms?*

P11.10 SOLUTION

A. Because price followers take prices as given, they operate at the output level at which their marginal costs equal price. Therefore,

$$P = MC_S$$

$$= \$1,000 + \$40Q_S$$

or

$$Q_S = -25 + 0.025P.$$

B. The demand curve for the large firm can be calculated algebraically by subtracting the supply curve of the price-following firms from the total industry demand, i.e., $Q_L = Q - Q_S$. Because the supply curve for the price followers is $Q_S = -25 + 0.025P$,

$$Q_L = Q - Q_S$$

$$= 2,000 - 0.1P - (-25 + 0.025P)$$

$$= 2,025 - 0.125P,$$

or

$$P_L = \$16,200 - \$8Q_L$$

C. Set

$$MR_L = MC_L$$

$$\$16{,}200 - \$16Q_L = \$2{,}000$$

$$16Q_L = 14{,}200$$

$$Q_L = 887.5$$

$$P = \$16{,}200 - \$8(887.5)$$

$$= \$9{,}100$$

D. The total quantity supplied by both the large and small firms can be found by substituting the price of $9,100 into the industry demand equation.

$$Q = 2{,}000 - 0.1P$$

$$= 2{,}000 - 0.1(9{,}100)$$

$$= 2{,}000 - 910$$

$$= 1{,}090$$

The total quantity supplied will be 1,090 units. The small firms should supply 1,090 - 887.5 = 202.5 units. At this quantity, their marginal costs will equal their marginal revenue:

$$MC_S = MR_S$$

$$\$1{,}000 + \$40Q = 9{,}100$$

$$40Q = 8{,}100$$

$$Q = 202.5$$

Chapter 12

PRICING PRACTICES

The fundamental prescription of managerial economics is that managers set marginal revenue equal to marginal cost for each product or product line to achieve maximum profits. If the value-maximizing theory of the firm is descriptive of actual business practice, then the pricing practices of success firms must be consistent with profit-maximizing behavior. It is therefore worth asking if the pricing practices of successful firms are consistent with profit maximization. If so, then the value maximization theory of the firm can be taken as relevant. If not, then the value maximization theory of the firm would have to be rejected as a practical guide to managerial practice.

This chapter begins with the observation that markup pricing is the most commonly employed pricing method. When the underlying basis for markup pricing methods is fully understood, these methods can be seen as a practical means for deriving profit-maximizing prices. The optimal markup is large when the underlying price elasticity of demand is low; the optimal markup is small when the underlying price elasticity of demand is high. With multiple markets or customer groups, the potential can exist to enhance profits by charging different prices and different price markups to each relevant market segment. This practice, called price discrimination, is profitable because it allows the firm to enhance revenues without increasing costs. In all instances, profit-maximizing prices are found by setting marginal revenue equal to marginal cost.

CHAPTER OUTLINE

I.   **MARKUP PRICING**

    A.   **Markup Pricing Technology:** Regular prices, discounts, rebates, and coupon promotions are pricing mechanisms used to discover the breadth and depth of customer demand, and to maximize profitability.

    B.   **Markup on Cost:** In cost-plus pricing, the difference between price and cost called profit margin or markup, is expressed as a percentage of cost:

$$\text{Markup on Cost} = \frac{\text{Price} - \text{Cost}}{\text{Cost}}.$$

    C.   **Markup on Price:** In the markup-on-price formula, the profit margin is expressed as a percentage of price:

$$\text{Markup on Price} = \frac{\text{Price} - \text{Cost}}{\text{Price}}.$$

D. **Role of Cost in Markup Pricing:** The standard cost or fully allocated cost concept is often applied to markup pricing policies.

1. Standard costs based on historical accounting costs can be misleading if not adjusted to reflect opportunity costs.

2. During peak periods of full capacity usage, fully allocated costs are relevant.

3. During off-peak periods of less than full capacity usage, only incremental costs are relevant.

E. **Role of Demand in Markup Pricing:** Empirical evidence indicates that firms adjust mark-ups for different products on the basis of varying demand elasticities.

1. Demand sensitivity analysis is used to ensure that mark-ups used in cost-plus pricing result in optimal prices.

II. **MARKUP PRICING AND PROFIT MAXIMIZATION**

A. **Optimal Markup on Cost:** Markup pricing is an efficient means for achieving the profit maximization objective. The profit-maximizing markup on cost is:

$$\text{Optimal markup on cost} = \frac{-1}{\varepsilon_p + 1},$$

here ε_p is the price elasticity of demand.

B. **Optimal Markup on Price:** The profit-maximizing markup on price is:

$$\text{Optimal markup on price} = \frac{-1}{\varepsilon_p}.$$

1. Empirical evidence strongly suggests that firms employ markup pricing strategies in a manner that is consistent with profit maximization.

C. **Another Optimal Markup Example:** In practice, firms often adjust markups on fully allocated costs to be consistent with the profit-maximizing markup on incremental costs.

1.   Both cost definitions and markup percentages must be studied to determine optimal pricing practices.

III.   PRICE DISCRIMINATION

A.   **Definition:** Price discrimination exists whenever different classes of customers are charged different markups for the same product.

1.   Price discrimination exists whenever:

$$\frac{P_1}{P_2} \neq \frac{MC_1}{MC_2}.$$

2.   Price discrimination exists whenever closely-related product prices differ in a way that is not proportional to the differences in the marginal cost of production and distribution.

3.   The objective of price discrimination is to enhance seller profits by setting MR = MC for each customer or customer group.

a.   Price discrimination allows sellers to capture a greater share of the total value of output.

B.   **Requirements for Profitable Price Discrimination:** Two primary requirements for profitable price discrimination are:

1.   The firm must be able to segment the market for a product.

a.   Multiple markets must exist and reselling from one market to another must be prevented.

2.   Different price elasticities of demand for the product must exist in the various submarkets.

C.   **Role Played by Consumers' Surplus:** Consumers' surplus is the difference between the price paid and the value of output to consumers.

1.   Price discrimination results in a transfer of consumers' surplus to producers (sellers).

D. **Degrees of Price Discrimination:** Price discrimination can be encountered in three different orders of magnitude.

  1. First degree: Separate prices for each consumer. This creates maximum profits for sellers.

  2. Second degree: Block-rates or quantity discounts based on usage.

  3. Third degree: Different prices for each customer class defined on the basis of age, sex, income, etc.

    a. Third degree is the most common type of price discrimination.

IV. **PRICE DISCRIMINATION EXAMPLE**

  A. **Price/Output Determination:** A firm that can segment its market maximizes profits by operating in such a way that marginal revenue equals marginal cost in each market segment.

  B. **Comparison With the One-Price Alternative:** Price discrimination increases revenues without affecting cost, thereby increasing profits.

    1. Without price discrimination, MR = MC for all customers as a group.

    2. With price discrimination, MR = MC for each customer or customer segment.

    3. Profitable price discrimination *always* benefits sellers at the expense of at least some customers.

  C. **Graphic Illustration:** Demand and marginal revenue curves for the combined market are drawn as the horizontal sum of submarket demand and marginal revenue curves.

    1. The optimal single price/output combination is indicated where MR = MC for the combined market.

    2. The optimal price/output combination for each market is indicated where MR = MC for each submarket.

    3. Profitable price discrimination allows the firm to better match marginal revenues and marginal costs.

V.   MULTIPLE UNIT PRICING STRATEGIES

   A.   Motivation: When products have different values for different customers, profits can sometimes be enhanced by using multiple unit pricing strategies.

      1.   Multiple unit pricing can result in some combination of per unit and "lump sum" fees.

   B.   Two-Part Pricing: Athletic clubs, time-share vacation resorts, golf courses, and a wide variety of "membership organizations" offer goods and services using two-part pricing.

      1.   A common two-part pricing technique is to charge all customers a fixed "membership" fee per month or per year, plus a per-unit usage charge.

      2.   With two-part pricing, each customer is charged a per-unit fee equal to marginal cost, plus a fixed fee equal to the amount of consumers' surplus generated at that per-unit fee.

   C.   Bundle Pricing: Another way firms with market power enhance profits is by a variant of two-part pricing called bundle pricing.

      1.   When significant consumers' surplus exists, profits can sometimes be enhanced if products are purchased together as a single package or bundle of goods or services.

         a.   Bundles can be of a single product, like soft drinks or legal services, or they can be comprised of closely related goods and services.

      2.   The optimal bundle price is derived in a manner similar to the optimal two-part price calculation.

         a.   The optimal level of output is determined by setting price equal to marginal cost, and solving for quantity.

         b.   The optimal bundle price is a single lump sum amount equal to the total area under the demand curve at that point.

VI.   MULTIPLE-PRODUCT PRICING

   A.   Demand Interrelations: Multiple product pricing analysis can be complicated by elaborate relationships between output demand and production costs.

       1.   Cross-marginal revenue terms indicate how revenues generated by one product are affected by a change in sales for other products.

   B.   **Production Interrelations:** Products may be produced in a fixed or variable ratio.

       1.   Joint products may compete for the resources of the firm or be complementary.

   C.   **Joint Products Produced in Variable Proportions:** If two or more products can be produced in variable proportions, they can be considered as individually distinct products.

       1.   For joint products produced in variable proportion, profit maximization requires $MR_A = MC_A$ and $MR_B = MC_B$.

   D.   **Joint Products Produced in Fixed Proportions:** If two or more products must be produced in a fixed ratio, they are joint products and must be considered as a package of output.

       1.   For joint products A and B where $Q = A = B$, profit maximization requires setting:

$$MR_A + MR_B = MC_Q$$

VII.   **EXAMPLE OF JOINT PRODUCT PRICING**

   A.   **Joint Products Without Excess Byproduct:** In this instance, profit-maximization requires setting $MR_A + MR_B = MC_Q$.

       1.   Marginal revenue from each byproduct makes a contribution toward covering MC_Q.

   B.   **Joint Production With Excess Byproduct (Dumping):** As previously, profit-maximization requires setting $MR_A + MR_B = MC_Q$. With excess byproduct, dumping occurs because there is insufficient byproduct demand at a price that yields a positive marginal revenue.

       1.   Marginal revenue from the primary product covers the marginal cost of production.

       2.   Marginal revenue from the byproduct is set equal to zero, the byproduct's marginal cost.

VIII.   TRANSFER PRICING

A.   **Transfer Pricing Problem:** Setting an appropriate price for the transfer of goods and services among divisions of a single firm can become complicated.

   1.   Vertical integration occurs when a single company controls various links in the production chain from basic inputs to final output.

B.   **Transfer Pricing for Products Without External Markets:** When transferred products cannot be sold in external markets, the marginal cost of the transferring division is the optimal transfer price.

   1.   Without external markets, marginal cost represents the relevant opportunity cost and appropriate transfer price.

C.   **Transfer Pricing for Products with Perfectly Competitive External Markets:** When transferred products can be sold in perfectly competitive external markets, the external market price is the optimal transfer price.

   1.   With perfectly competitive external markets, the external market price represents the relevant opportunity cost for within company use of a product.

D.   **Transfer Pricing for Products with Imperfectly Competitive External Markets:** When transferred products can be sold in imperfectly competitive external markets, the optimal transfer price is the marginal revenue derived from the combined internal and external markets.

   1.   With imperfectly competitive external markets, marginal revenue represents the relevant opportunity cost for within company use of a product.

IX.   GLOBAL TRANSFER PRICING EXAMPLE

A.   **Profit Maximization for an Integrated Firm:** The optimal transfer price ensures operation at the profit-maximizing activity level.

B.   **Transfer Pricing With No External Market:** The optimal transfer price ensures a perfect balance of within-firm supply and demand at the profit-maximizing activity level.

C. **Competitive External Market With Excess Internal Demand:** In the case of excess internal demand, the firm will employ inputs produced internally and by external suppliers.

D. **Competitive External Market With Excess Internal Supply:** In the case of excess internal supply, the firm will supply inputs to both the internal and external market.

X. **RIDDLES IN PRICING PRACTICE**

A. **Motivation:** Economic reasoning is a powerful tool that can be used to understand and improve pricing practices. Still, important mysteries remain in pricing practice.

1. Economists and marketing scholars don't know *why* buyers can be lured by a 99¢ price, and be turned off by a $1 price.

2. The relevance of input from psychology and other social and physical sciences should not be minimized. The ongoing design of effective pricing practices benefits from knowledge gained in a wide variety of areas.

XI. **SUMMARY**

PROBLEMS & SOLUTIONS

P12.1 *Optimal Markup.* Marketing consultant John Blutarsky as been retained to assess the pricing practices of Animal House Furniture, Inc. As Blutarsky's assistant, use the following demand elasticity estimates to calculate the profit-maximizing markup on cost and markup on price for a variety of sofa and easy chair products.

Furniture Item	Price Elasticity	Optimal Markup on Cost	Optimal Markup on Price
A.	-1		
B.	-4		
C.	-8		
D.	-20		
E.	-50		

P12.1   SOLUTION

Furniture Item	Price Elasticity	Optimal Markup on Cost	Optimal Markup on Price
A.	-1	----%	100.0%
B.	-4	33.3%	25.0%
C.	-8	14.3%	12.5%
D.	-20	5.3%	5.0%
E.	-50	2.0%	2.0%

P12.2 *Optimal Markup on Cost.* Air California is a regional airline serving a large number of west coast markets. Using recent operating data, the company wants to determine a profit maximizing price for service provided between the Orange County, CA, and Sacramento, CA, airports. During recent weeks, the company found that a one-way fare reduction from $75 to $69 had increased route traffic from 50 to 60 passengers per flight. On average, the company projects a cost per departure of $2,484.

A.   Using the $75 price as a base, calculate the point price elasticity of demand for the airline service. (Assume a linear demand curve.)

B.   In light of operating costs, will the new $69 fare result in an optimal markup on cost? If so, why? If not, why not?

P12.2   SOLUTION

A. $\varepsilon_P = \partial Q/\partial P \times P/Q$

$$= \frac{(60 - 50)}{(\$69 - \$75)} \times \frac{\$75}{50}$$

$$= -2.5$$

B.   Yes, the marginal cost per passenger is $41.40 (= 2,484/60). Given P = $69, the implied markup on cost is:

$$\text{Markup on cost} = \frac{\text{Price} - \text{Cost}}{\text{Cost}}$$

$$= \frac{\$69 - \$41.40}{\$41.40}$$

$$= 0.67 \text{ or } 67\%$$

Given MC = $41.40, the optimal price is:

$$P = MC\left(\frac{1}{1 + \dfrac{1}{\varepsilon_p}}\right)$$

$$= \$41.40 \left(\frac{1}{1 + \dfrac{1}{-2.5}}\right)$$

$$= \$69$$

Alternatively, using the optimal markup-on-cost formula:

$$\text{Optimal markup} \atop \text{on cost} = \frac{-1}{\varepsilon_p + 1}$$

$$= \frac{-1}{-2.5 + 1}$$

$$= 0.67 \text{ or } 67\%$$

P12.3   ***Optimal Markup on Price.*** *Quick Lube, Inc., provides while-you-wait oil lubrication services to customers throughout the Cleveland, Ohio market. In an effort to expand its customer base, Quick Lube recently offered $5 off its regular $25 price. Customer response was enthusiastic, with sales rising to 1,100 units from 700 units per week.*

    A.   *Calculate the arc price elasticity of demand for Quick Lube service.*

    B.   *Assume that the arc price elasticity (from part A) is the best available estimate of the point price elasticity of demand. Calculate Quick Lube's optimal markup on price.*

P12.3   **SOLUTION**

    A. $$E_P = \frac{\Delta Q}{\Delta P} \times \frac{P_2 + P_1}{Q_2 + Q_1}$$

$$= \frac{1,100 - 700}{\$20 - \$25} \times \frac{\$20 + \$25}{1,100 + 700}$$

$$= -2$$

    B.   Given $\varepsilon_P = E_P = -2$, the optimal markup on price is:

$$\text{Optimal Markup} \atop \text{on Price} = \frac{-1}{\varepsilon_P}$$

$$= \frac{-1}{-2}$$

$$= 0.5 \text{ or } 50\%$$

P12.4 ***Optimal Price.*** *Last week, Leo McGarry's Superette offered a 25¢ coupon on 12-packs of Diet Cola, regularly priced at $4. Coupons were used on 40% of all purchases, and resulted in an increase from 400 to 490 cases sold per week.*

    A. *Using the regular $4 price as a base, calculate the point price elasticity of demand for Diet Cola.*

    B. *Calculate the optimal markup on cost for Diet Cola.*

    C. *If McGarry's marginal cost per unit is $3 plus 20¢ in handling costs, calculate the profit-maximizing price on Diet Cola.*

    D. *Using P = $4 and Q = 400 as a base and the point price elasticity of demand formula, calculate expected unit sales, revenues and profits at the profit-maximizing activity level. (Note: For simplicity, assume MC = AVC).*

P12.4 **SOLUTION**

    A. Because coupons were used on 40% of all purchases, the average price reduction was 10¢ (=0.4 × 25¢). Thus,

$$\varepsilon_P \;=\; \partial Q/\partial P \times P/Q$$

$$=\; \frac{(490 - 400)}{(\$3.90 - \$4)} \times \frac{\$4}{400}$$

$$=\, \text{-}9$$

    B. Given $\varepsilon_P = \text{-}9$, the optimal markup on cost is:

$$\begin{array}{ll}\text{Optimal markup}\\ \quad\text{on cost}\end{array} \;=\; \frac{-1}{\varepsilon_P + 1}$$

$$=\; \frac{-1}{-9 + 1}$$

$$=\, 0.125 \text{ or } 12.5\%$$

    C. With an optimal markup of 12.5%, Bunker's profit-maximizing price on *Diet Cola* is:

$$\text{Markup} = \frac{\text{Price} - \text{Cost}}{\text{Cost}}$$

$$0.125 = \frac{\text{Price} - \$3.20}{\$3.20}$$

$$0.40 = \text{Price} - 3.20$$

$$\text{Price} = \$3.60$$

D. Expected unit sales at the profit maximizing activity level can be calculated using the point price elasticity formula:

$$\varepsilon_P = \partial Q/\partial P \times P/Q$$

$$-9 = \frac{(Q_2 - 400)}{(\$3.60 - \$4)} \times \frac{\$4}{400}$$

$$3.60 = 0.01(Q_2 - 400)$$

$$360 = Q_2 - 400$$

$$Q_2 = 760 \text{ cases per week}$$

$$TR = P \times Q$$

$$= \$3.60(760)$$

$$= \$2,736 \text{ per week}$$

$$\pi = TR - TC$$

$$= (P - AVC)Q$$

$$= (\$3.60 - \$3.20)760$$

$$= \$304 \text{ per week}$$

P12.5   *Peak Load Pricing. Cregg, Lyman & Moss, Inc., manufacture a battery-powered saw. Due to growing demand during the past few years, CLM has increased plant capacity for the saw to 300,000 units. The firm's expected output for next year was 250,000* *units, but it has received a special order for 100,000 units from a firm outside its normal market. The standard selling price is $50 per unit, but this firm has offered $40 per unit for the special order. Relevant cost data for the saw are as follows:*

Cost Per Unit	
Raw materials	$20
Direct labor	10
Variable overhead	3
Fixed overhead	2

Using the incremental profit framework, should CLM accept the special order?

P12.5   **SOLUTION**

Incremental Revenue calculation:
Price per unit		$ 40
Units		× 100,000
Incremental revenue		$4,000,000

Incremental Cost Calculation:
Raw materials		$2,000,000
Direct labor		1,000,000
Variable overhead		300,000
Opportunity cost:		
Capacity is 300,000		
units; 50,000 units		
of next year's		
expected demand will		
have to be foregone		
if the order is		
accepted:		
Sales revenue	2,500,000	
Variable costs	1,650,000	
Profit lost on		
foregone orders		850,000
Incremental Cost		$4,150,000
Incremental Profit		-$150,000

The firm should not accept the special order, because the incremental profit from the special order is negative.

P12.6   ***Peak Load Pricing.*** *The Modern Appliance Company manufactures an electric mixer-juicer. Sales of the appliance have increased steadily during the previous five years and, because of a recently completed expansion program, annual capacity is now 500,000 units. Production and sales for next year are forecast at 400,000 units, and production costs are estimated as:*

Cost Category	Amount
Materials	$3.00
Direct labor	2.00
Variable indirect labor	1.00
Overhead	1.50
Standard costs per unit	$7.50

In addition to production costs, Modern projects fixed selling expenses and variable warranty repair expenses of 75¢ and 60¢ per unit, respectively. Modern is currently receiving $10 per unit from its wholesale customers (primarily retail appliance stores), and expects this price to hold during the coming year.

After making these projections, Modern received an inquiry about the purchase of a large quantity of mixers-juicers from a discount department store chain. The discount chain's inquiry contained two purchase offers:

Offer 1.   The chain would purchase 80,000 units at $7.30 per unit. These units would bear the Modern label and the Modern warranty would be provided.

Offer 2.   The chain would purchase 120,000 units at $7 per unit. These units would be sold under the buyer's private label and Modern would not provide warranty service.

A.   *Evaluate the effect of each offer on pretax net income for next year.*

B.   *Should other factors be considered in deciding whether to accept one of these offers?*

C.   *Which offer, if either, should Modern accept? Why?*

P12.6   SOLUTION

A.   The incremental net income from the offers can be determined as follows:

	Offer 1		Offer 2	
Unit price		$7.30		$7.00
Unit variable costs:				
Materials	$3.00		$3.00	
Direct labor	2.00		2.00	
Variable indirect				
labor	1.00		1.00	
Variable warranty				
expense	0.60		--	
Unit variable costs		$6.60		$6.00
Unit incremental				
profit		$0.70		$1.00
Units to be sold		× 80,000		× 120,000
Total variable profit				
on units sold at				
special price		$56,000		$120,000
Less variable profit				
lost on regular sales:				
Regular price			$10.00	
Regular variable cost			- 6.60	
Regular variable profit			$3.40	
Units which cannot be				
sold at regular price				
if offer 2 is accepted			× 20,000	
Opportunity cost of lost				
regular sales				$ 68,000
Incremental profit		$56,000		$ 52,000

B.   Other factors to be considered by Modern include:

1.   The image of Modern's quality may be affected by sales of the appliance in the discount chain with Modern's label.

2.   Other buyers may demand the reduced price if Modern accepts Offer 1, and the discount chain undercuts them at the retail price.

3.   The sales lost if Modern accepts Offer 2 may affect future orders from regular customers.

C.   It depends upon how you evaluate the factors discussed in Part B above. The incremental profits of Offer 1 exceed those of Offer 2, but other factors might well dictate that Offer 1 not be accepted.

P12.7   ***Price Discrimination.*** *The Midcontinent Railroad Company runs a freight train daily between Indianapolis and Chicago. It has two major users of this service: Indiana Steel Companies and Midwestern Agriculture. The demand for freight cars and marginal revenue curves for each market are given by the equations:*

Indiana Steel Companies Demand

$$P_1 = \$550 - \$5Q_1$$

$$MR_1 = \partial TR_1/\partial Q_1 = \$550 - \$10Q_1$$

Midwestern Agriculture Demand

$$P_2 = \$300 - \$1.25Q_2$$

$$MR_2 = \partial TR_2/\partial Q_2 = \$300 - \$2.5Q_2$$

P_i *is the price charged by Midcontinent for hauling one freight car of materials between Indianapolis and Chicago, and* Q_i *represents the number of cars demanded by each user. Midcontinent's total and marginal cost functions for the daily train service is given by:*

$$TC = \$10,000 + \$50Q$$

$$MC = \partial TC/\partial Q = \$50$$

where Q is the number of freight cars hauled on a particular trip.

A.   *What conditions are necessary for profitable price discrimination by Midcontinent?*

B.   *What profit maximizing rule will Midcontinent employ to set prices as a price discriminator? Graphically determine the profit maximizing quantity of freight service Midcontinent will supply, show how it will divide this quantity between the* *steel and agricultural markets, and indicate the corresponding prices to be charged each company. Show that marginal revenue is equal in the two markets.*

C. *Assume that Midcontinent is prevented by law from engaging in price discrimination. What is the profit maximizing rule for determining profit and output under these conditions? Graphically determine Midcontinent's profit maximizing output and price under these conditions.*

P12.7 SOLUTION

A. For price discrimination to be profitable, Midcontinent must first be able to segment the market and prevent resale from one segment to another. Second, the elasticity of demand in one segment of the market must be lower than in the other if price discrimination is to be profitable.

B. With price discrimination, the profit maximizing rule is to equate marginal revenue with marginal cost in each market. Such an equality exists at points X and Y in the steel and agricultural market graphs, respectively. This indicates how total output (150 freight cars) should be allocated between steel (50 freight cars) and agriculture (100 freight cars), and the different prices to be charged each user.

The freight unit price for steel is $300, while that for agriculture is $175. Marginal revenue in each market is $50 and is equal to marginal cost.

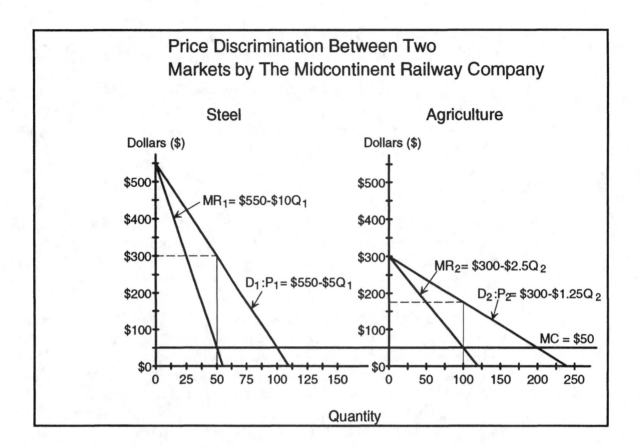

Price Discrimination Between Two
Markets by The Midcontinent Railway Company

C. Without price discrimination, the profit maximizing rule is to equate aggregate marginal revenue with marginal cost (point Z on graph). Here a vertical line from Z intersects the aggregate demand curve (point Y) determining the equal price ($200) to be charged in each market. A horizontal line at that price level will intersect the individual submarket demand curves (points W and X) and indicate the quantity of service (70 and 80 freight cars for steel and agriculture, respectively) that will be sold in each market.

The important point to remember is that total output and total costs are identical with and without price discrimination. However, because price discrimination allows the seller to charge higher average prices by setting MR = MC in each market, price discrimination will always increase seller profits.

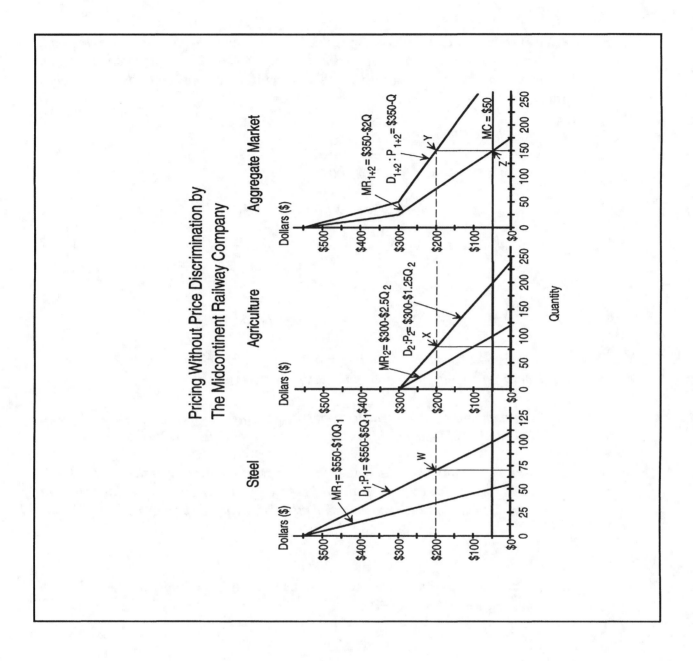

Pricing Without Price Discrimination by
The Midcontinent Railway Company

P12.8 **Price Discrimination.** *Brass & Brown, Inc. is an insulation contractor serving both residential and commercial customers in Las Vegas, Nevada. Demand and marginal revenue relations for treated cellulose fiber insulation, a popular product, have been estimated as:*

Residential Market

$$P_R = \$1,000 - \$0.0025Q_R$$

$$MR_R = \partial TR_R/\partial Q_R = \$1,000 - \$0.005Q_R$$

Commercial Market

$$P_C = \$750 - \$0.000625Q_C$$

$$MR_C = \partial TR_C/\partial Q_C = \$750 - \$0.00125Q_C$$

where Q is tons of insulation installed and P is dollars. Each ton of installed insulation results in $600 of marginal labor and materials expenses.

A. *Assuming the company can price discriminate between its two types of customers, calculate profit maximizing price, output and total profit contribution levels.*

B. *Calculate point price elasticities for each type of customer at the activity levels identified in part A. Are the differences in these elasticities consistent or inconsistent with your recommended price differences in part A? Why or why not?*

P12.8 **SOLUTION**

A. With price discrimination, profits are maximized by setting MR = MC in each market, where MC = $600.

Residential

$$MR_R = MC$$

$$\$1,000 - \$0.005Q_R = \$600$$

$$0.005Q_R = 400$$

$$Q_R = 80,000$$

and

$$P_R = \$1,000 - \$0.0025(80,000)$$

$$= \$800 \text{ per ton}$$

<u>Commercial</u>

$$MR_C = MC$$

$$\$750 - \$0.00125Q_C = \$600$$

$$0.00125Q_C = 150$$

$$Q_C = 120,000$$

and

$$P_C = \$750 - \$0.000625(120,000)$$

$$= \$675 \text{ per ton}$$

The profit contribution earned by the company is:

$$\pi = P_R Q_R + P_C Q_C - AVC(Q_R + Q_C)$$

$$= \$800(80,000) + \$675(120,000)$$

$$- \$600(80,000 + 120,000)$$

$$= \$25,000,000$$

B. Yes, a higher price for residential customers is consistent with the lower degree of price elasticity observed in that market.

<u>Residential</u>

$$\varepsilon_P = \partial Q_R/\partial P_R \times P_R/Q_R$$

$$= -400 \times (\$800/80,000)$$

$$= -4$$

<u>Commercial</u>

$$\varepsilon_P = \partial Q_C / \partial P_C \times P_C / Q_C$$

$$= -1,600 \times (\$675/120,000)$$

$$= -9$$

P12.9   ***Joint Product Pricing.*** *Corrado Soprano Enterprises produces two products in a joint production process. The products are produced in fixed proportions in a 1:1 ratio. Relevant cost functions are:*

$$TC = \$250,000 + \$200Q + \$0.25Q^2$$

$$MC = \partial TC / \partial Q = \$200 + \$0.5Q$$

where Q is a unit of output consisting of one unit of product A and one unit of product B.

A.   *Assume the demand and marginal revenue curves for Soprano's two products are:*

$$P_A = \$950 - \$0.125Q_A$$

$$MR_A = \partial TR_A / \partial Q_A = \$950 - \$0.25Q_A$$

and

$$P_B = \$250 - \$0.625Q_B$$

$$MR_B = \partial TR_B / \partial Q_B = \$250 - \$1.25Q_B$$

What are the optimal sales quantities and prices for each of these products? (Assume unsold production can be costlessly dumped.)

B.   *Assume now that Soprano incurs disposal cost of $75 for any excess production of product A or B manufactured but not sold. What are the optimal sales quantities and product prices under these conditions?*

P12.9   SOLUTION

A.   If each unit of production generates revenues for both products A and B, the appropriate output level is found as:

$$MR_A + MR_B = MC$$

$$\$950 - \$0.25Q + \$250 - \$1.25Q = \$200 + \$0.5Q \text{ (Because } Q = Q_A = Q_B)$$

$$2Q = 1,000$$

$$Q = 500$$

Thus, profit maximization with equal sales of each product requires that the firm operate at the level $Q = 500$. Marginal revenues for the two products are:

$$MR_A = \$950 - \$0.25Q_A = \$950 - \$0.25(500) = \$825$$

$$MR_B = \$250 - \$1.25Q_B = \$250 - \$1.25(500) = -\$375$$

Despite the fact that $MR_A + MR_B = \$825 - \$375 = \$450$ and equals marginal production costs ($MC = \$200 + \$0.5(500) = \$450$), the negative marginal revenue for B invalidates this solution. With the negative marginal revenue for B, this solution is incorrect if Soprano can dispose of B, or otherwise hold it off the market, without incurring additional costs. Soprano would like to produce more output to sell additional product A which more than covers marginal production costs. The negative marginal revenue on product B is therefore "holding back" production and sales of product A. If B can be costlessly held off the market, Soprano would sell B only up to the point where its marginal revenue is zero because, given production of A, the relevant marginal cost of B is zero.

$$MR_B = MC_B$$

$$\$250 - \$1.2Q_B = 0$$

$$1.25Q_B = 250$$

$$Q_B = 200$$

and

$$P_B = \$250 - \$0.625(200)$$

$$= \$125$$

Determination of the optimal production and sales level for A is found by equating the marginal revenue from A, the only product being sold from the marginal production unit, with the marginal cost of production.

$$MR_A = MC_A = MC_Q$$

$$\$950 - \$0.25Q = \$200 + \$0.5Q \quad \text{(Because } Q_A = Q)$$

$$0.75Q = 750$$

$$Q_A = 1,000$$

and

$$P_A = \$950 - \$0.125(1,000)$$

$$= \$825$$

Here, note that $MR_A = \$950 - \$0.25(1,000) = \$700$, and $MR_B = \$250 = \$1.25(200) = \$0$. Thus, $MR_A + MR_B = MC$, because $MC = \$200 + \$0.5(1,000) = \$700$. Unlike before, $MR_A = MC_A$ and $MR_B = MC_B$ as well. Thus, Soprano should produce 1,000 units of output, selling all 1,000 units of A at a price of $825. Only 200 units of B will be sold at a price of $125, with the remaining 800 units being destroyed or otherwise held off the market.

B.   The solution to part A assumes a cost-free disposal of excess B. Now, disposal of B will cost Soprano $75 per unit. In this situation, it will be more profitable for Soprano to continue selling B so long as its negative marginal revenue is less than the $75 per unit disposal cost. In other words, the marginal cost of selling as opposed to dumping B is -$75. Thus, the maximum sales quantity for B under these conditions is:

$$MR_B = MC_B - \text{Disposal cost saving}$$

$$\$250 - \$1.25Q_B = \$0 - \$75$$

$$1.25Q_B = 325$$

$$Q_B = 260$$

$$P_B = \$250 - \$0.625(260)$$

$$= \$87.50$$

The optimal production level is found by setting MR_A equal to MC_Q plus the disposal cost on unsold B which is being produced and dumped at the margin.

$$MR_A = MC_Q + \text{Disposal cost} = MC_A$$

$$\$950 - \$0.25Q = \$200 + \$0.5Q + \$75 \quad (\text{Because } Q_A = Q)$$

$$0.75Q = 675$$

$$Q_A = 900$$

$$P_A = \$950 - \$0.125(900)$$

$$= \$837.50$$

Once again, $MR_A + MR_B = MC$, with $MR_A = MC_A$ and $MR_B = MC_B$. Soprano will produce 900 units of output selling all 900 units of A produced. Only 260 units of B will be sold, and 640 units of B will be dumped at a cost of \$75 per unit.

When comparing the solutions to part A and part B, notice that imposition of a disposal cost (or pollution charge) reduces the amount of A and B produced, from 1,000 to 900, and disposal of B, from 800 to 640 units. Also note that P_A rises from \$825 to \$837.50, while P_B falls from \$125 to \$87.50.

P12.10 ***Joint Product Pricing****. Pee-Wee Petroleum, Inc., operates oil and gas producing wells in the Overthrust Belt region. On average, for each barrel of oil pumped to the surface, one thousand cubic feet of natural gas is also recovered. Therefore, the company views oil and gas as joint products where each unit of production involves 1 bbl: 1 mcf. Marginal costs are \$15 per unit of production.*

Although each output is sold in perfectly competitive commodity markets; transport, handling and related costs have the effect of reducing the net price received by Pee-Wee. The net price/output and marginal revenue relations for oil is:

$$P_O = \$20 - \$0.000075Q_O$$

$$MR_O = \partial TR_O/\partial Q_O = \$20 - \$0.00015Q_O$$

and for gas is:

$$P_G = \$3 - 0.000025Q_G$$

$$MR_G = \partial TR_G/\partial Q_G = \$3 - \$0.00005Q_G$$

where Q_O is barrels of oil and Q_G is mcf of natural gas sold per month.

A. Calculate the profit-maximizing price/output combination for oil and gas under current conditions.

B. Now assume that instability in the world oil market has caused the demand for domestic oil to double. Holding all else equal, calculate the new optimal price/output combination for oil and gas.

P12.10 SOLUTION

A. Begin analysis of this problem by examining the optimal activity level based on the assumption that all production of each byproduct will be sold. For profit maximization set,

$$MR = MR_O + MR_G = MC$$

$$\$20 - \$0.00015Q + \$3 - \$0.00005Q = \$15 \text{ (Because } Q = Q_O = Q_G)$$

$$0.0002Q = 8$$

$$Q = 40,000$$

Profit maximization with all production being sold requires that the firm produce 40,000 units of production involving 40,000 bbls of oil and 40,000 mcf of natural gas. Under this assumption, marginal revenues for each byproduct are:

$$MR_O = \$20 - \$0.00015(40,000) = \$14$$

$$MR_G = \$3 - \$0.00005(40,000) = \$1$$

Clearly, each byproduct is making a positive contribution to marginal costs. Because MR = \$14 + \$1 = \$15 = MC, Pee-Wee has no incentive to alter production from the $Q = Q_O = Q_G = 40,000$ optimal production and sales level.

Relevant prices are:

$$P_O = \$20 - \$0.000075(40,000) = \$17 \text{ per bbl}$$

$$P_G = \$3 - \$0.000025(40,000) = \$2 \text{ per mcf}$$

B. A doubling (or 100% increase) in oil demand means that a given quantity could be sold at twice the original price. Alternatively, twice the original quantity demanded could be sold at a given price. Therefore the new oil demand and marginal revenue curves can be written:

$$P_O' = 2(\$20 - \$0.000075Q_O)$$

$$= \$40 - \$0.00015Q_O$$

$$MR_O' = 2(\$20 - \$0.00015Q_O)$$

$$= \$40 - \$0.0003Q_O$$

Now, assuming all output is sold,

$$MR' = MR_O' + MR_G = \$15$$

$$\$40 - \$0.0003Q + \$3 - \$0.00005Q = \$15 \text{ (Because } Q = Q_O = Q_G)$$

$$0.00035Q = 28$$

$$Q = 80,000$$

Profit maximization with sale of all production requires that the firm produce and sell $Q = Q_O = Q_G = 80,000$. Under this assumption, marginal revenues for the two products are

$$MR_O' = \$40 - \$0.0003(80,000) = \$16$$

$$MR_G = \$3 - \$0.00005(80,000) = -\$1$$

Although $MR' = MR_O' + MR_G = \$15 = MC$, the above $Q = 80,000$ solution is suboptimal. $MR_P' = \$16 > \$15 = MC$ implies that a \$1 profit contribution is earned on each unit of production when just considering oil sales. The company would like to expand production beyond $Q = 80,000$ just in order to sell more oil. The negative marginal revenue on gas is "holding down" oil production at the margin.

Pee-Wee will only sell gas up until the point where $MR_G = 0$ because, given expanded production to sell oil, the marginal cost of gas is zero. Set,

$$MR_G = MC_G$$

$$\$3 - \$0.00005Q_G = \$0$$

$$0.00005Q_G = 3$$

$$Q_G = 60,000$$

$$P_G = \$3 - \$0.000025(60,000)$$

$$= \$1.50 \text{ per mcf}$$

The optimal production and sales level for oil is found by setting $MR_O' = MC_O = MC$, because oil is the only product being sold from the marginal unit of production.

$$MR_O' = \$40 - \$0.0003Q_O = \$15$$

$$0.0003Q_O = 25$$

$$Q_O = 83,333$$

$$P_O = \$40 - \$0.00015(83,333) = \$27.50 \text{ per bbl}$$

Therefore, Pee-Wee will produce 83,333 units of production and sell all 83,333 bbls of oil produced at \$27.50 per bbl, but only 60,000 mcf of gas at \$1.50 per mcf. The remaining 23,333 mcf of gas produced will be flared off (burned or dumped) at the well head, or otherwise held off the market (stored for future sale).

(*Note*: A doubling in oil demand doesn't have the effect of doubling oil prices because oil production increases.)

Chapter 13

REGULATION OF THE MARKET ECONOMY

Government regulation is a compelling subject because the ability to regulate, tax, subsidize or otherwise compel economic activity is a potent force that shapes the competitive environment. The process and results of government regulation are controversial because regulatory policy often makes some trade-off between efficiency and equity considerations. Appropriate government regulation is based on a balancing of costs and benefits to society in general, taking into account both administrative costs and hidden costs borne by the private sector. A careful analysis of government regulation of the market economy clearly suggests that although the intentions of many regulations may be laudable, they can have a net adverse impact on the general public. Recent changes in the method and scope of government regulation, including moves toward deregulation, reflect this fact and have the potential to affect the entire spectrum of economic activity. Not only are industrial firms affected, so too are financial institutions such as banks and savings and loans, insurance companies, and power and transportation utilities.

In this chapter, the role of government in the market economy is analyzed by considering the economic and political rationale for regulation and antitrust policy designed to maintain a workable level of competition in the economy. Some current regulatory problems are also investigated to illuminate the causes of deregulation and various possibilities for improving regulatory processes. This analysis shows that government regulation is sometimes no longer appropriate given recent changes in the economic environment.

CHAPTER OUTLINE

I. **COMPETITION AND THE ROLE OF GOVERNMENT**

   A. **How Government Influences Business:** Both economic and social considerations enter into decisions of what and how to regulate.

   1. Economic considerations relate to the cost and efficiency implications of regulatory methods.

   2. Equity, or fairness, criteria must also be carefully weighed when social considerations bear on the regulatory decision-making process.

      a. If a given change in regulatory policy provides significant benefits to the poor, society may willingly bear substantial costs in terms of lost efficiency.

B.   Economic Considerations: Government regulation is typically justified on the basis of its ability to correct "market failures" that lead to inefficiency and waste.

    1.   Market failure is the inability of unregulated market activity to provide desired goods and services at competitive prices.

    2.   Two types of market imperfections that can cause market failure are structural and incentive problems.

        a.   Structural problems are caused by too few buyers or sellers.

        b.   Incentive problems are caused by externalities like pollution.

C.   Social Considerations: Government regulation is also justified on the basis of social considerations. Primary among these are desires to:

    1.   Preserve consumer choice because a wide variety of production enhances personal freedom.

    2.   Limit economic and political power because unchecked economic and political power could threaten basic liberties.

II.   REGULATORY RESPONSE TO INCENTIVE FAILURES

A.   Property Rights Regulation: Property rights give firms the prerogative to limit use by others of specific land, plant and equipment, and other assets.

    1.   Service "in the public interest" is often promoted by offering firms valuable operating rights in exchange for specific operating concessions (e.g., public service broadcasts for local TV licenses).

    2.   Property rights regulation is hampered by imprecise operating criteria.

B.   Patents and the Tort System: The patent monopoly is granted by government to promote valuable research and development.

    1.   For applications filed on or after June 8, 1995, utility (or use) and plant (biological) patents are granted for a term that begins with the date of the grant and usually ends 20 years from the date of the patent application.

        a.   Maintenance fees totaling a few thousand dollars must be paid over the life of such patents.

2. Ornamental design patents last 14 years from the grant date, and involve no maintenance fees.

C. Subsidy Policy: A rapidly growing method of public support for desired business activity is implicit or outright subsidy.

1. A prominent example is the growing use of tradeable pollution emission allowances, a controversial form of subsidy.

a. Pollution allowances implicitly recognize the polluter's right to contaminate the environment.

2. Tax-free financing (municipal bonds at low interest rates) for private investment or housing projects are popular means of government subsidy.

D. Tax Policy: Taxes or fines encourage firms to minimize undesirable externalities such as air, water, or noise pollution.

1. Pollution taxes assert the public's right to a clean environment.

E. Operating Controls: Operating controls are various government directives designed to compel desirable business activity under penalty of law.

1. Operating controls often rely on nonmonetary incentives.

III. WHO PAYS THE COSTS OF REGULATION?

A. Demand and Supply Effects: The point of cost incidence is where, for example, taxes are collected, tolls are paid or pollution-reducing expenditures are made.

1. The burden of regulatory costs can be passed on to customers through higher output prices, to workers through lower wages, or suppliers through lower input prices.

2. The ability of producers to pass on regulatory costs depends on product demand elasticities.

a. With perfectly elastic product demand, producers including stockholders, employees and suppliers bear all regulatory costs.

b.   With perfectly inelastic product demand, consumers bear all regulatory costs.

B.   **Regulation Cost Sharing Example:** Elasticities of demand are seldom perfectly elastic or perfectly inelastic.

1.   Both producers and consumers typically share the burden of regulatory costs.

C.   **Efficient Regulation:** To be efficient, marginal benefits derived from regulation must cover marginal costs.
1.   Regulation often has important direct and indirect implications.

IV.   REGULATORY RESPONSE TO STRUCTURAL FAILURES

A.   **Dilemma of Natural Monopoly:** Natural monopoly exists if average production costs decline continuously as output expands. This situation presents a dilemma for policy makers because:

1.   A monopolist has the potential to achieve lower average costs than would a group of smaller competitors.

2.   A monopolist faces only limited competitive pressure to constrain prices. Excess profits, inefficiency and waste can result.

B.   **Utility Price and Profit Regulations:** Utility price and profit regulations seek to achieve the efficiency potential of natural monopoly, while limiting the potential for monopoly abuse

1.   Regulators set $P = AC$ to encourage output expansion and lower average costs while limiting monopoly profits.

2.   Audits of operating costs are also undertaken in an effort to limit excessive expenditures.

C.   **Utility Price and Profit Regulation Example:** Regulated utilities must determine the output level that is just sufficient to generate the allowed return in light of demand and cost conditions.

1.   In practice, utility price and profit regulation involves setting $P = AC$, where AC includes a "fair" rate of return on investment.

D. **Problems with Utility Price and Profit Regulation:** Significant problems in utility regulation limit its effectiveness. Among these problems are:

1. Defining a pricing schedule that will promote both equity and efficiency objectives is difficult given the large number of utility customer classifications.

2. Determining optimal output levels is difficult because demand and cost functions are unknown.

3. Reducing inefficiency and waste through regulatory surveillance is difficult because only actual, not necessarily minimum, costs are observed.

4. Regulation can lead to suboptimal input combinations by encouraging excessive or insufficient levels of capital investment.

5. Utility rate increases made necessary by inflation are often delayed or inadequate due to their political unpopularity. Political pressures can thus reduce utility operating efficiency.

6. An important drawback to current methods of utility regulation is their administrative and compliance cost.

7. Incentive regulation that rewards firms for meeting price and output goals has the potential to increase the efficiency of regulation.

   a. Regulators are often better at deciding regulatory objectives, as opposed to setting the means for achieving them.

V. ANTITRUST POLICY

A. **Overview of Antitrust Law:** Antitrust law is an example of case law.

1. In case law, judicial interpretation is relied upon in determining prohibited behavior; thus, legal precedent is extremely important.

2. In statutory law, specific acts such as murder are explicitly prohibited by the legislative branch.

3.   Antitrust policy is based on two statutes and their amendments:

     a.   Sherman Act (1890).

     b.   Clayton Act (1914).

B.   Sherman Act: The Sherman Act is the first piece of federal antitrust legislation.

1.   Section 1 forbids every contract, combination or conspiracy in restraint of trade and is aimed at cartels or cartel-like behavior.

2.   Section 2 prohibits monopolizing or any effort explicitly designed to drive competitors out of business.

3.   The imprecise nature of the Sherman Act reduces its effectiveness.

C.   Clayton Act: The Clayton Act is designed to overcome some of the ambiguity of the Sherman Act by explicitly prohibiting certain behavior.

1.   Section 2 outlaws price discrimination between firms that lessens competition. This section was later amended by the Robinson-Patman Act (1936).

     a.   Price discrimination between firms and consumers, such as senior citizen discounts for bus service, is legal.

2.   Section 3 makes leases or any sales contracts which lessen competition illegal. This provision is aimed at so-called tying contracts.

3.   Section 7 forbids stock mergers for monopoly. The Celler-Kefauver Act (1950) closed the asset acquisition loophole.

D.   Antitrust Enforcement: Responsibility for antitrust law enforcement lies with the Antitrust Division of the Department of Justice and the Federal Trade Commission.

1.   Criminal proceedings under the Sherman Act are pursued by the Justice Department with fines, imprisonment or injunctive relief being sought.

2.   Civil proceedings under the Clayton Act are typically pursued by the FTC with "cease and desist" orders being sought.

    E.   **Horizontal Merger Guidelines:** According to horizontal merger guidelines issued by the Department of Justice:

        1.   Mergers resulting in relatively unconcentrated markets are not likely to have adverse competitive effects and ordinarily will be approved.

        2.   Mergers producing a moderate increase in concentration in moderately concentrated markets are unlikely to have adverse competitive consequences and ordinarily will be approved.

        3.   Mergers producing a moderate increase in concentration in highly concentrated markets ordinarily will be approved.

            a.   Mergers producing a significant increase in concentration in highly concentrated markets ordinarily will not be approved.

    F.   **Recent Antitrust Policy Initiatives:** To the extent that recent antitrust policy initiatives hinder or otherwise interfere with invention and innovation, such initiatives come at a significant social cost, irrespective of any compensating virtues.

        1.   During recent years, some of the most important and controversial antitrust initiatives have come in increasingly important high-tech industries.

VI.   **PROBLEMS WITH REGULATION**

    A.   **Costs of Regulation:** An important consideration is the expense involved in terms of administrative and economic resource allocation costs.

        1.   Total regulation-induced cost estimates exceed $750 *billion* dollars per year in the United States, or more than $2,500 per capita.

    B.   **Size-Efficiency Problem:** Regulation and antitrust policy are sometimes criticized for attacking large firms whose large size and profitability were fairly obtained as a result of superior efficiency.

        1.   Market dominance is often achieved through efficiency (e.g., Intel, Microsoft).

    C.   **Capture Problem:** Regulation is sometimes carried out for the benefit of regulated firms rather than for the benefit of society as a whole.

        1.   In such instances, the regulatory process is said to be "captured" by the regulated.

VII.   DEREGULATION MOVEMENT

   A.   Major Steps Toward Deregulation: Dissatisfaction with the high costs and low public benefits of many regulations gave birth to a deregulation movement during the early 1970s.

   1.   Inefficient firms, consumers who buy partially subsidized goods and services, and workers who take home inflated wages all oppose deregulation.

   2.   To date, the net gains from deregulation are significant.

   B.   Regulation Versus Deregulation Controversy: Regulation is a tool that can be used to further the public interest, but only when regulation-induced incentives are understood and carefully considered.

   1.   Regulators must ensure that anticompetitive practices do not evolve in deregulated markets.

VIII.   REGULATORY REFORM FOR THE NEW MILLENNIUM

   A.   Promoting Competition in Electric Power Generation: The electric power industry is comprised of three different components: the generation of electric power, the transmission of electric power from generators to local utilities, and the distribution of electricity by local utilities to commercial and residential customers.

   1.   All three segments of the industry are currently subject to state and federal regulation.

   2.   Regulatory reform and greater competition have the potential to improve industry performance, espeically in the generation sector.

   B.   Fostering Competition in the Cable Television Industry: Cable television is available to more than 90% of U.S. households, and more than 60% of all such households subscribe to cable service.

   1.   The problem is that consumers in most communities receive cable services from a monopoly provider.

   2.   Regulators must encourage continued innovation in programming and in the development of new cable services, while at the same time restraining industry prices.

C. **Improving Regulation of Health and Safety:** In the United States, government seeks to control wrongful injury through the tort system and by an extensive and growing policy of health and safety regulation.

    1.   In regulating health and safety, as in other areas, government should focus on regulations with benefits that outweigh unavoidable costs.

D. **Reforming Environmental Regulation:** Significant uncertainties surround the costs and benefits of environmental regulation.

    1.   Economic incentives decrease compliance costs by allowing firms the flexibility to efficiently meet environmental regulations.

    2.   With economic incentives tied to environmental objectives, rather than to the means used to achieve them, firms and society in general benefit through a practical approach to protecting the environment.

IX. **SUMMARY**

PROBLEMS & SOLUTIONS

P13.1 **Market Failure.** *Water run-off from agricultural crops washes fertilizer, pesticides, and other chemicals into streams, rivers, and lakes. In some instances, the ground water itself becomes contaminated. Concerned citizens are appalled at the aesthetic and environmental implications of such pollution, as well as the potential health hazard to the local population.*

    A. *Pollution is a negative production externality and an example of market failure. What reasons might you cite for why markets fail?*

    B. *In analyzing remedies to the current situation, consider three general types of controls to limit pollution:*

- *Regulations -- licenses, permits, compulsory standards, and so on.*

- *Payments -- various types of government aid to help companies install pollution-control equipment. Aid can take the form of forgiven local property taxes, income tax credits, special accelerated depreciation allowances for pollution-control equipment, low-cost government loans, and so on.*

- *Charges -- excise taxes on polluting fuels (coal, oil, and so forth), pollution discharge taxes, and others.*

Review each of these methods of pollution control and do the following:

    (1) *Determine the incentive structure for the polluter under each form of control.*

    (2) *Decide who pays for a clean environment under each form of control. (Note that each form of control has definite implications about who owns the property rights to the environment.)*

    (3) *Defend a particular form of control on the basis of your analysis, including both efficiency and equity considerations.*

P13.1 **SOLUTION**

    A. Markets can fail due to:

        (i) Structural problems: Fewness in the number of buyers and/or sellers.

(ii)   Incentive problems: If some product benefit (cost) is not reflected in firm revenues (costs), then non-optimal production quantities and output prices will result due to improper firm incentives.

B.   Methods of pollution control:

(i)   Incentive structure:

   (a)   Regulation: Incentive is to avoid regulation, or be made a "special case."

   (b)   Payments: Incentive is to reduce pollution to earn subsidy.

   (c)   Charges: Incentive is to reduce pollution to avoid charges.

(ii)   Who pays for the clean environment?

   (a)   Regulation: Industry customers, employees, and stockholders pay to reduce pollution. Society's right to a clean environment is implied.

   (b)   Payments: Society pays to reduce pollution, implying that the company has a right to pollute.

   (c)   Charges: Industry customers, employees, and stockholders pay to reduce pollution. Again, society's right to a clean environment is implied.

(iii)   Defense of the alternatives:

Efficiency considerations favor payments and charges as more efficient methods of pollution control.

Equity or "ability to pay" considerations make the choice among pollution control methods less certain.

   (a)   Regulation: Insures due process, a day in court, for the polluter.

   (b)   Payments: Avoids penalty to polluters with "sunk" investment costs.

   (c)   Charges: Polluter should pay full costs of production consumption.

P13.2   ***Benefits of Regulation.*** *Each of the following problems illustrate instances where unregulated market activity might result in suboptimal market outcomes. Indicate whether the problem identified reflects market failure caused by a structural problem, or market failure caused by an incentive (enforcement) problem. Explain your answer.*

    A.   *Price-gouging by a pharmaceutical manufacturer protected by patents on an important medicine used to treat a major infectious disease.*

    B.   *Acid rain caused by factory pollution.*

    C.   *Excess profits for domestic manufacturers protected by import tariffs.*

    D.   *Excessive automobile insurance policy prices due to a lack of competition in the local market.*

    E.   *Excessive noise levels due to freeway traffic.*

P13.2   **SOLUTION**

    A.   Structural problem. Price-gouging by a pharmaceutical manufacturer protected by patents on an important medicine used to treat a major infectious disease is an example of market failure caused by structural problems. When too few competitors are present in a given market, high prices and excess profits can result.

    B.   Incentive (enforcement) problem. Acid rain caused by factory pollution is an example of market failure due to incentive problems. When factories emit excessive sulphur dioxide pollution they cause some of the environmental costs of producing output to be borne by third parties.

    C.   Structural problem. Excess profits for domestic manufacturers protected by import tariffs are an example of the social costs that result from limiting foreign competition.

    D.   Structural problem. Excessive automobile insurance policy costs due to a lack of sufficient competition in the local market reflects a structural problem in the market for insurance services.

    E.   Incentive (enforcement) problem. Excessive noise due to freeway traffic is an example of market failure due to a lack of proper incentives in the marketplace to reduce the level of noise pollution.

P13.3 ***Costs of Regulation.*** *In what is referred to as an industry-wide pattern labor agreement, the U.S. auto industry has agreed to pay generous health care benefits to employed and retired autoworkers. Following rapid unanticipated growth in health care costs over the past decade, the resulting health care liability to the auto industry has grown into the billions of dollars. To alleviate this burden, the auto industry sponsors a vigorous lobbying effort in Washington, D.C. to press for passage of an expensive government-guaranteed health care plan for all Americans. Under these circumstances, explain why passage of a government-guaranteed health care plan would increase, decrease or have no effect on:*

A. *Auto industry health care costs.*

B. *Auto industry profits.*

C. *Car prices.*

D. *National demand for health care.*

E. *National health care costs.*

P13.3 **SOLUTION**

A. Decrease. Passage of a government-guaranteed health care plan would decrease auto industry health care costs because these expenses would be paid out of general tax revenues.

B. Increase. Auto industry profits would rise following passage of a government-guaranteed health care plan because industry costs would fall (see Part A.)

C. Decrease. Passage of a government-guaranteed health care plan has the potential to result in some decrease in car prices. Because auto industry labor costs are at least somewhat variable, a decrease in health care costs could translate into lower marginal costs and somewhat lower car prices. However, the car price effect of a national health care plan is likely to be quite small.

D. Increase. Passage of a government-guaranteed health care plan would increase the national demand for health care. Unlike most goods and services that must be directly paid for by consumers, "free" health care is indirectly paid for through tax revenues.

E. Increase. Passage of a government-guaranteed health care plan would increase national health care costs given the burst in demand that can be anticipated.

P13.4   ***Capture Problem.*** *On November 21, 1986, The Wall Street Journal (p.29) carried an article titled "It'll Mean Another Two Semesters in the Red, but Who's Counting?" This article described efforts by the American Institute of Certified Public Accountants (AICPA) to require a fifth (graduate) year of study in accounting for joining the Institute. The following is an excerpt from that article:*

> *"Technical demands have become so great on accountants that they can't get five pounds of education in a four-pound bag," explains James MacNeil, director of the AICPA's education division. He says the extra year "would help graduates understand such new complexities as leveraged leases and buyouts and new types of securities being devised by Wall Street." (Hawaii, Utah, and Florida already require five years of study before taking the CPA exam, and several other states are giving the matter independent consideration.)*

> *Such arguments, however, have failed to sway many educators. "Most of the deans of the nation's 650 business schools oppose going to five years from four," says Charles Hickman, projects director for the American Assembly of Collegiate Schools of Business, based in St. Louis. "The big question raised by most deans is whether another roadblock should be raised to becoming a working accountant." Some opponents point out that since Florida imposed its five-year rule in 1983, the number of applicants for the CPA exam there has declined sharply each year.*

Briefly explain the following:

A.   *The causes and consequences of regulation according to the public interest theory of regulation.*

B.   *The causes and consequences of regulation according to the capture theory of regulation.*

C.   *How the preceding article supports or contradicts each.*

P13.4   **SOLUTION**

A.   According to the "public interest" theory of regulation, regulation is imposed on industry to protect larger social interests.

B.   According to the "capture" theory of regulation, regulation is imposed by industry, or other politically effective groups, in order to further the narrow self-interest of the regulated.

C. In support of the public interest theory of regulation, the requirement that CPA candidates have five rather than four years of graduate study can be viewed as an effort to enhance the quality of accounting services. If a fifth year of study is truly necessary in order to deal with new accounting complexities, then the quality of accounting information would be enhanced through such a requirement. States imposing such requirements could indeed be serving the public interest.

On the other hand, the lobbying of state legislatures by the accounting profession ("industry") for higher CPA candidate credentials has the effect of raising barriers to entry into the profession. If a national five-year requirement were imposed, the number of CPA candidates can be expected to decline sharply, as was seen in the state of Florida. With fewer CPA candidates, fewer CPAs will be accepted into the profession. With fewer CPAs available to certify financial statements, CPA salaries can be expected to rise. Therefore, if a fifth year of accounting study is not necessary in a technical sense, the effect of such a requirement would be to increase CPA incomes -- and provide evidence of state legislatures being "captured" by the accounting "industry."

P13.5 *Antitrust Law. Indicate whether or not each of the following examples of business behavior are legal or illegal under current antitrust law, and mention whether violations under the Sherman Act, Clayton Act, and/or Federal Trade Commission Act are involved. Explain your answer.*

A. *Charging higher markups for younger versus older consumers.*

B. *False and misleading advertising.*

C. *Mergers for monopoly.*

D. *Charging different markups to various business customers.*

E. *A business strategy of using patents to limit competition.*

P13.5 **SOLUTION**

A. Legal. The Clayton Act, as amended by the Robinson-Patman Act, explicitly prohibits price discrimination among business customers unless lower markups are required to meet the competition. However, price discrimination among final consumers is legal and widely practiced by business and government entities.

B. Illegal under the Federal Trade Commission Act. False and misleading advertising is a prime example of the type of unfair competition made illegal by the FTC Act.

C. Illegal under the Sherman and Clayton Acts. The Sherman Act explicitly forbade contracts, combinations, and conspiracies in restraint of trade. Similarly, the Clayton Act forbade mergers and asset acquisitions intended to create monopoly power.

D. Illegal under the Clayton Act. The Clayton Act, as amended by the Robinson Patman Act, explicitly prohibits price discrimination among business customers unless lower markups are required to meet the competition. Charging different markups to business customers is only legal in the unlikely event that no harm to competition would result.

E. Illegal under the Sherman and Federal Trade Commission Acts. A business strategy of using patents to limit competition is an example of monopolizing behavior and an unfair method of competition.

P13.6 *Consequences of Regulation.* *The Lawn Fertilizer Company takes raw mineral phosphate and converts it into a phosphate-based fertilizer. During the production process, fluoride gas is released into the air. This pollutant then settles on the citrus crops and grass in a wide area surrounding production facilities, retards the growth of crops and results in an inferior fruit product. The pollutant also settles on grass eaten by cattle, and produces an arthritic condition retarding their growth. As a result, agriculture and cattle interests have petitioned the State Environmental Protection Agency for pollution controls on LFC's conversion process. These controls would affect annual fixed and variable costs of the fertilizer industry, and add $30 million to their total asset base of $210 million.*

LFC and other firms in the fertilizer industry agree that something needs to be done to stop the pollution. However, caution is necessary because these changes could reduce the 10% "fair" rate of return on investment earned by the industry. Although they agree with the idea of pollution control, the fertilizer industry argues that an immediate pollution abatement program would lower industry profits, hamper future capital expansion, lower output, and force layoffs. The fertilizer industry advocates a slower program with a major emphasis on new facilities. This more gradual process will have a smaller impact on profits, output, and employment; and add only $5 million to the total asset base of the industry.

An independent committee acceptable to both sides was established to analyze relevant economic data. As a result of their analysis, the following industry demand, revenue and cost curves were discovered:

$$P = \$35,000 - \$0.5Q \qquad\qquad (Demand)$$

$$MR = \partial TR/\partial Q = \$35,000 - \$1Q \qquad (Marginal\ Revenue)$$

$$TC = \$100{,}000{,}000 + \$8{,}000Q + \$1Q^2 \qquad \text{(Total cost)}$$

$$MC = \partial TC/\partial Q = \$8{,}000 + \$2Q \qquad \text{(Marginal Cost)}$$

where P is price in dollars per hundred tons, Q is hundreds of tons of fertilizer, MR is marginal revenue, TC is total cost in dollars (before capital costs), and MC is marginal cost in dollars (before capital costs).

If controls advocated by the agriculture and cattle interests were immediately implemented, fertilizer industry cost curves would be adjusted to:

$$TC_1 = \$106{,}000{,}000 + \$8{,}200Q + \$1.1Q^2$$

$$MC_1 = \partial TC_1/\partial Q = \$8{,}200 + \$2.2Q$$

If controls advocated by the fertilizer industry were implemented, the cost curves would be adjusted to:

$$TC_2 = \$101{,}000{,}000 + \$8{,}050Q + \$1Q^2$$

$$MC_2 = \partial TC_2/\partial Q = \$8{,}050 + \$2Q$$

A. What is the current profit-maximizing price/output combination, level of profits, and rate of return on investment in the fertilizer industry?

B. What would be the profit-maximizing price/output combination, level of profits, and rate of return on investment in the fertilizer industry if the agriculture and cattle interests' recommendations were implemented?

C. What would be the profit-maximizing price/output combination, level of profits, and rates of return on investment in the fertilizer industry if their own recommendations were adopted?

D. Which recommendation should be implemented?

P13.6 SOLUTION

A. Set $M\pi = MR - MC = 0$ to find the current profit-maximizing output level:

$$M\pi = MR - MC$$

$$0 = \$35{,}000 - \$1Q - \$8{,}000 - \$2Q$$

$$0 = 27{,}000 - 3Q$$

$$3Q = 27{,}000$$

$$Q = 9{,}000(00) \text{ or } 900{,}000 \text{ tons}$$

$$P = \$35{,}000 - \$0.5Q$$

$$= \$35{,}000 - \$0.5(9{,}000)$$

$$= \$30{,}500 \text{ per hundred tons (or } \$305/\text{ton)}$$

$$\pi = -\$100{,}000{,}000 + \$27{,}000(9{,}000)$$

$$- \$1.5(9{,}000^2)$$

$$= \$21{,}500{,}000$$

$$\begin{array}{rcl} \text{Return on} \\ \text{investment} \end{array} = \dfrac{\pi}{\text{Total assets}}$$

$$= \dfrac{\$21{,}500{,}000}{\$210{,}000{,}000}$$

$$= 0.102 \text{ or } 10.2\%$$

(*Note*: Profit is falling for $Q > 9{,}000$, so $Q = 9{,}000$ is a point of maximum profits.)

B.   Based on the assumption that agriculture and cattle industry interests are adopted, set relevant $M\pi = MR - MC = 0$ to find the profit-maximizing output level:

$$M\pi = MR - MC_1$$

$$0 = \$35{,}000 - \$1Q - \$8{,}200 - \$2.2Q$$

$$0 = 26{,}800 - 3.2Q$$

$$3.2Q = 26{,}800$$

$$Q = 8{,}375(00) \text{ or } 837{,}500 \text{ tons}$$

$$P = \$35{,}000 - \$0.5Q$$

$$= \$35{,}000 - \$0.5(8{,}375)$$

$$= \$30{,}813 \text{ per hundred tons (or } \$308.13/\text{ton)}$$

$$\pi = TR - TC_1$$

$$= -\$106{,}000{,}000 + \$26{,}800(8{,}375)$$

$$- \$1.6(8{,}375^2)$$

$$= \$6{,}225{,}000$$

$$\text{Return on investment} = \frac{\pi}{\text{Total assets}}$$

$$= \frac{\$6{,}225{,}000}{\$240{,}000{,}000}$$

$$= 0.0259 \text{ or } 2.59\%$$

(*Note*: Profit is falling for Q > 8,375, so Q = 8,375 is a point of maximum profits).

C. Based on the assumption that fertilizer industry interests are adopted, set relevant $M\pi = MR - MC = 0$ to find the profit-maximizing output level:

$$M\pi = MR - MC_2$$

$$0 = \$35{,}000 - \$1Q - \$8{,}050 - \$2Q$$

$$0 = 26{,}950 - 3Q$$

$$3Q = 26{,}950$$

$$Q = 8{,}983.33(00) \text{ or } 898{,}333 \text{ tons}$$

$$P = \$35{,}000 - \$0.5Q$$

$$= \$35{,}000 - \$0.5(8{,}983.33)$$

$$= \$30{,}508 \text{ per hundred tons (or } \$305.08/\text{ton)}$$

$$\pi = TR - TC_2$$

$$= -\$101,000,000 + \$26,950(8,983.33)$$

$$- \$1.5(8,983.33^2)$$

$$= \$20,053,336$$

Return on investment $= \dfrac{\pi}{\text{Total assets}}$

$$= \dfrac{\$20,053,336}{\$215,000,000}$$

$$= 0.093 \text{ or } 9.3\%$$

(*Note*: Profit is falling for Q > 8,983.33, so Q = 8,983.33 is a point of maximum profits).

D. Obviously, there is no easy answer. Pollution abatement is not free; it will result in higher prices and/or lower profits. Importantly, after pollution abatement costs, industry profits may no longer be adequate. Although several issues might be raised, some of the more important considerations include:

1. Output and Price: As a result of implementing the agriculture and cattle interests' recommendations, price per ton would be $3.05 higher and industry output would be 60,800 tons lower than if the fertilizer industry's recommendations were implemented.

2. Because output would be much lower with TC_1 than with TC_2, the increase in unemployment in the fertilizer industry would probably be less with the fertilizer industry proposal.

3. The return on investment with TC_1 would fall to less than 3%, while TC_2 would fall to only 9.3%. The former decrease could substantially hamper necessary investment in the fertilizer industry.

4. What is the difference in the short-term and long-run effectiveness of the two pollution abatement programs recommended by the opposing industries?

P13.7 ***Utility Regulation.*** *The Electric Company is under review by a state regulatory commissions. Relevant revenue and cost curves including a "fair" rate of return agreed upon by both the firm and the commission are as follows:*

$$P = \$85Q - \$0.2Q^2 \qquad \text{(Demand)}$$

$$MR = \partial TR/\partial Q = \$85 - \$0.4Q \qquad \text{(Marginal Revenue)}$$

$$TC = \$900 + \$20Q + \$0.8Q^2 \qquad \text{(Total Cost)}$$

$$MC = \partial TC/\partial Q = \$20 + \$1.6Q \qquad \text{(Marginal Cost)}$$

where P is price (in dollars), Q is output (in thousands of megawatt hours) and TC is total cost (in thousands of dollars).

A. If the firm were operating as a pure monopolist, what would be its optimal price/output solution and level of economic profits?

B. What price should the commission set if it wishes to eliminate economic profits?

P13.7 **SOLUTION**

A. Set $M\pi = MR - MC = 0$ to find the profit-maximizing output level where:

$$M\pi = MR - MC$$

$$0 = \$85 - \$0.4Q - \$20 - \$1.6Q$$

$$2Q = 65$$

$$Q = 32.5(000) \text{ or } 32,500 \text{ megawatt hours}$$

$$P = \$85 - \$0.2(32.5)$$

$$= \$78.50$$

$$\pi = TR - TC$$

$$= \$85Q - \$0.2Q^2 - \$900 - \$20Q - \$0.8Q^2$$

$$= -\$1Q^2 + \$65Q - \$900$$

$$= -\$1(32.5^2) + \$65(32.5) - \$900$$

$$= \$156.25(000) \text{ or } \$156,250$$

(*Note*: Profit is falling for Q > 32.5, so Q = 32.5 is a point of maximum profits).

B.   To preclude monopoly profits, the commission must set:

$$P = AR = AC = TC/Q$$

$$\$85 - \$0.2Q = (\$900 + \$20Q + \$0.8Q^2)/Q$$

$$85Q - 0.2Q^2 = 900 + 20Q + 0.8Q^2$$

$$-1Q^2 + 65Q - 900 = 0$$

This is a quadratic equation of the form:

$$aQ^2 + bQ + c = 0$$

where a = -1, b = 65 and c = -900. Its two roots can be obtained using the quadratic formula where:

$$Q = \frac{-b \pm \sqrt{b^2 - 4ac}}{2a}$$

$$= \frac{-65 \pm \sqrt{(65^2) - 4(-1)(-900)}}{2(-1)}$$

$$= \frac{-65 \pm \sqrt{4,225 - 3,600}}{-2}$$

$$= \frac{-65 \pm 25}{-2}$$

$$= 20(000) \text{ or } 45(000) \text{ megawatt hours}$$

The "upper" Q is the relevant solution because regulatory commissions generally seek the "largest quantity of service consistent with the public interest." Therefore,

$$P = \$85 - \$0.2Q$$

$$= \$85 - \$0.2(45)$$

$$= \$76$$

$$\pi = -\$1(45^2) + \$65(45) - \$900$$

$$= \$0$$

P13.8 **_Minimum Wage Regulation._** *Young & Restless Design, Inc., is a manufacturer of fashionable dresses and evening gowns in New York City's garment district. The Y & R demand and marginal revenue relations are:*

$$P = \$1,000 - \$0.02Q,$$

$$MR = \partial TR / \partial Q = \$1,000 - \$0.04Q,$$

where Q is the quantity of dresses demanded per year (in hundred). Production of each unit of Q requires 100 hours of labor, 20 hours of capital-equipment time (sewing machines, etc.), and $50 of raw materials. Y & R has a total of 400,000 hours of capital equipment time available in its production facility each year and can purchase all the labor and materials it desires. The capital equipment investment by Y & R totals $6 million, and the firm requires a 12.5% return on capital. Assume that these are the only costs incurred and that Y & R has a profit maximization objective.

A. *You have been employed by the State Unemployment Service to evaluate the effect on employment of an increase in the minimum wage. As a first step in the analysis, develop Y & R's short-run demand curve for labor.*

B. *If Y & R currently pays a wage rate of $7 per hour for labor, calculate the short-run impact on employment of an increase to a $8 minimum wage.*

C. *Calculate Y & R profits at the $7 and $8 wage levels. What are the long-run employment implications of the higher minimum wage?*

P13.8 **SOLUTION**

A. Y & R's operating rule for profit maximization is to set:

$$MC = MR.$$

To determine the firm's marginal cost function note that:

$$MC = \text{Per Unit Material Cost} + \text{Per Unit Labor Cost}$$

$$= \$50 + 100P_L$$

where P_L is the unskilled labor wage rate. Then,

$$MC = MR$$

$$\$50 + 100P_L = \$1,000 - \$0.04Q$$

$$100P_L = \$950 - \$0.04Q$$

$$P_L = \$9.5 - \$0.0004Q$$

Because 100 labor hours are required for each unit of Q,

$$L = 100Q \text{ or } Q = L/100$$

and the short-run demand for labor equation is:

$$P_L = \$9.5 - \$0.0004Q$$

$$= \$9.5 - \$0.0004(L/100)$$

$$= \$9.5 - \$0.000004L$$

or

$$L = 2,375,000 - 250,000P_L$$

B.   Employment levels at $7 and $8 per hour are calculated using the demand for labor function derived in Part A:

$$L_1 = 2,375,000 - 250,000P_L$$

$$= 2,375,000 - 250,000(\$7)$$

$$= 625,000 \text{ worker hours}$$

$$L_2 = 2,375,000 - 250,000P_L$$

$$= 2,375,000 - 250,000(\$8)$$

$$= 375,000 \text{ worker hours}$$

Thus, a $8 minimum wage would reduce the quantity of labor demanded and employment by:

$$\text{Employment Loss} = L_1 - L_2$$

$$= 625{,}000 - 375{,}0$$

$$= 250{,}000 \text{ worker hours.}$$

Assuming 2,000 worker hours per year for each employee, this is a reduction of 125 (= 250,000/2,000) jobs.

C. The long-run job loss question is addressed by analyzing Y & R's profits at optimal output levels with a $7 and $8 wage rate, respectively. With $P_L = \$7$, output equals $Q = L/(L/Q) = 625{,}000/100 = 6{,}250$. With $P_L = \$8$, output equals $Q = L/(L/Q) = 375{,}000/100 = 3{,}750$. Y & R's total revenue function is:

$$TR = P \times Q$$

$$= (\$1{,}000 - \$0.02Q)Q$$

$$= \$1{,}000Q - \$0.02Q^2$$

The total cost function is constructed as follows:

$$TC = \text{Fixed Cost} + (\text{Per Unit Material Cost}) \times Q$$

$$+ (\text{Per Unit Labor Cost}) \times Q$$

$$\text{Fixed Cost} = 0.125(\$6{,}000{,}000)$$

$$= \$750{,}000$$

$$\text{Per Unit Material Cost} = \$50$$

$$\text{Per Unit Labor Cost} = 100P_L, \text{ where } P_L \text{ is the labor wage rate}$$

Therefore,

$$TC = \$750{,}000 + \$50Q + 100P_LQ$$

$$\pi = TR - TC$$

$$= \$1,000Q - \$0.02Q^2 - \$750,000 - \$50Q - 100P_LQ$$

$$= -\$0.02Q^2 + \$950Q - 100P_LQ - \$750,000$$

With $P_L = \$7$ and $Q = 6,250$, total profit is:

$$\pi = -\$0.02(6,250^2) + \$950(6,250) - 100(\$7)(6,250) - \$750,000$$

$$= \$31,250$$

With $P_L = \$8$ and $Q = 3,750$, total profit is:

$$\pi = -\$0.02(3,750^2) + \$950(3,750) - 100(\$8)(3,750) - \$750,000$$

$$= -\$468,750 \ (\text{A loss})$$

At the $7 wage rate, economic profits are positive (recall that the $750,000 fixed cost includes the required return on capital), the firm will operate and have an incentive to expand in the long run. At $P_L = \$8$, economic profits are negative, indicating that the required return on capital is not being met. At this higher wage rate, the firm will not be able to attract the capital necessary to continue operating in the long run. The long-run impact of the increase in the minimum wage could be a loss of all such jobs at the firm.

P13.9   *Severance Taxes. Rocky Mountain Natural Resources, Inc., processes enriched ore to extract silver and lead. Each ton of processed ore yields one ounce of silver and one pound of lead. Marginal processing costs equal $5 per ton. After insurance, transportation and other marketing costs, the net price and marginal revenue of silver received by Rocky Mountain are:*

$$P_S = \$10 - \$0.00025Q_S,$$

$$MR_S = \partial TR_S/\partial Q_S = \$10 - \$0.0005Q_S,$$

and for lead are:

$$P_L = \$2 - \$0.0001Q_L,$$

$$MR_L = \partial TR_L/\partial Q_S = \$2 - \$0.0002Q_L,$$

Q_S *is ounces of silver and* Q_L *is pounds of lead.*

A. Calculate Rocky Mountain's optimal sales quantities and prices for silver and lead.

B. Calculate Rocky Mountain's optimal sales quantities and prices in the event of a 5% state silver revenue tax.

C. Calculate Rocky Mountain's optimal sales quantities and prices in the event of a 5% state lead revenue tax.

D. Which state tax is preferable in terms of minimizing short-run employment effects in the mining industry?

P13.9   SOLUTION

A. Because each unit of production generates revenue from both metals, the optimal activity level is reached when aggregate marginal revenue (silver plus lead) is equated with marginal cost:

$$MR = MR_S + MR_L \; = \; MC$$

$$\$10 - \$0.0005Q + \$2 - \$0.0002Q \; = \; \$5 \;\; (\text{Because } Q_S = Q_L = Q)$$

$$12 - 0.0007Q \; = \; 5$$

$$0.0007Q \; = \; 7$$

$$Q \; = \; 10{,}000$$

and

$$P_S \; = \; \$10 - \$0.00025(10{,}000) = \$7.50 \text{ per ounce}$$

$$P_L \; = \; \$2 - \$0.0001(10{,}000) = \$1 \text{ per pound}$$

To be optimal, marginal revenues for each joint output must be greater than or equal to zero. At this activity level:

$$MR_S \; = \; \$10 - \$0.0005(10{,}000) = \$5$$

$$MR_L \; = \; \$2 - \$0.0002(10{,}000) = \$0$$

Therefore, the quantities and prices derived above are optimal. The marginal revenue from silver covers all marginal production costs. The marginal revenue from lead equals zero, which is the marginal production cost of lead given ore processing for silver production.

B.   The effect of a silver revenue tax is to reduce MR_S. As in Part A, consider:

$$MR = MR_S + MR_L \ = \ MC$$

$$(1 - 0.05)(\$10 - \$0.0005Q) + \$2 - \$0.0002Q \ = \ \$5 \text{ (Because } Q_S = Q_L = Q)$$

$$9.50 - 0.000475Q + 2 - 0.0002Q \ = \ 5$$

$$11.50 - 0.000675Q \ = \ 5$$

$$0.000675Q \ = \ 6.50$$

$$Q \ = \ 9,630$$

and

$P_S \ = \ \$10 - \$0.00025(9,630) = \$7.59$ (Price paid by consumers)

$P_S \ = \ (1 - 0.05)\$7.59 = \$7.21$ (Price received by Rocky Mountain)

$P_L \ = \ \$2 - \$0.0001(9,630) = \$1.037$

To be optimal, marginal revenues to Rocky Mountain for each joint output must be nonnegative at this activity level.

$$MR_S \ = \ \$9.50 - \$0.000475(9,630) = \$4.93$$

$$MR_L \ = \ \$2 - \$0.0002(9,630) = \$0.07$$

Because the marginal revenues from each joint product are positive, each contributes toward covering marginal processing costs of $5, and the prices and quantities derived above are optimal.

C.   The effect of a lead revenue tax is to reduce MR_L. As above, set:

$$MR_S + MR_L \ = \ MC$$

$$\$10 - \$0.0005Q + (1 - 0.05)(\$2 - \$0.0002Q) = \$5 \quad (\text{Because } Q_S = Q_L = Q)$$

$$10 - 0.0005Q + 1.90 - \$0.00019Q = 5$$

$$11.90 - 0.00069Q = 5$$

$$0.00069Q = 6.90$$

$$Q = 10,000$$

and

$$P_S = \$7.50 \qquad\qquad (\text{As in part A})$$

$$P_L = \$1 \qquad\qquad (\text{Paid by consumers})$$

$$P_L = (1 - 0.05)\$1 = \$0.95 \qquad\qquad (\text{Received by Rocky Mountain})$$

Marginal revenues to Rocky Mountain at this activity level are again nonnegative because:

$$MR_S = \$10 - \$0.0005(10,000) = \$5$$

$$MR_L = \$1.90 - \$0.00019(10,000) = \$0$$

As in Part A, the marginal revenue from silver covers all marginal production costs. The marginal revenue from lead again equals zero, which is the marginal production cost of lead given ore processing for silver production. Prices and quantities shown above are optimal.

D. The lead revenue tax will have no short-run effect on output and employment, and is therefore preferable to a silver revenue tax.

In general, a tax on byproduct revenues affects neither output nor employment in the short-run. Such a tax on primary product revenues will always reduce both. Unlike a byproduct tax, a primary product revenue tax always causes consumer prices to rise for each product.

P13.10 **Costs and Benefits of Regulation.** *GellerBing, Inc., produces two chemical products, chemical A and chemical B, in a constant 1:1 ratio. GellerBing has long followed the practice of dumping excess or waste production into the Mississippi River, and currently incurs no cost from this activity. Total and marginal cost functions are:*

Chapter 13

$$TC = \$1,200,000 + \$100Q + \$0.08Q^2$$

$$MC = \partial TC/\partial Q = \$100 + \$0.16Q$$

where Q represents a unit of production consisting of 1 unit of A and 1 unit of B.

Total and marginal revenue curves for the two products are:

Product A:

$$TR_A = \$825Q_A - \$0.045Q_A^2$$

$$MR_A = \partial TR_A/\partial Q_A = \$825 - \$0.09Q_A$$

Product B:

$$TR_B = \$400Q_B - \$0.1Q_B^2$$

$$MR_B = \partial TR_B/\partial Q_B = \$400 - \$0.2Q_B$$

A. Calculate the optimal price/output combination for each product, assuming GellerBing operates as a profit maximizing firm. Calculate profits under this assumption.

B. Assume now that the State Pollution Control Board imposes a fine of $50 per unit on any excess or waste production that is dumped into the Mississippi River. Calculate optimal output, prices and profits in this situation.

C. Calculate the smallest fine per unit that would cause GellerBing to stop all dumping.

D. Who is helped and who is hurt by imposition of the dumping fine?

P13.10   SOLUTION

A. Deriving the correct solution to this problem requires that one look at the production and sales options available to the firm. One option is to produce and sell equal quantities of chemicals A and B. In this case, the firm sets $M\pi = MR - MC = 0$:

$$M\pi = MR_A + MR_B - MC$$

$$0 = \$825 - 0.09Q + \$400 - \$0.2Q$$

$$-\$100 - \$0.16Q$$

$$0 = \$1,125 - \$0.45Q$$

$$0.45Q = 1,125$$

$$Q = 2,500 \text{ units}$$

The profit-maximizing output level for production and sale of equal quantities of chemicals A and B is 2,500 units. However, one must check to be sure that the marginal revenues of both chemicals are positive at this sales level before claiming that this is an optimal activity level. Marginal revenues for each chemical evaluated at an output level of 2,500 units are:

$$MR_A = \$825 - \$0.09(2,500) = \$600$$

$$MR_B = \$400 - \$0.2(2,500) = -\$100$$

Notice that $MC = \$100 + \$0.16(2,500) = \$500$. Despite the fact that $MR_A + MR_B = \$600 - \$100 = \$500 = MC$, the $Q = 2,500$ units activity level is suboptimal. Given production of Q to sell chemical A, the marginal cost of chemical B is zero; it is free. Output of chemical A is being "held down" by the negative marginal revenue associated with sales of chemical B. This invalidates the entire solution developed above. The problem must be set up in such a way as to recognize that GellerBing will stop selling chemical B at the point where its marginal revenue becomes zero because, given production for chemical A, the marginal cost of chemical B is zero. Set:

$$MR_B = MC_B$$

$$\$400 - \$0.2Q_B = \$0$$

$$0.2Q_B = 400$$

$$Q_B = 2,000 \text{ units}$$

Thus, 2,000 units of chemical B is the maximum that will be sold. Absent regulation, any excess units will be dumped into the Mississippi River. The price for B at 2,000 units is:

$$P_B = TR_B/Q_B$$

$$= \$400 - \$0.1Q_B$$

$$= \$400 - \$0.1(2,000)$$

$$= \$200$$

To determine the optimal production level of chemical A, set the marginal revenue of A equal to the marginal cost of producing another unit of the output package.

$$MR_A = MC_A = MC_Q$$

$$\$825 - \$0.09Q = \$100 + \$0.16Q$$

$$0.25Q = 725$$

$$Q_A = 2,900 \text{ units} \quad (\text{Because } Q_A = Q)$$

and

$$P_A = TR_A/Q_A$$

$$= \$825 - \$0.045Q_A$$

$$= \$825 - \$0.045(2,900)$$

$$= \$694.50$$

The firm maximizes profits by producing 2,900 units of output, selling all 2,900 units of chemical A at a price of $694.50, and 2,000 units of chemical B at a price of $200. Nine hundred units of chemical B will be dumped into the Mississippi. Total profits for GellerBing are:

$$\pi = P_AQ_A + P_BQ_B - TC$$

$$= \$694.50(2,900) + \$200(2,000) - \$1,200,000$$

$$- \$100(2,900) - \$0.08(2,900^2)$$

$$= \$251,250$$

B.   The imposition of a waste disposal fine alters GellerBing's relevant cost functions. Because it costs the firm a $50 fine for every unit of B dumped into the Mississippi. The sale of any units of B with marginal revenues greater than a -$50 will result in increased profits. The marginal cost of producing and *selling* chemical B is -$50. The profit-maximizing sales quantity for B is determined by setting MR_B = -$50.

$$MR_B = MC_B \text{ - Fine savings}$$

$$\$400 - \$0.2Q_B = \$0 - \$50$$

$$0.2Q_B = 450$$

$$Q_B = 2{,}250 \text{ units}$$

and

$$P_B = \$400 - \$0.1(2{,}250)$$

$$= \$175$$

To determine the optimal quantity of production for chemical A, the marginal revenue of A is set equal to the marginal cost of producing one more unit of the output package, recognizing that there is a $50 added cost associated with dumping of the marginal unit of B produced.

$$MR_A = MC_Q$$

$$\$825 - \$0.09Q = \$100 + \$0.16Q + \$50$$

$$0.25Q = 675$$

$$Q_A = 2{,}700 \text{ units} \quad (\text{Because } Q_A = Q)$$

and

$$P_A = \$825 - \$0.045(2{,}700)$$

$$= \$703.50$$

Total profits for GellerBing are:

$$\pi = P_A Q_A + P_B Q_B - TC - \$50Q_B$$

$$= \$703.50(2,700) + \$175(2,250) - \$1,200,000$$

$$- \$100(2,700) - \$0.08(2,700^2) - \$50(450)$$

$$= \$217,500$$

C. The first section of part A shows the $Q = 2,500$ unit profit-maximizing output level for the firm assuming it produces and sells equal quantities of the two products. In that circumstance, $MR_B = -\$100$ at an output and sales level of 2,500 units. Any fine less than \$100 per unit will result in at least some dumping because marginal fine costs are more than covered by marginal revenues derived from sale of chemical A. Any fine greater than or equal to \$100 is sufficient to eliminate all dumping.

D. Given a per unit fine on dumping of \$50, GellerBing maximizes profit by trimming production to 2,700 from 2,900 units. Both with and without a fine on dumping, all of chemical A that is produced is sold. Given the lower sales quantities of chemical A when a fine is imposed on dumping, the price to Chemical A customers rises by \$9 from \$694.50 to \$703.50. Sales of chemical B rise from 2,000 units to 2,250 units, and the price of B falls by \$25 from \$200 to \$175. chemical A customers are worse off as a result of the fine being imposed; chemical B customers are better off. Imposition of the fine has the beneficial effect of reducing pollution. With a \$50 fine, dumping of B falls by 50% from 900 units (= 2,900 - 2,000) to 450 units (= 2,700 - 2,250). This benefit of regulation is somewhat offset by the fact that some customers face higher prices, payments to suppliers and employment opportunities will decrease.

A major loser following imposition of the dumping fine is GellerBing in terms of the resulting impact on profits. Before imposition of the fine, company profits of \$251,250 represent roughly 10.4% of the company's \$2.4 million in sales. After imposition of the dumping fine, profits of \$217,500 amount to about 9.5% of roughly \$2.3 million in sales. Profits have declined by \$33,750, or 13.4%. This new lower profit level may not be sufficient to sustain the company's need to build new plant and equipment in the long run.

Chapter 14

RISK ANALYSIS

Managers of successful companies incorporate risk analysis into everyday decision making. The certainty equivalent method converts expected risky profit streams into certain sum equivalents to eliminate value differences that result from different risk levels. For risk-averse decision makers, the value of a risky stream of payments is less than the value of a certain stream, and the application of certainty equivalent adjustment factors results in a downward adjustment to the value of expected returns. For risk-seeking decision makers, the value of a risky stream of payments is greater than that of a certain stream, and application of certainty equivalent adjustment factors results in an upward adjustment in the value of expected returns. In both cases, risky dollars are converted into certain-sum equivalents. Another method used to reflect uncertainty in the basic valuation model is the risk-adjusted discount rate approach. In this technique, the interest rate used in the denominator of the basic valuation model depends on the level of risk associated with a given cash flow. For highly risk-averse decision makers, higher discount rates are implemented; for less risk-averse decision makers, lower discount rates are employed. Using this technique, discounted expected profit streams reflect risk differences and become directly comparable.

This chapter is an essential component of managerial economics because it shows how managers deal effectively with risk. Attitudes toward risk taking are a matter of personal and corporate preferences. As such, they cannot be derived through economic analysis. However, in light of personal and corporate risk preferences, managerial economics can be effectively employed to determine an appropriate course of action.

CHAPTER OUTLINE

I. **CONCEPTS OF RISK AND UNCERTAINTY**

    A. **Economic Risk and Uncertainty:** To make effective investment decisions, managers must appreciate the difference between risk and uncertainty.

        1. Economic risk is the chance of loss because all possible outcomes and their probability of occurrence are unknown.

        2. Uncertainty exists when the outcomes of managerial decisions cannot be predicted with absolute accuracy but all possibilities and their associated probabilities are known.

    B. **General Risk Categories:** Risk analysis is facilitated when economic risk can be categorized and quantified.

1. Business risk is the chance of loss associated with a given managerial decision.

2. Market risk is the chance that a portfolio of investments can lose money because of overall swings in the financial markets.

3. Inflation risk is the danger that a general increase in the price level will undermine the real economic value of corporate agreements or assets.

4. Interest-rate risk is another type of market risk that can severely affect the value of corporate investments and obligations.

5. Credit risk is the chance that another party will fail to abide by contractual obligations.

6. Liquidity risk is the difficulty of selling corporate assets or investments at favorable prices under typical market conditions.

7. Derivative risk is the chance that volatile financial derivatives such as commodities futures and index options could create losses by increasing rather than decreasing price volatility.

C. **Special Risks of Global Operations:** Special risks are borne by companies that pursue a global rather than just a domestic investment strategy.

1. Cultural risk is the chance of loss due to product market differences derived from distinctive social customs.

2. Currency risk is the chance of loss due to price swings in the relative value of domestic and foreign currencies.

3. Global investors experience government policy risk because foreign government grants of monopoly franchises, tax abatements, and favored trade status can be tenuous.

4. Expropriation risk is the chance that business property located abroad might be seized by host governments.

II.   PROBABILITY CONCEPTS

A. **Probability Distribution:** The probability of an event is the chance, or odds, that the incident will occur.
1. Business risk is the chance of loss associated with a managerial decision.

2. If the probability of occurrence is assigned to each possible event, the listing is called a probability distribution.

3. A payoff matrix illustrates the dollar outcome associated with each possible state of nature.

B. Expected Value: Expected value is the anticipated realization from a given payoff matrix and probability distribution.

1. Expected-profit is expressed by the equation:

$$\text{Expected Profit} = E(\pi) = \sum_{i=1}^{n} \pi_i \times p_i,$$

where π_i is profit and p_i is probability.

C. Absolute Risk Measurement: Tight probability distributions imply low risk because the chance that actual outcomes will differ from expected values is small.

1. Absolute risk is measured by the standard deviation and is the square root of the variance:

$$\text{Standard Deviation} = \sigma = \sqrt{\sum_{i=1}^{n} [\pi_i - E(\pi)]^2 p_i}.$$

D. Relative Risk Measurement: Relative risk is the variation in possible returns compared to the expected payoff amount.

1. A popular measure of relative risk is the coefficient of variation:

$$\text{Coefficient of Variation} = v = \frac{\sigma}{E(\pi)}.$$

2. When comparing decision alternatives with costs and benefits that are not of approximately equal size, the coefficient of variation measures relative risk better than the standard deviation.

E.   **Other Risk Measures:** The contribution of a single investment project to the overall return variation of the firm's asset portfolio is measured by beta.

   1.   Beta is a measure of the systematic variability or covariance of one asset's returns with returns on a portfolio of assets.

III.   **STANDARD NORMAL CONCEPT**

A.   **Normal Distribution:** A normal distribution has a symmetrical distribution about the mean or expected value.

   1.   The smaller the standard deviation, the smaller the probability of an outcome that is very different from the expected value.

   2.   For a normal distribution:

   a.   Actual outcomes lie within ±1 standard deviation of the mean roughly 68 per cent of the time.

   b.   The probability that actual outcomes will be within two standard deviations of the expected outcome is approximately 95 per cent.

   c.   There is greater than a 99 per cent probability that actual outcomes occur within three standard deviations of the mean.

B.   **Standardized Variables:** A standardized variable has a mean of zero and a standard deviation equal to one.

   1.   Any distribution of revenue, cost, or profit data can be standardized with the following formula:

$$z = \frac{x - \mu}{\sigma},$$

where z is the standardized variable, x is the outcome of interest, and μ and σ are the mean and standard deviation of the distribution, respectively.

   2.   When $z = 1.0$, the point of interest is 1σ away from the mean; when $z = 2$, the value is 2σ away from the mean, and so on.

3. The probability of an outcome falling within two standards of the mean is 95.46 per cent; 99.74 per cent of all outcomes fall within three standard deviations of the mean.

C. **Use of the Standard Normal Concept: An Example:** The standard normal concept is often used to estimate the probability of profitable operation.

IV. **UTILITY THEORY AND RISK ANALYSIS**

A. **Possible Risk Attitudes:** Three possible attitudes toward risk are present.

1. Risk aversion characterizes individuals who seek to avoid or minimize risk.

2. Risk neutrality describes decision makers who focus on expected returns and disregard the dispersion of returns (risk).

3. Risk seeking portrays decision makers who prefer risk.

B. **Relation Between Money and its Utility:** At the center of the risk aversion concept is the notion of diminishing marginal utility for money.

1. Risk aversion implies that the total utility of money rises at a diminishing pace for additional increments of money (marginal utility of money is falling).

2. Those who are indifferent to risk perceive a strictly proportional relationship between total utility and money (marginal utility of money is constant).

3. Risk seekers perceive a more-than-proportional relation between total utility and money (marginal utility of money is rising).

C. **An Example of Risk Aversion:** Utility theory dictates that investments are chosen on the basis of their ability to enhance decision-maker utility or well-being.

V. **ADJUSTING THE VALUATION MODEL FOR RISK**

A. **Basic Valuation Model:** The basic valuation model states that the value of the firm equals the discounted present worth of future profits:

$$V = \sum_{t=1}^{n} \frac{\pi_t}{(1 + i)^t}.$$

1. Under conditions of certainty, the numerator of this expression is profit, and the denominator is a time-value adjustment using the risk-free rate of return i.

2. Under conditions of uncertainty, profits shown as π equal the expected value of profits during each future period.

B. Certainty Equivalent Adjustments: Any expected risky amount can be converted to an equivalent certain sum using the certainty equivalent adjustment factor, α, calculated as the ratio of a certain sum divided by an expected risky amount, where both dollar values provide the same level of utility:

$$\begin{array}{l}\text{Certainty}\\ \text{Equivalent}\\ \text{Adjustment}\\ \text{Factor}\end{array} = \alpha = \frac{\text{Equivalent Certain Sum}}{\text{Expected Risky Sum}}.$$

1. $\alpha < 1$ implies risk aversion.

2. $\alpha = 1$ implies risk indifference.

3. $\alpha > 1$ implies risk preference.

4. The basic valuation model can be converted into a risk-adjusted valuation model that explicitly accounts for risk:

$$V = \sum_{t=1}^{n} \frac{\alpha E(\pi_t)}{(1 + i)^t}.$$

In this risk-adjusted valuation model, expected future profits, $E(\pi_t)$, are converted to their certainty equivalents, $\alpha E(\pi_t)$, and are discounted at a risk-free rate, i.

C. Certainty Equivalent Adjustment Example: If a potential project's required investment and risk levels are known, the α implied by a decision to accept the investment project can be calculated.

1. Risk-averse individuals should invest in projects if calculated α's are *less* than or equal to those for accepted projects in the same risk class.

D. **Risk-Adjusted Discount Rates:** Another way to incorporate risk in managerial decision making is to adjust the discount rate or denominator of the basic valuation model.

1. As risk increases, higher expected returns on investment are required to compensate investors for the additional risk.

2. The basic valuation model can be adapted to account for risk through adjustment of the discount rate, k, where:

$$V = \sum_{t=1}^{n} \frac{E(\pi_t)}{(1 + k)^t},$$

3. The risk-adjusted discount rate k is the sum of the risk-free rate of return, R_F, plus the required risk premium, R_p:

$$k = R_F + R_P$$

E. **Risk-Adjusted Discount Rate Example:** Investment projects with higher as opposed to lower risk-adjusted value should be chosen to maximize the value of the firm.

VI. **DECISION TREES AND COMPUTER SIMULATION**

A. **Decision Trees:** A decision tree is a visual mapping of the sequential decision-making process.

1. Decision trees are designed for analyzing decision problems that involve a series of choice alternatives that are constrained by previous decisions.

   a. Decision points are instances when management must select among several choice alternatives.

   b. Chance events are possible outcomes following each decision point.

2. The decision that offers the largest risk-adjusted net present value is the optimal choice.

3. The expected value and risk of each decision alternative must be calculated to help arrive at an appropriate managerial decision.

B. Computer Simulation: Computer simulation involves the use of computer software and sophisticated desktop computers to create a variety of decision outcome scenarios.

  1. Using computer simulation, hypothetical "what if?" questions can be asked and answered on the basis of measurable differences in underlying assumptions.

  2. Computer simulations require probability distribution estimates for investment outlays, unit sales, product prices, input prices, and asset lives.

      a. Full-scale simulations are expensive and time consuming, and restricted to projects such as major plant expansions or new-product decisions.

      b. Limited-scale simulations are used to project outcomes for projects or strategies.

C. Computer Simulation Example: Computer simulation randomly selects revenue and cost levels from each relevant distribution, and uses this information to estimate future profits, net present values, or the rate of return on investment.

  1. The simulation process is repeated a large number of times to identify the central tendency or expected value of projected returns.

  2. Computer simulation illustrates the frequency pattern and range of future returns that can be plotted and analyzed.

VII. USES OF GAME THEORY IN RISK ANALYSIS

A. Game Theory and Auction Strategy: Mathematician John von Neuman and economist Oskar Morgenstern discovered that deciding when to bluff, fold, stand pat, or raise is not only relevant when playing cards, but also when opposed by aggressive competitors in the market place.

  1. One of the most interesting business uses of game theory is to analyze bidder strategy in auctions.

  2. The most familiar type of auction is an English auction where an auctioneer keeps raising the price until a single highest bidder remains.

      a. The advantage of an English auction is that it is widely regarded as a fair and open process.

b. It is an effective approach for obtaining high winning bid prices.

3. The winner's curse results when overly aggressive bidders pay more than the economic value of auctioned off items.

4. Another commonly employed auction method is a sealed-bid auction where all bids are secret, and the highest bid wins.

   a. A compelling advantage of the sealed-bid approach is that it is relatively free from the threat of collusion.

   b. The downside to the approach is that it often encourages bidders to act cautiously.

5. A relatively rare sealed-bid auction method is a Vickrey auction, where the highest sealed bid wins, but the winner pays the price of the second-highest bid.

   a. A disadvantage of the technique is that it creates the perception that the buyer is taking advantage of the seller by paying only the second highest price.

6. Another uncommon auctioning method is the so-called reverse or Dutch auction.

   a. In a Dutch auction, the auctioneer keeps lowering a very high price until a winning bidder emerges.

   b. The winning bidder is the first participant willing to pay the auctioneer's price.

   c. A disadvantage of this approach is that bidders tend to act cautiously out of fear of overpaying for auctioned items.

B. **Maximin Decision Rule:** The maximin (or secure strategy) criterion states that the decision maker should select the alternative that provides the best of the worst possible outcomes.

1. This criterion instructs one to maximize the minimum possible outcome.

C. **Minimax Regret Decision Rule:** The minimax regret criterion states that the decision maker should minimize the maximum possible regret (opportunity loss) associated with a wrong decision *after the fact*.

1.   This criterion instructs one to minimize the difference between possible outcomes and the best outcome for each state of nature.

D.   **Cost of Uncertainty:** An unavoidable opportunity loss is the cost associated with uncertainty.

1.   The cost of uncertainty is measured by the minimum expected opportunity loss.

a.   Using this concept, it is possible to assess the value of gaining additional information before choosing among decision alternatives.

2.   Firms often engage in activities aimed at reducing the uncertainty of various alternatives before making an irrevocable decision.

VIII.   **SUMMARY**

PROBLEMS & SOLUTIONS

P14.1   **Expected Value.** *Glen Ford Motors, Inc., estimates that three out of every fifty individuals who take demonstration test drive will actually purchase a Ford Explorer. The firm's gross profit margin per vehicle is $500 and the cost of a test ride is $10.*

A.   *What is the expected profit of each test ride given?*

P14.1   **SOLUTION**

A.   The probability of an individual who takes a test ride actually purchasing a car is 3/50 = 0.06. Because Glen Ford's gross profit margin is $500, the expected gross profit margin per test drive is:

$$\text{Expected Profit} = \frac{\text{Purchase probability} \times}{\text{Gross margin} - \text{Test ride cost}}$$

$$= 0.06(\$500) - \$10$$

$$= \$20$$

P14.2   **Probability Concepts.** *The Cellular Telephone Corporation has just completed development work on a new line of cellular telephones. Preliminary market research indicates two feasible marketing strategies: (a) concentration on developing general consumer acceptance by advertising through newspapers, television, and other media; or (b) concentration on distributor acceptance of the cellular telephone through intensive sales calls by company representatives, extensive development of software support (user programs), and so forth. Eleanor Rigby, Celluar Telephone's marketing manager, has developed sales estimates under each alternative plan, and has arranged rough payoff matrices according to her assessment of likely product acceptance under each plan. These data are illustrated below:*

Strategy 1: Consumer-Oriented Promotion

Probability	Sales Outcome
0.1	$500,000
0.4	1,500,000
0.4	2,500,000
0.1	3,500,000

Strategy 2: Distributor-Oriented Promotion

Probability	Sales Outcome
0.3	$1,000,000
0.4	1,500,000
0.3	2,000,000

A. Assume that the company has a 50% profit margin on sales. Calculate the expected profits for each plan.

B. Construct a simple bar graph of the possible profit outcomes for each plan. On the basis of the appearance of the two graphs, which plan appears to be more risky?

C. Calculate the standard deviation and coefficient of variation associated with the profit distribution of each plan.

D. Assume that management of Celluar Telephone has a utility function like the one illustrated below. Which marketing strategy should Rigby recommend?

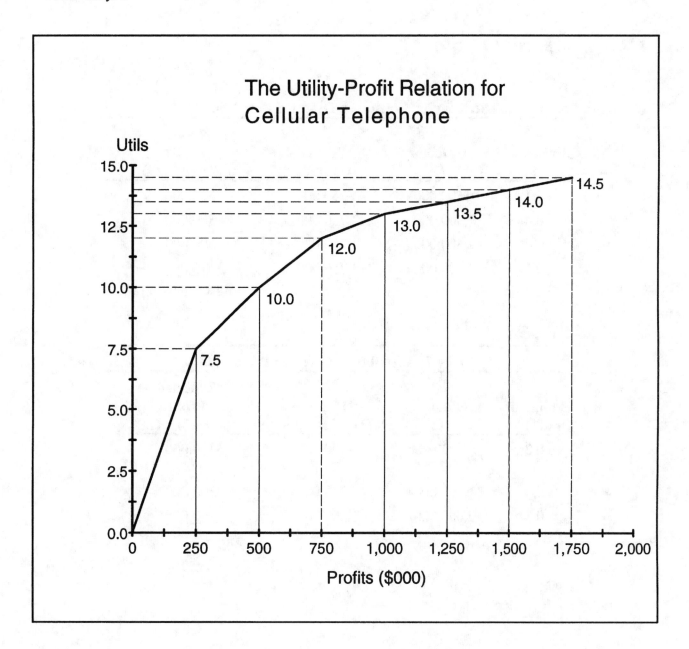

The Utility-Profit Relation for Cellular Telephone

P14.2 **SOLUTION**

A.

Strategy 1: Consumer-Oriented Promotion

Probability (1)	Sales Outcomes (2)	Profit (3) = (2) × 0.5	Expected Profit (4) = (3) × (1)
0.1	$500,000	$250,000	$25,000
0.4	1,500,000	750,000	300,000
0.4	2,500,000	1,250,000	500,000
0.1	3,500,000	1,750,000	<u>175,000</u>

$$E(\pi_1) = \$1,000,000$$

Strategy 2: Distributor-Oriented Promotion

Probability (1)	Sales Outcomes (2)	Profit (3) = (2) × 0.5	Expected Profit (4) = (3) × (1)
0.3	$1,000,000	$500,000	$150,000
0.4	1,500,000	750,000	300,000
0.3	2,000,000	1,000,000	<u>300,000</u>

$$E(\pi_2) = \$750,000$$

B.

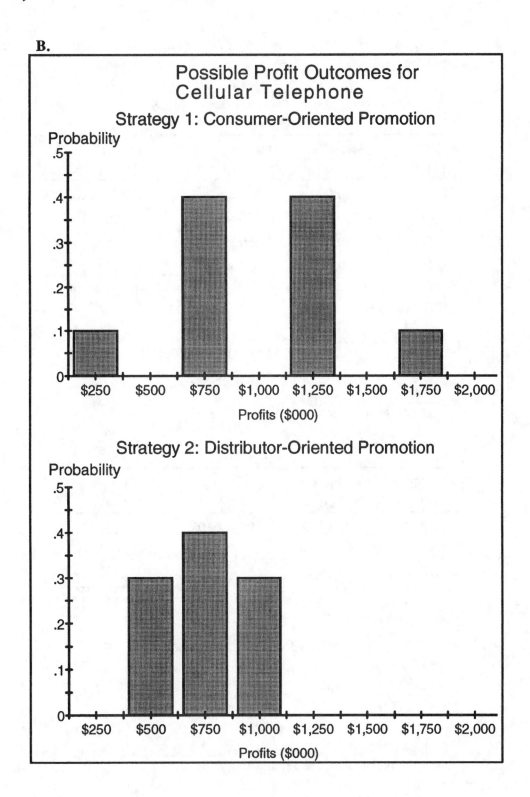

Strategy 1 appears to be more risky than strategy 2 due to the greater variability of outcomes.

C.

Strategy 1:

Probability (1)	Deviations (2)	(Deviations)^2 (3)	(1) × (3) = (4)
0.1	-750,000	5.625×10^{11}	5.625×10^{10}
0.4	-250,000	6.250×10^{10}	2.5×10^{10}
0.4	250,000	6.250×10^{10}	2.5×10^{10}
0.1	750,000	5.625×10^{11}	5.625×10^{10}
			$\sigma_1^2 = 16.25 \times 10^{10}$

$$\sigma_1 = \sqrt{\$16.25 \times 10^{10}} = \$4.0311 \times 10^5 = \$403,110$$

$$V_1 = \frac{\$403,110}{\$1,000,000} = 0.403$$

Strategy 2:

Probability (1)	Deviations (2)	(Deviations)^2 (3)	(1) × (3) = (4)
0.3	-250,000	6.25×10^{11}	1.875×10^{10}
0.4	0	0	0
0.3	250,000	6.25×10^{10}	1.875×10^{10}
			$\sigma^2 = 3.75 \times 10^{10}$

$$\sigma_2 = \sqrt{\$3.75 \times 10^{10}} = \$1.9365 \times 10^5 = \$193,650$$

$$V_2 = \frac{\$193,650}{\$750,000} = 0.258$$

These calculations make more precise the conclusion reached in part B that strategy 1 is the more risky marketing approach.

D.

		Strategy 1:	
Probability (1)	**Profits (2)**	**Utils (3)**	**Expected Utility (4) = (3) × (1)**
0.1	$250,000	7.50	0.75
0.4	750,000	12.00	4.80
0.4	1,250,000	13.50	5.40
0.1	1,750,000	14.50	<u>1.45</u>

$$E(U_1) = 12.40 \text{ utils}$$

		Strategy 2:	
Probability (1)	**Profits (2)**	**Utils (3)**	**Expected Utility (4) = (3) × (1)**
0.3	$500,000	10	3.0
0.4	750,000	12	4.8
0.3	1,000,000	13	<u>3.9</u>

$$E(U_2) = 11.7 \text{ utils}$$

Rigby should recommend strategy 1 because of its higher expected utility. In this case, the higher expected profit of strategy 1 more than offsets its greater riskiness.

P14.3   *Expected Utility. Penny Lane is considering two alternative investments, each costing $7,000. Present values of possible outcomes and their probabilities of occurrence are:*

Investment A

	Outcome		
	1	*2*	*3*
Present Value	$6,000	$8,000	$10,000
Probability of occurrence	0.25	0.50	0.25

Investment B

	Outcome		
	1	*2*	*3*
Present Value	$5,000	$9,000	$10,000
Probability of occurrence	0.30	0.50	0.20

A. Calculate the expected present values of the two investments.

B. Calculate the standard deviation for each investment. Which alternative is riskier?

C. If Lane has a constant marginal utility of income as indicated by the utility function $U = 30 + 2X$, where X is thousands of dollars of present value, which investment should she choose? Why?

D. If Lane's utility of income is given by the function $U = 30X - X^2$, which investment should she select? Why?

P14.3 **SOLUTION**

A.

INVESTMENT A

Present Value (1)	Probability (2)	Expected Present Value (3) = (1) × (2)
$6,000	0.25	$1,500
8,000	0.50	4,000
10,000	0.25	2,500
		$E(PV_A) = \$8,000$

INVESTMENT B

Present Value (1)	Probability (2)	Expected Present Value (3) = (1) × (2)
$5,000	0.3	$1,500
9,000	0.5	4,500
10,000	0.2	2,000
		E(PV$_B$) = $8,000

B.

$$\sigma_A = \sqrt{0.25(\$6,000 - \$8,000)^2 + 0.50(\$8,000 - \$8,000)^2 + 0.25(\$10,000 - \$8,000)^2}$$

$$= \sqrt{\$2,000,000}$$

$$= \$1,414.21$$

$$\sigma_B = \sqrt{0.3(\$5,000 - \$8,000)^2 + 0.5(\$9,000 - \$8,000)^2 + 0.2(\$10,000 - \$8,000)^2}$$

$$= \sqrt{\$4,000,000}$$

$$= \$2,000$$

Investment B is more risky than investment A.

C. When $U = 30 + 2X$, expected utility is:

INVESTMENT A

Probability (1)	PV (2)	X (3)	Utility (U = 30 + 2X) (4)	Expected Utility (5) = (4) × (1)
0.25	$6,000	6	42	10.5
0.50	8,000	8	46	23.0
0.25	10,000	10	50	12.5
				$E(U_A) = 46$ utils

INVESTMENT B

Probability (1)	PV (2)	X (3)	Utility (U = 30 + 2X) (4)	Expected Utility (5) = (4) × (1)
0.3	$5,000	5	40	12
0.5	9,000	9	48	24
0.2	10,000	10	50	10
				$E(U_B) = 46$ utils

With a linear utility function (constant marginal utility), Lane would be indifferent between the two investments. So long as the alternatives have equal expected dollar returns, they must provide the same expected utility to an individual exhibiting an indifference to risk.

D.   When utility $U = 30X - X^2$, expected utility is:

INVESTMENT A

Probability (1)	PV (2)	X (3)	Utility (U = 30X - X²) (4)	Expected Utility (5) = (4) × (1)
0.25	$6,000	6	144	36
0.50	8,000	8	176	88
0.25	10,000	10	200	50
				$E(U_A) = 174$ utils

INVESTMENT B

Probability (1)	PV (2)	X (3)	Utility ($U = 30X - X^2$) (4)	Expected Utility (5) = (4) × (1)
0.3	$5,000	5	125	37.5
0.5	9,000	9	189	94.5
0.2	10,000	10	200	40.0

$$E(U_A) = 172 \text{ utils}$$

Investment A should be selected because of its higher expected utility. In this case, Lane exhibits risk aversion (diminishing marginal utility), and, hence, with equal expected dollar returns, he prefers the alternative with less risk. We know Lane has a diminishing marginal utility of income because marginal utility will fall as income grows.

P14.4   ***Certainty Equivalent Adjustment Factors.*** *Blue Chip Investors, Ltd. offers limited partnership investments to individual investors. A current $1.5 million offering consists of 25 equal shares priced at $60,000 each. Proceeds from the offering will be used to purchase and renovate a local apartment complex. BCI projects a total investment return for the project of $4 million, or $160,000 per share, to be paid in one lump sum at the end of 7 years.*

A.   *Using a 6% risk-free rate of return, calculate the discounted present value of projected returns for a single unit.*

B.   *Calculate and interpret the minimum certainty equivalent adjustment factor α necessary to justify investment in the project.*

P14.4   SOLUTION

A.   PV of future returns   =   Projected returns × (PVIF, n= 7, i = 6%)

= $160,000(0.6651)

= $106,416

B.   From the certainty equivalent adjustment factor formula note that:

$$\alpha = \frac{\text{Certain Sum}}{\text{Expected Risky Return}}$$

$$= \frac{\$60,000}{\$106,416}$$

$$= 0.56$$

In order for investors to justify investment in the project, each dollar of expected risky return must be worth at least 56¢ in certain dollars.

P14.5 **Certainty Equivalents.** *The Hungry Heifer, Inc., is considering opening a new restaurant in Hanover, Indiana. Projecting net profits for such an outlet is quite subjective, but Norm Peterson, Hungry Heifer's marketing director, estimates:*

Probability	Annual Net Profits
0.125	$135,000
0.750	225,000
0.125	315,000

During the past year, The Hungry Heifer opened new restaurants in four different markets. In analyzing these investment decisions, you discover the following:

Market	Certainty Equivalent	Coefficient of Variation
A	0.80	0.10
B	0.75	0.15
C	0.70	0.19
D	0.60	0.22

A. *Calculate the expected return, standard deviation and coefficient of variation of annual net profits for the Hanover restaurant.*

B. *Given Hungry Heifer's historical decisions, calculate the range for the maximum acceptable investment requirement for the Hanover restaurant given an anticipated ten-year project life, and a 6% risk-free rate of return.*

P14.5 **SOLUTION**

A. $E(R) = \$135,000(0.125) + \$225,000(0.750) + \$315,000(0.125) = \$225,000.$

$$\sigma = \sqrt{(\$135,000 - \$225,000)^2(0.125)}$$

$$\overline{+\ (\$225{,}000\ -\ \$225{,}000)^2(0.750)}$$

$$\overline{+\ (\$315{,}000\ -\ \$225{,}000)^2(0.125)}$$

$$=\ \sqrt{\$1.0125\ \times\ 10^9\ +\ \$1.0125\ \times\ 10^9}$$

$$=\ \$45{,}000$$

$$V\ =\ \frac{\sigma}{E(R)}\ =\ \frac{\$45{,}000}{\$225{,}000}\ =\ 0.2$$

B. By definition,

$$\alpha\ =\ \frac{\text{Certain sum}}{\text{Expected risky return}}$$

$$=\ \frac{\text{Investment requirement}}{E(R)}$$

Therefore, it is obvious that an acceptable investment requirement for an investment with a one year life would be:

$$\text{Investment Requirement}\ =\ \alpha\ \times\ E(R)$$

For the Hanover restaurant, which has a life span of more than one year, the range within which an acceptable investment requirement will be found using the relation:

$$\text{Investment Requirement}\ =\ \sum_{t=1}^{n}\frac{\alpha\ \times\ E(R)}{(1\ +\ i)^t}$$

The Hanover restaurant has a $V = 0.2$, which is between $V_C = 0.19$ and $V_D = 0.22$. This implies that an acceptable certainty equivalent lies between $\alpha_C = 0.70$ and $\alpha_D = 0.60$.

In this instance, an acceptable investment requirement is found within the range:

$$\text{"High" Investment Limit} = \sum_{t=1}^{n} \frac{\alpha_C \times E(R)}{(1 + i)^t}$$

$$= \sum_{t=1}^{10} \frac{0.70(\$225,000)}{(1.06)^{10}}$$

$$= (\text{PVIFA}, n=10, i=6\%)(0.70)(\$225,000)$$

$$= (7.3601)(0.70)(\$225,000)$$

$$= \$1,159,216.$$

$$\text{"Low" Investment Limit} = \sum_{t=1}^{n} \frac{\alpha_D \times E(R)}{(1 + i)^t}$$

$$= \sum_{t=1}^{10} \frac{0.60(\$225,000)}{(1.06)^{10}}$$

$$= (\text{PVIFA}, n=10, i=6\%)(0.60)(\$225,000)$$

$$= (7.3601)(0.60)(\$225,000)$$

$$= \$993,614.$$

Thus, the maximum acceptable investment requirement which would be consistent with Hungry Heifer's past management decisions will be found within the range \$993,614 to \$1,159,216.

P14.6   **The Standard Normal.** *Dan Cooper, is owner-operator of D.B. Cooper's Sky Diving School, Inc., in Portland, Oregon. Cooper is considering a boost in advertising to increase sales. Cooper plans to make his media decision using the following data on the expected success of television versus newspaper promotions:*

	Market Response	Probability	Revenues
Newspaper	Poor	0.18	\$3,400
	Good	0.64	5,000
	Very good	0.18	6,600

Television	Poor	0.245	4,000
	Good	0.51	6,500
	Very good	0.245	9,000

Assume that the returns from each promotion are normally distributed, and that net revenues are before advertising expenses.

A. *Calculate the expected return, standard deviation, and coefficient of variation for each promotion.*

B. *Which promotion is most risky? Why?*

C. *If the newspaper promotion costs $3,752 while the television promotion costs $2,825, what is the probability each will generate a profit?*

D. *Which promotion should be chosen?*

P14.6   SOLUTION

A.   Newspaper Promotion

$$E(R_N) = \$3,400(0.18) + \$5,000(0.64) + \$7,600(0.18)$$

$$= \$5,000$$

$$\sigma_N = \sqrt{(\$3,400 - \$5,000)^2(0.18) + (\$5,000 - \$5,000)^2(0.64)}$$
$$\overline{+ (\$6,600 - \$5,000)^2(0.18)}$$

$$= \$960$$

$$V_N = \frac{\sigma_N}{E(R_N)} = \frac{\$960}{\$5,000} = 0.192$$

Television Promotion

$$E(R_{TV}) = \$4,000(0.245) + \$6,500(0.51) + \$9,000(0.245)$$

$$= \$6,500$$

$$\sigma_{TV} = \sqrt{(\$4{,}000 - \$6{,}500)^2(0.245) + (\$6{,}500 - \$6{,}500)^2(0.51)}$$

$$\overline{+ (\$9{,}000 - \$6{,}500)^2(0.245)}$$

$$= \$1{,}750$$

$$V_{TV} = \frac{\sigma_{TV}}{E(R_{TV})} = \frac{\$1{,}750}{\$6{,}500} = 0.269$$

B. The television promotion has a higher standard deviation and coefficient of variation than does the newspaper promotion, and is thus the more risky of the two promotion alternatives.

C. To calculate the probability that each promotion will generate a profit one must consider the normal curve and relevant values of the standard normal. In graphic terms, one must calculate the share of the total area under the normal curve which is to the right of each breakeven point, the relevant point of interest.

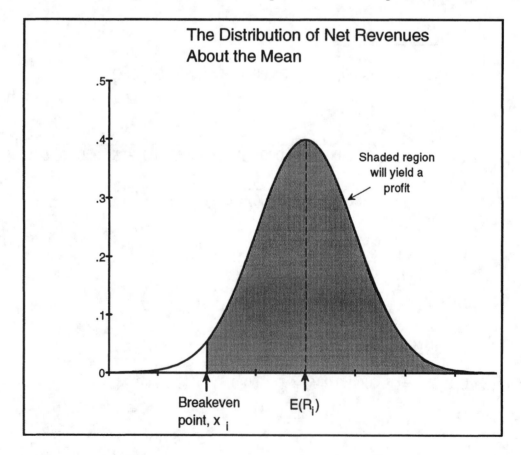

Newspaper Promotion Profit Probability

$$z = \frac{x_N - E(R_N)}{\sigma_N}$$

$$= \frac{\$3,752 - \$5,000}{\$960}$$

$$= -1.3$$

The standard normal distribution function value for $z = -1.3$ is 0.4032. This means that 0.4032 or 40.32% of the total area under the normal curve lies between x_N and $E(R_N)$, and implies a profit probability for the newspaper promotion of 0.4032 + 0.5 = 0.9032 or 90.32%.

Television Promotion Profit Probability

$$z = \frac{x_{TV} - E(R_{TV})}{\sigma_{TV}}$$

$$= \frac{\$2,825 - \$6,500}{\$1,750}$$

$$= -2.1$$

The standard normal distribution function value for $z = -2.1$ is 0.4821. This means that 0.4821 or 48.21% of the total area under the normal curve lies between x_{TV} and $E(R_{TV})$, and implies a profit probability for the television promotion of 0.4821 + 0.5 = 0.9821 or 98.21%.

D. Without evidence on the firm's risk attitudes, we can't say which promotion should be undertaken. Although the TV promotion has a higher expected profit and profit probability, it is the more risky of the two promotion possibilities.

P14.7 *Game Theory. Jim Carey, owner of Universal Cinema, Inc., must decide between two alternative bookings. The first is a new movie called "Grouch," and features a cartoon character who seeks to ruin the holidays by stealing Christmas presents from little children. Despite featuring an established star in the leading role, Carey fears the movie may "bomb" (fail) because the subject matter may prove controversial. Thus, Carey expects only a 50% chance of "Grouch" proving to be a hit. If the movie is a hit,*

Carey anticipates $500,000 in weekly revenue during the initial booking. Only $100,000 in revenue is expected if it proves to be a bomb.

As an alternative to booking "Grouch," Carey can rebook the second run of an action packed thriller called "Castaway." Because "Grouch" will be featured by other theaters in the Universal Cinema market area, Carey projects revenue for "Castaway" of $50,000 if "Grouch" is a hit, and $75,000 if "Grouch" bombs. Both movies would be rented by Universal Cinema from regional distributors on a fixed fee basis of $200,000 per week for "Grouch," and $40,000 for "Castaway."

A. *Construct a net profit (revenues minus fixed fee) payoff matrix for the two alternatives. Which would be chosen using the maximin criterion?*

B. *Construct a net profit regret or opportunity loss matrix for the two alternatives. Which would be chosen using the minimax regret criterion?*

C. *Which alternative would be chosen if Universal Cinema solely wished to maximize its expected net profit?*

D. *Calculate the cost of uncertainty in this problem.*

E. *Briefly describe when the choices made in parts A, B and C would be appropriate.*

P14.7   SOLUTION

A.

Payoff Matrix

States of Nature

Decision Alternatives	1. "Grouch" is a hit	2. "Grouch" bombs
A. Book "Grouch"	$300,000 (=$500,000-$200,000)	-$100,000 (=$100,000-$200,000)
B. Book "Castaway"	$10,000 (=$50,000-$40,000)	$35,000 (=$75,000-$40,000)

Booking "Grouch" exposes Carey to the possibility of a $100,000 loss which would be incurred if the movie bombs. This worst payoff outcome can be avoided by choosing to book "Castaway" instead. Thus, decision B is the maximin strategy.

B.

Regret Matrix

States of Nature

Decision Alternatives	1. "Grouch" is a hit	2. "Grouch" bombs
A. Book "Grouch"	$0 (=$300,000-$300,000)	$135,000 (=$35,000-(-$100,000))
B. Book "Castaway"	$290,000 (=$300,000-$10,000)	$0 (=$35,000-$35,000)

Booking "Castaway" exposes Carey to the possibility of a $290,000 opportunity loss in the event "Grouch" proves to be a hit. This worst opportunity loss outcome can be avoided by booking "Grouch" instead. Thus, decision A is the minimax strategy.

C. Using an expected profit criterion suggests:

$$E(\pi_A) = \$300,000(0.5) + (-\$100,000)(0.5) = \$100,000$$

$$E(\pi_B) = \$10,000(0.5) + \$35,000(0.5) = \$22,500$$

Thus, decision A is the preferred alternative based upon a criterion of simply choosing the alternative with the highest expected net profit.

D. The expected opportunity loss under each alternative is:

$$E(\text{Loss}_A) = \$0(0.5) + \$135,000(0.5) = \$67,500$$

$$E(\text{Loss}_B) = \$290,000(0.5) + \$0(0.5) = \$145,000$$

The cost of uncertainty is the minimum or unavoidable expected opportunity loss of $67,500.

E. If Carey is extremely risk averse, as would be true if a $100,000 loss would be a disastrous outcome for Universal Cinema, then the maximin strategy B would be most appropriate. A less risk averse decision maker would choose A, the minimax strategy. Decision making based on an expected profit criterion, part C, is most appropriate in the case of risk neutral decision makers.

Any of these three alternative individual decision strategies might prove appropriate depending on decision maker risk attitudes. It is always necessary to

examine *both* decision maker attitudes and decision alternatives prior to making any
recommendation regarding the "best" alternative.

P14.8   ***Probability Concepts.*** *Kung Fu Exports, Ltd., is faced with a very uncertain market for*
next summer's ginseng root harvest. Kung Fu has the opportunity to contract now for
purchase of 1,000 pounds of ginseng root at $80 per pound. Alternatively, they can wait
until summer and pay the current market rate at that time. With a good harvest, ginseng
will sell for $70 per pound. With a poor harvest, ginseng will sell for $100 per pound.

    A.   *Assuming risk indifference, at what probability of a good harvest would the firm*
contract now for 1,000 pounds of ginseng root?

    B.   *If there is a 90% probability of a good harvest, what would the firm pay for an*
option to purchase 1,000 pounds at $80?

P14.8   **SOLUTION**

    A.   Let X equal the probability of a good harvest needed to induce the firm to contract
now. For indifference, the expected cost of waiting to purchase must be equal to
the expected cost of a current purchase.

$$\begin{matrix} \text{Expected} \\ \text{Cost of Waiting} \end{matrix} = \begin{matrix} \text{Expected Cost} \\ \text{of Current} \\ \text{Purchase} \end{matrix}$$

$$X(\$70,000) + (1 - X)(\$100,000) = \$80,000$$

$$70,000X + 100,000 - 100,000X = 80,000$$

$$30,000X = 20,000$$

$$X = 0.67 \text{ or } 67\%$$

    B.   The option described would allow the firm to wait until all uncertainty had been
resolved before making its purchase decision. Assuming risk indifference, the cost
of uncertainty measures the maximum amount the manager would pay for such an
option.

The cost of uncertainty is measured as the minimum expected opportunity loss
associated with the two alternatives.

$$E(Loss_{\text{Current purchase}}) = \$0(0.1) + \$10,000(0.9)$$

$$= \$9,000$$

$$E(Loss_{\text{Wait to purchase}}) = \$20,000(0.1) + \$0(0.9)$$

$$= \$2,000$$

Therefore, the firm should be willing to pay up to $2,000 for the option.

P14.9   ***Cost of Uncertainty.*** *The Doodle Pen Company has just priced a new fiber tip pen at 50¢ each. The firm is trying to decide whether to use method A or method B for production. Under method A, the fixed costs of producing the pen are $1,000 and variable costs are 30¢ per unit. With method B, fixed costs are $3,000, and variable costs per unit are 20¢. The estimated probability distribution for sales volume is:*

Unit Sales	Probability
5,000	0.25
30,000	0.50
50,000	0.25

A.   *Construct the payoff matrix for this problem.*

B.   *Calculate the expected payoff for each alternative.*

C.   *Calculate the expected opportunity loss for each alternative.*

D.   *What is the cost of uncertainty in this problem?*

E.   *Should Doodle be willing to spend an amount equal to the cost of uncertainty to remove all uncertainty in this case? Why or why not?*

P14.9   SOLUTION

A.   Profits using method A are given by the equation:

$$\pi_A = P \times Q - TC_A$$

$$= \$0.50Q - \$1,000 - \$0.30Q$$

$$= \$0.20Q - \$1,000$$

Profits under the three possible states of nature will be:

$$\pi_{A1} = \$0.2(5,000) - \$1,000 = \$0$$

$$\pi_{A2} = \$0.2(30,000) - \$1,000 = \$5,000$$

$$\pi_{A3} = \$0.2(50,000) - \$1,000 = \$9,000$$

Profits using method B are:

$$\pi_B = P \times Q - TC_B$$

$$= \$0.50Q - \$3,000 - \$0.20Q$$

$$= \$0.30Q - \$3,000$$

Profits under the three states of nature will be:

$$\pi_{B1} = \$0.3(5,000) - \$3,000 = -\$1,500$$

$$\pi_{B2} = \$0.3(30,000) - \$3,000 = \$6,000$$

$$\pi_{B3} = \$0.3(50,000) - \$3,000 = \$12,000$$

The payoff matrix for the problem is:

Payoff Matrix

Decision Alternatives	States of Nature		
	Q = 5,000	Q = 30,000	Q = 50,000
Method A	$0	$5,000	$9,000
Method B	-$1,500	$6,000	$12,000

B.   The expected payoff for method A is:

$$E(\pi_A) = \$0(0.25) + \$5,000(0.50) + \$9,000(0.25)$$

$$= \$4,750$$

The expected payoff for method B is:

$$E(\pi_B) = (-\$1,500)(0.25) + \$6,000(0.5) + \$12,000(0.25)$$

$$= \$5,625$$

C. The opportunity loss or regret matrix for the problem is:

Regret Matrix

Decision Alternatives	States of Nature		
	Q = 5,000	Q = 30,000	Q = 50,000
Method A	$0	$1,000	$3,000
Method B	$1,500	$0	$0

The expected opportunity loss for each alternative is:

$$E(\text{Loss}_A) = \$0(0.25) + \$1,000(0.5) + \$3,000(0.25)$$

$$= \$1,250$$

$$E(\text{Loss}_B) = \$1,500(0.25) + \$0(0.5) + \$0(0.25)$$

$$= \$375$$

D. The cost of uncertainty is equal to the minimum expected opportunity loss of $375, which is the expected opportunity loss associated with production method B.

E. The cost of uncertainty is the expected gain associated with making the right decision after the fact. A firm attempting to maximize expected profits without regard to risk should be willing to spend precisely that amount to remove all uncertainty. A risk-averse individual would spend at least that amount, and possibly significantly more, to remove the potential variation in profits.

P14.10 ***Decision Tree Analysis.*** *Klingon Vulcan, Inc., produces electronic equipment that readily lends itself to design alternatives. Layout changes under consideration would have an effect on both the expected demand and costs of an important product. Klingon Vulcan managers expect a major reaction from competitors during the first year if any design innovations are successful, but none thereafter. If design changes are undertaken, the firm has estimated the following relevant data for the next two years (the firm's planning horizon):*

YEAR 1

Design	Success	Competitor	Total Incremental Revenue	Total Incremental Cost
A	Yes (0.85)	Yes (0.75)	$50,000	$40,000
	No (0.15)	No (0.85)	20,000	30,000
	Yes (0.85)	No (0.25)	55,000	42,000
	No (0.15)	Yes (0.15)	17,000	29,000
B	Yes (0.75)	Yes (0.55)	60,000	48,000
	No (0.25)	No (0.80)	18,000	30,000
	Yes (0.75)	No (0.45)	65,000	50,000
	No (0.25)	Yes (0.20)	15,000	28,000

YEAR 2

Design	Probability	Total Inc. Rev.	Total Inc. Cost
A	0.65 given "successful" 1st year	$70,000	$55,000
	0.35 given "successful" 1st year	10,000	25,000
	1.0 given "failure" in 1st year	0	0
B	0.70 given "successful" 1st year	$80,000	$60,000
	0.30 given "successful" 1st year	5,000	20,000
	1.0 given "failure" in 1st year	0	0

A. Construct a decision tree for the problem.

B. Assume that incremental revenues come in at the end of the year, costs are incurred at the beginning of the year, and a 12% discount rate. Compute the NPV of each alternative at each branch terminal.

C. Which is the more risky alternative in terms of potential variation in total return?

D. Which design should Klingon Vulcan select?

P14.10   SOLUTION

   A.

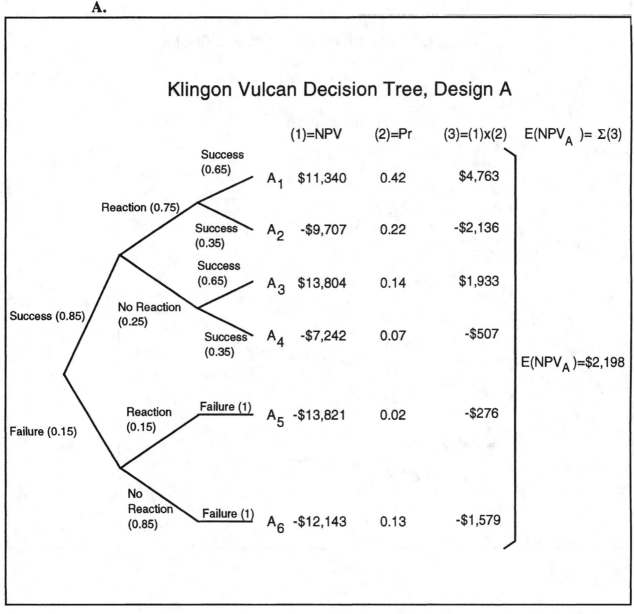

Klingon Vulcan Decision Tree, Design A

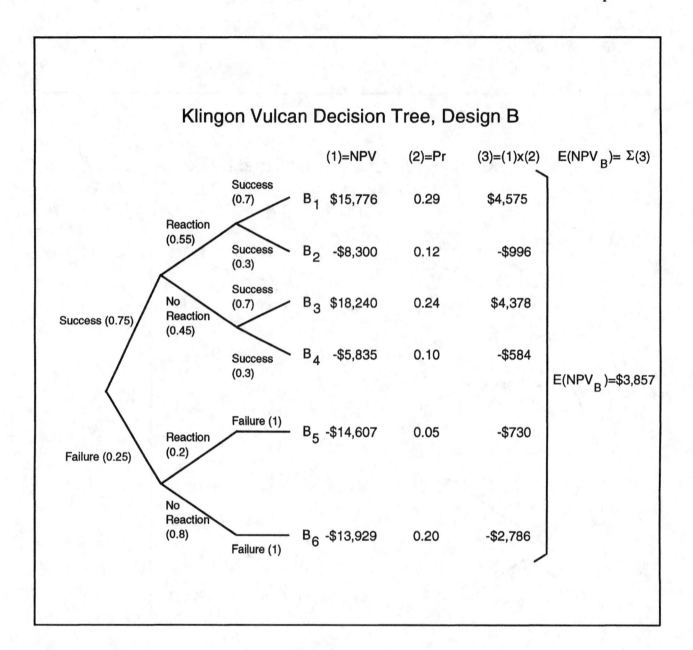

B. Net Present Value calculations:

<u>Project A</u>

$$NPV_{A1} = \frac{\$50,000}{(1.12)^1} - \$40,000 + \frac{\$70,000}{(1.12)^2} - \frac{\$55,000}{(1.12)^1}$$

$$= \$11,340$$

$$NPV_{A2} = \frac{\$50,000}{(1.12)^1} - \$40,000 + \frac{\$10,000}{(1.12)^2} - \frac{\$25,000}{(1.12)^1}$$

$$= -\$9,707$$

$$NPV_{A3} = \frac{\$55,000}{(1.12)^1} - \$42,000 + \frac{\$70,000}{(1.12)^2} - \frac{\$55,000}{(1.12)^1}$$

$$= \$13,804$$

$$NPV_{A4} = \frac{\$55,000}{(1.12)^1} - \$42,000 + \frac{\$10,000}{(1.12)^2} - \frac{\$25,000}{(1.12)^1}$$

$$= -\$7,242$$

$$NPV_{A5} = \frac{\$17,000}{(1.12)^1} - \$29,000 = -\$13,821$$

$$NPV_{A6} = \frac{\$20,000}{(1.12)^1} - \$30,000 = -\$12,143$$

$$E(NPV_A) = 0.42(\$11,340) + 0.22(-\$9,707) + 0.14(\$13,804)$$

$$+ 0.07(-\$7,242) + 0.02(-\$13,821) + 0.13(-\$12,143)$$

$$= \$2,198$$

Project B

$$NPV_{B1} = \frac{\$60,000}{(1.12)^1} - \$48,000 + \frac{\$80,000}{(1.12)^2} - \frac{\$60,000}{(1.12)^1}$$

$$= \$15,776$$

$$NPV_{B2} = \frac{\$60,000}{(1.12)^1} - \$48,000 + \frac{\$5,000}{(1.12)^2} - \frac{\$20,000}{(1.12)^1}$$

$$= -\$8,300$$

$$NPV_{B3} = \frac{\$65,000}{(1.12)^1} - \$50,000 + \frac{\$80,000}{(1.12)^2} - \frac{\$60,000}{(1.12)^1}$$

$$= \$18,240$$

$$NPV_{B4} = \frac{\$65,000}{(1.12)^1} - \$50,000 + \frac{\$5,000}{(1.12)^2} - \frac{\$20,000}{(1.12)^1}$$

$$= -\$5,835$$

$$NPV_{B5} = \frac{\$15,000}{(1.12)^1} - \$28,000 = -\$14,607$$

$$NPV_{B6} = \frac{\$18,000}{(1.12)^1} - \$30,000 = -\$13,929$$

$$E(NPV_B) = 0.29(\$15,776) + 0.12(-\$8,300) + 0.24(\$18,240)$$

$$+ 0.10(-\$5,835) + 0.05(-\$14,607) + 0.20(-\$13,929)$$

$$= \$3,857$$

C.   The risk of these two alternatives can be examined by calculating the coefficient of variation for each.

Project A

Outcome (1)	Deviation from mean (2)	(Deviation)^2 (3)	Probability (4)	(3) × (4) = (5)
$11,340	$9,142	$83,576,164	0.42	$35,101,989
-9,707	-11,905	141,729,030	0.22	31,180,387
13,804	11,606	134,699,240	0.14	18,857,894
-7,242	-9,440	89,113,600	0.07	6,237,952
-13,821	-16,019	256,608,360	0.02	5,132,167
-12,143	-14,341	205,664,280	0.13	26,736,356

$$\sigma_A^2 = \$123,246,745$$

$$\sigma_A = \sqrt{\$123,246,745} = \$11,102$$

$$V_A = \frac{\sigma_A}{E(NPV_A)} = \frac{\$11,102}{\$2,198} = 5.051$$

Project B

Outcome (1)	Deviation from mean (2)	(Deviation)^2 (3)	Probability (4)	(3) × (4) = (5)
$15,776	$11,919	$142,062,560	0.29	$41,198,142
-8,300	-12,157	147,792,650	0.12	17,735,118
18,240	14,383	206,870,690	0.24	49,648,966
-5,835	-9,692	93,934,864	0.10	9,393,486
-14,607	-18,464	340,919,300	0.05	17,045,965
-13,929	-17,786	316,341,800	0.20	63,268,360

$$\sigma_B^2 = \$198,290,037$$

$$\sigma_B = \sqrt{\$198,290,037} = \$14,082$$

$$V_B = \frac{\sigma_B}{E(NPV_B)} = \frac{\$14,082}{\$3,857} = 3.651$$

Project B's coefficient of variation is approximately 28% smaller than that of Project A, indicating that it is a considerably less risky alternative.

D.   Typically, it is difficult to determine what choice a decision maker should make between risky alternatives without explicit information concerning their risk aversion or utility function. However, in this case, because design B has both a greater expected return and a lower risk it dominates design A and would be chosen regardless of the decision maker's degree of risk aversion. Note, however, that this does not preclude the possibility that a very risk averse individual might decline both projects, because they are quite risky. Design B, although superior to design A, still entails a good deal of risk relative to the expected return. One cannot say for sure that Klingon Vulcan would choose to go ahead with design B without more knowledge about the risk-return tradeoff function used in such decision problems.

Chapter 15

CAPITAL BUDGETING

To derive and manage an optimal capital budget, economically sound capital budgeting decision rules must be developed and employed. Such rules consistently lead to the acceptance of projects that will increase the value of the firm. When the discounted present-value of expected future cash flows exceeds the cost of investment, the project represents a worthy use of scarce resources and should be accepted. When the discounted present-value of expected future cash flows is less than the cost of investment, the project represents an inappropriate use of scarce resources and should be rejected. In other words, an investment project is attractive and should be pursued as long as the discounted net present-value (NPV) of cash inflows is greater than the discounted net present-value of the investment requirement, or net cash outlay. Because the attractiveness of individual projects increases with the magnitude of this difference, high NPV projects are inherently more appealing and are preferred to low NPV projects. Any investment project that is incapable of generating sufficient cash inflows to cover necessary cash outlays, when both are expressed on a present-value basis, should not be undertaken. NPV analysis represents a practical application of the marginal concept, in which the marginal revenues and marginal costs of investment projects are considered on a present-value basis. Use of the NPV technique in the evaluation of alternative investment projects allows managers to apply the principles of marginal analysis in a simple and clear manner. The widespread practical use of the NPV technique also lends support to the view of value maximization as the prime objective pursued by managers in the capital budgeting process.

CHAPTER OUTLINE

I.   **THE CAPITAL BUDGETING PROCESS**

    A.   **What is Capital Budgeting?:** Capital budgeting is the process of planning expenditures that generate cash flows expected to stretch beyond one year.

        1.   Capital refers to financial resources used to fund production.

        2.   A budget is a detailed plan of projected cash inflows and outflows over future periods.

    B.   **Project Selection Process:** A firm's growth and development depends on a constant flow of ideas for new products and ways to make existing products better and cheaper.

        1.   Well-managed firms go to great lengths to develop good capital budgeting proposals.

C.   **Project Classification Types:** Firms generally classify projects into a number of categories, and analyze projects in each category somewhat differently.

   1.   Replacement projects consist of expenditures necessary to replace worn-out or damaged equipment.

   2.   Cost reduction projects include expenditures to replace serviceable but obsolete plant and equipment.

   3.   Safety and environmental projects are mandatory investments that are often nonrevenue-producing in nature.

   4.   Expansion projects increase the availability of existing products and services.

II.   **STEPS IN CAPITAL BUDGETING**

   A.   **Sequence of Project Valuation:** In theory, the capital budgeting process involves six logical steps.

      1.   The cost of the project must be determined.

      2.   Management must estimate the expected cash flows from the project, including the value of the asset at a specified terminal date.

      3.   The riskiness of projected cash flows must be estimated.

      4.   Given the riskiness of projected cash flows and the cost of funds under prevailing economic conditions as reflected by the riskless rate, R_F, the firm must determine the appropriate discount rate, or cost of capital, at which the project's cash flows are to be discounted.

      5.   Expected cash flows must be converted to a present-value to obtain a clear estimate of the investment project's value to the firm.

      6.   The present-value of expected cash inflows is compared with the required outlay, or cost, of the project.

         a.   If the present-value of cash flows derived from a project exceeds the cost of investment, the project should be accepted.

B. **Cash Flow Estimation:** The most important and difficult step in capital budgeting is cash flows estimation.

    1.   For the capital budgeting process to be successful, expected cash inflows and outflows must be estimated within a consistent and unbiased framework.

C. **Incremental Cash Flow Evaluation:** In capital budgeting, it is critical that decisions be based strictly on cash flows, the actual dollars that flow into and out of the company during each time period.

    1.   Relevant cash flows for capital budgeting purposes are the incremental cash flows attributable to a project.

        a.   Incremental cash flows are the period-by-period changes in net cash flows due to an investment project:

$$Project\ CF_t = \frac{CF_t\ for\ Corporation}{with\ Project} - \frac{CF_t\ for\ Corporation}{without\ Project}.$$

    2.   Accounting income statements provide a crucial basis for estimating the relevant cash flows from investment projects.

        a.   Accounting information must be adjusted to reflect the economic pattern of inflows and outflows so that value-maximizing investment decisions can be made.

III. **CASH FLOW ESTIMATION EXAMPLE**

A. **Elements of Cash Flow Analysis:** This example illustrates several important aspects of cash flow analysis and shows how they relate to one another.

    1.   Cash flow analysis involves estimating cash inflows and investment outlays associated with a project.

    2.   Computer spreadsheet software makes sophisticated cash flow analysis possible for even highly complex projects.

IV. **CAPITAL BUDGETING DECISION RULES**

A. **Fundamental Criterion:** An economically sound capital budgeting decision rule consistently accepts projects that lead to an increase in the value of the firm.

1. Projects involving incremental costs that exceed incremental revenues should be rejected.

B. **Net Present-value Analysis:** NPV analysis measures the current-dollar difference between the marginal revenues and marginal costs for individual investment projects:

$$NPV_i = \sum_{t=1}^{n} \frac{E(CF_{it})}{(1 + k_i)^t} - \sum_{t=1}^{n} \frac{C_{it}}{(1 + k_i)^t}$$

where NPV_i is the NPV of the ith project, $E(CF_{it})$ represents the expected cash inflows in the tth year, k_i is the risk-adjusted discount rate, and C_{it} is cash outflows.

1. If NPV > 0, the project should be accepted.

2. If NPV < 0, the project should be rejected.

C. **Profitability Index or Benefit/Cost Ratio Analysis:** The PI or B/C ratio shows the *relative* profitability of any project, or the present-value of benefits per dollar of cost:

$$PI = \frac{PV \text{ of Cash Inflows}}{PV \text{ of Cash Outflows}} = \frac{\sum_{t=1}^{n} [E(CF_{it})/(1 + k_i)^t]}{\sum_{t=1}^{n} [C_{it}/(1 + k_i)^t]}.$$

1. PI > 1 indicates a desirable investment project and NPV > 0.

2. PI < 1 indicates an undesirable investment project and NPV < 0.

3. For alternative projects of unequal size, PI and NPV criteria can give different project rankings.

D. **Internal Rate of Return Analysis:** The internal rate of return is the discount rate that equates the present-value of future receipts to the initial cost of a project. To calculate the internal rate of return k_i^*, simply set the NPV formula equal to zero:

$$NPV_i = 0 = \sum_{t=1}^{n} \frac{E(CF_{it})}{(1 + k_i^*)^t} - \sum_{t=1}^{n} \frac{C_{it}}{(1 + k_i^*)^t}.$$

1.   The discount rate that produces a zero net present-value is the internal rate of return earned by the project.

2.   Projects should be accepted when IRR > k, and rejected when IRR < k.

3.   When capital is scarce, the IRR can be used to derive a project rank ordering from most desirable to least desirable projects.

E.   **Payback Period Analysis:** The payback period is the expected number of years of operation required to recover an initial investment:

Payback Period = Number of Years to Recover Investment.

1.   The payback period is the breakeven time period.

2.   The shorter the payback period, the more desirable the investment project.

V.   CHOOSING AMONG ALTERNATIVE PROJECTS

A.   **Decision Rule Conflict Problem:** Appropriate decision criteria consider the time value of money, and rank projects according to their impact on the value of the firm.

1.   Ranking consistency is a feature of relevant capital budgeting criteria.

B.   **Reasons for Decision Rule Conflict:** NPV, PI and IRR criteria consider time value and valuation effects, but each incorporate assumptions that differently affect project rankings.

1.   NPV is an *absolute* measure of project attractiveness.

a.   NPV analysis can create a bias for larger as opposed to smaller projects.

2.   PI is a *relative* measure of project attractiveness.

a.   When capital is scarce, the PI method can lead a better project mix.

3.   In the IRR method, excess cash flows are reinvested at the IRR.

a.   The IRR can overstate project attractiveness when reinvestment of excess cash flows at the IRR is not possible.

C.   **Ranking Reversal Problem:** A conflict can arise between NPV and IRR rankings when projects differ in the size and timing of cash flows.

   1.   Changes in the appropriate discount rate can lead to reversals in project rankings.

   2.   A ranking reversal occurs when a switch in project standing occurs with an increase in the relevant discount rate.

   3.   The crossover discount rate is an interest factor that equates NPV for two or more projects. It is a ranking reversal point.

D.   **Making the Correct Investment Decision:** Many comparisons between alternative investment projects involve neither crossing NPV profiles nor crossover discount rates.

   1.   Logic suggests that the NPV ranking should dominate because that method results in a value maximizing selection of projects.

   2.   For a firm with limited resources, the PI approach allocates scarce resources to projects with the greatest relative effect on value.

VI.   **COST OF CAPITAL**

A.   **Component Cost of Debt Financing:** The component cost of debt is the interest rate that investors require on debt, adjusted for taxes.

   1.   The after-tax cost of debt financing is:

$$k_d = \text{(Interest Rate)} \times (1.0 - \text{Tax Rate}).$$

B.   **Component Cost of Equity Financing:** The component cost of equity is the rate of return stockholders require on common stock.

   1.   The cost of equity consists of a risk-free rate of return, R_F, plus a risk premium, R_P:

$$k_e = R_F + R_P.$$

   2. k_e and R_P are sometimes estimated using the capital asset pricing model (CAPM). Risk is measured by the variability of return relative to the variability of returns on all stocks, or the beta coefficient, ß:

$$R_i = \alpha_i + \beta_i R_M + e$$

where R_i is the weekly or monthly return on a given stock, and R_M is a similar market return

    a.   Low-risk stocks have betas less than 1.0; high-risk stocks have betas greater than 1.0.

    b.   The CAPM estimate of the required rate of return on any given stock is:

$$k_e = R_F + \beta(k_M - R_F),$$

where $k_M - R_F$ is the market risk premium.

3.   Another common technique estimates the required return on equity as four or five percent plus the risk premium paid on a firm's long-term bonds.

4.   A further method for determining the cost of equity is to use a constant growth model. If earnings, dividends, and the stock price all grow at the same rate, then:

$$\frac{\text{Required Return}}{\text{on Equity}} = \frac{\text{Expected Dividend}}{\text{Current Stock Price}} + \frac{\text{Expected Growth}}{\text{Rate}},$$

$$k_e = \frac{D_1}{P_0} + g.$$

C.   **Weighted Average Cost of Capital:** The firm should be viewed as an ongoing concern, and the cost of capital should be calculated as a weighted average of the various types of funds it uses.

1.   The weighted average cost of capital is the marginal cost of a composite dollar of debt and equity financing.

2.   The proper set of weights to employ in computing the weighted average cost of capital is determined by the firm's optimal capital structure.

3.   The optimal capital structure is the combination of debt and equity financing that minimizes the firm's overall weighted average cost of capital.

VII.   **OPTIMAL CAPITAL BUDGET**

A. **Definition:** The optimal capital budget is the funding level required to underwrite a value-maximizing level of new investment.

B. **Investment Opportunity Schedule:** The investment opportunity schedule (IOS) shows the pattern of returns for all of the firm's potential investment projects.

    1. To define the optimal capital budget, both the returns *and* costs of potential projects must be considered.

C. **Marginal Cost of Capital:** The marginal cost of capital (MCC) is the extra financing cost necessary to fund an additional investment project, expressed on a percentage basis.

    1. When IOS = MCC, all profitable investment projects have been accepted.

D. **Postaudit:** The postaudit is a careful examination of actual and predicted results, coupled with a detailed reconciliation of any differences.

    1. In the postaudit process, conscious or subconscious biases can be observed and eliminated; new forecasting methods can be sought as their need becomes apparent.

VIII.   SUMMARY

PROBLEMS & SOLUTIONS

P15.1 ***Decision Rule Criteria****. Indicate whether the net present-value, profitability index, and/ or internal rate of return method of capital budget evaluation is most appropriate in each of the following decision situations. Explain your answer.*

    A. *Access to capital is strictly limited.*

    B. *Cash flows obtained during the life of the project can only be reinvested at the cost of capital rate.*

    C. *The company's entire capital budget is just sufficient to fund its most attractive investment opportunity.*

    D. *The company has easy access to ample capital resources.*

    E. *Capital is scarce and the size of investment projects tends to vary widely.*

P15.1 **SOLUTION**

    A. Profitability index method. When access to capital is strictly limited, use of the profitability index method will insure that projects with the highest relative net payoff are undertaken first.

    B. Net present-value and/or profitability index methods. If cash flows obtained during the life of the project can only be reinvested at the cost of capital rate, then use of the NPV or PI method will result in the most accurate representation of the value of alternate investment projects. Use of the IRR method, which is based on an assumption of reinvestment at the IRR rate, would result in an overstatement of the attractiveness of the firm's most attractive investment projects.

    C. Internal rate of return method. When the company's entire capital budget is required to fund its most attractive investment opportunity, project cash flows can be reinvested at the IRR rate, and use of the IRR method is most appropriate.

    D. Net present-value and/or the internal rate of return methods. Depending on cash flow reinvestment opportunities, when a company has easy access to ample capital resources, either the NPV or IRR method can be relied upon to provide a useful ranking of the relative desirability of various projects.

E. Profitability index method. When capital is scarce and the size of investment projects tends to vary widely, use of the profitability index method will insure that projects with the highest relative net payoff are undertaken first.

P15.2 ***Project Ranking***. *Indicate whether each of the following statements is true or false. Explain why.*

A. *By accepting all projects with NPV > 0, the value of the firm is maximized.*

B. *The IRR of a project equals the cost of capital when PI = 1.*

C. *Under capital rationing, the NPV approach is preferred to the PI for ranking project attractiveness.*

D. *Holding all else equal, doubling the size of project revenues and costs leaves the IRR unaffected.*

E. *When NPV > 0, the IRR is below the cost of capital.*

P15.2 **SOLUTION**

A. True. By definition, value maximization requires undertaking all NPV > 0 projects.

B. True. When the IRR equals the cost of capital, the PV of cash flows equals the cost of the project, and PI = 1.

C. False. With capital rationing, use of the PI criterion ensures that projects with the highest return per dollar of investment will be adopted.

D. True. Holding all else equal, changes in the size of projects leave the IRR unaffected.

E. False. When the IRR is below the cost of capital, NPV < 0.

P15.3 ***NPV Analysis***. *Dr. Robert Romano, chief of staff at County General Hospital, is contemplating the purchase of additional magnetic resonance imaging (MRI) equipment. Romano's staff has generated the following projections for a five-year planning horizon:*

	Model 911 Targa	Model 911 GT2
Cost	$2 million	$2.75 million
PV of expected cash flow when k = 12%	$3 million	$4 million

A.   Calculate the net present-value for each type of equipment. Which is more desirable according to the NPV criterion?

B.   Calculate the profitability index for each. Which is more desirable according to the PI criterion?

C.   Under what conditions would either or both pieces of equipment be purchased?

P15.3 Solution

A.   Model 911 Targa

$$NPV_{Targa} = PV \text{ Cash Flow - Cost}$$

$$= \$3,000,000 - \$2,000,000$$

$$= \$1,000,000$$

Model 911 GT2

$$NPV_{GT2} = PV \text{ Cash Flow - Cost}$$

$$= \$4,000,000 - \$2,750,000$$

$$= \$1,250,000$$

Because $NPV_{GT2} > NPV_{Targa}$ the GT2 is ranked ahead of the Targa alternative, using the NPV criterion. However, because NPV > 0 for each, both are highly acceptable and would be profitable.

B.   <u>Model 911 Targa</u>

$$PI_{Targa} = \frac{PV\ Cash\ Flow}{Cost}$$

$$= \$3,000,000/\$2,000,00$$

$$= 1.50$$

<u>Model 911 GT2</u>

$$PI_{GT2} = \frac{PV\ Cash\ Flow}{Cost}$$

$$= \$4,000,000/\$2,750,000$$

$$= 1.45$$

Because $PI_{Targa} > PI_{GT2}$, the Targa is ranked ahead of the GT2 alternative using the PI criterion. However, because PI > 1 for each service, both are acceptable and would be profitable.

C.   Should the company have relatively abundant capital resources, or at least $4.75 million available for investment, both types of equipment would be purchased. However, when capital resources are scarce, use of the PI criterion, and purchase of the Targa would result in scarce funds being used where their relative impact on value is greatest.

P15.4   *NPV Analysis. The Three's Company is considering two mutually exclusive capital budgeting projects. These projects have equal lives of 2 years, and similar costs of $8,000. Relevant cash flow data for the two projects are as follows:*

	Project 1		
	Year 1		*Year 2*
Pr	*Cash Flow*	*Pr*	*Cash Flow*
0.35	$4,000	0.25	$5,000
0.40	5,000	0.50	6,000
0.25	6,000	0.25	7,000

	Project 2		
Year 1		**Year 2**	
Pr	*Cash Flow*	*Pr*	*Cash Flow*
0.20	$(200)	0.10	$1,000
0.30	4,000	0.30	4,500
0.30	5,000	0.35	6,500
0.20	7,000	0.25	8,000

A.   What is the expected value of the annual cash flows from each project?

B.   Using 10% for the more risky project and 8% for the other, and using variability of cash flows as an indicator of risk, what is the risk-adjusted NPV of each project?

C.   Which project should Three's accept?

P15.4   **SOLUTION**

A.

	Project 1		
Year 1:		**Year 2:**	
0.35(4,000) =	$1,400	0.25(5,000) =	$1,250
0.40(5,000) =	2,000	0.50(6,000) =	3,000
0.25(6,000) =	1,500	0.25(7,000) =	1,750
$E(CF_{11})$ =	$4,900	$E(CF_{12})$ =	$6,000

	Project 2		
Year 1:		**Year 2:**	
0.20(-200) =	$ -40	0.10(1,000) =	$ 100
0.30(4,000) =	1,200	0.30(4,500) =	1,350
0.30(5,000) =	1,500	0.35(6,500) =	2,275
0.20(7,000) =	1,400	0.25(8,000) =	2,000
$E(CF_{21})$ =	$4,060	$E(CF_{22})$ =	$5,725

B.   Project 2 appears to be more risky because by inspection the variability of cash flows is obviously higher. Thus, project 1 will be discounted at 8% and project 2 will be discounted at 10%.

Project 1

$$NPV_1 = E(CF_{11}) \times (PVIF, N = 1, i = 8\%)$$

$$+ E(CF_{12}) \times (PVIF, N = 2, i = 8\%) - C$$

$$= \$4,900(0.926) + \$6,000(0.857) - \$8,000$$

$$= \$1,679.40$$

Project 2

$$NPV_2 = E(CF_{21}) \times (PVIF, n = 1, i = 10\%)$$

$$+ E(CF_{22}) \times (PVIF, n = 2, i = 10\%) - C$$

$$= \$4,060(0.909) + \$5,725(0.826) - \$8,000$$

$$= \$419.39$$

C.   Project 1 should be chosen because it has the higher risk-adjusted NPV.

P15.5   *Investment Project Choice. Boris Badenov is a management trainee with Rocky &*
Bullwinkle, Inc. Badenov has been asked to evaluate two innovative pieces of machinery
that might be used to replace obsolete equipment. The following annual cost savings
(cash flows) will be generated over the four-year useful lives of the new machines:

	Probability	Cash Flow
Alternative 1	*0.3*	*$2,900*
	0.5	*3,500*
	0.2	*4,100*
Alternative 2	*0.3*	*$0*
	0.5	*4,000*
	0.2	*8,000*

Whichever piece of machinery is chosen, the total investment cost is the same,
$4,000.

A. *Badenov uses a discount rate of 12% for cash flows with a high degree of dispersion and a 10% rate for less risky cash values. Which machine has the highest expected net present-value?*

P15.5   SOLUTION

A.   The expected values of cash flows for each alternative are:

	Alternative 1	
Probability	Cash Flow	Expected Cash Flow (1) × (2)
0.3	$2,900	$ 870
0.5	3,500	1,750
0.2	4,100	820
		E(CF$_1$) = $3,440

	Alternative 2	
Probability	Cash Flow	Expected Cash Flow (1) × (2)
0.3	$ 0	$ 0
0.5	4,000	2,000
0.2	8,000	1,600
		E(CF$_2$) = $3,600

Alternative 2 is riskier because it has the greater variability in its cash flows. This is obvious from an inspection of the distributions of possible returns and could be verified by calculating the standard deviations of each alternative.

Alternative 1

$$\sigma_1 = \sqrt{(\$2,900 - \$3,440)^2(0.3) + (\$3,500 - \$3,440)^2(0.5)}$$

$$\overline{+ (\$4,100 - \$3,440)^2(0.2)}$$

$$= \$420$$

$$V_1 = \frac{\sigma_1}{E(CF_1)} = \frac{\$420}{\$3,440} = 0.122$$

Alternative 2

$$\sigma_2 = \sqrt{(\$0 - \$3,600)^2(0.3) + (\$4,000 - \$3,600)^2(0.5)}$$

$$\overline{+ (\$8,000 - \$3,600)^2(0.2)}$$

$$= \$2,800$$

$$V_2 = \frac{\sigma_2}{E(CF_2)} = \frac{\$2,800}{\$3,600} = 0.778$$

Obviously, Alternative 2 is to be evaluated at the 12% cost of capital, while alternative 1 requires only a 10% cost of capital.

$$NPV_1 = \sum_{t=1}^{4} \frac{\$3,440}{(1.10)^t} - \$4,000$$

$$= \$3,440(PVIFA, n = 4, i = 10\%) - \$4,000$$

$$= \$3,440(3.170) - \$4,000$$

$$= \$6,905$$

$$NPV_2 = \sum_{t=1}^{4} \frac{\$3,600}{(1.12)^t} - \$4,000$$

$$= \$3,600(PVIFA, n = 4, i = 12\%) - \$4,000$$

$$= \$3,600(3.037) - \$4,000$$

$$= \$6,933$$

Because alternative 2 has the higher risk adjusted net present-value, it is the appropriate investment.

P15.6 **NPV Analysis.** *Louie De Palma, cab dispatcher for Sunshine Cab Company, must choose between two mutually exclusive investment projects. Each project costs $6,000 and has an expected life of four years. Annual net cash flows from each project begin one year after the initial investment is made and have the following characteristics:*

	Probability	Annual Net Cash Flow
Project A	0.05	$2,200
	0.40	3,300
	0.25	3,800
	0.30	3,600
Project B	0.15	$ 300
	0.35	3,700
	0.22	6,900
	0.28	6,200

De Palma has decided to evaluate the riskier project at a 14% cost of capital and the less risky project at 12%.

A. *What is the expected value of the annual net cash flows from each project?*

B. *What is the risk-adjusted NPV of each project?*

P15.6 **SOLUTION**

A. $E(CF_A)$ = $2,200(0.05) + $3,300(0.40) + $3,800(0.25) + $3,600(0.30)

= $3,460

$E(CF_B)$ = $300(0.15) + $3,700(0.35) + $6,900(0.22) + $6,200(0.28)

= $4,594

B. Project B is the riskier project because it has the greater variability in its expected cash flows. Accordingly, project B is evaluated at a 14% cost of capital versus 12% for project A. The net present-values for each project are:

NPV_A = $3,460(PVIFA, n = 4, i = 12%) - $6,000

= $3,460(3.037) - $6,000

$$= \quad \$4,508$$

$$NPV_B \quad = \quad \$4,594(PVIFA, n = 4, i = 14\%) - \$6,000$$

$$= \quad \$4,594(2.914) - \$6,000$$

$$= \quad \$7,387$$

The above calculations indicate that De Palma should accept project B despite its higher risk.

P15.7   **Cash Flow Estimation.** *The ASU Co-op, a nonprofit student organization, runs a Laundromat located in the main dormitory complex at a large southwestern university. The latest monthly operating statement for the Laundromat is presented below.*

Revenues		
5,000 loads at $1.50 per load		*$7,500*
Costs:		
Rent	*$750*	
Maintenance	*500*	
Depreciation	*500*	
Electricity	*2,500*	
Water	*1,500*	
Miscellaneous Expenses	*1,000*	*$6,750*
Profit		*$ 750*

The month represented by this statement is typical, although there is considerable variation from month to month. Of the expenses incurred in the operation of the Laundromat, only electricity, water, and miscellaneous expenses are directly related to the level of output. These variable cost average $1 per load (=($2,500 + $1,500 + $1,000)/1,000). (Note: Maintenance is done under a service contract for a fixed fee).

Currently, the Co-op is considering the purchase of dry-cleaning equipment for the Laundromat. The dry-cleaning equipment costs $50,000 and has an expected life of three years with a zero salvage value. At a price of $3 per load, it is estimated that 1,000 loads of dry-cleaning per month will be the average use factor for the equipment. Cleaning fluid and electricity costs per load are 50¢ and 20¢, respectively. Additional annual maintenance costs of $500 are also expected. And finally, it is expected that by installing dry-cleaning equipment overall usage of laundry equipment will fall by 500 loads per month.

A.   *Develop the relevant cash flows for an analysis of this decision.*

B. *Assume the Co-op has the capital necessary to purchase the dry-cleaning equipment and that it places a 6% opportunity cost on those funds. Should the equipment be purchased? Why or why not?*

P15.7   SOLUTION

A.

<u>Initial Investment:</u>	$50,000
<u>Incremental Annual Revenues:</u>	
(1,000 loads/mo. × 12 × $3)	$36,000
<u>Incremental Annual Costs:</u>	
Cleaning Fluid: (1,000 loads/mo. × 12 × $0.50)	6,000
Electricity (1,000 loads/mo. × 12 × $0.20)	2,400
Maintenance	500
Loss of profit contribution from laundry (500 loads/mo. × 12 × $0.50)	<u>3,000</u>
	<u>$1,900</u>
<u>Incremental Annual Cash Flows</u>	<u>$24,100</u>

B. $NPV = \sum_{t=1}^{3} \frac{\text{Incremental Annual Cash Flows}}{(1.06)^t} - \text{Initial Investment}$

$$= \sum_{t=1}^{3} \frac{\$24,100}{(1.06)^t} - \$50,000$$

$$= \$24,100(PVIFA, n = 3, i = 6\%) - \$50,000$$

$$= \$24,100(2.673) - \$50,000$$

$$= \$14,419.30$$

The dry-cleaning equipment has a positive net present-value and, therefore, should be purchased.

P15.8   NPV and PI. *Z-Best Corporation is a small and rapidly growing company that specializes in carpet-cleaning and restoring fire- and flood-ravaged buildings. The company has the opportunity to complete the following services contracts:*

	Project A: Hotel del Coronado Restoration	Project B: DBL-Miraman Station Cleanup
Cost	$ 500,000	$200,000
PV of expected cash flow @ k = 15%	1,000,000	500,000

A. Calculate the net present-value for each service. Which is more desirable according to the NPV criterion?

B. Calculate the profitability index for each service. Which is more desirable according to the PI criterion?

C. Under what conditions would either or both of the services be undertaken?

P15.8   SOLUTION

A.   <u>Project A</u>

$$NPV_A = \text{PV Cash Flow - Cost}$$

$$= \$1{,}000{,}000 - \$500{,}000$$

$$= \$500{,}000$$

<u>Project B</u>

$$NPV_B = \text{PV Cash Flow - Cost}$$

$$= \$500{,}000 - \$200{,}000$$

$$= \$300{,}000$$

Because $NPV_A > NPV_B$, Project A service is ranked ahead of the Project B alternative, using the NPV criterion. However, because NPV > 0 for each service, both are acceptable and profitable.

B.   <u>Project A</u>

$$PI_A \; = \; \frac{PV \; Cash \; Flow}{Cost}$$

$$= \; \$1,000,000/\$500,000$$

$$= \; 2$$

<u>Project B</u>

$$PI_B \; = \; \frac{PV \; Cash \; Flow}{Cost}$$

$$= \; \$500,000/\$200,000$$

$$= \; 2.5$$

Because $PI_B > PI_A$, the project B alternative is ranked ahead of the project A alternative using the PI criterion. However, because PI > 0 for each service, both are acceptable and profitable.

C.   Should the company have relatively abundant capital resources, or at least $700,000 available for investment, both services should be initiated. However, when capital resources are scarce, use of the PI criterion, and initiation of project B first, would result in scarce funds being used where their relative impact on value is greatest.

P15.9   ***Project Ranking.*** *Dr. Elizabeth Corday is considering three investment alternatives for expanding her medical practice. Project A, involves expanding her waiting room to speed the flow of patients. Project B, involves the purchase of new diagnostic equipment, thereby allowing her to handle patients faster. Project C, involves opening a new office in a suburban mall location. Expected net cash flows (before investment costs) over the next five years and investment requirements for each project are given below:*

	Project		
	A	*B*	*C*
Annual Net Cash Flows	*$8,000*	*$20,000*	*$35,000*
Investment Cost	*20,000*	*50,000*	*100,000*

A.   *Rank each project according to the NPV criterion using an 8% cost of capital.*

B.   *Using the same cost of capital, rank each project according to the PI criterion.*

C.   *Rank each project according to the IRR criterion.*

P15.9   SOLUTION

A.   In the NPV approach, NPV = PV cash flows - Cost. Therefore,

$$NPV_A = \$8,000(PVIFA, n = 5, i = 8\%) - \$20,000$$

$$= \$8,000(3.9927) - \$20,000$$

$$= \$11,941.60$$

$$NPV_B = \$20,000(PVIFA, n = 5, i = 8\%) - \$50,000$$

$$= \$20,000(3.9927) - \$50,000$$

$$= \$29,854$$

$$NPV_C = \$35,000(PVIFA, n = 5, i = 8\%) - \$100,000$$

$$= \$35,000(3.9927) - \$100,000$$

$$= \$39,744.50$$

Because $NPV_C > NPV_B > NPV_A$, a project rank ordering using the NPV criterion is C > B > A.

B.   In the PI approach, PI = PV cash flows/Cost. Therefore,

$$PI_A = \$8,000(3.9927)/\$20,000$$

$$= 1.597$$

$$PI_B = \$20,000(3.9927)/\$50,000$$

$$= 1.597$$

$$PI_C = \$35,000(3.9927)/\$100,000$$

$$= 1.397$$

Because $PI_A = PI_B > PI_C$, a project rank ordering using the PI criterion is A = B > C.

It is interesting to note how project B, which is 2.5 times larger than project A, is preferred to project A using the NPV criterion despite their equivalence using the PI approach. Note also how the relatively large size of project C causes it to be preferred using the NPV approach despite the fact that it is the least attractive project on a PI basis.

C. The IRR is the interest rate which equates the PV of cash flows and investment costs. Thus,

$$PV \text{ cash flows} = \text{Cost}$$

$$CF(PVIFA, n = 5, i = IRR) = \text{Cost}$$

$$(PVIFA, n = 5, i = IRR) = \frac{\text{Cost}}{\text{CF}}$$

$$\text{For project A:} \quad (PVIFA, n = 5, i = IRR) = \frac{\$20,000}{\$8,000}$$

$$= 2.5$$

From the present-value tables, notice that this interest factor falls between 28% and 32%. Interpolating finds:

i	PVIFA(n = 5)
28%	2.5320
28% + ?	2.5000
32%	2.3452

because this factor covers 0.171 or 17.1% (= 320/1,868) of the distance between 28% and 32%, the relevant $IRR_A = 28.6\%$ [= 28% + 0.171(4%)].

The IRR for project B is the same as above because:

For project B: $(\text{PVIFA}, n = 5, i = \text{IRR}) = \dfrac{\$50,000}{\$20,000}$

$$= 2.5000$$

And finally,

For project C: $(\text{PVIFA}, n = 5, i = \text{IRR}) = \dfrac{\$100,000}{\$35,000}$

$$= 2.857$$

From the present-value tables, one can see that this interest factor falls between 20% and 24%. By interpolation:

i	PVIFA(n = 5)
20%	2.9906
20% + ?	2.8570
24%	2.7454

because this factor covers 0.545 or 54.5% (= 1,336/2,452) of the distance between 20% and 24%, the relevant $\text{IRR}_A = 22.2\%$ [= 20% + 0.545(4%)].

Therefore, because $\text{IRR}_A = \text{IRR}_B > \text{IRR}_C$, a project rank ordering using the IRR criterion is A = B > C.

P15.10   ***Cost of Capital.*** *Nirvana Products, Inc., is a rapidly growing chain of retail outlets offering brand-name merchandise at discount prices. A security analyst's report issued by a national brokerage firm indicates that debt yielding 13%, composes 50% of Nirvana's overall capital structure. Furthermore, both earnings and dividends are expected to grow at a rate of 12% per year.*

Currently, common stock in the company is priced at $20 and it should pay $0.60 per share in dividends during the coming year. This yield compares favorably with the 6% return currently available on risk-free securities and the 12% average for all common stocks, given the company's estimated beta of 1.5.

A.   *Calculate Nirvana's component cost of equity using both the capital asset pricing model and the dividend yield plus expected growth model.*

B.   *Assuming a 40% marginal federal-plus-state income tax rate, calculate Nirvana's weighted average cost of capital.*

P15.10   SOLUTION

A.   In the capital asset pricing model (CAPM) approach, the required return on equity is:

$$k_e = R_F + b(k_M - R_F)$$

where k_e is the cost of equity, R_F is the risk-free rate, b is stock-price beta, and k_M is the return on the market as a whole. Therefore,

$$k_e = 6\% + 1.5(12\% - 6\%)$$

$$= 15\%$$

In the dividend yield plus expected growth model approach, the required return on equity is:

$$k_e = \frac{D}{P} + g$$

Where D is the expected dividend during the coming period, P is the current price of the firm's common stock, and g is the expected growth rate.
Therefore,

$$k_e = \frac{\$0.60}{\$20} + 0.12$$

$$= 0.15 \text{ or } 15\%$$

B.   Given a 40% state plus federal income tax rate, the after-tax component cost of debt is:

$$\text{After-tax component cost of debt, } k_d = \text{Interest rate} \times (1.0 - \text{tax rate})$$

$$= 0.13 \times (1.0 - 0.4)$$

$$= 0.078 \text{ or } 7.8\%$$

Therefore,

$$\text{Weighted average} \atop \text{cost of capital} = {\text{Debt percentage} \times k_d \atop + \text{Equity percentage} \times k_e}$$

$$= 0.5(0.078) + 0.5(0.15)$$

$$= 0.114 \text{ or } 11.4\%$$

Chapter 16

ORGANIZATION STRUCTURE AND CORPORATE GOVERNANCE

Problems in corporate governance exist to the extent that there are unresolved material conflicts between the self-seeking goals of (agent) managers and the value maximization goal of (principal) stockholders. "Agency costs" incurred by stockholders are reflected in expenses for managerial monitoring, excessive managerial compensation, the over-consumption of perquisites by managers, and lost opportunities due to excessive risk avoidance. Questions about corporate effectiveness are ultimately questions about corporate governance. Corporate governance is the system of controls that helps the corporation effectively manage, administer and direct economic resources. If a corporation fails to effectively command its economic resources, this corporate failure can often be blamed on a similar failure of its corporate governance mechanism.

In some instances, corporate internal control systems at giant U.S. corporations have failed to deal effectively with economic changes, especially slow growth and the requirement for exit from declining industries. However, in many parts of the economy, new and smaller organizations are emerging to take the place of giant corporations. In these agile organizations, management incentives are closely tied to performance, decentralization is common, and obligations to creditors and stockholders are clearly specified.

Thus, although it is entirely valid to express concerns with the adaptive capability of some specific corporations, pronouncements concerning the "death" of the modern corporation seem premature. The corporate form has endured and flourished because it is a useful and effective means for gathering and deploying economic resources. Don't bet against it.

CHAPTER OUTLINE

I. **ORGANIZATION STRUCTURE**

    A. **What is Organization Structure?** The optimal design of the firm is the organization type that most successfully meets customer demands.

        1. Organization structure is described by the vertical and horizontal relationships among the firm, its customers and suppliers.

            a. A vertical relation is a business connection between companies at *different* points along the production-distribution chain from raw materials, to finished goods, to delivered products, e.g. GM and U.S. Steel.

      b.   A horizontal relation is a business affiliation between companies at the *same* point along the production-distribution chain, e.g., GM and Toyota.

    2.   The optimal boundaries and structure of the firm are not static, they are dynamic and responsive to the changing needs of the marketplace.

      a.   If economics of scale are important, large corporations evolve to minimize production costs.

      b.   If economies of scale are slight to nonexistent, small and nimble corporations evolve to exploit niche markets.

      c.   When economies of scope are relevant, it becomes attractive to offer customers bundles of related products and services.

B.   Transaction Costs and the Nature of Firms: The firm is a collection of contractual agreements among owners, managers, workers, suppliers and customers. It has no physical presence; it exists only as a legal device.

    1.   The efficiency of firms depends upon the ability of participants to find effective means to minimize the transactions costs of coordinating productive activity.

    2.   Transaction costs include:

      a.   information costs,

      b.   decision costs,

      c.   enforcement costs.

    3.   Search or information costs encompass expenses encountered in discovering the type and quality of goods and services demanded by consumers.

    4.   Bargaining or decision costs include expenditures involved with successfully negotiating production agreements.

    5.   Policing or enforcement costs include charges necessary to make sure that all parties live up to their contractual commitments.

C. **Coase Theorem:** According to Coase, firms exist as an economic force because they are an effective means of minimizing transaction costs.

    1.   It would be prohibitively expensive for each of us to organize production of all goods and services that we desire.

    2.   According to what is now referred to as the Coase Theorem, resource allocation will be efficient so long as transaction costs remain low and property rights can be freely assigned and exchanged.

II.   AGENCY PROBLEMS: SOURCES OF CONFLICT WITHIN FIRMS

A. **What is the Firm's Agency Problem?** An agency problem is present to the extent that unresolved material conflicts exist between the self-seeking goals of (agent) managers and the value maximization goal of (principal) stockholders.

    1.   Agency costs are the explicit and implicit transaction costs necessary to overcome the natural divergence of interest between agent managers and principal stockholders.

    2.   Agency problems exist because of conflicts between the incentives and rewards that face owners and managers. Such conflicts commonly arise given owner-manager differences in:

        a.   risk exposure,

        b.   investment horizons,

        c.   familiarity with investment opportunities.

B. **Risk Management Problems**: Significant differences in the risk exposure of managers and stockholders often leads to problems.

    1.   When employees share in gains but not in losses, an excessive risk-taking problem can emerge.

    2.   When employees do not share in gains but are penalized for losses, a risk-avoidance problem can emerge.

    3.   An "other peoples' money" problem can occur because employees tend to be less vigilant with corporate resources than with their own money (apologies to Danny DeVito).

4.   To combat managerial myopia, more and more companies are insisting that managerial compensation be directly tied to long-term performance.

C.   **Investment Horizon Problems:** Investment horizon problems can occur because top executives and many other managers tend to have fairly short careers.

1.   Any tendency toward focusing on short-term results is reenforced by compensation plans that rely on near-term corporate performance.

2.   To combat the potential for shortsighted operating and investment decisions, sometimes referred to as the managerial myopia problem, most corporations tie a significant portion of total compensation to the company's long-term stock price performance.

a.   Stock options and other payments tied to stock-price appreciation now account for 30 per cent to 35 per cent of top executive pay.

3.   Given the advanced age of most top executives and many senior managers, firms must be on guard against what is sometimes referred to as the end-of-game problem.

a.   The end-of-game problem is the most serious manifestation of myopic decision making, or inefficient risk avoidance.

D.   **Information Problems:** Another source of agency problems is tied to management's inherently superior access to information inside the firm, or the information asymmetry problem.

1.   Knowledgeable critics of managerial inefficiency are troubled about the inherent difficulty of gauging excess compensation, unprofitable empire building, and other elements of managerial malfeasance when managers control the flow of information about firm and managerial performance.

III.   ORGANIZATION DESIGN

A.   **Resolving Unproductive Conflict Within Firms:** Successful firms are an effective means for collecting and processing a vast array of sometimes conflicting information about customer demands, technology, input prices, raw material supplies, and so on.

1. The design of the organization is appropriate if it facilitates constructive communication. Prime needs to be met are:

   a. allocate decision making authority,

   b. monitor and evaluate performance,

   c. reward productive behavior.

2. An effective organization design is one that allocates decision authority to that person or team of persons best able to perform a given task or influence a particular outcome.

B. **Centralization Versus Decentralization**: A fundamental question facing management of all companies is the basic issue of when and how to centralize versus decentralize decision making authority.

1. With centralized decision authority, detailed judgments concerning how to best manage corporate resources, deal with suppliers and customers, and so on, are handled by top-line executives within a "top down" organization.

2. With decentralized decision authority, front-line employees, often those in direct communication with customers, are empowered to make fundamental judgments concerning how to best serve customer needs in a "flat" organization.

C. **Assigning Decision Rights**: The question of centralization versus decentralization focuses on defining the appropriate numbers of levels within the organization.

1. A flat organization has few or a single level of decision making authority.

2. A vertical organization features multiple ascending levels of decision making authority.

3. At its most basic level, the production process encompasses a sequence of related tasks, or assignments necessary to effectively meet customer needs.

4. In turn, related tasks are bundled into jobs, when such packaging facilitates cost savings and a more productive use of firm resources.

5. Many larger organizations facing the need to successfully deal with increasingly complex tasks have turned to team concepts.

D.   **Decision Management and Control:** Decision management is the vital process of generating, choosing and implementing management decisions. Decision control is the essential process of assessing how well the decision management process functions.

    1.   It is useful to characterize the decision management and control process as consisting of four distinct parts:

        a.   generate attractive decision proposals,

        b.   choose the best decision,

        c.   implement the best decision,

        d.   assess decision success.

    2.   Constructive management demands an ongoing assessment of the decision making process and the success, or lack thereof, of past decisions.

        a.   Correct investment and operating decisions are made on the basis of economic expectations, or a reasonable before-the-fact forecast of monetary implications.

        b.   Judging the wisdom of past decisions involves much more than a simple after-the-fact analysis of economic realizations, or financial outcomes.

IV.   **INCENTIVE COMPENSATION**

A.   **Match Worker Incentives With Managerial Motives:** Incentive compensation, or "pay for performance," has the potential to act as a powerful catalyst for a convergence of interests and effort between the management and owners of a corporation. To maximize effectiveness, such incentive compensation plans must be designed correctly and communicated effectively.

    1.   By allocating important decision rights to front-line employees, workers are better able to serve customers.

    2.   By empowering front-line workers, the company is able to attract and retain workers who seek jobs that demand and reward individual initiative.

B. **Individual Pay For Performance:** Many compensation plans fail to achieve desired ends because they focus on input-oriented measures rather than output-oriented criteria. The obvious challenge is to base compensation on measures of productivity that are output oriented.

1. Pay for performance simply means to adjust the level of compensation according to measurable indicators of worker productivity.

   a. Productivity that stems from the worker's natural dexterity, intelligence, or general education is derived from the worker's general human capital, where human capital is the capitalized value of future productivity derived from worker skills.

   b. Specific human capital is any special aptitude, education, or skill that gives rise to added productivity in a unique work setting.

2. Workers that seek jobs outside the firm are able to command a general labor market wage that offers a fair risk-adjusted rate of return on general human capital, sometimes called the reservation wage rate.

C. **Divisional Pay for Performance:** Organizations are often divided into subunits, or divisions, with independent decision-making authority, operating budgets, and performance evaluations.

1. An increasingly popular method for judging the performance of divisional profit centers is called economic value added (EVA) analysis.

   a. Because EVA measures the value added to the enterprise through superior divisional performance, it is a useful measure of the exceptional productivity of divisional employees.

   b. Suitable divisional pay for performance plan sets bonus payments based upon the relative productivity of individual employees or groups of employees as measured by their contribution to the amount of EVA generated by the division.

V. CORPORATE GOVERNANCE

A. **Role Played by Boards of Directors:** The most important and closely monitored corporate governance mechanism is the company board of directors.

1.   Corporate governance is the system of controls that helps the corporation effectively manage, administer and direct economic resources.

B.   **Corporate Governance Mechanisms Inside the Firm:** Corporate control mechanisms inside the firm are useful means for helping alleviate the potential divergence of interests between managers and stockholders.

 1.   Organization design, including the degree of vertical integration and the horizontal scope of the corporation, are examples of essential corporate governance mechanisms inside the firm.

 2.   Another useful means for controlling the flow of corporate resources is provided by internal markets established among divisions to better balance the supply and demand conditions for divisional goods and services.

C.   **Franchise Agreements:** Franchise agreements are prime examples of voluntary contractual arrangements outside the firm that can be viewed as corporate governance mechanisms.

 1.   Franchise agreements give local companies the limited right to offer goods or services developed or advertised on a national basis.

D.   **Strategic Alliances:** Strategic alliances are formal operating agreements between independent companies that also can be viewed as corporate governance mechanisms.

 1.   These combinations are increasingly used to improve foreign marketing.

 2.   Strategic alliances also arise when participating companies enjoy complementary capabilities.

E.   **Mandatory Corporate Governance Mechanisms Outside the Firm:** Compulsory mechanisms outside the firm include the wide variety of federal, state and local laws and regulations that govern corporate behavior.

 1.   Calculated or inadvertent violations of federal laws have the potential to impose significant costs on shareholders and other residual claimants.

 2.   Short-term "hit and run" managers may possess incentives to "cut" legal and ethical corners. The design and administration of federal laws is a means of outside monitoring designed to ensure a coincidence of managerial incentives, stockholder interests, and broader social objectives.

VI.   OWNERSHIP STRUCTURE AS A CORPORATE GOVERNANCE MECHANISM

    A.   Dimensions of Ownership Structure: Ownership structure of the firm is the complex array of divergent claims on the value of the firm.

        1.   In financial economics, the capital structure of the firm has been traditionally described in terms of the share of total financing obtained from equity investors versus lenders (debt).

        2.   Today, interest has shifted from capital structure to ownership structure, as measured along a number of important dimensions, including:

            a.   inside equity,

            b.   institutional equity,

            c.   widely-dispersed outside equity,

            d.   bank debt,

            e.   widely-dispersed outside debt.

        3.   Inside equity is the share of stock closely held by the firm's chief executive officer (CEO), other corporate insiders including top managers, and members of the board of directors.

        4.   When ownership is concentrated among a small group of large and vocal institutional shareholders, called institutional equity, managers often have strong incentives to maximize corporate performance.

    B.   Is Ownership Structure Endogenous? The probability that outside investors will discover evidence of managerial inefficiency or malfeasance is increased when institutional ownership is substantial. Managers of firms with high institutional ownership are relatively more susceptible to unfriendly takeover bids.

        1.   Fiduciary responsibility and the dynamics of ownership concentration have the potential to make institutional stockholders especially effective in the managerial monitoring process.

2.   Insider and institutional stock ownership represent alternative forms of ownership concentration that combine to form an effective method for monitoring managerial decisions.

3.   Four general forces affecting corporate ownership structure are:

a.   amenity potential,

b.   regulatory potential,

c.   quality control potential,

d.   ownership control potential.

4.   Amenity potential is derived from the ability to influence the type of goods produced. Such benefits can be derived from ownership of mass media and professional sports teams, for example.

5.   Extensive rate-of-return regulation, or regulatory potential, limits the capacity of managers to influence firm performance.

6.   In the case of firms that produce goods and services with the potential for high quality variation, or quality control potential, a more concentrated ownership structure may be required to give shareholders the amount of control necessary to mollify other suppliers and customers.

7.   The ownership control potential of the firm is the wealth gain achievable through more effective monitoring of managerial performance.

VII.   SUMMARY

PROBLEMS AND SOLUTIONS

P16.1 **Organization Structure.** *Determine whether each of the following statements is true or false. Explain why.*

    A. *A horizontal relation is a business connection between companies at the same point along the production-distribution chain.*

    B. *The unintended loss of valued employees to competitors is a type of decision cost.*

    C. *A merger between Internet content provider America Online, Inc., and Internet access provider AT&T WorldNet, Inc., would be horizontal in nature.*

    D. *When a corporation fires an underperforming CEO, it is an admission that the organization was unable to minimize transactions costs.*

    E. *Effective pay for performance requires that all employees retain an equity interest in the firm.*

P16.1 **SOLUTION**

    A. True. A vertical relation is a business connection between companies at *different* points along the production-distribution chain.

    B. True. Bargaining or decision costs include expenditures involved with successfully negotiating production agreements, including implicit or explicit labor agreements.

    C. False. A horizontal relation is a business affiliation between companies at the *same* point along the production-distribution chain.

    D. True. The efficiency of firms is defined by the ability of participants to find effective means to minimize the transactions costs of coordinating productive activity. The firing of an underperforming CEO implies a coordination failure.

    E. False. Pay for performance requires that all employees be compensated according to how well they have achieved specific tasks. Profit sharing and gain sharing, for example, are two effective means for motivating employees. Employee stock ownership can be an effective motivating device, but it is not the only means for providing needed performance incentives.

P16.2 **Agency costs.** *Indicate whether each of the following transaction costs is explicit or implicit, and describe how it is a manifestation of a particular type of agency problem.*

A. *A CEO with an options-laden compensation plan pursues a risky and value-reducing merger plan in the hope for short-term stock gains.*

B. *A manager fails to achieve optimum efficiency by engaging workers in a long and acrimonious strike.*

C. *Senior executives propose an overly generous pension benefits plan during their last few years of employment.*

D. *Value-reducing new product introductions are adopted in order to boost near-term accounting performance.*

E. *Executives switch from the tax-saving LIFO to FIFO inventory accounting method in order to boost short-term accounting profit performance and managerial compensation.*

P16.2 SOLUTION

A. Explicit. Significant differences in the risk exposure of managers and stockholders can lead to an excessive risk-taking problem on the part of overly ambitious empire-building managers.

B. Explicit. This and other examples of the "other peoples' money" problem arise when decision makers control resources that they do not own.

C. Explicit. To guard against the end-of-game problem, boards of directors often set long-term goals, compensation and benefits for senior managers.

D. Implicit. To combat shortsighted operating and investment decisions, the managerial myopia problem, most corporations tie a significant portion of total compensation to long-term performance.

E. Explicit. The information asymmetry problem is tied to management's inherently superior access to information inside the firm. When managers smooth or boost accounting performance to increase compensations, shareholders suffer an explicit cost.

P16.3 *Ownership structure. Describe each of the following factors as being responsible for increasing, decreasing, or having no effect on the amount of concentrated inside equity. Explain why.*

A. *High national media advertising requirements.*

B.   *A corporate history of sterling operating performance.*

C.   *Intense product-market competition.*

D.   *Intense security analyst coverage of corporate performance.*

E.   *A relaxation of antitrust policy.*

P16.3   SOLUTION

A.   Increase the amount of concentrated inside equity. High advertising requirements are apt to increase the amount of concentrated inside equity. In the case of firms that produce goods and services with the potential for high quality variation, or quality control potential, a more concentrated ownership structure may be required to give shareholders the amount of control necessary to give high quality assurance to suppliers and customers.

B.   Decrease the amount of concentrated inside equity. A corporate history of good operating performance means that the management team in place is capable of providing effective stewardship of shareholder assets. Because there is little to be gained by winning control of efficiently run corporations, there is little so-called ownership control potential for efficient firms, and scant potential wealth gain achievable through more effective monitoring of managerial performance.

C.   Decrease the amount of concentrated inside equity. When product-market competition is intense, the loss potential due to managerial malfeasance is small, and the need to further align managerial and owner incentives is slight. Vigorous competition is a quick and effective check on underperforming management.

D.   Decrease the amount of concentrated inside equity. Intense security analyst coverage of corporate activities is apt to decrease the need for concentrated inside equity. Independent auditors, security analysts, and journalists all provide a watchdog function that can be an effective monitoring device.

E.   Increase the amount of concentrated inside equity. Antitrust and regulatory policy is a type of external monitoring device. Any reduction in external monitoring increases the need for the type of internal monitoring provided by high levels of inside equity. For example, diffuse ownership structures are common for utilities because their regulatory potential limits the capacity of managers to influence firm performance. Concentrated ownership is more common in the case of unregulated monopolies.

P16.4   *Excessive risk taking/investment horizon problems.* *Pfizer, Inc., is known for producing exciting new products, including drugs to treat migraine headaches, heart rhythm disorders, arthritis, and treatments for sexual dysfunction. The pace of Pfizer's research productivity has jumped sharply from the early 1990s, when it introduced an average of one product a year. By 2002, for example, Pfizer had literally hundreds of projects in the works. The company also plans to enter new therapeutic areas, such as cancer, obesity and age-related conditions, that it hopes will yield new products further into the future.*

    A.   *Explain how the design and execution of corporate R&D programs has the potential to create excessive risk-taking and investment horizon problems.*

    B.   *R&D managers typically have huge personal incentives to turn in favorable year-to-year growth in the revenues and earnings derived from specific projects. This can sometimes have the unfortunate effect of focusing managerial attention on near-term accounting performance to the detriment of long-term value maximization. Explain how managerial compensation can be designed to avoid such myopic behavior.*

P16.4   SOLUTION

    A.   Significant differences in the risk exposure of managers and stockholders has the potential to create an excessive risk-taking problem. In Pfizer's case, the company continues to rapidly grow an impressive and broad pipeline of new product developments. Upbeat presentations regarding the company's R&D programs have clearly impressed investors and helped lift Pfizer's stock price.

        The risk is, of course, that the pursuit of short-term stock gains might lead the company to launch risky R&D projects where expected rewards fail to justify reasonable estimates of costs in light of the risk entailed. Although it is obviously enticing to attack such dreaded diseases as cancer, obesity, and other diseases of aging, the company must ensure that projects can be justified on a risk-reward basis. In addition, long term problems and unanticipated side effects are sometimes ignored when managers adopt an overly short-run perspective. In the case of Pfizer, for example, the company had to temper its amazing success with Viagra, a male impotence drug, with product labeling that states some users of the drug have experienced priapism, a painful, prolonged erection that can cause serious damage.

    B.   Agency problems tied to differences between the investment horizons of stockholders and management can emerge when salary and bonus payments are tied to short-term rather than long-term performance. This can be especially troublesome when the payoffs to hard-to-predict R&D efforts are considered. To combat such myopic behavior, more and more companies are insisting that managerial compensation be directly tied to long-term performance. An efficient means for establishing this link is to demand that top management hold a significant stock position that cannot be sold until some time *after* retirement. In Pfizer's case, the company might be well advised to encourage or demand that R&D managers and top executives make open market purchases of the firm's common stock. This is a trend that seems to be spreading in the pharmaceuticals industry, and for good reason. Information about Pfizer, Inc., can be found on the company Web Site. (http://www.pfizer.com)

P16.5 **Coase Theorem.** *On February 18, 2002, United Airlines announced a tentative contract agreement with the International Association of Machinists and Aerospace Workers, the union representing its 12,800 mechanics and aircraft cleaners. The agreement came on the fourth day of urgent talks, and less than 36 hours before a strike deadline. Notwithstanding assurances that an agreement would be reached, United experienced a steep decline in passenger bookings, reflecting public fears of a shutdown. Despite enormous costs in terms of lost business, labor strife between management, pilots, mechanics, and other employees seems to be a way of life at United and other major airlines.*

A. *Use the Coase Theorem to explain why labor-management standoffs in the airline industry reflect failures in corporate governance due to flawed organization structures.*

B. *Suggest a permanent means for resolving ongoing labor disputes between airline management and worker unions.*

P16.5 SOLUTION

A. According to Coase, firms exist as an economic force because they are an effective means for minimizing transaction costs. It would be prohibitively expensive for each of us to organize production of all goods and services that we desire. According to what is now referred to as the Coase Theorem, resource allocation will be efficient so long as transaction costs remain low and property rights can be freely assigned and exchanged.

Company management in the airline industry struggles to contain fixed costs and improve razor-thin margins. At the same time, uncontrollable fuel and capital acquisition costs often change in ways that make it difficult, if not impossible, to estimate and control these important variable cost categories. This makes labor costs one of the few controllable costs in the industry, and an obvious target of cost-conscious management during ties of weak revenues or high operating expenses.

Periodic standoffs between airline management and various worker unions are examples of organization failure, or the inability of such firms to effectively resolve fundamental disputes within the organization concerning the division of revenues and profits.

B. The airline industry offers an integral service that is relied upon heavily by both business and leisure travelers. Through the air freight part of the business, the airline industry also becomes part of dozens of industries that do everything from build computers to ship expensive drugs and consumer products. If a major airline like United stops operating normally for even a few days at a time, some of the most advanced sectors of the U.S. economy take a terrific blow. Customers demand reliability, and the airline business and its customers suffer greatly without dependable service from the pilots, mechanics, and other workers.

Work stoppages that strand business and leisure customers have enormous economic costs. United Airlines, like any airline, needs the cooperation of the pilots, mechanics, and other workers. At the same time, all workers need aircraft to fly. As a result, workers need management. Perhaps the clearest and simplest means of ensuring a convergence of worker and management interests in the airline industry is to require all parties to take on a significant ownership interest in the company.

P 16.6 *Organization Design. BTG, Plc., is an unusual company that acquires the rights to important inventions and hustles for patent royalties. BTG executives call themselves "merchant scientists." The company holds 8,500 patents covering nearly 300 different technologies. For example, it owns patents on the basic cholesterol test done using blood samples, and magnetic resonance imaging (MRI) technology. Because all patents expire, BTG is constantly scrambling for new ones. BTG once counted heavily on academia for new inventions, but universities and research labs are increasingly doing their own licensing. BTG now looks to corporate America, and offers its services to help companies exploit underused intangible assets.*

Created as an agency of the British government in 1949 after U.S. companies patented penicillin, a British discovery, BTG once had monopoly rights on any publicly funded research in Britain. It lost those rights in the 1980s, was privatized in 1992 and became a publicly-owned corporation in 1995.

A. *BTG has engineered and patented an innovative Torotrak transmission that cuts fuel consumption by 20%, but faces resistance from the auto industry which has big investments in traditional transmissions. Explain how BTG might overcome such resistence and make its invention a commercial success.*

B. *BTG's business lends itself to endless patent disputes. Explain how the company might favorably resolve such problems.*

P16.6 SOLUTION

A. To overcome auto industry resistence and make its invention a commercial success, BTG was forced to build a production facility in northern England to manufacture its new transmissions. This was a costly move that contributed to BTG's decision to spin off its entire Torotrak transmission operation. "Had we not invested in it, it would have died," BTG executives acknowledge. Meanwhile, the company continues in its quest to get industry adoptions. So far, the news on this front has not been promising. In January 2002, Torotrak announced that General Motors (GM) have given notice that they will not exercise their option for a production licence for Torotrak's Infinitely Variable Transmission (IVT) technology. The IVT demonstrator vehicles that GM reviewed successfully proved that the technology works, but commercial considerations led GM to decide not to undertake any further internal development work for the foreseeable future.

B. BTG's business lends itself to endless patent disputes, but the company strives to work out cross-licensing deals rather than pay lawyers. In 1982, for example, BTG filed for patents on the discovery by Oxford University scientists of the gene for a rare form of hemophilia. With a gene-replacement drug in mind, the company filed world-wide rights for both the gene and a protein derived from it. As it turns out, the Washington Research Foundation, a nonprofit institute in Seattle representing researchers at the University of Washington, had already filed patents in the U.S. for the gene.

To avoid lengthy litigation and court costs, BTG approached the foundation and worked out a revenue-sharing agreement under which it took over all licensing. BTG then secured American Home Products Corp. as an exclusive licensee for the new drug, called BeneFix., which it began marketing in 1997. Further information can be obtained at the BTG Web Site. (http://www.btgplc.com)

P 16.7 Contracting Issues. The country's largest book retailer, Barnes & Noble, Inc., sparked a wave of criticism with its $600 million buyout bid for Ingram Book Group, the largest book wholesaler in the United States, in November 1998. Ingram Books, based in Nashville, Tenn., had annual sales in excess of $1 billion from the distribution of consumer books, books-on-tape, textbooks and specialty magazines to a wide variety of customers, including Barnes & Noble, Borders, independent bookstores, libraries and Internet bookseller, Amazon.com, Inc.

News of the proposed deal pushed up Barnes & Noble stock price almost 11% on heavy trading volume, but critics called the acquisition anticompetitive. In June 1999, under heavy fire from independent booksellers and negative signals from the Federal Trade Commission, Barnes & Noble withdrew its bid. Independent booksellers rejoiced over their victory. Barnes and Noble announced plans to build new distribution channels, presumably with the $600 million in cash and stock left over from the failed *bid. Meanwhile, Ingram grumbled that the FTC didn't understand the company, and Barnes & Noble continued to shrug off suggestions that the deal would hurt competition.*

A. *Explain economic differences among a vertical merger, strategic alliance and a long-term contractual relationship between Borders and Ingram Book Group.*

B. *Does the fact that Borders and Ingram Book Group sought a merger agreement imply significant contracting costs in the industry?*

P16.7 SOLUTION

A. Economic differences among a vertical merger, strategic alliance and a long-term contractual relationship between Borders and Ingram Book Group are matters of degree and formality. A vertical merger between the two would minimize subsequent contracting costs because all such negotiations become internal and all parties have the same objective: to maximize total net profits going forward. A vertical merger, combined with an effective transfer pricing policy within the firm, would result in an elimination of the costs and risk involved with dividing up the total profit contribution earned.

Strategic alliances and a long-term contractual relationships are alternative and less formal methods of contracting among legal entities. In this case, a merger with Ingram would have expanded the size of Barnes & Noble's book-distribution system and sharply increased the speed with which Barnes & Noble gets copies of books to customers. Speed in distribution is not a small matter when competition with Internet bookseller Amazon.com is considered. In fact. The "need for speed" was the prime driver behind this failed merger proposal. With eleven strategically located distribution centers, more than 80% of the combined company's online and retail-store customers would have been eligible for overnight delivery.

In commenting on the merger proposal, Barnes & Noble noted that independent booksellers constitute a substantial portion of Ingram's business and are responsible for a major share of its profits. The company argued that it would have been foolhardy for Barnes & Noble to do anything but try to increase its business with other independent booksellers.

B. Yes, the fact that Borders and Ingram Book Group sought a merger agreement implies that contracting costs in the industry are significant. Although a vertical merger between the two would minimize contracting costs, a less formal and less comprehensive strategic alliance or long-term contractual relationship is subject to the risk of third-part intervention. For example, if Amazon.com were to buy Ingrams, Borders might rightfully fear an interruption in its beneficial supplier-retailer relationship with Ingrams.

To be sure, Ingrams has an incentive to maximize profits going forward whether or not it is independent or part of a larger organization that includes Borders, Amazon.com, or some other retailer. If the wholesale market for books were perfectly competitive, there would be no reason to fear negative competitive consequences from vertical relationships. Indeed, with perfectly competitive supply, there would be no reason to pursue long-term vertical relationships. (Notice that McDonald's sells milk but doesn't own dairy farms.) At a minimum, the fact that Borders sought a long-term vertical relationship with Ingrams implies a close strategic fit between the two. A merger may or may not have led to a durable competitive advantage over rivals such as Amazon.com.

Interestingly, in March 2001, Borders Group announced that it has signed an agreement to make Ingram the primary provider of book fulfillment services for Borders Group's special order and online sales. The transaction included the sale to Ingram of a large percentage of the book inventory housed in Borders Group's Fulfillment Center in La Vergne, Tenn., which previously handled the function assumed by Ingram. In this case, a strategic alliance may achieve many of the benefits sought in their failed merger proposal.

P16.8 **Incentive Compensation.** *Consumer-products juggernaut Procter & Gamble, Inc., shook up the advertising industry when it introduced a revolutionary compensation method that rewards advertising agencies for increases in company sales. Under P&G's historical compensation system, advertising agencies were paid roughly 13% to 15% of the amount P&G spent through them on advertising. Under the traditional system, critics contended that there was a big incentive to favor television. That's because agencies got a lot bigger paycheck for a $150,000 television commercial than for a $2,000 to $20,000 billboard.*

P&G wants a "media-neutral" advertising expenditure policy without any inherent advantage for network TV at the expense of other media such as the Internet, billboards, magazines and public-relations events.

A. *Is there any necessary conflict between advertising expenditure efficiency and a commission-based compensation plan for advertising agencies?*

B. *Can changes in technology explain why P&G might alter its method of compensating advertising agencies?*

P16.8 SOLUTION

A. No. Of course, it's true that advertising agencies got a lot bigger paycheck for a $150,000 television commercial than for a $2,000 to $20,000 billboard. However, it's worth remembering that ad rates are set in a competitive market based upon advertising effectiveness. A $100,000 television commercial can be expected to generate far more customer awareness and sales revenue than an ad on a $2,000 to $20,000 per month billboard. In fact, in an efficient advertising market, the television ad would generate 5 to 50 times the value of such a billboard. Similarly, the amount paid in advertising agency commissions can be expected to vary proportionately with the amount of value added at the margin. The fact that P&G wants a "media-neutral" advertising expenditure policy without any inherent advantage for network TV at the expense of other media such as the Internet, billboards, magazines and public-relations events makes good economic sense. So too do traditional forms of ad agency compensation.

B. Yes. Effective people meters, price-tracking technology, scanner data, and computer software suited to measuring advertising effectiveness on the Internet all make it easier than ever before for P&G and other advertisers to effectively track advertising effectiveness. In fact, measurement technology now makes a significant contribution to advertising effectiveness, and thereby reduces the relative importance of the creative input traditionally provided by advertising agencies. Changes in advertising technology help explain why the traditional commission system is increasingly losing ground as advertisers gravitate toward base fees to cover fixed costs, plus various incentives. As the commission system has faded, agency profit margins have been squeezed. Traditional ad agencies grumble that it's tough to make a living churning out online ads, for example, because a commission-based system makes it less than lucrative to devote much time and effort to online-ad efforts.

P16.9 ***Information Asymmetry Problem.*** *Global Crossing, Ltd., a Bermuda-based telecom giant, was putting the finishing touches on its 100,000-mile fiber-optic network in 2001 when it entered into a series of transactions that many now regard as deceptive. For example, a small Orlando, Florida, company called EPIK Communications Inc. paid $40 million for the right to divert some of its telephone and data traffic through Global's Latin American fiber routes. Exactly offsetting that payment, Global spent $40 million for unspecified future use of EPIK's facilities, which include a 1,850-mile fiber network linking Atlanta and Miami. Using a series of such transactions with other telecom carriers, Global's revenues soared to $3.79 billion by 2000 from $419.9 million in 1998. Global also became a regular fixture in Washington, DC. The company and its executives donated $2.6 million in the 2000 presidential campaign, surpassing even notorious Enron Corp. in that regard.*

Unfortunately, in the wake of the dwindling revenue growth, soaring costs, and growing investor skepticism concerning the company's accounting practices, Global was forced to file for bankruptcy court protection in January, 2002. At the time, it was the fourth-largest bankruptcy filing in U.S. history. It also marked a stunning collapse for shareholders who saw the stock price steadily decline from a high of $61.06 per share, and a market capitalization of $47.6 billion in February 2000.

A. Explain how the rise and fall of Global Crossing, Ltd., Inc., might be described as a manifestation of the information asymmetry problem.

B. How could this problem have been avoided?

P16.9 SOLUTION

A. Accounting methods always leave room for managerial interpretation, and this flexibility can and has been used to understate expenses and inflate reported earnings. When CEO compensation and stock-based rewards are tied to various accounting performance targets, it's a bit like asking students to fill out their own final grade report. At a minimum, shareholder's shouldn't be surprised when accounting data places firm and managerial performance in a favorable light. Shareholder's must take steps to guard against significant manipulation of accounting standards and/or accounting bias that results in a meaningful distortion of accounting performance.

B. The most obvious and simplest corporate governance mechanisms used to guard against manipulation of the firm's accounting statements are corporate practices that insure independence on the part of auditors and members of the board of directors. Perhaps the best corporate practice is to have the independent auditor report to the board itself, or to a subcommittee comprised of independent board members (not members of top management). Boards of directors also tend to be most independent when the chairman of the board is not a member of top management, but rather an independent board member.

   Independent security analysts also have a role to play in monitoring the quality of information reported by the firm. Though security analysts often do a good job of keeping shareholders informed, they obviously dropped the ball, or globe in the case of Global Crossing. See Dennis K. Berman and Deborah Solomon, "Global Crossing's Use of Swaps To Boost Revenue Wasn't Unusual," *The Wall Street Journal Online*, February 13, 2002 (http://online.wsj.com)

P16.10 Corporate Governance. *In March 2002, an unrepentant Jeffrey Skilling, former Enron Corp. chief executive, testified before Congress that the company had tight controls on financial risk but that he couldn't be expected to oversee everything and "close out the cash drawers... every night." Skilling, whose testimony to Congress was severely challenged by lawmakers, even sought to defend himself in an interview on CNN's "Larry King Live." "I think the Congress is acting as judge and jury," he said, and "that is to be expected in an election year." Meanwhile, from company computers obtained by Justice Department prosecutors, evidence was obtained that Enron paid its executives one-time bonuses totaling some $320 million. The stock targets, ending in*

2000, were reached at the same time investigators say Enron officials were improperly inflating company profits by as much as $1 billion, thereby buoying the stock price.

A. *Explain how the design and administration of state and federal laws can be seen as a means of outside monitoring designed to ensure a coincidence of managerial incentives, stockholder interests, and broader social objectives.*

B. *Explain how the economic effects of law enforcement actions on the value of the firm can be expected to differ according to the relative importance of intangible factors in firm valuation.*

P16.10 SOLUTION

A. Calculated or inadvertent violations of state and federal laws have the potential to impose significant costs on shareholders and other residual claimants. The pursuit of illegal short-term strategies can represent a form of self-dealing by managers who seek to reap short-term personal gain while escaping detection. Actual or suspected violations of federal laws have the potential to result in significant costs measured in terms of investigation expenditures, litigation expenses, fines and seizures, and lost reputational capital for the firm--all of which can measurably reduce future cash flows and current market values. Within this context, laws can be seen as part of the institutional framework that contributes to the range of control mechanisms that originate inside and outside the firm to comprise an effective system of corporate governance. Because short-term "hit and run" managers may possess incentives to "cut" legal and ethical corners, the design and administration of laws and regulations can be seen as a means of outside monitoring designed to ensure a coincidence of managerial incentives, stockholder interests, and broader social objectives. Law enforcement activities can be viewed as an important element in the institutional framework of corporate governance.

B. Economic effects of federal law enforcement actions on the value of the firm can be expected to differ across firms according to the relative importance of intangible factors in firm valuation. The value of the firm is derived from assets in place and growth opportunities stemming from research and development (R&D), advertising, and other such expenditures. Firms whose value stems mainly from growth opportunities, or complex trading strategies such as in the case of Enron, may be especially susceptible to law enforcement actions because of the enhanced potential to adversely impact the firm's reputational capital and growth options.

Chapter 17

PUBLIC MANAGEMENT

As trustees of valuable public resources, managers in the public sector must administer economic resources in a responsible manner. This task is made difficult by problems involved with assessing the true levels of demand and cost for government-administered goods and services. Because individuals not paying for many public goods cannot be excluded from consumption, there is a tendency for consumers to avoid payment responsibility. A so-called free-rider problem emerges because each consumer believes that public goods will be provided irrespective of his or her contribution towards covering their costs. Consumers of public goods are also reluctant to reveal strong personal demand for public goods because they fear correspondingly high payment demands. Like the free-rider problem, this hidden preferences problem makes assessing the true demand for public goods difficult. As a result, a variety of nonmarket-based mechanisms have evolved that can be used to effectively administer government programs in light of relative marginal social benefits and costs.

After considering the theoretical framework for public sector management, this chapter considers a variety of economic issues facing public-sector managers. First among these is macroeconomic growth and stabilization policy. An economic environment that includes free markets, well-designed and efficient regulation, where necessary, and legal protection of property rights fosters economic betterment over time.

CHAPTER OUTLINE

I. **RATIONALE FOR PUBLIC MANAGEMENT**

    A. **Public Versus Private Goods:** The traditional rationale for public management of economic resources is the perception of markets failing to efficiently provide and equitably allocate economic goods and services. Another important function of government is to provide goods and services that cannot be provided and allocated in optimal quantities by the private sector.

        1. If the consumption of a product by one individual does not reduce the amount available for others, the product is referred to as a public good (e.g., radio broadcasts).

        2. A private good is one where consumption by one individual limits consumption by others. Food, clothing and shelter are all private goods because the number of potential consumers of a fixed amount is strictly limited.

3.   The distinguishing characteristic of public goods is the concept of nonrival consumption. In the case of public goods, use by certain individuals does not reduce availability for others.

4.   A good or service is characterized as nonexclusionary if it is impossible or prohibitively expensive to confine the benefits of consumption to paying customers.

5.   Because public goods can be enjoyed by more than one consumer at the same point in time, aggregate demand is determined through the vertical summation of the demand curves of all consuming individuals.

    a.   When "free riders" fail to financially support public goods, less than the optimal amount of the public good will be provided.

    b.   A hidden preferences problem emerges in the provision of public goods because individuals have no economic incentive to accurately reveal their true demand for public goods.

B.   Public Choice Theory: Public choice theory is the philosophy of how government decisions are made and implemented.

1.   It explicitly recognizes the possibility of government failure, or circumstances where public policies reflect narrow private interests, rather than the general public interest.

2.   Public choice theory examines how government decisions are made and implemented by analyzing the behavior of four major groups.

    a.   Voters in the political process are the counterpart of consumers in the marketplace.

        (1)   According to public choice theory, voters are less informed about political decisions than about market decisions due to their rational ignorance.

    b.   Politicians, are the political-system counterpart of entrepreneurs and managers in the private market system.

    c.   Special-interest groups are organized lobbyists that actively support the passage of laws and regulations that further their own narrow economic interests.

d.   Public employees, or bureaucrats, are not passive executors of adopted policies; they actively seek to influence these policies to further personal interests.

C.   **Policy Implications of Public Choice Theory**: The characterization of the political process by public choice theorists is sometimes viewed as overly cynical.

1.   In practice, many voters are well informed and unselfish in their political beliefs.

2.   Politicians sometimes refuse to compromise basic principles simply to maximize chances for reelection.

3.   Public interests prevail more often than one might expect; powerful special-interest groups are sometimes defeated.

4.   Government bureaucracies are often staffed by well-intentioned and committed public servants.

II.   BENEFIT-COST ANALYSIS

A.   **Benefit-Cost Analysis Theory**: Implicit in the choice of a government-sponsored program or public works project is the desire to achieve some underlying social objective.

1.   If investment in a public project makes at least one individual better off and no one worse off, then the project is described as Pareto satisfactory.

2.   When all such government programs and investment projects have been undertaken, the situation is deemed to be Pareto optimal.

3.   A government program or project is deemed attractive under the potential Pareto improvement criterion when beneficiaries could fully compensate losers and still receive some positive net benefit.

4.   The marginal social costs of any good or service equal the marginal cost of production plus any marginal external costs, such as pollution, that are not directly borne by producers or their customers.
      a.   In the absence of marginal external costs, marginal private costs and marginal social costs are equal at all levels of output.

5. Marginal social benefits are the sum of marginal private benefits plus marginal external benefits.

    a. Marginal private benefits are enjoyed by those who directly pay for any good or service; marginal external benefits are enjoyed by purchasers and non-purchasers alike, and are not reflected in market prices.

    b. When no externalities are present, marginal social benefits equal marginal private benefits.

6. The optimal production of public-sector goods and services follows the same rules as optimal private-sector production.

    a. When the ratio *MSB/MSC* > 1, the value of marginal social benefits exceeds the value of marginal social costs.

    b. When the ratio *MSB/MSC* < 1, then the value of marginal social benefits is less than the value of marginal social costs.

    c. If the ratio *MSB/MSC* = 1, the value of marginal social benefits exactly equals the value of marginal social costs.

B. **Benefit-Cost Analysis Methodology**: Benefit-cost analysis is the public-sector analog to the profitability index decision criterion.

    1. Benefit-cost analysis is often used when the economic consequences of a project or a policy change are likely to extend beyond one year.

    2. Benefit-cost analysis is complex because it seeks to measure both direct and indirect effects of government programs and public-sector investment projects.

C. **Social Rate of Discount**: Determining the appropriate social rate of discount, or interest-rate cost of public funds, is critical to the selection of appropriate alternatives in benefit-cost studies.

    1. A low rate favors long-term investments with substantial future benefits; a higher rate favors short-term projects with benefits that accrue soon after the initial investment.

    2. A common approach at the Federal and state levels is to discount the benefits and costs associate with public projects based on the government's cost of borrowed funds.

D. **Social Net Present-value Analysis**: Designating a standard upon which to accept or reject decision alternatives is a critical consideration in the evaluation of government programs and public-sector investment projects.

1. If adequate public funds are available for all decision alternatives, the appropriate decision criterion must rank-order decision alternatives so that net social benefits are maximized.

2. If public funds are inadequate to fund all desirable decision alternatives, the appropriate decision criterion must rank-order decision alternatives so that marginal social benefits are maximized per dollar of marginal social cost.

3. Under the social net present-value (*SNPV*) criterion, marginal social benefits and marginal social costs during the life of each program or project are discounted back to the present using an appropriate social discount rate.

   a. Public-sector projects are desirable when the *difference* between the present-value of direct and indirect benefits and the present-value of direct and indirect costs is greater than or equal to zero.

E. **Benefit-Cost Ratio Analysis**: When public-sector budgets are limited or capital expenditures are otherwise restricted, the evaluation of social programs or public-sector investment projects must reflect this fact.

1. A variant of *SNPV* analysis that is often used in complex capital budgeting situations is called benefit-cost (B/C) ratio analysis.

2. The *B/C ratio* shows the *relative* attractiveness of any social program or public-sector investment project, or the present-value of marginal social benefits per dollar of marginal social cost.

   a. In *B/C ratio* analysis, any social program with *B/C ratio* > 1 should be accepted and any program with *B/C ratio* < 1 should be rejected.

   b. The *B/C ratio* and *SNPV* methods always indicate the same accept/reject decisions for independent programs, because *B/C ratio* > 1 implies *SNPV* > 0 and *B/C ratio* < 1 implies *SNPV* < 0.

   c. For alternative programs of unequal size, *B/C ratio* and *SNPV* criteria can give different program rankings.

F. **Internal Rate of Return Analysis**: The social internal rate of return (*SIRR*) is the interest or discount rate that equates the present-value of the future receipts of a program to the initial cost or outlay.

1. The equation for calculating the social internal rate of return is simply the *SNPV* formula set equal to zero.

2. Like a rank ordering of all *SNPV* > 0 programs from highest to lowest *B/C ratios*, a rank ordering of potential investment programs from highest to lowest *SIRR*s allows public-sector managers to effectively employ scarce public funds.

G. **Limitations of Benefit-Cost Analysis**: Although benefit-cost analysis is conceptually appealing, it has several limitations that must be considered.

1. Existing measurement techniques are inadequate for comparing diverse public programs.

2. Benefit-cost analysis requires public-sector managers to quantify all relevant factors in dollar terms.

    a. Qualitative factors must be considered to prevent the omission of important indirect and intangible impacts.

3. Evaluation problems occur when a non-efficiency objective, such as reducing the level of highway noise pollution around a school yard, must be considered alongside an efficiency objective.

4. Significant measurement problem can arise because of uncertainties surrounding future marginal social benefits and marginal social costs.

III. **ADDITIONAL METHODS FOR IMPROVING PUBLIC MANAGEMENT**

A. **Cost-Effectiveness Analysis**: Once the resource allocation decision has been made, the purpose of cost-effectiveness analysis is to determine how to best employ resources in a given social program or public-sector investment project. The key operational question is how to maximize stated goals at the least possible cost.

1. One common approach is to hold output or service levels constant, and then evaluate cost differences resulting from alternative program strategies.

2. In an alternative approach to cost-effectiveness analysis, costs are held constant while different service levels or output quantities are compared.

3. Cost-effectiveness analysis is especially adept for evaluating the effectiveness of social programs and public-sector investment projects where output can be identified and measured in qualitative terms, but is difficult to express in monetary terms.

B. Privatization: With privatization, public-sector resources are sold or otherwise transferred to the private sector in the hope that the profit motive might spur higher product quality, better customer service, and lower costs for production and distribution.

1. By transferring goods and services to the private sector, competition can be called upon to provide necessary managerial discipline and control.

2. Opponents of privatization argue that evaluating the success of private firms in providing public goods is made difficult by inadequate performance measures and lax performance monitoring.

IV. MACROECONOMIC GROWTH AND STABILIZATION POLICY

A. Business Cycles and Long-Term Economic Performance: The dominant feature of per capita real gross domestic product (GDP), or output, in the United States since 1870 has been its steady growth.

1. The business cycle refers to fluctuations of output around a long-term trend, or recessions followed by recoveries and expansions.

2. Stabilization policy is designed to offset temporary economic disruptions.

3. Even if no policy mistakes are made, it is unrealistic to expect that well-chosen public policies can eliminate recessions.

B. Monetary Policy: Monetary policy refers to actions taken by the Federal Reserve (the Fed) that influence bank reserves, the money stock, and interest rates.

1. An expansionary monetary policy lowers short-term interest rates by increasing the availability of money and credit. Lower interest rates encourage spending, particularly on investment projects. If the economy is operating well below capacity, increased spending is likely to lead to increased output.

2. Once the economy is at or near capacity, rapid monetary expansion leads to inflation (a sustained increase in prices) rather than output growth.

3.   Tight monetary policy reduces the growth rate of the money stock, increases short-term interest rates, and eventually lowers inflation.

C.   **Fiscal Policy:** Fiscal policy refers to the spending and taxing policies of the Federal Government. Fiscal policy can influence total demand in the economy by changing taxes and government spending.

1.   Expansionary fiscal policy implements tax cuts, government spending increases, or both, to increase economic activity during business downturns.

2.   Fiscal policy can also affect incentives to work, save, invest, and innovate.

3.   Automatic stabilizers act as buffers when the economy weakens by automatically reducing taxes and increasing government spending.

4.   Discretionary policy refers to changes in spending and taxes.

D.   **Limits of Monetary and Fiscal Policy**: The foundation for activist economic policy was weakened considerably by the historical experience of the 1960s and 1970s.

1.   Leads and lags in economic activity, forecasting problems, and uncertainty make fine-tuning unreliable at best.

2.   Changes in economic expectations and certain indirect effects of government actions place severe limits on the effectiveness of fiscal and monetary stabilization policy.

3.   The reduction in private investment associated with an increase in government spending is known as the crowding out phenomenon.

V.   **ECONOMIC GROWTH POLICY**

A.   **Public and Private Benefits of Growth:** Productive investments in institutions, technology, and human and physical capital all contribute to growth.

1.   Resources required for these investments are generally obtained when people save and invest out of a desire to increase their own or their children's income.

2.   Short-term growth can also be accomplished by forcing current generations to sacrifice so that future generations may be better off.

3. Growth can be reduced when the capital stock is run down or when governments borrow from future generations to increase consumption today.

B. **Economic Growth and the Environment:** Properly understood, economic growth means not just "more" but "better." Living standards rise not just because people consume more goods and services, but because the quality of those goods and services improves.

1. Innovations in technology that accompany economic growth allow resources to be used more efficiently, and sometimes even decrease the amount of resource consumption.

2. As the United States has grown economically, it has devoted an increasing share of national income to environmental protection.

3. A useful definition of sustainable development is growth in which every generation passes on a stock of "net resources" no lower in per capita value than the stock it received.

   a. Net resources include natural and environmental resources as well as knowledge, technology, and physical and human capital.

C. **Limits to Growth?** Some believe that economic growth is ultimately constrained by finite natural resources. This view traces its roots at least as far back as Thomas Malthus, who wrote in 1798 that the population has a natural tendency to grow faster than food production, and hence is constrained by starvation, pestilence, and war.

1. The "limits-to-growth" hypothesis gained new popularity in the 1970s and again in the 1990s, with attendant forecasts of disaster.

2. The limits-to-growth view neglects the fact that competitive markets adjust to scarcity.

   a. When goods, services, or raw materials become scarce, prices rise and both consumers and producers are motivated to find more efficient ways of obtaining and using them.

   b. Rising energy prices encourage conservation; rising land prices encourage improvements in agricultural techniques that increase the output of food per acre.

VI.   TRADE POLICY

   A.   International Trade: The voluntary exchange of goods and services across national boundaries increases the well-being of all participants by promoting peace and economic efficiency.

   1.   International trade allows each country to concentrate on its most productive activities.

   2.   Foreign competition forces domestic monopolies or oligopolies to lower prices; imported goods provide consumers with greater choice.

   B.   Public Benefits of Free Trade: Expanding opportunities for international trade have effects similar to those of technological improvements: For the same amount of inputs and resources, more output will be produced.

   1.   Open trade may be especially beneficial to the growth of the developing economies and former Communist nations that have less competitive markets and a great need for investment and modern capital goods.

   2.   By creating new competition, providing domestic producers with access to large international markets, and improving the environment for investment, international trade can make a far greater contribution to economic development than does traditional government-to-government foreign aid.

   C.   North American Free Trade Agreement (NAFTA): In August 1992, the United States, Canada, and Mexico reached an agreement to create a free-trade area with more than 400 million consumers and roughly $13 trillion in annual output.

   1.   NAFTA links the United States with its first- and third-largest trading partners.

   2.   NAFTA stimulates growth, promote investment in North America, enhance the ability of North American producers to compete, and raise the standard of living of all three countries.

   3.   NAFTA will also speed up technological progress and provide innovating companies with a larger market.

VII. PUBLIC MANAGEMENT OF HEALTH CARE

A. **Economics of Health Care**: Economic theory and methodology can help explain the performance of the American health care market. Evidence strongly suggests that both the providers and purchasers of health care services respond to economic incentives.

    1. Two features of health care services have significant implications for costs.

        a. It is difficult for consumers to independently evaluate the quality of health care services.

        b. Licensing regulation in every State can increase the cost of health care by restricting the number of providers and limiting competition.

    2. All insurance, whether privately or publicly provided, affects the incentives of the insured. The change in incentives that results from the purchase of insurance is known as the moral hazard problem.

        a. Insurance provides incentives for the overconsumption of health care services.

B. **Market-Based Health Care Reform**: Uncontrollable increases in health care expenditures and a growing number of uninsured have led to a proliferation of proposals for U.S. health care reform.

    1. Comprehensive, market-based reform plans are designed to expand access to health insurance and to improve the functioning of the private markets for health care services.

C. **Public Management of Health Care Reform**: In an evolving plan for comprehensive health care reform, the Administration has proposed an alternative "managed competition" approach.

    1. Managed competition would greatly increase the role of government in the health care system and limit the range of health insurance options available to Americans.

    2. Managed competition seeks to address what the Administration views as four key problems with the U.S. health care system.

a.   The current system fails to provide comprehensive health security for millions of Americans, both insured and uninsured.

b.   Under the current system, people that are less healthy pay more for insurance than those that are more healthy.

c.   The Administration argues that the current health care system lacks effective competition and necessary incentives for cost-conscious decisions.

d.   Large and growing public health care expenditures place a burden on public sector budgets with adverse consequences for long-term economic growth.

D.   **Outlook for Health Care Reform**: Substantive health care reform in the United States is likely to evolve over a number of years. Experience with government-run health care programs such as Medicare and Medicaid suggests that such plans have difficulty in managing costs and service quality in the health care field.

1.   It is speculative to project that the U.S. health care system in the new milllenium will be shaped along the lines of market-based proposals, the Clinton managed competition plan, or even by more traditional "play-or-pay" or national health insurance proposals.

2.   Pay-or-play plans are structured around requirements that firms either provide basic health insurance to employees and their dependents ("play") or pay a payroll tax to cover enrollment in a public health care plan ("pay").

3.   Proposals for national health insurance envision replacing the private health insurance market with a single national health insurer.

a.   National health insurance would be funded through taxes and care would be either free (as in Canada) or provided at a low cost-sharing level.

VIII.   SUMMARY

PROBLEMS & SOLUTIONS

P17.1 ***Public Versus Private Goods.*** *Publicly-funded educational television provides a valuable service across the United States and Canada. Innovative children's programming, award-winning environmental and nature telecasts and imaginative historical documentaries are all delivered free on "ultra high frequency" (UHF) television stations across America.*

A. *Give a public good argument in favor of public funding for educational television.*

B. *Does educational television display both nonrival consumption and nonexclusion characteristics?*

C. *Explain how private-sector providers of educational television might operate profitably in the United States*

P17.1 **SOLUTION**

A. The distinguishing characteristic of public goods is the concept of nonrival consumption. In the case of public goods, use by certain individuals does not reduce availability for others. For example, when an individual watches a network broadcast of a popular TV program such as *The Nightly Business Report*, this does not interfere with the enjoyment of that same TV program by others. In contrast, if an individual consumes a 12 ounce can of *Diet Coke*, this same can of soda is not available for others to consume.

Educational television clearly displays the nonrival consumption concept. Moreover, education is typically regarded a public good because of tangible and intangible external social benefits. Social benefits of a more highly educated populace include higher income tax revenues, reduced crime, higher voter participation, and so on.

B. No. Because educational television programs can be enjoyed equally by more than one person at the same point in time, they display the nonrival consumption attribute and represent a type of public good. This is despite the fact that public television does not exhibit the characteristic of nonexclusion because access to educational television programming can be restricted. Educational TV is not exclusive because such programs could be provided by cable TV operators that charge subscribers a fee for watching.

C. A great number of public goods are not typified by the nonexclusion concept. Examples include public support for educational television, National Public Radio, recreational services provided by national parks and forests, weather forecasts by the National Weather Service, and so on. In these and many other instances, use by nonpaying customers can be easily precluded by private-sector providers. For example, public television's popular *Nightly Business Report* program could be easily restricted to paying sponsors, much like cable television restricts viewing to paying subscribers.

P17.2   ***Public vs Private Goods.*** *Use the nonrival concept to classify each of the following goods and services as public goods or private goods. Also indicate whether or not the good or service in question can be characterized by the nonexclusion concept. Explain your answer.*

    A.   *Fire protection.*

    B.   *Major league baseball game attendance.*

    C.   *National defense.*

    D.   *Long-distance phone service.*

    E.   *The "Wall Street Week" public television program provided on "free" broadcast TV.*

P17.2   **SOLUTION**

    A.   Public good that is nonexclusionary. Enjoyment of fire protection by one consumer does not reduce its enjoyment by others. Hence, it is nonrival in consumption and a public good. It is also nonexclusionary because it would be impossible or prohibitively expensive to confine the benefits of fire protection to paying customers.

    B.   Private good that is not nonexclusionary. In the case of major league baseball games, attendance by certain individuals can in fact reduce availability for others, especially during the pennate race when attendance is high. Baseball games are, therefore, a private good. Because attendance is restricted to paying customers, baseball games cannot be described as nonexclusionary.

    C.   Public good that is nonexclusionary. Enjoyment of national defense by one consumer does not reduce its enjoyment by others. Hence, it is nonrival in consumption and a public good. It is also nonexclusionary because it would be impossible or prohibitively expensive to confine the benefits of national defense to paying customers.

D. Private good that is not nonexclusionary. In the case of long-distance telephone service, use by certain individuals can in fact reduce availability for others, especially during the peak periods when telephone usage is high. It is, therefore, a private good. Because long-distance phone service is in fact restricted to paying customers, it cannot be described as nonexclusionary.

E. Public good that is nonexclusionary. When an individual watches a "free" over-the-air (UHF or VHF) broadcast of a popular PBS program this does not interfere with the enjoyment of that same PBS program by others. As a result, PBS and all other over-the-air broadcasts are a type of nonexclusionary public good. The enjoyment of TV broadcasts can be made exclusive by restricting viewing to cable TV customers.

P17.3   ***Social Rate of Discount.*** *Assume that the rate of return on long-term government bonds is 6%, a typical after-tax return on investment in the private sector is 8%, the marginal corporate and individual tax rate is 40%, and consumption averages 94% of total income.*

     A. *Based on the information provided, calculate an economically appropriate social rate of discount.*

     B. *Is an increase in the marginal corporate tax rate likely to increase, decrease, or have no effect on the appropriate social rate of discount?*

P17.3   **SOLUTION**

     A. The appropriate social rate of discount is a weighted average of the opportunity cost of consumption and investment spending diverted from the private sector to public-sector use.

     Using the assumptions provided, an appropriate average social rate of discount is 6.44%, calculated as follows:

$$\begin{aligned}
\begin{matrix} Social\ rate \\ of\ discount \end{matrix} &= \begin{pmatrix} Percentage\ of \\ funds\ diverted \\ from\ private-sector \\ consumption \end{pmatrix} \times \begin{pmatrix} Before-tax \\ opportunity \\ cost\ of \\ private-sector \\ consumption \\ (Govt.\ bond\ rate) \end{pmatrix} \\[2em]
&+ \begin{pmatrix} Percentage\ of \\ funds\ diverted \\ from\ private-sector \\ investment \end{pmatrix} \times \begin{pmatrix} \dfrac{\begin{matrix} After-tax \\ opportunity \\ cost\ of \\ private-sector \\ investment \end{matrix}}{(1\ -\ Tax\ rate)} \end{pmatrix}
\end{aligned}$$

$$= (94\%) \times (6\%) + (6\%) \times \left(\frac{8\%}{(1 - 40\%)} \right)$$

$$= 6.44\%$$

B.   Increase. An increase in the marginal corporate tax rate has a simple, or first-order, effect of increasing the appropriate social rate of discount because it reduces the denominator of the second term shown in part A. This stems from the fact that the average *pretax* rate of return on private-sector investment is a useful estimate of the opportunity cost of funds diverted from private investment. On a simple mathematical basis, as the corporate income tax rises, the required *pretax* rate of return required on social programs or public-sector investment projects rises.

P17.4   **Public Management Theory.** *A traditional rationale for public management of economic resources is the perception of private market failures to efficiently provide and equitably allocate economic goods and services.*

A.   *Cite at least two reasons why unregulated private-sector markets sometimes fail.*

B.   *Cite some practical examples of goods and services provided by the public sector that might be justified by the problems cited in part A.*

P17.4   **SOLUTION**

A.   A primary cause of market failure is a lack of competition due to too few buyers or sellers, sometimes called failure by market structure. In such instances, government regulation and antitrust policy are often used to protect consumers and workers, and to discourage and/or regulate monopoly.

Another source of market failure is due to a lack of proper prices and economic incentives caused by positive or negative externalities tied to production or consumption, sometimes called failure by incentive. To overcome problems posed by externalities such as pollution, a wide variety of pollution control regulation is imposed and monitored throughout the private sector.

B. A common function of government is to provide goods and services that cannot be provided and allocated in optimal quantities by the private sector. A wide variety of government-provided services have been justified on the basis of a lack of private-sector competition due to too few buyers or sellers. Prominent examples include: the U.S. mail service; municipal water, sewer and electricity service; local municipal garbage collection; and so on.

At the same time, other public-sector services have been justified on the basis that there is a lack of proper prices and economic incentives caused by externalities tied to production or consumption. Conspicuous illustrations include municipal, state, and national parks; water irrigation and dam projects; the public provision of elementary, secondary and college education; and so on.

P17.5 **Free Rider Problem.** *Public goods that incorporate both the nonrival consumption and nonexclusive attributes involve a number of difficulties in demand estimation.*

A. *What is the free rider problem?*

B. *How is the free rider problem overcome in practice?*

C. *Is the free rider problem relevant for all public goods, or only for those that also display the nonexclusion characteristic?*

P17.5 **SOLUTION**

A. When individuals not paying for a certain public good cannot be excluded from consumption, there is a tendency for consumers to avoid payment responsibility. A free-rider problem emerges because each consumer believes that the public good will be provided irrespective of his or her contribution towards covering its costs. When several people share the cost of providing public goods, consumers often believe that their individual failure to provided financial support will have no effect on the provision of the good. When many individuals behave this way, however, less than the optimal amount of the public good will in fact be provided.

B.   This problem is generally overcome when the government initiates a tax on the general public to pay for the provision of important public goods, like national defense. In the private sector, free-rider problems are sometimes resolved through group consensus to support local zoning covenants, charitable associations, and so on.

C.   The free rider problem is only relevant for public goods that also display the nonexclusion characteristic. As discussed in Part A, when individuals not paying for a certain public good cannot be excluded from consumption, there is a tendency for consumers to avoid payment responsibility.

P17.6   **Demand Estimation for Public Goods.** *Assume that ardent concert goers and casual concert goers have revealed their demands for summertime classical concerts in the park, a public good, as follows:*

$$P_1 = \$4{,}000 - \$100Q, \qquad \text{(Ardent concert goers demand)}$$

$$P_2 = \$500 - \$50Q, \qquad \text{(Casual concert goers demand)}$$

where P is price and Q is the number of concerts per year in the local park.

A.   *Calculate the total or aggregate demand for summertime concerts.*

B.   *The marginal cost of summertime concerts is $3,000 each. Determine the socially optimal amount of publicly-supported summertime concerts.*

P17.6   **SOLUTION**

A.   Total or aggregate demand for public goods is determined by a vertical summation of ardent concert goer and casual concert goer demand curves:

$$\text{Total demand} = P_1 + P_2$$

$$= \$4{,}000 - \$100Q + \$500 - \$50Q$$

$$= \$4{,}500 - \$150Q$$

B.   The socially optimal amount of summertime classical concerts in the park is determined by the intersection of demand and supply:

$$\text{Demand} = \text{Supply}$$

$$P_1 + P_2 = MC$$

$$\$4,500 - \$150Q = \$3,000$$

$$150Q = 1,500$$

$$Q = 10$$

And,

$$P = \$4,500 - \$150(10) = \$3,000 \qquad \text{(Demand)}$$

$$P = \$3,000 \qquad \text{(Supply)}$$

P17.7 **Demand Estimation for Public Goods.** *Assume that students and nonstudents have revealed their group demands for junior college education, a public good, as follows:*

$$Q = 1,500 - 0.25P, \qquad \text{(Student demand)}$$

$$Q = 4,000 - P, \qquad \text{(Nonstudent demand)}$$

where Q is the number of students educated per year and P is the price of tuition at the local 2-year junior college.

A. *Calculate the total or aggregate demand for secondary education.*

B. *The marginal cost of college education is given by the expression:*

$$MC = \$1,000 + Q,$$

where MC is marginal cost and Q is again the number of students.

Determine the socially optimal amount of publicly-supported college education.

P17.7 **SOLUTION**

A. Total or aggregate demand for public goods such as college education is determined by a vertical summation of individual student and nonstudent demand curves. First, it is necessary to express student and nonstudent demand in terms of Q as a function of P.

For student demand:

$$Q = 1,500 - 0.25P$$

$$-0.25P = Q - 1,500$$

$$P = \$6,000 - \$4Q$$

For nonstudent demand:

$$Q = 4,000 - P$$

$$-P = Q - 4,000$$

$$P = \$4,000 - Q$$

Then,

$$\text{Total demand} = \text{Student demand} + \text{Nonstudent demand}$$

$$= \$6,000 - \$4Q + \$4,000 - Q$$

$$= \$10,000 - \$5Q$$

B.   The socially optimal amount of publicly-supported college education is determined by the intersection of demand and supply:

$$\text{Demand} = \text{Supply}$$

$$\text{Student demand} + \text{Nonstudent demand} = MC$$

$$\$10,000 - \$5Q = \$1,000 + Q$$

$$6Q = 9,000$$

$$Q = 1,500$$

And,

$$P = \$10,000 - \$5(1,500) = \$2,500 \qquad \text{(Demand)}$$

$$P = \$1,000 + \$1(1,500) = \$2,500 \qquad \text{(Supply)}$$

P17.8   ***Size of Government.***   *Over the past several decades, the scope and magnitude of government activity has increased dramatically in the United States and in many foreign countries. In the United States, the Federal government has built dams and highways, conducted research, expanded the arts, and increased it's regulatory authority over many facets of the economy. Through the federal revenue sharing program, the Federal government has also directed millions of dollars to state and local governments to support education, crime-prevention programs and highway construction.*

In the United States, the purchase of goods and services by all levels of government exceeds 20% of GDP, with a budget in excess of \$2 trillion and more than 3 million employees. Spreading taxpayer resistance, to the growth in government has spawned increasing efforts to curb the size of government while improving the quality and efficiency of government services.

A.   *Discuss the primary strengths of the unregulated private- sector allocation of economic resources.*

B.   *Discuss how the presence of positive external social benefits give rise to a demand for government.*

P17.8   **SOLUTION**

A.   Private markets can identify and be responsive to individual preferences through the interaction of supply and demand. In the absence of important externalities, marginal social benefits associated with any good or service are directly reflected in equilibrium prices and quantities. At the same time, marginal social costs of production are reflected in the market supply curve.

Perfectly functioning competitive markets yield output prices and quantities that exactly balance marginal social benefits and marginal social costs. In terms of demand, consumers dictate the strength of their preferences to producers. In terms of supply, production is allocated among the most efficient marginal producers.

In sum, perfectly functioning competitive markets provide customers *what* they want in a least-cost fashion.

B.   Positive external social benefits give rise to a demand for government because private markets are unable to ensure cooperative allocations that maximize social welfare. When positive marginal social benefits are enjoyed following the consumption or production activity of others, the failure to reward those responsible for positive externalities leads to underconsumption or to underproduction. Conversely, when negative marginal social costs are suffered following the consumption or production activity of others, the failure to penalize those responsible for negative externalities leads to overconsumption or to overproduction.

P17.9   ***Public Choice Theory.*** *According to public choice theory, four different groups comprise the U.S. political system: voters, politicians, special-interest groups and bureaucrats. Each of these groups play an important role in influencing the level and quality of services provided. Members of each group behave rationally to maximize their welfare the same way that individuals do in market economies. As a result, these groups generate competing interests in the political environment that can compromise the general welfare and lead to inefficient or ineffective government programs, policies and regulations.*

    A.   *Who plays the role of managers in the public choice theory of government?*

    B.   *Describe some of the characteristics of these "managers" that can contribute to government failure.*

P17.9   **SOLUTION**

    A.   According to public choice theory, politicians play a role in the public sector much like the role played by managers in the private sector. Like managers of private firms seeking to maximize his or her interest by maximizing profits, politicians operate in a political system where maximizing one's personal benefit is achieved by increasing one's chances for re-election.

    B.   Because politicians operate in a political system where maximizing one's personal benefit is achieved by increasing one's chances for re-election, politicians often curry favor with special-interest groups whose interests make contrast sharply with the public interest. As a result, government failure can result when politicians respond to the wishes of small well-organized and well-funded special-interest groups at the expense of the less vocal and uninformed general public.

        For example, many federal and state legislators develop business relationships with private firms that contribute campaign funds to their re-election efforts. In return, the firms get rewarded with government contracts or the enactment of special legislation. These relationships become stronger and more long-term, and potentially more damaging to the public interest, if these legislators continue to get re-elected.

P17.10   ***Benefit-cost Analysis.*** *AIDS, acquired immune deficiency syndrome, is the final stage of the disease caused by the human immunodeficiency virus (HIV). In most victims, HIV causes a deterioration in the immune system by killing a class of white blood cells called "T4 helpers." After a period of five to ten years, too few of these T4 helper cells* *remain, and the HIV victim succumbs to an opportunistic infection such as pneumonia. During the period between HIV infection and the onset of AIDS, victims are infectious, asymptomatic carriers. Because HIV alters the victim's genetic material and is highly prone to mutation, finding a cure is extremely difficult and any vaccine is likely to be ineffective in a substantial minority of those vaccinated. Moreover, no natural immunity has been observed. So far, the disease is fatal for nearly everyone who gets it. For all of these reasons, AIDS has become the most dreaded disease in the world today.*

Since the AIDS outbreak during the 1980s, public sector managers have been confronted with a complex social and economic problem in the field of epidemiology, the study of epidemics and epidemic diseases. Even under "optimistic" scenarios, AIDS is expected to remain a leading cause of death for persons in the 25 to 44 age group for the forseeable future. In the United States, treatment cost estimates run as high as $50 billion per year, and will continue to have a dramatic influence on the cost and availability of hospital care, health and life insurance, employee benefits, and public services. Although the dreadful personal cost of the AIDS epidemic in terms of lost life and personal suffering is immeasurable, the fact that AIDS strikes primarily young people in their most productive years intensifies its economic and social impact. To mitigate these costs, public-sector managers must evaluate the benefits associated with a number of alternative means of focusing current research efforts and treatment methods designed to control the human suffering and economic costs of the AIDS epidemic.

A. *From an economic standpoint, the value of a human life is sometimes measured as the discounted present-value of a person's expected lifetime earnings. Is this a reasonable basis for public-sector managers to use in placing a dollar value on the lives saved through finding a cure for AIDS?*

B. *The "willingness to pay" approach, bases life value estimates on the payments one would require to accept a small risk of death or, alternatively, the payments one would be willing to make to reduce the risk of death. Is this a reasonable basis for public-sector managers to use in placing a dollar value on the lives saved through finding a cure for AIDS?*

C. *Which approach, the human capital approach of part A or the willingness to pay approach of part B, is likely to yield higher life value estimate? Explain.*

P17.10 **SOLUTION**

A. In a general sense, money spent on the prevention, treatment and cure of AIDS cannot be used in other areas, such as in the treatment of cancer or to improve the safety of air traffic control facilities. Therefore, to evaluate the efficacy of public expenditures and public policies aimed to save human lives, public-sector managers must make some determination, using either subjective or objective criteria, of the value of human life.

The human capital approach, determines the value of a human life as the discounted present-value of a person's expected lifetime earnings. An obvious disadvantage of this approach is that it is one-dimensional. By focusing only on earning power it implies that the lives of nonworkers have no economic value.

B.   The "willingness to pay" approach, bases life value estimates on the payments one would require to accept a small risk of death or, alternatively, the payments one would be willing to make to reduce the risk of death. In implementing this approach, questionnaires have been used to determine the amount people would be willing to pay to participate in a program that would reduce the risk of death due to a given disease. It is worth mentioning that the results of these surveys are not totally reliable because the hypothetical nature of the questions makes it difficult for people to answer truthfully and accurately.

C.   Without specific information on disease incidence and the distribution of income it is not possible to say which approach, the human capital approach or the willingness to pay approach, is likely to yield higher life value estimate.

Obviously, if one has contracted AIDS, he or she would pay whatever it takes to obtain a cure. The only obvious limit is the amount of income or wealth available. If AIDS were most common among the wealthy, then a willingness to pay approach would suggest relatively high life value estimates. If AIDS were most common among the poor, then a willingness to pay approach would suggest relatively low life value estimates.

Similarly, if AIDS were most common among the highly educated, then a human capital approach would suggest relatively high life value estimates. If AIDS were most common among the uneducated, then a human capital approach would suggest relatively low life value estimates.

(*Note:* This topic was purposely chosen to be thought provoking. No one can be so presumptuous as to value something so sacred as human life. Nevertheless, everyday public policy decisions are based on economic values that must be debated and understood.)